Studies in Interactional Sociolinguistics 4

General Editor: John J. Gumperz

Politeness

Some universals in language usage

Companions to this volume

Discourse strategies John J. Gumperz
Language and social identity edited by John J. Gumperz
The social construction of literacy edited by Jenny Cook-Gumperz
Discourse markers Deborah Schiffrin

Politeness
Some universals in language usage

PENELOPE BROWN

and

STEPHEN C. LEVINSON

Max-Planck-Institute for Psycholinguistics,
Nijmegen

CAMBRIDGE
UNIVERSITY PRESS

Published by the Press Syndicate of the University of Cambridge
The Pitt Building, Trumpington Street, Cambridge CB2 1RP
40 West 20th Street, New York, NY 10011–4211, USA
10 Stamford Road, Oakleigh, Melbourne 3166, Australia

First published 1978 as part of Esther N. Goody (ed.): *Questions and politeness*
Reissued 1987 with corrections, new introduction and new bibliography
Reprinted 1988, 1989, 1990, 1992, 1994, 1996

Printed in Great Britain at the
Athenæum Press Ltd, Gateshead, Tyne & Wear

British Library cataloguing in publication data

Brown, Penelope
Politeness: some universals in language usage.
– (Studies in interactional sociolinguistics; 4)
1. Sociolinguistics   2. Social interaction
I. Title   II. Levinson, Stephen C.
III. Series
306'.4   P40

Library of Congress cataloguing in publication data

Brown, Penelope
Politeness: some universals in language usage.
(Studies in interactional sociolinguistics; 4)
"The bulk of the material in this volume first appeared in a collection
in the series Cambridge papers in social anthropology, volume 8" –
Bibliography.
Includes index.
1. Sociolinguistics.   2. Etiquette.   3. Conversation.
4. Pragmatics.   5. Speech acts (Linguistics).   6. Social interaction.
I. Levinson, Stephen C.   II. Title.   III. Series.
P40.5.E75B76 1987   401'.9   86–23255

ISBN 0 521 30862 3   hardback
ISBN 0 521 31355 4   paperback

To the memory of Erving Goffman

CONTENTS

*1

SYMBOLS AND ABBREVIATIONS

*	ungrammatical
r	rude
p	polite
c.i.	conversationally implicates
FTA	face-threatening act
S	speaker
H	hearer, addressee
P	power
D	social distance
R_x	rating of imposition
W_x	seriousness (weightiness) of FTA x
C	context
MP	Model Person
T	second-person singular pronoun ('tu')
V	second-person plural honorific pronoun ('vous')
⊢	1. entailment 2. assertion sign
⊃	if-then (material conditional)
iff	if and only if
φ	as 'a' in hall
´	stress

FOREWORD · *John J. Gumperz*

The bulk of the material in this volume first appeared in a collection in the series Cambridge Papers in Social Anthropology, volume 8. Its reissue will now make it available to a much wider audience. In the years since it first appeared it has come to be accepted as the classic treatment on politeness in communication. As an integrative treatment of phenomena previously dealt with in a variety of disciplines it is now widely cited by linguists, psychologists and students of social interaction. A major reason for this interest is that politeness, as the authors define it, is basic to the production of social order, and a precondition of human cooperation, so that any theory which provides an understanding of this phenomenon at the same time goes to the foundations of human social life.

In addition to their status as universal principles of human interaction, politeness phenomena by their very nature are reflected in language. Societies everywhere, no matter what their degree of isolation or their socioeconomic complexity, show these same principles at work; yet what counts as polite may differ from group to group, from situation to situation, or from individual to individual. If we can find some underlying grammatical and social regularities which account both for this type of variation and for the recurrent patterns, we will have taken a major step in demonstrating and not just claiming the basically social nature of human language. One of the reasons for the attention that this work has created, is the fact that an abstract theoretical framework has been proposed which does indeed account for the bulk of the cross-linguistic and cross-cultural data, and which also yields predictions which can be (and in some cases have been) tested through independent experiments.

Apart from its general import, the book makes a number of important theoretical and methodological points relevant to current interests in both linguistics and sociolinguistics. Politeness principles are reflected in linguistic universals which are in many ways equivalent to those discovered by grammarians. However, the methods by which these universals are derived constitute a significant departure from current practice. Grammarians rely on informants' responses to systematic elicitation procedures to deduce abstract rules which are then related to hypotheses about the human mind. Brown and Levinson's work, in contrast, takes its source data primarily from situated conversational exchanges, and generalizations are made with reference to empirically testable universals of discourse and interaction. By so doing, while using new kinds of data, they are also able to draw on and integrate a long tradition of research in social anthropology, conversational discourse analysis, and in syntax and linguistic pragmatics.

The new introduction, which takes the form of a critical examination of the 1978 work in the context of research since then, explores these and related issues of theory. It brings together the recent theoretical work on inference in conversation, and discusses work by anthropologists, psychologists and linguists of various persuasions who have attempted to use or test the Brown and Levinson principles. In addition, it surveys the implications of their approach for a number of issues such as those of power and control, first and second language learning, conversation analysis and ritual, which are basic to interactional sociolinguistics. Although intended specifically for this volume, this introduction in itself is both a good guide to current directions in sociolinguistics and linguistic pragmatics and an argument for the important role sociolinguistics can play in illuminating the bases of social life.

INTRODUCTION TO THE REISSUE: A REVIEW OF RECENT WORK[1]

Preface

> The human personality is a sacred thing; one dare not violate it nor infringe its bounds, while at the same time the greatest good is in communion with others. (Durkheim 1915:299)

The reissue of 'Universals in language usage: politeness phenomena' over a decade after it was written, perhaps calls for some explanation, especially as, for economy of production, we have have had to minimize revisions to a new introduction and bibliography. One reason is that we believe the issues addressed there (and originally, or at least most influentially, by Goffman 1967, 1971) have a perennial importance, for they raise questions about the foundations of human social life and interaction. For example, in the original introduction to this work, Goody (1978a:12) notes how the phenomena we review below seem to require an enormously complex kind of reflexive reasoning about other agents' desires, and she suggests that this reasoning, with its roots in interpersonal ritual, 'may be fundamental in an evolutionary sense to social life and human intelligence'. She goes on to suggest (1978a:15), in the context of a discussion of 'joking relations', that it is the essence of these that they carry the 'presumption of non-threatening intention'. From a gross ethological perspective, perhaps we can generalize somewhat: the problem for any social group is to control its internal aggression while retaining the potential for aggression both in internal social control and, especially, in external competitive relations with other groups (Maynard-Smith, in press). In this perspective politeness, deference and tact have a sociological significance altogether beyond the level of table manners and etiquette books (Goffman 1971:90); politeness, like formal diplomatic protocol (for which it must surely be the model), presupposes that potential for aggression as it seeks to disarm it, and makes possible communication between potentially aggressive parties.[2] But how? Goffman suggests that it is through the diplomatic fiction of the *virtual offence*, 'or worst possible reading' of some action by A that potentially trespasses on B's interests, equanimity or personal preserve (1971:138ff). By orienting to the 'virtual offence', an offender can display that he has the other's interests at heart. Equally, a failure to orient to the virtual offence counts as a diplomatic breach. Thus is constructed a precise semiotics of peaceful vs. aggressive intentions (where the measure of precision is sometimes in fractions of a second —

1

see e.g. Davidson 1984), which in assigning such momentous significance to what are often trivial substantive acts requires a constant vigilance over the manner in which social interaction is conducted. This semiotic system is then responsible for the shaping of much everyday interaction, and in so shaping it, constitutes a potent form of social control.

But although issues of politeness raise sociological speculations of this scale, they also touch on many other interests and many other fields. The time at which this essay was first written was particularly propitious, for it witnessed the beginning of a confluence of interests in linguistics, anthropology and 'micro'-sociology. Since then significant advances have been made in the study of language use and social interaction. Issues bearing upon politeness have emerged as being of central interest in sociolinguistics, pragmatics, applied linguistics, social psychology, conversation analysis and anthropology, generating an enormous body of research bearing directly on our thesis. In this introduction we shall try to spell out these issues, evaluating recent work (but necessarily selectively) and its bearing on our original essay (see also the review essay by Lavandera, in press).

We shall not in this introduction summarize our thesis: this is done on pp. 59ff. We need only say here that the original essay attempts to show in considerable detail how certain precise parallels in language usage in many different languages can be shown to derive from certain assumptions about 'face' — individuals' self-esteem. We phrase the derivation in terms of three main strategies of politeness, 'positive politeness' (roughly, the expression of solidarity), 'negative politeness' (roughly, the expression of restraint) and 'off-record (politeness)' (roughly, the avoidance of unequivocal impositions), and claim that the uses of each are tied to social determinants, specifically the relationship between speaker and addressee and the potential offensiveness of the message content. If this account is even approximately along the right lines, we believe it has important implications for a number of issues and disciplines. Some of these we address at length in sections 7 and 8[3] of the essay, but let us highlight here the sorts of implications we believe it has for the disciplines concerned.

In the case of *sociolinguistics*, the theory argues for a shift in emphasis from the current preoccupation with speaker-identity, to a focus on dyadic patterns of verbal interaction as the expression of social relationships; and from emphasis on the usage of linguistic forms, to an emphasis on the relation between form and complex inference. Further, interest in cultural detail, as in the ethnography of speaking, should be supplemented with attention to crosslinguistic generalizations. In the case of *linguistic pragmatics* a great deal of the mismatch between what is 'said' and what is 'implicated' can be attributed to politeness, so that concern with the 'representational functions' of language should be supplemented with

2

attention to the 'social functions' of language, which seem to motivate much linguistic detail; applications of linguistics, whether to second language learning or to interethnic communication difficulties, need to pay proper attention to these essential 'social functions'. The implication for *sociology* and *anthropology* is, first and most generally, that more attention should be given to the interactional basis of social life, if only to aid progress at other analytical levels – this because the area offers significant links across the divide between 'macro' and 'micro' levels of sociological analysis (Gal 1983). Second, the possibility of the reduction of 'ritual' to principles of rational action ought to be challenging to the Durkheimian thesis of the irreducibility of social facts. Thirdly, politeness universals, together with their cultural skewings, suggest the need for a different kind of comparative sociology, attuned to just this sort of interplay, and alive to the possibility of interesting ethological underpinnings to human cultural elaborations.

These core issues and implications are still very much alive, and this introduction reviews some recent work that has a bearing on at least some of them and on the details of our account of politeness phenomena. In section *1.0[3] we attend to challenges to the general Gricean framework in which the theory is couched; in *2.0 we reassess some of our claims in the light of new evidence; in *3.0 we review a number of fields in which there happens to have been a great deal of work that has a bearing on our thesis; and in *4.0 we turn to directions for future research. However, in this discussion we must perforce presuppose familiarity with the framework developed in this book, and readers may prefer to return to this review after reading the body of the text.

1.0 General framework
1.1 Gricean framework

The original essay presumes that Grice's theory of conversational implicature and the framework of maxims that give rise to such implicatures is essentially correct. (See pp. 94–5 below for a sketch of this framework, and discussion in Levinson 1983:Ch. 3.) Naturally, such an important theory has been subject to a number of attempts at revision. Horn (1984), for example, suggests that Grice's four maxims, together with their nine sub-maxims, can in fact be reduced to three: retaining Quality and the first maxim of Quantity (his Q), the rest can be subsumed within an enlarged Relevance maxim (his R). Detailing a series of conflicting requirements based on Q and R, Horn suggests that our negative politeness is based on

3

R-implicatures ('hint, don't say more than is necessary'), while positive politeness is based on Q-implicatures ('say as much as required'), with a consequent tension between the two strategies. More radical still is the Sperber and Wilson attempt (1986; see also Wilson and Sperber 1981) to reduce all the maxims to one super-maxim of Relevance, which is less of a maxim (on their view) than a natural human propensity to maximize the informational value of environmental stimuli. On this view, implicatures of politeness would presumably arise in the same way that all implicatures do, namely, on the assumption that what the speaker said was relevant (maximized information pertinent to the context), certain (polite) presumptions would have to be made.

There are places in which the original essay relies on the classical Gricean formulation, for example in the discussion of the 'off-record' strategies in section 5.5. However, the only essential presumption is what is at the heart of Grice's proposals, namely that there is a working assumption by conversationalists of the rational and efficient nature of talk. It is against that assumption that polite ways of talking show up as deviations, requiring rational explanation on the part of the recipient, who finds in considerations of politeness reasons for the speaker's apparent irrationality or inefficiency. In any case, we do not believe that these recent modifications of the Gricean programme are wholly successful, and specifically do not consider that wholesale reduction of the maxims has been well motivated (see Levinson, in press).

Another recent proposal by Leech (1983), in a quite contrary spirit, suggests that the Gricean framework of maxims should be proliferated: the field of linguistic pragmatics is the study of goal-directed linguistic behaviour, and this is governed by a 'textual rhetoric' and an 'interpersonal rhetoric', each constituted by a set of maxims. Thus within the 'interpersonal rhetoric', we find not only Grice's Cooperative Principle (CP) with all the maxims in their traditional form, but also a Politeness Principle (PP), with six (or more) maxims of Tact, Generosity, Approbation, Modesty, etc. (1983:16, 132). That the CP and PP are coordinate principles is shown, he claims, by the fact that without the PP, the CP would make erroneous predictions – the PP explains why, despite the maxims of Quality and Quantity, people sometimes quite appropriately say things that are false or less informative than is required (pp. 80–1).

There are a number of reasons for resisting this line of argument. One is that, if we are permitted to invent a maxim for every regularity in language use, not only will we have an infinite number of maxims, but pragmatic theory will be too unconstrained to permit the recognition of any counter-examples. A second is that the distribution of politeness (who has to be polite to whom) is socially controlled: it is not as if there were some basic modicum of politeness owed by each to all; in contrast, language usage principles of the Gricean sort do indeed generally obtain, principled exceptions though there are. Another reason is more pertinent to this book: every discernable pattern of language use does not, *eo ipso*, require a maxim or principle to produce it. The Gricean maxims are not merely statements of regular patterns in behaviour; they are background presumptions, which by virtue of that special status are robust to apparent counterevidence. Thus a partial answer to a question does not typically undermine the presumption of cooperation; it is more likely to be interpreted as (say) implicating inability to meet the requisite canons of factual information. In other words the assumption of cooperative behaviour is actually hard to undermine: tokens of apparent uncooperative behaviour tend to get interpreted as in fact cooperative at a 'deeper level'. Now if politeness principles had maxim-like status, we would expect the same robustness: it should, as a matter of fact, be hard to be impolite. Instead, when one said 'Shut your mouth' or the like, we would expect an attempt to construct an inference of the sort: 'The speaker has broken the maxim of Tact (or some such subprinciple); however, given the Politeness Principle, we must assume that the speaker is in fact following the PP; the only way to preserve this assumption is to assume that he is not in a position to observe the maxim of Tact, say, because he is in a hurry; it is clear that we can work this out; therefore he P-implicates that he is in a hurry.' We take this to be a *reductio*, and an argument against setting up politeness principles as coordinate in nature to Grice's Cooperative Principle (see also Kasher, in press).

Our own position, as developed below, is that Grice's CP (however it is finally conceptualized) is of quite different status from that of politeness principles. The CP defines an 'unmarked' or socially neutral (indeed asocial) presumptive framework for communication;[4] the essential assumption is 'no deviation from rational efficiency without a reason'. Politeness principles are, however, just such principled reasons for deviation. Linguistic politeness is therefore implicated in the classical way, with maximum theoretical parsimony, from the CP. It is true, however, that polite motivations for such deviations perhaps have a special status in social interaction by virtue of their omni-relevance. Nevertheless, this omni-relevance does not endow them with the presumptive nature enjoyed by the CP: politeness has to be communicated, and the absence of communicated politeness may, *ceteris paribus*, be taken as absence of the polite attitude. (And, incidentally, the specific phenomena motivating every one of Leech's six politeness maxims were discussed and, it seems to us, quite adequately accounted for by our more parsimonious apparatus.)

In our model, then, it is the mutual awareness of 'face' sensitivity, and the kinds of means-ends reasoning that this induces, that together with the

CP allows the inference of implicatures of politeness. From the failure to meet the maxims at face value, plus the knowledge of face-preserving strategies, the inferences are derived. However, recent work does suggest that this model is somewhat under-described. Instead of deriving the details of linguistic form directly from face-preserving strategies as we attempt, it may be better to let the mechanisms of generalized conversational implicature get us half-way, as it were. We can do this by showing how the details of the linguistic forms, and specifically their semantic structure, invite certain general inferences independently of face considerations (see Atlas and Levinson 1981; Leech 1983:159ff; Levinson 1983;122ff; and Sperber and Wilson 1986:Ch. 4); we can then let face considerations take us to the more specific polite implicatures. Let us take an example from Leech (1983:Ch. 7): why are the following, construed as offers, increasingly polite?

(1)   Will you have anything to eat?
(2)   Will you have something to eat?
(3)   Won't you have anything to eat?
(4)   Won't you have something to eat?

Leech's argument goes very roughly as follows. The 'negative polarity' form *anything* indicates non-factuality, and is therefore the normal quantifier required in polar questions (as in (1) and (4)), because a question, like a negative statement, does not presume the factual status of the proposition (or propositional function) expressed. In contrast, the 'positive polarity' item *something* (as in (2) and (4)) does presume factuality, and therefore forces a more complex analysis for the logical forms of sentences like (2) and (4) — as indicated by the following informal rendition of the contrast between (1) and (2):

(1′)   I ask whether you will eat anything.
(2′)   I ask whether it is a fact that you will eat something.

Here (2′) includes a proposition ('it is a fact that p') about a proposition ('p'), without thereby adding much in the way of semantic content; there is therefore (Leech argues 1983:166–71) a Manner implicature to the presumption that the embedded proposition ('you will eat something') is actively entertained in the context.[5] On the assumption that the speaker entertains this proposition, he is presuming what is (supposedly) beneficial to the addressee, and given that to so presume is polite, the speaker in using (2) is being more polite than he would be by use of (1) with its simpler logical form.

In a similar way Leech gives an account of how the negative (3) is still more polite than the positive (1). As long noted, a negative statement is in general relatively uninformative; therefore, by the maxim of Quantity, we seek an explanation for the use of a negative statement, usually finding the explanation in the use of the negative to deny the positive, where the latter is entertained in the context.[6] The polite interpretation of the question in (3) would appear to go thus: the speaker questions the addressee's denial of the speaker's implied assumption (entertained in the context) that the addressee will have something to eat. Thus the speaker attributes polite denial to the addresssee, while giving him a chance to change his mind: the implicated import of the sentence may be glossed 'I hope and expect you to have something to eat, but now it appears you will not have anything to eat; is this really so?' (Leech 1983:110). Sentence (4) of course compounds the polite implicatures from the use of the positive polarity *something* and the negative form (although there is more to it than that, as Leech 1983:170 details). Again, generalized conversational implicature will get us part of the way to the polite interpretation, while specific assumptions about the nature of polite behaviour (in these examples, the nature of polite offers) will get us the rest.

Whatever the merits of this particular argument, the general line of account seems correct. However, it is clear that the ways in which morphosyntactic options reflect differing semantic structures, which in turn induce contrastive implicatures, is exceedingly complex, and is likely to be the focus of a great deal of future work in linguistic pragmatics, work which in turn should throw considerable light on the details of the linguistic expression of politeness.

1.2 Intention and strategies

Our framework presupposes the other great contribution by Grice, namely his account of the nature of communication as a special kind of intention designed to be recognized by the recipient (1971). That account itself presupposes that what agents do is related systematically to their intents, and thus that intentions of actors are reconstructable by observers or recipients of actions. The systematic relation is presumed to be given by some rational means-ends reasoning, of the sort sketched in 3.1.3 and 4.2 of the essay below.

Clearly such a framework begs a great number of questions, and it has been challenged on grounds as different as conceptual impossibility, psychological implausibility and cultural bias. Let us take these one by one. The conceptual difficulties with such a theory of communication centre on the apparent infinite regress involved in a recipient of a message trying to figure out what its sender reckoned the recipient would reckon the speaker would reckon (and so on, *ad infinitum*) the recipient might infer from the communicative behaviour in question. There have, since Grice's original essay, been various attempts to solve this philosophical puzzle, especially as it involves establishing the shared background of *mutual knowledge* on which the inference of communicative intention seems to rely (see e.g. Schiffer 1972). Sperber and Wilson (1982, 1986) argue that some weaker concept of *mutual manifestness* will be sufficient to preserve the essence of the Gricean account.

As for the psychological implausibility of all this, Clark and Carlson (1982a, b) have energetically defended the model, arguing that the regressive reasoning is finessed by simple heuristics. After all, the idea that ego has a model of alter's beliefs about ego, and about ego's beliefs about alter's beliefs about ego, etc., seems altogether likely, up to some point. Further succour for the Gricean view may be given by recent work in artificial intelligence, which has shown that, again up to a point, a machine may be programmed to take such factors into account, and that doing so lends naturalness to a verbal interchange between man and machine (see especially Allen 1983). The details of these AI programs offer some support for our sketch of the kinds of reasoning that might be involved: the programs contain inference rules that instantiate some of the most distinctive properties of the Kenny Logic we employed (compare Allen's 'nested planning rule' 1983:124 with p. 88 below). However, despite these attempts to show the plausibility and practicality of the Gricean account of communication, there is one very basic problem that has not been properly attended to. Our account, like these others, basically suggests that understanding is a matter of reconstructing speakers' communicative intentions, and that this is done by running a logic of practical reasoning 'backwards' as it were. The essential problem here is a logical one: no logical system, including Kenny Logic, offers any way of going from conclusions back to premises – they are not symmetrical systems. Thus, even if we had a perfected system of means-ends reasoning, it would remain a conceptual mystery how we are able to reconstruct other agents' intentions from their actions (Levinson 1985). Yet that we do so, or attempt to do so, is hardly open to question, and is presupposed by at least some uses of the term 'strategy', including ours (whatever its unclarities, see Riley 1981)[7]. And in the sense of that term in which people can be seen to be doing something before doing, or in order to do, something else, there is a great range of subtle evidence from conversation analysis of the routine use of strategy (Heritage 1981; Pomerantz 1980; Davidson 1984; Drew 1984; Levinson 1985; also work on 'pre-sequences', reviewed in Levinson 1983:345ff).

We turn finally to the charge of cultural bias in the Gricean account of communication, and in our own emphasis on rational sources for behaviour. We foresaw this charge (p. 58), seeing that we appeared to be making the same sort of (alleged) error that economists make when looking at economic systems as divorced from the 'irrationalities' of social values (see e.g. Sen 1979). Our defence still seems to us adequate: if we make the assumption of rationality, and the behavioural facts then tally, there must be something right about it. However, the *a priori* critique has now been joined by a line of counter-argument based on detailed ethnographic and sociolinguistic findings. In a number of recent studies of Pacific island societies, it has been claimed that cultural notions of personhood are sufficiently different to make the Western emphasis on the intentional agent of very dubious application there (Ochs 1984; Duranti 1983b, 1985; Rosaldo 1982; see also discussion in Schegloff, in press). These cultural ideas are then claimed to show up in the details of linguistic behaviour: thus Ochs (1984) claims that because Samoans do not share our Western emphasis on personal intentions, Samoans do not normally 'other-correct' (i.e. correct other speakers by guessing what they are trying to say; see Schlegloff et al. 1977 for the relevant distinctions). She goes on to claim that the Gricean view of communication is nothing but our own folk-theory canonized as philosophy (1984:335; see also Candlin 1981). Independently, Rosaldo (1982) attributes the absence of a speech act of promising among the Ilongots (a tribal group of the Philippines) to a lack of interest in personal sincere intentions (as opposed to public undertakings, expressed by oaths); this she claims undermines the cross-cultural applicability of Searle's speech act formulations, with their 'undue emphasis upon the speaker's psychological state' (p. 227). In both these societies, the emphasis appears to be on what is literally said, rather than on what might have been intended or implicated, and on the social consequences of what is said. The implication of these arguments is not merely that no inferences about politeness could be cross-culturally valid, but that there can be no universal framework of communication based on intention recognition.

It is hard to judge the import of these apparent ethnographic counter-examples to the Gricean framework. For example, Ochs (1984:333) indicates that Samoan lower-status individuals (including all children) have to learn to take the perspective of higher-ranking individuals, and that surely would involve the attribution of intention: taking the perspective of others is indeed the heart of the Gricean account. At most, we think, these facts argue for a slight shift in emphasis in the relative importance of what is said vs. what is implicated or attributed, a shift tied to the hoary sociological distinctions, variously conceived, between communities where positional status is emphasized and those where persons are treated as 'individuals'. Our particular claims will only be undermined by counter-examples of just the opposite kind from the Samoan facts, for example where only high-status individuals have to take account of the perspective of lower-status individuals; meanwhile, our framework successfully predicts the observed direction of perspective-taking, and does so partially on the basis of Gricean assumptions, which thus appear to survive the attack.[8]

2.0 Reassessments
2.1 Some reservations

It is natural that we should ourselves now have some reservations about certain aspects of the theory or its presentation, which we now record.

First, there are some obvious ways in which the presentation is, in places, somewhat dated. One of these is due to the fact that the frameworks of grammatical analysis now favoured are very different from the transformational framework that we were presupposing. However, this is mostly a matter of formulation, and does not affect our thesis in any appreciable way. Moreover, we may note that the Generative Semantics framework, long defunct, to which we refer occasionally below, had the great merit of directing serious attention to the relation between grammar and pragmatics, interests currently undergoing revival, sometimes with direct reference to the sorts of issues raised in this book (see e.g. Horn 1984).[9]

Another framework that we would now rely on less heavily is speech act theory. At the time of writing we took this theory to provide a basis for a mode of discourse analysis, as others of empirical bent had also done (see e.g. Labov and Fanshel 1977; by the time the paper went to press we already had reservations, p. 232ff). For many reasons, we now think this not so promising (see e.g. Levinson 1983:286ff); speech act theory forces a sentence-based, speaker-oriented mode of analysis, requiring attribution of speech act categories where our own thesis requires that utterances are often equivocal in force. The alternative is to avoid taking such categories as the basis of discourse analysis, choosing other more directly demonstrable categories as done in conversation analysis, and then to give a derivative account of the intuitions underlying speech act theory. For example, the notion of a 'request' can in part be characterized as an utterance-type occurring in certain recurrent types of sequences of utterances, a view that escapes some of the conceptual problems of 'indirect speech acts' (see e.g. Levinson 1983:356ff; for recent developments in conversation analysis see below *3.4). In any case, we recognized (in section 6.3) that 'face-threatening acts' or FTAs need not be realized in sentence-like units, and the upshot of all this is that we must now acknowledge that the speech act categories that we employed were an underanalysed shorthand, but one which, were we to try again today, would still be hard to avoid.

We also have some methodological reservations to record. One area where we have been rightly taken to task is for mixing data of quite different kinds: ours was an unholy amalgam of naturally occurring, elicited and intuitive data (which would have mattered less if it had been more clearly distinguished). The state of the art in discourse analysis would hardly let us get away with this today. However, there were certain intrinsic difficulties in obtaining clearly parallel data in three languages, and the data were not (on the whole) collected specifically with this project in mind. In addition, we had frequent recourse to other published materials, with distinct goals and methods of their own. Thus any cross-linguistic project of this scope and ambition is going to have to make do with less than fully adequate data. This does not make the lapse any less regrettable, and we record it with regret. As a matter of record, though, nearly all examples of dialogue came from naturally occurring tape-recorded speech, with just a few examples of English dialogue constructed for illustrative purposes. Where grammatical points were being made, elicited data from Tamil and Tzeltal were frequently employed, but even here extensive use was made of recorded examples. Naturally, we did not feel free to construct examples in languages we are not native speakers of.[10]

Thirdly, we now have some doubts about the precision and falsifiability of our model. Our theory takes the classical form of expectations derived from initial premises (cf. the 'hypothetico-deductive method'). However, since the reasoning linking premises to expectations is a practical reasoning whose formal properties are (to say the least) not fully understood, there is room for considerable 'slippage', especially as we in fact relied on an intuitive sense of means-ends relationships between goals and utterance-types. Another problem is that if we take some face-redressive goal like 'be pessimistic about the success of the FTA', this suggests that an utterance like 'You don't want to pass the salt' should be polite; that it is not, of course, is due to the fact that it attributes impolite desires to the addressee: in short, our system 'over-generates' and needs to be complemented with a set of 'filters' that check that a chosen utterance form has no impolite implicatures for other reasons (as outlined in *1.1 above), as in this case it does because of a rather complex reflexive reasoning that takes account of the implied presumptions about the addressee's beliefs (see Leech 1983:170). We are thus less sanguine now than we were about the possibility of real precision in this area because of the enormous complexities of the reasoning involved.

In a related way, we may have over-claimed about the 'precision' of our system as an ethnographic tool, a means of discovering the nature of social relationships in a culture. The method relies on our equation that the 'gravity' of an FTA is a function of the social relation between speaker and addressee on the one hand and the intrinsic face-threatening content of the FTA on the other (our 'R' factor). One problem here is that we underplay the influence of other factors, especially the presence of third parties, which we now know to have much more profound effects on verbal interaction than we had thought (see Bell 1984; Goffman 1981, on 'footing'; Levinson, n.d.). Another problem is that to use the method as an ethnographic tool, one needs to know a lot about the particular cultural factors involved in the assignment of R-values; for example, one needs to know that asking where someone is going is impolite in Tamil, we think because of cultural concepts of destiny. Without this knowledge, no computation of perceived social relationships from language usage is sound.

However, where R-factors and the influences of audiences are understood, and where generalizations are taken from sufficient instances of observed language usage, it is indeed possible to use the distribution of polite forms as a highly sensitive index of the distribution of social equality and inequality, intimacy and distance, as shown (we believe) for example by Brown (1979, 1980), Levinson (1982).

If our theory is perhaps less precisely articulated than we thought, the doubt may arise that it is in fact so loose that it makes claims verging on the vacuous, the unfalsifiable. Consider, for example, our prediction that an off-record strategy should be associated with large requests, or distant or elevated addressees. However, we note that utterances that have the 'hint'-like nature of off-record utterances may be used in circumstances where no defensible alternative interpretation is available, i.e. they are in fact 'on-record', in which case they may occur with lesser requests or to less distant or elevated addressees. The problem here of course is that it is not so easy to verify empirically some notion like 'having in context only one defensible interpretation'.

In any case, though we admit that there are areas of our theory that may be hard to test empirically, there is no doubt that the theory makes strong (perhaps overstrong) predictions: for example, the asymmetry of strategy choice between participants in asymmetrical social relationships of authority/subservience, and the exact nature of that asymmetry with more face-redressive strategies employed by the lower ranking participant. Thus there would be many kinds of clear counter-examples to the theory, none of which seem to have been substantiated, although there have been a number of experimental results at least in part contrary to our predictions. We now turn to these, and to other considerations provoking reassessment of some of our particular claims.

2.2 Detailed reassessments

There have been a number of reports of empirical tests of our specific claims, including some attempts to operationalize and quantify those claims, and there has been a great deal of detailed work on particular usage phenomena which we incorporated, often fairly cursorily, in positive and negative politeness strategies — work for example on honorifics, on speech acts of particular sorts, on use of grammatical features like the 'vivid present', the passive and dative, particles and evidentials, and on conversational uses of irony and metaphor. We will briefly assess a selection from this work in relation to modifications suggested to our general and specific arguments.

2.2.1 Cultural notions of 'face'. Central to our model is a highly abstract notion of 'face' which consists of two specific kinds of desires ('face-wants') attributed by interactants to one another: the desire to be unimpeded in one's actions (negative face), and the desire (in some respects) to be approved of (positive face). This is the bare bones of a notion of face which (we argue) is universal, but which in any particular society we would expect to be the subject of much cultural elaboration. On the one hand, this core concept is subject to cultural specifications of many sorts — what kinds of acts threaten face, what sorts of persons have special rights to face-protection, and what kinds of personal style (in terms of things like graciousness, ease of social relations, etc.) are especially appreciated (see section 7.2)[11]. On the other hand notions of face naturally link up to some of the most fundamental cultural ideas about the nature of the social persona, honour and virtue, shame and redemption and thus to religious concepts — points well made, for example, by Geertz's (1960) description of Javanese religion.

Much can be found in traditional ethnographic description that bears on this field of concepts,[12] and naturally it may be thought that our universalistic account is an inexcusable cultural denudation, or worse, ethnocentric projection. But our point is that despite the rich cultural elaborations, the core ideas have a striking familiarity. Take for example Yang's (1945:167–72) careful description of this conceptual domain in a Chinese village — he lists seven factors involved in losing or gaining face, each of which seems entirely in line with our own cultural assumptions, down to the same facial metaphor.[13] Or, to take an example from the ethnography of speaking, where the focus has always been on cultural differences, Basso (1979), in a study of Western Apache Indian joking performances portraying Whitemen, says that 'Whitemen and Apaches come to social encounters with conflicting ideas of what constitutes deferential comportment — ideas . . . ultimately grounded in conflicting conceptions of what it means to be a person and the kinds of actions that can discredit a person's worth in public situations' (1979:64). However, perusal of his description of the details of Apache self-esteem and demeanour reveals little or nothing that conflicts with our universalistic distillation of face wants into negative and positive face; Apaches differ from Whitemen not in their basic face wants (for self-approval and freedom from imposition), but in definitions of *who* they want to attend to their positive face, and in the assessment of what constitute particularly threatening FTAs. So they see interaction in the manner of white American positive politeness, where behaviour appropriate to long-term intimates comes from semi-strangers, as irredeemably invasive of their person. (The same observation is made with respect to Athabaskans by Scollon and Scollon 1981, who found our framework of direct comparative utility.) Such cross-cultural conflicts grounded in different views of what constitutes 'good' behaviour in interaction is precisely what our model was designed to accommodate (see *3.2).

It was, however, based in part on existing ethnographic descriptions of how different people elaborate notions of face, self-esteem, and personhood. Clearly, though, there is a need for more in the way of ethnographic descriptions of the ways in which people articulate face notions, rights to personal preserves, and how these affect daily life — how confrontations or shamings are managed, how people gossip (see Haviland 1977), how they clear their name from disparagement, and how face regard (and sanctions for face disregard) are incorporated in religious and political systems. A more specific issue, however, is whether our model collapses two kinds of politeness in an ethnocentric way. Harris, for example (1984), emphasizes the necessity of distinguishing between the institutional status-based requirements of face vs. the more personal side of face which is involved in popular notions of tact and kindness to the personal, individual, feelings of others, a distinction which may partially correlate with on-record vs. off-record forms of politeness. Attention to one aspect of face may be independent of attention to the other (so, for example, a doctor may be polite in informing his patient that he is dying, without being tactful, or vice versa).[14] (Leech (1977, 1983) also makes this distinction, although quite differently, and we discuss this below.)

But it is not clear that our folk notion of tact is relevant in all societies. It perhaps reflects the bias of a culture obsessed with individual rights and wants, and so with tact (as e.g. Wierzbicka 1985b claims). Rosaldo (1982), in a critique of speech act theory based on ethnography among the Philippine Ilongot, argues that the Ilongot do not interpret each others' speech in terms of the expression of sincere feelings and intentions, but stress

Wierzba 1,

14

TACT

the expectations due to group membership, role structures, and situational constraints; her description suggests to us that Ilongot notions of politeness would minimize a component of tact. Such cultural differences doubtless exist and work down into the linguistic details of the particular face-redressive strategies preferred in a given society or group. Nevertheless, for the purposes of cross-cultural comparison developed here, we consider that our framework provides a primary descriptive format within which, or in contrast to which, such differences can be described.

Leech (1983) offers a somewhat different model for cross-cultural comparison of politeness strategies. He distinguishes 'tact' (1983:109) from other modes of politeness on quite different lines, in terms of a maxim maximizing the benefit, and limiting the cost, to the addressee (which thus cross-cuts the categories of positive and negative politeness while capturing essential elements of both). He then contrasts a maxim of 'tact' ('perhaps the most important kind of politeness in English-speaking society', 1983:107) to maxims of generosity, modesty, approbation, agreement and sympathy, and suggests that cross-cultural variability will lie in the relative importance given to one of these maxims vis-à-vis another (1983:80). Thus he suggests that Japanese mores make it impossible to agree with praise by others of oneself, indicating that the maxim of modesty takes precedence in Japan over the maxim of agreement (1983: 136; but see Pomerantz 1978, for parallels in English). Only further cross-cultural work in this alternative framework will test its utility.[15]

2.2.2 P, D, R: underanalysed? In broad terms, research seems to support our claim that three sociological factors are crucial in determining the level of politeness which a speaker (S) will use to an addressee (H): these are relative power (P) of H over S, the social distance (D) between S and H, and the ranking of the imposition (R) involved in doing the face-threatening act (FTA). Grimshaw (1980a, b, c and 1983) gives prominence to the same three factors, as do (in different ways) Bates 1976, Lakoff 1977b, Lakoff and Tannen (1979) and Leech (1980, 1983). There is also strong experimental support in the compliance-gaining literature for the importance of the P and R factors in determining politeness assessments; for example, from Falbo and Peplau (1980), Baxter (1984), and Holtgraves (1984) (for the P variable), and from Cody, McLaughlin and Schneider (1981) and Lustig and King (1980), for the importance of R.

However, a number of experiments have shown opposing results to the predictions of our model for the D variable. For example, Holtgraves (1984) found that subjects judged a high degree of encoded politeness as indicating *higher* reciprocal liking between speaker and addressee, and

Baxter (1984) found that subjects prescribed that they would use *greater* politeness for close (i.e. friend) relationships. Slugoski (1985) argues this is due to the nature of friendship relationships, which do not legitimize instrumental goals (and hence bald on record utterances), and that therefore our D variable should be further broken down to distinguish familiarity from affect (intimates don't necessarily like each other, and liking predicts politeness directions which are opposite to those predicted by unfamiliarity). Slugoski demonstrates that the distinction (between affect and social distance) is also necessary in interpreting ironic utterances as either insults or compliments.

Some of these results are fairly baffling, and (as the experimenters note) often equivocal with respect to our theory. But Slugoski's finding that 'liking' is so important in distinguishing an attack (insult) from an expression of admiration (compliment) is hardly surprising. Nevertheless, we can only concede that 'liking' might be an independent variable affecting choice of politeness strategy. If so, as Slugoski argues (1985:96), some more complex arithmetical compounding of these factors might be required. It would be interesting to investigate this by looking at cultures where 'friendship' is less confounded with social distance; for example in India, where cross-caste friendships can be especially strong.

We pointed out (in 3.4.2) that P, D, and R are composite categories which are compounded of culturally specific factors. For example, as Rosaldo (1982:230) has argued, the composition of the P variable is very different in egalitarian as opposed to hierarchical societies. She goes on, though, to question whether variables like our P, D, and R are too simple to capture the complexities of the ways in which members of different cultures assess the nature of social relationships and interpersonal behaviour.

In our view, P, D, and R (as defined in 3.4.2) can be seen to subsume most of the culturally specific social determinants of FTA expression, but we must concede that there may be a residue of other factors which are not captured within the P, D, and R dimensions. In addition to the liking factor, the presence of an audience is another, as we mentioned above, which operates in part to affect definitions of situational 'formality', and so enters into the context-variability of P, D, and R assessments. It seems likely that formality (and other sorts of situation and setting classifications – see e.g. Levinson 1979a; Brown and Fraser 1979) will have a principled effect on assessments of FTA danger, and there may well be cross-culturally valid generalizations as to the direction of this effect. (See Bloch 1975; Irvine 1979; Laver 1981; Atkinson 1982; for some recent discussions of interactional aspects of formality.)

Of course there are dimensions to social relations other than those of power and social distance that show up verbally in different ways: for example, coded social statuses like that of warrior or Brahmin, in South India (Levinson 1977), or the *ade* relationship among the Kaluli of New Guinea (Schieffelin 1984), and we cannot hope to capture all the nuances of such relationships with our P, D, and R variables (but see Stiles 1981). But for cross-cultural comparison these three, compounded of culturally specific dimensions of hierarchy, social distance, and ranking of imposition, seem to do a remarkably adequate job in predicting politeness assessments.

2.2.3 On and off record, and the hierarchy of politeness.

A related set of considerations arises in relation to the various attempts to verify (or discredit) our claims as to the intrinsic ranking of politeness strategies in terms of a cost/benefit analysis; in our schema, positive politeness precedes (is less face-redressive than) negative, and negative precedes off record, because of an assessment of the risks involved in choosing each of these super-strategies. (See definitions and discussion on pp. 68–74 below.) First, two distinctions must be made: we must distinguish the overall ranking of these super-strategies from within-strategy ranking of politeness levels (for example, elaboration of politeness levels within conventionally indirect requests). And we must distinguish overt behaviour — how speakers actually use these strategies in interaction, in relation to P, D, and R assessments — from subjective ranking of perceived politeness. The questions we shall address here, then, are (1) to what extent is our cost/benefit analysis supported by this research? and (2) to what extent do subjective politeness rankings match those predicted by our model?

Experimental support for the cost/benefit approach has come from psychologists Clark and Schunk (1980, 1981), who demonstrated (contra Kemper and Thissen 1981) that experimental subjects do indeed rank English conventionally indirect speech acts in the order of politeness predicted by our theory (see pp. 142–44 below). (See also Walters 1980; Fraser and Nolan 1981, for similar rankings of indirect requests in Spanish; and Bates 1976, for Italian.)

On the other hand, certain weaknesses in our formulation have been suggested by other research attempting to apply our ranking system to new data. A number of workers have claimed (e.g. Harris, 1984; Strecker, in prep.) that our super-strategies can be mixed in discourse, that is, that we may obtain, for example, positive politeness markers within negative politeness strategies like indirect requests or off-record positive politeness. To be true counter-examples to our claims it will not be sufficient to show that in a short stretch of talk between two interlocutors two or more strategies were employed. For that stretch might contain more than one

FTA, each FTA with different R values, the distinct R values motivating different strategies. Nor will it be sufficient to show that hint-like utterances were used with explicit positive or negative face redress, for the 'hints' may in fact have been *de facto* on record. Nevertheless, these authors have persuaded us that we may have been in error to set up the three super-strategies, positive politeness, negative politeness, and off record, as ranked unidimensionally to achieve mutual exclusivity. However, one possible source of confusion here is this: when describing positive politeness, on the one hand, we included the use of 'markers' of social closeness like intimate address forms; and when describing negative politeness, on the other hand, we included the use of 'markers' of deference like honorifics. Now, although address forms and honorifics may, in certain cases which we described, be FTA-sensitive, i.e. the choice of a form and the choice to use them at all may be influenced by R-factors, yet on the whole such elements are tied relatively directly to the social relationship between speaker and addressee. The consequence of such direct 'markers' of social relationship is that they may occur with an FTA of any R-value, and thus equally with markers of positive and negative politeness; if shifts are permissible at all, we should merely expect a shift towards a more 'formal' address form than normally used (which may of course still be somewhat 'intimate') when R-values increase between the same interlocutors. Thus, certain aspects of, for example, positive politeness like 'intimate' address forms may happily occur in off-record usages motivated by high R factors. What we did not expect, and have not found, is that there might be a shift to more 'intimate' address forms with an *increase* in R.

One problem encountered in assessing the 'ranking' of positive as opposed to negative politeness is the different nature of the two. Scollon and Scollon (1981), who applied our model to the analysis of interethnic interaction between Athabaskan Indians in Canada and native English-speakers, made the point that positive politeness, which is relevant to all aspects of a person's positive face, is a quite different phenomenon from negative politeness, which is specific for the particular FTA in hand. They argue that positive politeness is naturally escalated in interaction (a positively polite utterance is naturally responded to by one upgrading the degree of positive politeness), and hence unstable; in contrast, negative politeness, lacking the escalating feedback loop, tends to be stable, suggesting (implicitly) that these two super-strategies cannot be ranked on a unidimensional scale. However, while acknowledging the fundamental differences between positive and negative politeness, we do not see them as incompatible with a systematic use in one case versus another — their ranking follows naturally from the Durkheimian perspective: rituals of approach are for lesser deities, those of avoidance for the ultimate deity (Durkheim 1915).

Other research has challenged our intrinsic ranking of politeness super-strategies, suggesting for example that off-record requests might not always be ranked as more polite than negatively polite on-record indirect speech acts. Blum-Kulka (1985) found, in a series of experiments designed to test perceptions of politeness and indirectness in English and Hebrew, that the highest politeness level in both languages was awarded to negatively polite indirect speech acts and not to hints, off-record requests. She suggests that, in requests at any rate, politeness and indirectness are linked for conventional indirect requests but not necessarily in cases of non-conventional indirectness. In part this result may have been due to the experimental design: because the use of off-record hints to do requests of a certain R level is limited to certain kinds of alters, in experimental scenarios subjects might well rank the off-record hints as less polite (since they would presume certain kinds of addressees). Furthermore, the request to rank 'politeness' level explicitly might conjure up associations of school-book notions of etiquette which do not fit happily with off-record un-explicitness. Also, the requests chosen for her experiment all assumed a relatively low R (requests not unreasonable in the context specified from S to H), so indirectness might have seemed inappropriately devious (as indicating a higher-risk FTA than was actually involved).

A genuine counter-case to our ranking of off record and negative polite-ness would exist if it could be shown that, to two different addressees, one higher in P than S and the other not higher, subjects used negative polite-ness strategies to the higher-ranking H, and off-record ones to the lower-ranking H, and, to our knowledge, no politeness ranking experiments have shown this. However, Blum-Kulka's results do suggest that in some societies (as suggested by Lakoff 1974a, 1977b), an 'efficiency' factor is involved in the assessment of payoffs of off-record vs. on-record strategies for making requests; i.e. it is perceived as rude to require a superior to calcu-late the illocutionary potential of an off-record request. We call this an 'efficiency' factor, following Lakoff's idea that this is related to cultural valuations of the superior's 'time', etc. The use of off-record speech actions is restricted by this efficiency factor and by another culturally specific expectation: that mere co-presence in an interaction is implicitly demand-ing, as it requires the superior's attention. This is certainly not the case in all societies (e.g. India, or see Philips 1974 on Warm Springs Indians), so we do not see efficiency as an intrinsic component of negative politeness for all kinds of FTAs, as do, for example, Lakoff (1977b) and Leech (1983).

One source of the impression that off-record strategies 'mix' with posi-tive and negative ones should be mentioned. When utterances constructed like hints are actually, in the context, on record (that is, when only one interpretation is acceptable in the context), they are sometimes positively polite (as with irony or understatement) and sometimes negatively polite (as with indirect speech acts). The motivation for the use of off-record strategies in on-record negative politeness is obvious enough (see 5.4.1 below), but their use in positive politeness is less obvious. A possible explanation for the positive-politeness impact of strategies like irony and understatement, for example, would lie in two characteristics of positive politeness: the reliance on mutual knowledge to decode utterances, such mutual knowledge of attitudes and values normally obtaining only between in-group members, and the fact that positive politeness uniquely allows the introduction of extraneous material (not relevant to the particular FTA in hand). There is also the point raised in recent conversation analytic work (e.g. Drew 1984) that (between interlocutors of the appropriate relationship) off-record strategies can 'invite' positively polite take-ups; by reading an ambiguous utterance as a criticism, for example, the addressee 'colludes' in the negative attitude which was indirectly conveyed. (See also Drew's analysis of pre-emptive self-invitations, discussed in *3.4. below.) However, the fact that strategies may be shuffled from off record 'down' (in terms of face redress) into positive or negative politeness, while not necessarily creating problems for the interactants, may be problematical for the analyst.[16]

In general, despite the various deviations from our expected hierarchy that have emerged from some of these experimental tests, no one (to our knowledge) has come up with clear evidence of a counter-ranking: where (for example) positive politeness is used for greater FTAs, negative politeness for smaller ones, or where off record is used for smaller FTAs (or to lower-status Hs) than negative or positive politeness. It may not be unproblematic to construct valid indices of the social variables P, D, and R (as the Baxter and Slugoski studies indicate), but insofar as this is achieved, the predictions of our model should be testable.

At present, in the absence of definitive evidence that we got the ranking wrong, there are good arguments for insisting that off-record strategies are generally more polite than on-record. For one thing, as we argued in detail below (section 5.4.1, strategy 1), the appearance of utterances constructed as off-record hints in cases where they are actually on-record requests (giving H a token 'out' in interpreting the utterance as a request) would not otherwise be motivated. In a similar way, the diachronic origin of honorifics in off-record strategies (cf. section 8.1.3.7) also argues for the greater degree of politeness for indirectness. A third point is that off-record strategies are a solution half-way between doing the FTA on record and not doing it at all; therefore, in the absence of context-specific implicatures to the contrary, we would expect them to be more polite than on-record performances of the FTA. Fourthly, the off-record super-strategy is a natural extension of negative politeness (in adding an additional element of avoidance), analogous to Radcliffe-Brown's 'avoidance' relation as the relationship of extreme respect (1952). And a final source of support for our ranking comes from research in second-language usage; for example, Chun et al. (1982), and Day et al. (1984), found that 'correction' of a non-native speaker's utterances by a native-speaker interlocutor tended to be more 'on record' if they were friends, and off record for higher D relations.

In our view, present evidence is too equivocal to entail the abandonment of our original scheme. But we do concede that the possibility that the off-record strategy is independent of, and co-occurrent with, the other two super-strategies is something which definitely requires close investigation.

2.3 Problems of quantification and operationalization

A number of attempts to test our hypotheses directly by applying them to actual language usage data, either experimentally induced or naturally occurring, have run into difficulties in operationalizing the model and in coding the data. Shimanoff (1977) for example, tried to use our politeness strategies as categories for quantitative tests of the hypothesis that women's speech would be more highly elaborated for politeness; no sex differences were found, and a number of difficulties in applying the model appeared. For example, 3% of her sample of 300 strategies involved 'crossovers', where negative politeness strategies were serving positive politeness functions and vice versa. And Baxter (1984), as mentioned above, had experimental subjects rank utterances with respect to likelihood of use in eight situations, and perceived politeness; she found subjects reported that they would use more politeness in close relationships, and ranked positive-politeness strategies as more polite (in some respects) than negative-politeness ones. Blum-Kulka's experimental results (1985) mentioned above likewise displayed an inverted order to assessments of politeness for indirect speech acts and off-record hints.

To what extent do these results reveal inadequacies in our model, and to what extent problems in the operationalizations favoured by the experimenters? It should be pointed out, first of all, that our strategies were never intended as an exhaustive taxonomy of utterance styles, but rather as an open-ended set of procedures for message construction, and they therefore do not necessarily provide sensible categories for quantitative

research. Secondly, experiments attempting to get subjects to rank politeness assessments need to manipulate or control for each of the three factors D, P, and R, and to report exactly what utterances the subjects were
required to assess, in order for the results to be interpretable in terms of
our theory.

But thirdly, and more critically, there are intrinsic difficulties in trying
to obtain quantitative measures of politeness strategies in naturalistic
interactional data. Problems with frequency counts that emerged in the
attempts by Shimanoff (1977) and Brown (1979) include:

1   The count of redressive features may be high but native-speaker
     intuitions are that the utterance is not very polite, or vice versa. This
     may be due to the fact mentioned above, that our strategies are an
     open-ended list; polite redress (or impolite counters to overt polite-
     ness markers) may be being done in ways (e.g. intonational or
     kinesic) which are not captured by the counts. Also, as argued
     throughout (see *1.1), politeness is *implicated* by the semantic struc-
     ture of the whole utterance, not communicated by 'markers' or
     'mitigators' in a simple signalling fashion which can be quantified.

2   Not all instances of a given strategy may be being used to do polite-
     ness, since (as we stressed, p. 93) politeness is not the only motiva-
     tion for using these strategies; they may for example be used to put
     on a social 'brake' or 'accelerator' in the development of social rela-
     tionships, or an off-record utterance may be used to avoid responsi-
     bility for actions unrelated to face concerns.

3   The semantics and pragmatics of utterances must be taken into
     account in assessing degree of face redress; if the overt content of
     an utterance is rude, for example, politeness strategies won't neces-
     sarily redeem it. And the speech act function of utterances, and their
     R ranking in the culture, must be coded before our politeness model
     can be applied to assess degrees of face redress.

In our view, therefore, quantitative evaluations of polite redress in
natural language data must always be preceded by, and supplemented with,
qualitative ones. Controlled experimental tests of our model should, however, be possible, given the specific predictions it makes about the ranking
of super-strategies, the ranking of politeness levels within strategies, and
the summative nature of P, D, and R assessments.

2.4 Recent work on linguistic themes

2.4.1 Honorifics. Honorifics provide obvious and important evidence for
the relation between language structure, politeness and social forces in

general, yet because of the ethnocentric nature of much sociolinguistics they have been relatively neglected. However, recently there has been a considerable increase in interest, and there is sufficient further evidence against which to test our earlier generalizations.[17]

In the body of the work, we refer to honorifics under a number of headings: first, and most obviously, as motivated by a strategy of giving deference (5.4.3 Strategy 5, p. 178ff); secondly, as diachronically motivated by a strategy of impersonalization (5.4.4 Strategy 7; p. 198ff), this predicting the person-number switches found for example in polite pronouns of address; thirdly as providing evidence for a tendency for higher strata in complex societies to be concerned especially with negative politeness, while lower strata elaborate internal positive politeness (7.2, p. 245ff); fourthly, as providing good evidence for the non-arbitrary nature of polite forms, being for the most part 'frozen' or grammaticalized outputs of productive politeness strategies (8.1.3.7, p. 276ff).

Recent work confirms the importance of all these themes. Let us take first the diachronic sources of polite pronouns. Three cross-linguistic surveys confirm our generalizations (independently, Levinson 1978, based on a sample of 38 languages; Head 1978, based on about 100 languages; Wenger 1982, based on more detailed examination of 11 languages). These surveys confirm that pluralization, substitution of third person for second person, and other person switches, are widespread throughout the world, and common in that order[18]; the regularities are such that a number of quite detailed implicational universals can be stated (see Head 1978; Levinson 1978; Wenger 1982). Thus (contrary to Brown and Gilman 1960, who assumed these were diffused culture traits), there must be strategically motivated sources for these switches — deference is not encoded in language by the use of *arbitrary* forms, but by the use of *motivated* forms (see also Haiman 1985:154). This is of course the hub of all our claims, here illustrated in one area but on a world-wide scale: polite forms cannot be fully understood within a Saussurean structural perspective of an arbitrary system of oppositions that thus varies from culture to culture; rather they are systematically motivated by a reasoning from the proper treatment of the social person, and thus have the universality they empirically do. We may also note that a number of our detailed hypotheses, like the diachronic development of addressee honorifics from referent honorifics, now have supporting evidence (see e.g. Wenger 1982).

We therefore argue that honorifics are frozen conversational implicatures, constituting some of the best examples of Grice's category of *conventional implicature* (Levinson 1979b, 1983:127ff). However, the conventional implicatures attached to honorifics do not exhaust their social significance — because a particular dyadic pattern of exchange is what distinguishes deference (high P) from mutual formality (high D) (Brown and Levinson 1979:296-7; see also Bean 1978:Ch. 8.). Levinson (1978) notes that one can also state universals on the social valuation of dyadic exchanges of honorifics (as on p. 250 below), and this can be related to a potentially universal *exchange symbolism* (see *3.5 below and Levinson 1982:116ff).

The kernel idea of our politeness theory, that some acts are intrinsically threatening to face and thus require 'softening', finds ratification in microcosm in the domain of honorifics. For there is enough cross-linguistic evidence for the FTA-sensitivity of the use of honorifics that one can confidently predict that, for example, honorifics will especially co-occur (often at an upgraded level) with requests (see e.g. Bean 1978: 39-40, for Kannada; Hill and Hill 1978:139 for modern Nahuatl; Paulston 1976:376 for Swedish; McClean 1973:93 for Nepali; Haviland 1982:61 for the Australian language Guugu Yimidhirr; Duranti 1981 for Samoan — the last cites co-occurrence with disagreements).

Of all our generalizations in this area, the idea that politeness strategies, and thus the use of honorifics, might be used differently in the high and low levels of stratified societies, with higher levels emphasizing V and lower ones T, was the most daring and the least substantiated at the time. Since then we have found some limited confirmatory evidence, if only at the level of informal observations and stereotypes (see e.g. McClean 1973:91; Slobin 1963:199). In so far as this pattern is confirmed, our hypothesis about the probable importance of social network (p. 246) receives backing from the growing evidence for the power of that level of social organization as a sociolinguistic determinant (Milroy 1980). However, there is also some distinct counter-evidence to the hypothesis: Lambert and Tucker (1976) found that, according to children's reports, Canadian middle-class families use more internal *tu* than working-class families; and Bates and Benigni (1975) found the same pattern for Italian address. However, in the Italian study, upper-class informants expressed the belief that lower-class informants used more familiar forms, and the authors conclude that either the sort of hypothesis we are maintaining is a middle-class myth, or there has in fact been radical change (1975:276-9). One cross-cutting factor here, it has been argued (Levinson 1978), is another generalization about group tendencies in the use of honorifics, namely the tendency for rural families to be more authoritarian, and thus to use more asymmetrical T/V and other politeness forms, than families of similar socio-economic status in cities (for evidence see e.g. Paulston 1976; Lambert and Tucker 1976; Hollos 1977:223) — for the Bates and Benigni working-class population seem to be quite largely rural migrants from South Italy. Thus generalizations about class-stratified patterns of honorific use will always have to be restricted to relatively stable, traditional stratified populations. With this proviso in mind, the hypothesis still seems to us to be open, and worth pursuing. Incidentally, the great sociological utility of honorifics in the study of stratification is demonstrated in detail in two independent studies in the same region of India (Levinson 1977 and 1982; Den Ouden 1979; see also Bean 1978:118ff).

The relationship of honorifics to the use of our more open-ended politeness strategies is something that requires further investigation. For example, it is noteworthy in Tamil that some direct requests (specifically those of low R) may occur from subordinates to superordinates, providing that such requests are mitigated with the appropriate honorifics; this might suggest that in some languages the burden of politeness might be carried more by the grammaticalized system of honorifics and less by matters of language use. However, this inference does not seem to be generally correct; there is not, as it were, a certain quantity of politeness to be conveyed by one channel (the grammaticalized honorifics) or another (strategic language use) — politeness is usually redundantly expressed in both. Thus, Mackie (1983) finds that our politeness strategies are used by Japanese children even before they have acquired the complex honorific system in full.

Cross

2.4.2 Cross-cultural data on speech acts and FTAs. In the past ten years, many books and papers have appeared, exploring how particular kinds of speech act are realized in different contexts and in different languages, and much of this research deepens our understanding of cross-cultural parallels in politeness strategies for particular kinds of 'face-threatening acts' or FTAs. Our review here can do no more than sample this large literature (see bibliography in Verschueren 1978 and in press).

The heavy emphasis on requests, that derives from psychological and linguistic studies of speech acts, was reflected in our presentation of the politeness strategies, and is still prevalent in the literature, although it is now being supplemented by information on many other kinds of potentially face-threatening act. In addition to the work on requests by linguists, carried out within the framework of speech act theory, there is a large body of work on 'compliance-gaining' in the communications literature, for example (see Baxter 1984, and the bibliography therein), and work on children's acquisition of pragmatic competence still maintains a strong focus on requests (see references in *3.3 below). There is a great deal of other material on requests in English (e.g. Clark and Lucy 1975; Ervin-Tripp 1976, 1981; Gibbs 1979; Jacobs and Jackson 1983). Cross-cultural work on requests includes the large-scale project reported in Blum-Kulka and Olshtain 1984, which investigated requests and apologies in Hebrew, Danish, German, Canadian French, and British, American and Australian English; Haverkate (1979) and Walters (1979) explored requests in Spanish; and there have been other studies comparing requests in English with those in Greek (Drossou 1985, Tannen 1981c), and in German (House and Kasper 1981), comparing white Australian and Aboriginal English in Northeastern Queensland (Eades 1982a), white and black Americans (Weigel and Weigel, 1985), and examining requests amongst Israelis (Blum-Kulka et al. 1985), the Ilongot (Rosaldo 1982), and the Wolof of Senegal (Irvine 1985), to mention just a few.

Relatively formulaic polite 'routines' have also received a fair share of attention. Particularly interesting, as Goffman (1967) insisted, are apologies and associated ways of repairing delicts with face-threatening consequences: Owen 1983 is an in-depth study of apologies and remedial interchanges in English, with a framework for cross-cultural comparison (built on similar principles to our account of face-redressive strategies) with sample applications, while Coulmas (1981) compares thanks and apologies in certain European languages and in Japanese; Fraser (1981), Edmondson (1981), Cohen and Olshtain (1981) and Olshtain (1983) offer additional perspectives on apologies. Cross-cultural work on other politeness formulae includes Firth 1972, Goody 1972, Ferguson 1976, Tannen and Öztek 1981, Laver 1981. We also have much new information on how people do particular FTAs, for example compliments in English (Manes 1983; Manes and Wolfson 1981; and see Pomerantz references below), and among Spanish-American bilinguals (Valdés and Pino 1981), announcements (of intended actions, including threats and warnings) in German (Rehbein 1981), and American English invitations (Wolfson, D'Amico-Reisner and Huber 1983). In addition, an important development is attention to speech actions of these kinds in a sequential context — for example, politeness uses of pre-sequences (Beach and Dunning 1982), invitations (Davidson 1984), requests (Wootton 1981), compliments (Pomerantz 1978, 1984a), the seeking of information (Eades 1982a, b); but we discuss these developments in *3.4 below.

Another area in which research has proliferated is the examination of conflict and confrontation in interaction; how this is done — and what constitutes a slight — has obvious implications for any theory of politeness. Benoit (1983) examines children's threats, Bleisener and Siegrist (1981) look at conflicts between doctors and hospital patients, McLaughlin, Cody and Rosenstein (1983) and McLaughlin, Cody and O'Hair (1983) explore 'account' sequences (after initial hostilities) in conversation, Bonikowska (1985a, b) and House and Kasper (1981) look at the speech act(s) of complaining (and Schegloff n.d. explores the attribution of complaining, intentions to prior speakers), D'Amico-Reisner (1983) examines disapproval sequences. There is in addition a growing literature on the management of arguments in conversation (Boggs, 1978; Lein and Brenneis 1978, Goodwin 1980a, b, 1982, 1983; Goodwin and Goodwin, in press; Jackson and Jacobs 1980, 1981; Jacobs and Jackson 1982; and Maynard 1985), in relation to the preference for agreement which is an observable feature of conversation (Pomerantz 1984a). Related work on confrontatory interactional styles includes Kochman 1981, 1983, 1984, on Black/White styles of confrontation in the US, and Tannen 1981a, b and Schiffrin 1984 on aggressiveness in US Jewish conversational style. (See also section *3.2 on miscommunication and interactional style.)

Clearly, there is now a great deal more evidence concerning the cross-cultural realization of face-threatening speech actions. Much of this material is descriptive and classificatory and does not attempt cross-linguistic comparison; but there are also significant attempts to formulate frameworks for such comparison (see e.g. Olshtain and Blum-Kulka 1983; Wierzbicka 1985a) and to criticize them (e.g. Rosaldo 1982).

Some of this might at first appear to be quite challenging to our thesis: for example, the relative absence of mitigating or face-redressive features associated with, say, requests in some communities (see e.g. Rosaldo 1982; Weigel and Weigel 1985; Wierzbicka 1985b); or the apparent preference for confrontation in some interactional styles (Goodwin 1980a, 1983). However, by and large, we believe that the evidence falls in line with our predictions, and that the exceptions are the kind allowed for by the specific socio-cultural variables we introduced (see 7.2 below; *2.0 above).

2.4.3 Other linguistic realizations of politeness strategies.

Aside from the construction and use of address forms, honorifics and indirect speech acts, which have received most attention, detailed studies have appeared of some of the other phenomena we described as involved in constructing linguistic realizations of positive and negative politeness strategies. For example, our claim (pp. 194-96) that passive and dative constructions can be used negatively politely, to distance S and H from the FTA, has been supported by Berk-Seligson's (1983) study of grammatical case usage in Costa Rican Spanish, where she illustrates how non-active constructions (especially dative and reflexive passive) are used to avoid attribution of blame to persons in adverse situations, and argues that this phenomenon is common in many dialects of New World Spanish.

Other areas of current interest which bear upon politeness issues include the communication of affect, an area at present of special interest within the ethnography of speaking. Stimulated by Ochs (in press b) on

Samoan, B. Schieffelin (Schieffelin, in press; Schieffelin and Feld, in press), Feld (1982) and E. Schieffelin (1980) on the Kaluli of New Guinea, others have begun describing how affective states are communicated in different societies and languages (e.g. Irvine 1981, 1982). Insofar as the display of affect is socially constructed, with cultural and situational expectations about what and how feelings should be displayed, work here links in directly with our discussions of face-threatening acts (3.2), positive politeness strategies (5.3), and cultural ethos (7.2.1). Other work from a more strictly linguistic perspective also contributes to our understanding of the intensifying mechanisms which convey socially appropriate levels of affect (see e.g. Labov 1984 on intensifers in Black English Vernacular, and linguistic work on discourse particles and evidentials, e.g. Goldberg 1982; James 1983; Gibbons 1980; Wierzbicka, ed., in preparation). Here again the tension between universals and cultural particulars is a matter of primary concern.

Irony is another phenomenon we considered (pp. 221-2 and 262-5) which has received considerable attention recently, partially as a critical case used to challenge or refine Grice's theory (e.g. Kaufer 1981; Sperber and Wilson 1981; Sperber 1984; Clark and Gerrig 1984; Slugoski 1985; Slugoski and Turnbull 1985). Work here, as well as empirical work on the use of irony in conversation (e.g. Brown 1979: 470-501; Roy 1976, 1977, 1978; Tannen 1984a: Ch. 6) tends to support our analysis of how on-record irony operates as a positively polite stressing of in-group knowledge and commonality of attitudes. Studies of joking behaviour (e.g. Basso 1979, for Western Apache) and ritual abuse (Parkin 1980) also support this point.

Other linguistic realizations of positive politeness strategies have received empirical attention, for example the use of slang (Gordon 1983), and of tense manipulations as a form of point-of-view switching to emphasize commonality of perspective (Johnstone n.d.; Schiffren 1981; Wolfson 1982). A study of deixis in kin term usage (Carter 1984) provides evidence that quite young children can do this kind of point-of-view switching.

In short, this (very partial) review of recent work demonstrates that there is now available a great deal more detailed information bearing on the particular linguistic realizations of politeness strategies which we formulated. Had we had access to all this material originally, our account of these details would doubtless have been more precise and better founded.

3.0 Recent developments

Turning now from the linguistic details to more general issues, there are several areas of current research where findings have tied in closely with our concerns in this paper. We will focus on four of these. First, from a number of different disciplines critical attention is being focussed on the language use of nonpowerful or disadvantaged groups (women, ethnic minorities, second-language learners, for example), and here the question of cultural particulars vs. universal patterns is foregrounded. Secondly, there is interesting work in the child language field on the acquisition of politeness strategies and children's use of indirect speech acts. Thirdly, there is a great deal of current work on the structure of conversation, which although carried out within a frame of reference quite different from the one we operate within here, has turned up many properties of conversational organization which tie in directly with matters of politeness. And fourthly, there is a recent attempt to apply our framework of politeness to the analysis of ritual. We will briefly survey research in these areas and assess its contribution to the concerns of the present volume.

3.1 Language, power and control

The work done within this rubric raises two questions central to our model. On the one hand, are there, as the model would predict, discernable patterns of language usage characteristic of members of nonpowerful groups, and on the other, are the difficulties encountered in communicating across linguistic subculture boundaries interpretable in terms of parameters provided in the model? We made some stabs at predictions about these matters in 7.2 below, but recent work has prompted us to develop these ideas further.

3.1.1 Women and language use. One body of research that might be expected to support or contradict our framework is the burgeoning work on women's language use. Here we can only selectively review work of immediate pertinence.[19]

There are of course differences between the speech of men and women that may have nothing whatever to do with our framework — linguistic indicators of female identity for example (as in Koasati, Haas 1964); or certain paralinguistic features (Laver 1968; Loveday 1981.) Also, much of the work in this field has dealt with sexism in linguistic structure and in the content of speech, matters peripheral to our concerns here. But directly relevant is the line of research attempting to describe the features of gender-differentiated styles (or 'genderlects'), sparked off by the arguments popularized by Lakoff (1975, 1977a, 1979) that women are more 'polite' than men. Empirical tests of Lakoff's specific claims (that women use more tag questions, hesitation markers, and 'trivializing' adjectives, for example), have by and large failed to substantiate them in detail (see for example Dubois and Crouch 1975; Crosby and Nyquist 1977; Brouwer, Gerritsen and de Haan 1979; Edelsky 1979; Brouwer 1982; Baroni and d'Urso 1984), but the argument that women have a distinctive 'style', due to their distinctive position in society, is still being actively pursued, despite the persistence of negative evidence (no clear sex differences found) in much of the research.

In trying to understand the often very elusive and subtle differences between language use of men and women, we need to be crystal clear about exactly where and how the differences are supposed to manifest themselves. For example, we need first to distinguish behaviour in same-sex dyads and cross-sex dyads. We also need to distinguish effects due to sex of speaker from those due to sex of addressee. And we need constantly to remember the obvious but always pertinent fact that gender is just one of the relevant parameters in any situation, and is indeed potentially irrelevant in a particular situation.[20] Thus we need to specify closely some claim of the sort that 'women are more polite than men' — more polite than whom, to whom, about what and in what circumstances?

As we make clear below (7.2), our framework makes available just a few possible parameters that can account for variation in politeness levels. The most obvious of these is the P variable: if gender is, as seems to be generally the case, a contributory factor in the perception of social asymmetry, power and authority, then we might expect to find that women are more polite to some arbitrary interlocutor than are men from the same status-bearing group (family, caste, class, etc.); also that, for any arbitrary speaker, there ought to be more politeness shown to a male than a female addressee of the same status-bearing group. However, any such simple predictions are likely to be confounded by the fact that if gender may play a role in P assignments, it certainly plays a (sometimes compensating) role in D assignments.[21]

If we now turn to the literature, we find that the evidence is equivocal: the many negative results where predicted sex differences were not found suggests uni-causal explanations in terms of P (i.e. that women are universally subordinate to men and therefore more polite) will not do justice to the complexities. Some studies do show the importance of P; for example, work on interruptions (e.g. Zimmerman and West 1975; West 1979) shows that, not only do men tend to interrupt women, but high-status men interrupt low-status men, high-status women interrupt low-status women, and adults interrupt children, suggesting that P is the important factor here.[22]

Insofar as P factors account for the differences between men's and women's speech, these differences are, in a sense, epiphenomenal – neither the social underpinnings (the P differential) nor the linguistic manifestations are specific to gender. An obvious testable corollary of this reductionist claim is that when women are in positions of high authority vis-à-vis some interlocutor, we should expect these women to be less polite than speakers of lower status of either sex (a finding of the work by Ochs, in press a, on Samoan, and others).

However, there are indications that not all gender differences in the use of language are accounted for just by the P-factor. If they were, (a) high status women should talk exactly like high status men (insofar as gender is irrelevant to that estimation of status, and the other factors D and R are held constant); (b) the characteristics of 'female speech' should be entirely context-dependent, only manifesting themselves in circumstances where gender plays a crucial role in P (or D assessments). But the claim that there are true 'genderlects' perhaps presumes something more than this, namely that there are stabilized patterns of language use characteristic of male and female identities; and this is in part an empirical matter, but in part a matter of definition, of what constitutes a 'stabilized pattern of language use', and how variable across contexts is it allowed to be.

A second source of variation in politeness levels provided by our model is the D factor. We hypothesized (pp. 245–6) one effect of differentials in D assessments, namely, that women would be more likely to develop positive politeness strategies to a high degree, at least insofar as they operate dense social networks, these kinds of network possibly being quite generally associated with lower-status groups. The issues here are closely related to one raised in the work of Labov and his associates on sociolinguistic variables in large Western cities, on the tendency of women to 'hypercorrect'. A quite general finding is that women typically use more prestigious dialect variables (more 'standard' phonological forms) than men do in comparable situations (Labov 1966; Trudgill 1974b; Cheshire 1982). Work by Milroy (1980) has shown that this phenomenon appears to be attributable not directly to sex but to the relative *absence* of dense female networks: in the Belfast working-class communities she studied, men typically had denser social networks than women – density being associated with divergence from the standard dialect. (And in the exceptional community where women had denser networks than men, men were the leading users of the standard linguistic forms.) This suggests that in the large Western cities where these studies have been carried out, women may well not be analogous to other lower status groups (based on class, caste, or ethnicity) in their tendency to develop dense networks, although in other societies like Tenejapa that does seem to be the pattern (see also

Gal 1979), with the expectable association of positive politeness with female–female interaction. Finally, we should mention here an attempt (Deucher 1985) to link the female 'hypercorrection' data directly to polite accommodation to male (and other high-status) investigators (see also Bell's 1984 reassessment of this area).

Notice, though, that insofar as sex differences in language use are captured in the kinds of linguistic dimensions described in our politeness strategies, it is possible that they are due to perceived differences in the one variable in our model that is not dependent on social attributes of the interlocutors, namely the R-factor that measures the perceived intrinsic 'danger' of an FTA. For this is clearly sometimes assessed differently in different subcultures, and it may be that where gender groups are sufficiently segregated, there is a systematic higher rating of FTAs by women. Where this was the determinant of greater politeness by women, there would be precise predictions: for example, two men of equal status and social distance (say, cousins) should use less-face-redressive measures than two women of equal status and social distance (cousins). This kind of account was in fact developed by Brown (1979) to deal with the characteristics of female speech in Tenejapa, a society where the sexes are relatively segregated. We think it is unlikely to be the case where they are not, as among the urban middle classes in industrialized societies.

In short, despite the volume of work on sex differences in language, the various possible contributory variables (P, D, R, sex of speaker vs. hearer, etc.) have not been carefully enough controlled for this research to be used to test our hypotheses in the way that we might have hoped. Whether it is in general true cross-culturally that 'women are more polite than men', and if so, whether this is a simple and direct consequence of the systematic contribution of gender to P and D assignments, remain open questions. Meanwhile, current research on gender and speech is moving in other directions.[23]

We may mention here that in addition to studies of gender and language use there is an increasing literature on other aspects of speech by groups or individuals of lower status or lower power, which may be brought to bear on these questions, including work on medical encounters (e.g. Treichler et al. 1985; see also other papers in Kramarae et al. 1984), classroom interaction (e.g. Cazden 1979), judicial proceedings (O'Barr 1982), police interviews and magistrates courts (Thomas 1983b, 1985). (See also the articles in van Dijk 1985:vol. 4.) In the communications literature, our politeness framework has been employed to analyse strategies of control in employer–employee relations; for example, Fairhurst et al. (1984) explored the employer's use of positive face support in controlling poor performances, and showed that positive face support was associated with a higher performance rating of the employee. And Kline (1981) devised coding schemes for measuring positive and negative face support and applied them to managers' strategies of control. Indeed, it has been suggested that the analysis of linguistic politeness might have quite general application in social skills training (Good, in press). All of this material on 'unequal encounters' (Thomas 1983b) will potentially provide many useful insights into the ways in which asymmetrical social relationships are displayed in, and perpetuated through, interactants' use of linguistic strategies.

3.2 Cross-language, cross-cultural interference in interaction

Another area concerned with the linguistic manifestations of social inequality is the study of interethnic communication, focussing on the performance of minority group members in communication tasks defined by majority group norms (see reviews by Verschueren 1984; Tannen, in Van Dijk 1985: vol. 4). Pioneering work here by Gumperz and colleagues (1978a, b, 1982a, b) has shown that the most subtle linguistic cues, ranging from the placement of intonational nucleus to the rhetorical structure of an argument, can systematically differ between majority and minority varieties of the 'same' language, with the consequence that exasperation, incompetence, aggression and so on may be unintentionally signalled. Since in Western democracies, at least, much in the way of opportunity is channelled through the brief and crucial 'gate-keeping' interview (Erikson and Schultz 1979), failure to match another ethnic group's standards of linguistic decorum may be fatal to individual social advancement.

The interest of this kind of research to investigations of politeness is at least threefold. First, the possibility of such miscommunication, especially amongst ethnic groups in long and daily contact, might be thought to undermine our claims about the essential universality of politeness strategies. Of course, though, it does nothing of the sort: it demonstrates that the most subtle differences in the prosodic or pragmatic features of a linguistic variety are sufficient to engender mismatches in perceived politeness (Labov 1978), even without differences in the perception of the social relationships and FTAs being negotiated. Secondly, and relatedly, this work is interesting confirmation of the key role of Goffman's concept of the 'virtual offence', which predicts that the non-communication of the polite attitude will be read not merely as the absence of that attitude, but as the inverse, the holding of an aggressive attitude.[24] Thirdly, and most importantly, work on interethnic miscommunication constitutes an entirely different and intriguing method for discovering cultural norms of politeness. This method, the discovery of social norms through the study of their systematic violation, has long been advocated by Garfinkel (1972; Heritage 1984b:Ch. 4), and has been put to good effect here not only by Gumperz, but also by other work to which we now turn.

Scollon and Scollon (1980, 1981, 1983) have explicitly analysed inter-ethnic communication partly within the framework of our politeness theory to produce an assessment of interactional difficulties between Canadian Athabaskan Indians and (monolingual) English speakers. One basic finding was that Athabaskan interactional style is characterized by the negative ('deference') politeness based on the assumption of reciprocal social distance (high D) (1981:Ch. 7), with a serious mismatch to the positive ('solidarity') politeness assumed by English-speaking Americans in gatekeeping interviews. The mismatch is a 'double-bind' condition, where the Athabaskan feels incapable of adopting the positive politeness of an intimate relationship, but is then involved in the asymmetrical giving of respect symbolic of low status (1981:186-7). Scollon and Scollon in fact recommend that 'gatekeepers' in interethnic interviews should adopt negative politeness strategies because of the intrinsic dangers of the assumption of positive politeness. Interestingly, working in a quite unrelated framework, Basso (1979) has developed similar themes in his sensitive ethnographic work on Apache views of interactions with Whitemen.

Brown (n.d.) and Brown and Levinson (in prep.) in a similar vein have analysed Aboriginal/Non-Aboriginal interaction in Northern Queensland; Chick (1985) has analysed South African Black/White interaction. Other studies in more limited domains have described (and explicitly or implicitly, contrasted) interactional styles in American Jewish society (Tannen 1981a, b; Lakoff and Tannen 1979), among Greeks, Greek-Americans and Americans (Tannen 1981c, 1982), between Cree Indians and 'whitemen' (Darnell 1985), between American men and women (Maltz and Borker 1982), between German and English (House and Kasper 1981), and Japanese and English (Barnlund 1975; Loveday 1982).

The practical implications of this work are many, primarily perhaps for the training of 'gatekeepers'. However, as Schegloff (n.d.) points out, the maintainance of intersubjectivity is a frail affair even where there are no obvious problems of linguistic or ethnic differentiation, a maintainance that depends on the possibility of 'repair' (including correction). Since the techniques used to accomplish repair in any one language or variety appear to be invariant to the kind of problem or error that requires it (Schegloff, Jefferson and Sacks 1977), one practical consequence is the importance of establishing shared repair techniques.

But most important for our present concerns is the cross-group perspective on details of politeness strategies explored by this research: as in-depth studies of cultural differences in interpretive strategies and inter-action accumulate, we should be able to refine our analysis of the ways in which the quality of interaction determines particular cultural assessments of the P, D, and R factors, and specify more precisely the relationship between cultural particulars and the universal principles of interaction which seem to underlie them.

3.2.2 Second language learning.

Closely related interests are pursued in the extensive body of research on learning a second language. Here issues of cross-language, cross-cultural interference are of prime concern, and in this work the focus on differences has tended to obscure cross-linguistic parallels in the construction of utterances.

Some of the research in this field has directly addressed the question of the transfer of politeness strategies from one language to the other. Studies of native/non-native English speakers' judgements of politeness in indirect speech acts (Carrell and Konneker 1981; Fraser and Nolan 1981; Scarcella 1980; Scarcella and Brunak 1981; Walters 1980, 1981) have demonstrated that politeness rankings of differently formulated requests, for example, are highly correlated for native and non-native speakers (as we predict they would be), although there is some evidence that learners perceive more politeness distinctions than do native speakers, suggesting that they may be over-sensitive to distinctions of grammatical form (mood, modals, and tense) in different request forms. Thomas (1983a) criticizes this work for underplaying the effect of context on such rankings. Other work has examined the interaction of sex and age with politeness factors in second language users (Rintell 1979, 1981; Zimin 1981), finding evidence of transfer from native (in this case Spanish) pragmatic strategies into English.

A second line of enquiry has focussed on cultural differences in norms and values underlying our P, D, and R assessments — the extent to which speakers from different cultural backgrounds emphasize hierarchy vs. equality, or individualism vs. social harmony, for example, and the nature of the social person (public vs. private self) — in relation to degree of directness in formulating utterances (see, for example, Blum-Kulka 1982, 1983; Loveday 1982; Richards and Sukwiwat 1983), and to rhetorical patterns in speech (Clyne 1981; Loveday 1983; Tannen 1984b; Varonis and Gass 1985).

A third dimension involves looking at speakers' strategies for facilitat-ing mutual understanding between native and non-native speakers (Faerch and Kasper 1984). For example Chun et al. (1982) and Day et al. (1984), extend our on/off record distinction to assess the form of native speaker corrections of non-native speaker utterances; in line with our predictions they found that on-record corrections were more likely when the interlocutors were friends. (See also Schegloff, Jefferson and Sacks 1977; Jefferson n.d.)

While all this work has focussed on cultural differences, and has clearly demonstrated that even minor differences in interpretive strategies carried over from a first to a second language (e.g. whether an upgliding or downgliding intonation pattern conveys a polite offer) can lead to misunderstandings and cross-group stereotyping of interactional style, there is (as pointed out in the prior section) no inherent contradiction between this evidence of the pervasive effects of linguistic and cultural differences and our own insistence on underlying universal (or 'generic') properties of the linguistic construction of utterances, which we see as deriving from universal constraints on human interaction. For our model of politeness, the significance of the work on second language interference as well as that on cross-cultural interaction lies in the great accumulation of detailed information about how speakers of different languages use and interpret politeness strategies, and how the factors P, D, and R are differently assessed (Thomas 1984). In the main, it supports our claim that it is differential assessments of these three factors which produce those variations in interactional style which we called 'ethos'.

3.3. Child language and the acquisition of politeness

Another area of research to which the student of politeness looks with interest is the field of child language. A considerable amount of the extensive literature on child language development has focussed on the acquisition of particular types of speech act, especially requests or 'directives', and on the acquisition of politeness formulae and strategies (see, for example, Garvey 1975; Ervin-Tripp 1977, 1979, 1982; Ervin-Tripp et al. 1984; Ervin-Tripp and Gordon, in press; James 1978; Read and Cherry 1978; Gleason 1980; Wood and Gardner 1980; Newcombe and Zaslow 1981; and papers in Ervin-Tripp and Mitchell-Kernan 1977; Ochs and Schieffelin 1979; Wolfson and Judd 1983). Most of this work has been on English, but there are a number of studies of other languages (e.g. Bates 1976 on Italian; Hollos 1977 on the acquisition of the T/V system in Hungarian; Hollos and Beeman 1974 on directives in Norwegian and Hungarian; Mackie 1983 on Japanese; Ochs in press b on Samoan; Schieffelin 1979, in press, on the Kaluli of New Guinea). A parallel line of research has explored aggressive and 'rude' behaviour in children (Benoit

1983; Boggs 1978; Lein and Brenneis 1978; Katriel 1985; see also *2.4.2 above). Others have looked at how children acquire sex-differentiated communicative norms and interactional styles (see e.g. Edelsky 1977, and review in Maltz and Borker 1982).

A number of interesting points have been raised by this work. It appears, for example, that children as young as 2½ years old can use and understand question forms of directives; Bates (1976) found Italian 2½-year-olds were using the Italian form of 'please', and upgrading the politeness of their requests in response to unsuccessful direct first attempts, and by the age of 4 were using formal address forms in play. Newcombe and Zaslow (1981) also found 2½-year-olds in English using question forms and even indirect hints as directives. However, they suggest that the children were not necessarily using such hints for politeness reasons but rather, especially where the hints were statements of need, because they expected adults to attend to their needs. Therefore, when compliance wasn't forthcoming, the tendency was to repeat their requests in a more explicit form, rather than 'softening' them as the Italian children in Bates' study did. A few examples of truly subtle hints were identified, however, suggesting that by a very young age, perhaps by 3, children are able to employ strategic hints for politeness (or other) reasons.

Mackie's work on Japanese (1983) claims that children control polite strategies like hedging, long before they learn the elaborate formal system of honorifics. She argues that Japanese children don't begin to learn honorifics until they enter school, at about age five, and it takes many years to acquire the full system of subject/object honorifics. The first- and second-grade children in her study used no referent honorifics, and only one used addressee honorifics (the desu/masu formal style), but all demonstrated the ability to use several degrees of politeness, constructed of things like tone of voice, sentence-final particles (hedges), and preference for agreement.

Studies such as these suggest children begin acquiring strategic variation in utterance formation naturally, along with the acquisition of language, and that formal markers of politeness (honorifics, address variables) come later and are more explicitly taught. It is clear from the limited amount of material already available that studies of how children use language in different languages and cultures will, almost regardless of their intended focus, greatly contribute to our understanding of the processes by which politeness is incorporated into a child's verbal repertoire. Issues of special interest would be whether the features we claim to be universal precede the acquisition of language-specific forms of politeness (as the precedence of the acquisition of strategies over honorifics hints); whether the acquisition of linguistic politeness can be correlated with the growth of skill in

37

handling social interaction in general; and what role specific cultural
beliefs about 'face' play in socialization.

3.4 Politeness, discourse and conversation analysis

If issues of politeness have the wide ramifications we envisage, then clearly
such matters should inform the structure of day to day conversation. In
6.3, we referred to some ways in which this might be the case, but since
then much published work in conversation analysis has greatly deepened
our understanding not only of conversational 'mechanics', but also of the
way in which modulations of these serve to communicate the essentials of
social relationships.

One area of particular pertinence is what conversation analysts call
preference organization (see Atkinson and Heritage 1984: Part II; Levinson 1983:332ff). The term refers to the phenomenon that after specific
kinds of conversational turn, responses are often strictly non-equivalent:
one kind of response, termed the *preferred*, is direct, often abbreviated
and structurally simple, and typically immediate; in contrast, other kinds,
termed *dispreferred* are typically indirect, structurally elaborated, and
delayed (Pomerantz 1975, 1978, 1984a). The preferred type of response is
usually more frequent also, but the term 'preference' refers to the structural disposition, to the fact that conversational organization conspires to
make it easier to use the preferred type of turn, not to participants' wishes.
In this sense it can be shown that there are preferences for matters as
diverse as: (i) agreement (vs. disagreement); (ii) repair by self (vs. repair
by other of mistake or unclarity by self); (iii) acceptances (vs. rejections)
of requests and offers; (iv) answers (vs. non-answers) to questions; in addition, preferences also hold across sequence types, for example, (v) offers
by A (as opposed to requests by B to A); (vi) recognition by other of self
on telephone (vs. self-identification); and so on.

If one asks what determines which kinds of response are preferred vs.
dispreferred, in this structural sense corresponding to unmarked vs. marked
in form respectively, a large part of the answer must surely lie in face
considerations (Heritage 1984a, 1984b:268). For example, taking the
above list, agreement is preferred because disagreement is an FTA (as
noted in 5.3); self-repair because correction by other may imply that self
is misguided or incompetent (3.2.1); acceptances of offers or requests
because the alternative refusals would imply lack of consideration (5.3.2);
as might non-answers to questions. In the case of (v), the preference for
an offer-acceptance sequence over a request-acceptance sequence, clearly

there is less face risk in A's inducing B to make an offer than in A making a request of B, because B may refuse the request, but not withdraw the offer. And in the case of (vi), the preference for recognition without overt self-identification on the telephone can be attributed to the deleterious positive-face implications of failure of immediate recognition (like name forgetting). Thus face considerations seem to determine which of two alternative responses after another turn will be normally associated with the unmarked, preferred turn format. (Incidentally, the use of the unmarked simple form to do the stereotypical, expected and structurally predisposed action, while any departure from this will serve to signal the complement of that interpretation, fits in with a Neo-Gricean theory of implicature developed in Horn 1984, and in Levinson, in press).

Sometimes, face considerations motivate conflicting requirements. For example, Pomerantz has explored the interaction of the preference for agreement with compliments on the one hand (1978) and self-denigrations on the other (1984a). To agree with a compliment is, Pomerantz notes, to run counter to a constraint against self-praise. To preserve something of both the preference for agreement and the constraint, various intermediate turn types are often used: agreements with praise-downgrade; agreements about praiseworthiness but with praise shifted to third party; return compliments. Self-denigrations also raise problems for the general preference for agreement, running counter to a constraint against criticism of others: again, intermediate solutions involve, for example, agreement with self-inclusion; implicit agreement by silence or minimal acknowledgement. All three of the principles here seem to lie firmly in the realm of face-motivated behaviour: the preference for agreement follows from positive face considerations (see 5.3 strategy 5), as does the constraint against criticism of alter, of course; while the constraint against self-praise follows from face considerations in a way parallel to the way in which honorifics work — just as to raise the other is to imply a lowering of the self, so a raising of the self may imply a lowering of the other.

A feature of preference organization that is of special interest here is that it makes possible a whole range of face-preserving strategies and techniques. For example, given that preferred turns should immediately follow a first turn, the slightest delay is often sufficient to signal that the recipient does not in fact intend to produce the preferred action (will reject the request, invitation, etc.); this makes it possible for the speaker of the first turn to resume with a modification, in an attempt to make the initial action more acceptable (Davidson 1984; Pomerantz 1984b), or even to withdraw it (Goodwin 1979), even though no overt rejection has taken place.

We noted that some kinds of entire sequence (of conversational turns) are preferred to others. Again, face considerations help to explain this, as Heritage has pointed out (1984a). We noted for example the preference for inducing offers over making requests. But how does one induce an offer? One way is to give a prior indication that a request may be coming up, and this may be done by means of a 'pre-request', a turn that typically checks out whether some precondition for a request obtains (e.g. 'Do you still have that good bicycle?'), thus making it clear that a request may follow — which may be pre-empted by an offer. In this sort of way, face considerations motivate many kinds of pre-sequences (see review in Levinson 1983:345ff). But they also motivate more indirect 'fishings' still, where reports of events may be used to elicit other reports (Pomerantz 1980), offers, etc. (Drew 1984). Drew gives the following sort of example: if A announces the acquisition of some new furniture, and B then pre-empts an invitation to come and see it by requesting permission to do so, B conveys 'the essence of sociability' — a pre-emptive display of caring about what is important to the other. Thus by reporting events that make such a display possible and pertinent, A can make relevant such a pre-emptive self-invitation without in any way requiring it — B can quite appropriately offer congratulations or other appreciations of a lesser sort. Pre-sequences and 'fishings' thus allow the off-record negotiation of business with face implications well in advance of the possible on-record transaction. Thus nearly all of the structural predispositions that have been studied under the rubric of preference, and many aspects of pre-sequences, seem to be motivated by face considerations.

There is much other work in conversation analysis that is pertinent to our themes, but let us single out one topic in particular, how 'troubles' are broached and received (the subject of extended research by Jefferson 1980, 1984a, b; Jefferson and Lee 1981). A's announcement of a misfortune (which may be, as in the case of a death or a divorce, a matter that one is socially obliged to communicate) poses various interactional problems. A may appear to be upset, not in control, not properly maintaining 'face' (3.2.2); to counteract which reports of 'troubles' are often delivered by the 'troubled' with laughter 'exhibiting that, although there is this trouble, it is not getting the better of him; he is managing' (Jefferson 1984b:351). Although laughter by speaker typically invites laughter by recipient, here of course recipient refrains from laughter and treats the report as a serious matter. Thus A attends to the face implications of A's 'not managing', while B attends to the face implications of A's trouble. Although of course if B properly refrains from laughter while A reports the misfortune, A may nevertheless find a subsidiary topic offering comic relief (again, displaying self-control), and manage to induce reluctant laughter from B, who will nevertheless typically display 'a tremendous caution about and sensitivity to engaging in laughter in the course of a troubles telling' (1984b:358).

Reports of misfortunes raise additional interactional problems: how to disengage from the topic without seeming to belittle its import. In fact, Jefferson finds that in the majority of cases the only available solution seems to be to end the conversation without introducing further topics (1984a). Alternatives may be to 'restart' the conversation with the 'How are you' or 'What have you been doing?' typically reserved for the beginning; or to seek a change in topic that is nevertheless focussed on the troubled participant's welfare, 'in effect, a breaking away from talk about a trouble exhibits deference to it by preserving the interactional reciprocity that is a feature of such talk' (1984a:194). Alternatively, the trouble-teller may lay the ground for a 'step-wise transition' to a new topic by introducing, in the final stages of troubles-telling, ancillary material that invites elaboration in other topical directions. In short, the face implications of the reports of troubles are quite sufficient to structure the entire conversation from the point of their introduction.

Although we have scarcely done justice to its depth and subtlety, all this work conspires to show how complex and intricate are the ways in which conversational organization is interwoven and informed by the concern with participants' self-esteem and its preservation. This work is essential for establishing the empirical basis for speculations of the sort we have indulged in. While our framework could hardly be said to predict all these details, it does suggest a more abstract level of explanation to which conversation analysis might usefully refer, perhaps reconstructing our ideas in line with the emerging empirical observations. It is a matter of regret that so little conversation analysis has been done in non-Western languages, especially by native speakers of them, but this lacuna will we hope be filled in the near future.[25]

Naturally, politeness is prototypically exhibited in conversation and other kinds of face-to-face interchange, and so other approaches to discourse analysis, using different kinds of text (predominantly narrative) have contributed less to our theme. A notable exception here, though, is the linguistic approach by Labov and Fanshel (1977) which concentrates on the analysis of a therapeutic interview. They attempt to enrich the philosophical theory of speech acts by building in social felicity conditions; for example, they suggest (p. 78ff) that there are felicity conditions on requests requiring that (the speaker believes that) the addressee has the obligation to do what is requested, and the speaker the right to tell the addressee to do it. Thus one can construct an indirect request by mentioning one of these conditions. Further, they propose a distinction between 'mitigation' and 'aggravation', and claim that reference to needs and abilities is generally mitigating (as in *Do you have enough time to dust this room?*) while reference to obligation (as in *Shouldn't the room be dusted?*) is generally aggravating (1977:85). Thus a scale of politeness (or 'mitigation') of indirect request forms can be predicted which more or less coincides with the accounts by us below and by Leech (1983).

We cannot here discuss the Labov and Fanshel approach in detail (see Levinson 1983:286ff, 1986); suffice it to say that insofar as it succeeds as an account of politeness it does so because it builds the FTA nature of speech acts into their felicity conditions, and does so illegitimately (we believe) because there do not in fact appear to be such social felicity conditions (e.g. one can ask a stranger for change where there is neither obligation to give nor right to tell the addressee to provide change). In addition, no account is given of *why* references to abilities and needs are 'mitigating' while references to obligations are 'aggravating' (in requests, but why are they 'mitigating' in offers? cf. Leech 1983:107ff). Here advances in conversation analysis have shown that the theory of indirect speech acts, wherein the questioning of a felicity condition can serve to perform the relevant speech act, can be recast in sequential terms: so-called indirect speech acts are in fact pre-sequences designed for co-operative pre-emption or tactful evasion (Schegloff 1979; Levinson 1983: 356ff); to question needs and abilities is to offer an escape route, which is in fact the escape route most typically used (Wootton 1981), an important fact noted by Labov and Fanshel themselves (1977:86ff).

Labov and Fanshel's analysis raises many further pertinent issues. One is the conventional nature of 'frozen mitigators' (1977:83ff; cf. Levinson, 1983:274), much addressed in the speech acts literature (see *2.4.2 above)[26]. Another important question they raise is whether family life is not in fact more characterized by 'aggravation' than 'mitigation' (1977: 84; cf. Wootton 1981; Ervin-Tripp et al. 1984), and thus whether our interests in politeness should not be better balanced by an interest in confrontation (see section *2.4.2).

We have selected for review just two trends in a rapidly growing literature concerned with the sequential analysis of verbal interaction from many different perspectives, many of which inevitably touch on issues germane to politeness (for a compendious review, see Van Dijk 1985)[27], and some of which are directly focussed in that direction (see e.g. Owen 1983 on remedial interchanges). However, the essential lesson from all this work is that the kind of perspective which we have emphasized, which focusses on the internal structure of conversational turns that realize FTAs, is properly and necessarily complemented by a focus on what came before and what comes next, for it is those two contingencies that the internal structure of a turn is specifically adapted to: thus an upgraded offer (Davidson 1984) looks back to a polite, perhaps implicit, refusal and forward to a possible acceptance.

3.5 Politeness as ritual

The 'ritual' character of politeness has been much stressed by Goffman and others. One diagnostic of ritual is often held to be repetitive or pre-patterned behaviour. Although our theory plays down the importance of politeness routines by stressing the 'generative' production of linguistic politeness, polite formulae clearly form an important focal element in folk notions and in the distinction between 'personal' tact and 'positional' politeness (*2.2.1 above), where the latter is associated with formulaic decorum (Coulmas 1979, 1981).

However, here we wish to focus on politeness as a model or prototype for other kinds of ritual. In recent work, Strecker (in preparation) has tried to show that many of the politeness strategies that we elucidate have clear parallels or exploitations in the structure of ritual and ceremony. We cannot do justice here to his suggestions, but find them intriguing, and prompted by his work we here record our own thoughts on the interrelation of interpersonal politeness and the formal rites that have preoccupied anthropologists.

That there must be simple and direct links we dimly saw when we borrowed the distinction between negative and positive politeness from Durkheim's distinction between negative and positive rites, which is worth quoting in full:

> By definition sacred beings are separate beings. That which charac-
> terizes them is that there is a break of continuity between them and
> the profane beings. ... A whole group of rites has the object of realiz-
> ing this state of separation which is essential. Since their function is
> to prevent undue mixings and to keep one of these two domains
> from encroaching upon the other, they are only able to impose
> abstentions or negative acts (1915:299).

However, he adds,

> Men have never thought that their duties towards religious forces
> might be reduced to a simple abstinence from all commerce; they
> have always believed that they upheld positive and bilateral relations
> with them, whose regulation and organization is the function of a
> group of ritual practices. To this special system of rites we give the
> name of *positive cult* (1915:326),

43

and he goes on to adduce rites of sacrifice, initiation and 'representation'.

Goffman has suggested that the interest of interpersonal ritual is partly, in our Western urban settings, as a kind of residue from our earlier ritually dominated forms of public life:

> In contemporary society rituals performed to stand-ins for super-natural entities are everywhere in decay, as are extensive ceremonial agendas involving long strings of obligatory rites. What remains are brief rituals one individual performs for or to another, attesting to civility and good will on the performer's part and to the recipient's possession of a small patrimony of sacredness. What remains, in brief, are interpersonal rituals. These little pieties are a mean version of what anthropologists would look for in their paradise. But they are worth examining. (1971:63).

But we wish to reverse the suggestion: interpersonal rituals are not some poor residue of the 'staged' rituals of some prior age, they are rather the primordial origin, and the omnipresent model for rituals of all kinds. As Durkheim (1915:73) put it, seeming to take this view:

> The human personality is a sacred thing; one dare not violate it nor infringe its bounds, while at the same time the greatest good is in communion with others.

The key prototype for the sacred thing is the social person; grand rites are, on this view, projected from the interpersonal to the larger stage of the set-piece ceremony. Perhaps we could even embrace a Malinowskian 'extensionalism': the prototypes for all ritual are familial, or at least based in the kinship domain, so that the prototype positive and negative rites are distributed across the parents and uncles and aunts as predicted by Levi-Strauss's 'kinship atom' (e.g. in matrilineal societies, the father receives positive rites from the child, the mother's brother negative rites, and in patrilineal societies the pattern is reversed).

If, following Strecker, we can find in the treatment of the sacred, in the details of high ritual, the same minutiae of symbolic expression that we can find in verbal politeness, perhaps this 'extensionalism' can be shown to have real foundation. One element in such a theory would have to be Leach's (1966) rejection of the definition of ritual as a type of event, specifically a non-instrumental, obliquely communicative kind of activity — instead, as he urges, we must see it as a *mode* of action that may accompany the most instrumental of activities. Then there is a natural continuum from the prototype familial interpersonal rituals, through the elaborate interpersonal rituals of adult life to the highly cathected sacred rites that are so prominent in traditional societies (as suggested by e.g. Geertz's 1960 description of the religion of Java).

Here, we would like to focus on just one kind of parallel between inter-personal ritual and institutionalized rites, and this is the way in which our ideas about typical dyadic rituals of interpersonal communication (p. 250ff) suggest a startlingly simple theory of a universal *symbolism of exchange*. Our starting point is from the details of a particular kind of linguistic exchange, namely the use of the polite (or V) and intimate (T) pronouns. We deal below (in 5.4.3, Strategies 5 and 7) with these from the point of view of linguistic politeness, but here we are interested in their use in line with a much more general pattern of exchange. Brown and Gilman (1960) drew attention to the generality of the following pattern: in relations of intimacy, A and B exchange T pronouns; in relations of social distance (or non-intimacy) A and B exchange V pronouns; in rela-tions of dominance where A ranks higher than B, A gives T and receives V. Although, as they noted, there is here an iconic relation between asym-metrical social relations and asymmetrical usage, that alone will not explain the direction in which the particular pronouns are used, or why symmetrical T should have the value it does in contrast to V. Further, their appeal to particular historical conditions (the double Roman Emperors of the fourth century), is not sufficient for what we now know is a world-wide generality for this particular pattern (see Head 1978; Levinson 1978; Wenger 1982); hence the attempt below to relate an explanation to universal principles of politeness.

However, through work done in an Indian context, it became clear to us that the pattern extended beyond linguistic exchanges. Marriott, Mayer, Dumont and others (see Marriott 1976) have shown conclusively that the complex patterns of food and service exchange between castes in Indian villages have a symbolic valuation as follows: in relations of social equality or alliance, castes exchange cooked food; in relations of dominance, the higher caste provides cooked food and the lower caste reciprocates with services. Most Indianists have looked at this purely in terms of a Hindu metaphysic concerned with exchange and ritual purity, but the pattern properly construed is in fact quite general. From a detailed study of the relation between verbal and non-verbal exchanges in a Tamil village (Levin-son 1982), it is clear that the use of the T pronoun patterns in a highly complex series of precise parallels like the use of cooked food, and the use of the V pronoun patterns more or less like the provision of services. What on earth do the T pronoun and cooked food have in common? In essence, both are 'intimate stuff'. What then do the V pronoun and the provision of services have in common? By contrast, they are 'non-intimate stuff'. With this clue one may look more broadly within the Indian village for parallels, and find that who will approach and sit with whom, who will delouse whom, who will physically avoid whom, and so on, all pattern, where cultural restrictions allow, in the same sort of way; that is, symbols of intimacy (commensality, grooming, approach and propinquity) are used like the T pronoun, *both* as symbols of intimacy and domination. And fitting neatly into these patterns one can find the use of positive politeness and bald-on-record politeness strategies (as detailed below) being used both symmetrically as symbols of equality and asymmetrically (downwards, as it were) as symbols of domination. In India, there is evidence (see Beck 1972:172; Levinson 1982) that the relations of social equality and hierarchy that are first expressed, disputed and finally stabilized in the interpersonal rituals of linguistic (and interactional) exchange are then slowly converted into the more rigid idiom of the institutionalized rituals of commensality (as in the order of eating at a Brahman feast). In short, not only are the rituals of the exchange of 'intimate stuff' on the interpersonal level paralleled on the level of 'staged' ritual, but the interpersonal rituals can be shown to have priority.

Further reflection will show that these are not peculiarly Indic patterns. An English country gentleman, like an Indian landlord, to this day can feast his tenants, but would refrain from accepting food from them; one-way 'commensality' is dominance. Again, a social superior (teacher, boss) may use the form of English address, the first name, otherwise used reciprocally amongst intimates, but receive title plus last name (otherwise used reciprocally among non-intimate equals) in exchange. The widespread nature of these patterns is well known. Intimate stuff used non-intimately takes on a different, but highly predictable, meaning, namely the symbolism of dominance (a prototype for which can be found, perhaps, in the relation between parent and child).

With some temerity we suggest that this simple reasoning might be applied quite generally to the analysis of rituals of exchange. Consider Mauss's (1966) remarks about the 'gift': why on some occasions is the gift an expression of solidarity (cf. below under 5.3.3), and on others an expression of hostility and domination? Symmetrical non-competitive giving would have the same symbolism as T-exchange, but attempts to out-give, to arrive at a state where one party cannot reciprocate in kind, is by our simple principle of asymmetrical exchange of intimate stuff, to claim dominance, as in the Kwakiutl potlatch. Part of this is just anthropological commonplace, as Leach remarks (1976.6): 'If you return my gift in kind ... the behaviour expresses equality of status. But if the reciprocity involves gifts which are different in kind ... the behaviour expresses inequality of status'. But it is the nature of the gifts that flow in opposite directions that establishes who is dominant, and the peculiar predictability of the one-way use of 'intimate stuff' that is our special contribution here.

We have dwelt on rituals of exchange, but there are other connections (many raised by Strecker, in preparation) between interpersonal rituals and grand rites. But perhaps the most important is the role of ritual in social control, a role long emphasized by social anthropologists. Bloch (1975:5ff) for example specifically links verbal politeness to political control through the constraints it imposes on next actions by addressees. Bloch, thinking primarily of traditional oratory, sees these constraints as directly imposed by the sequential rules of formal speech, but perhaps a more subtle perspective is the one indicated by Goffman's concept of the 'virtual offence' (p. 1 above): politeness, in exactly specifying the semiotics of offence, and in so making offensiveness as much a loss to the instigator's as to the target's 'face', produces the social order of everyday life out of the primordial chaos of self-seeking individuals.

4.0 Conclusions

This review of recent work will, we hope, have indicated both in general and in detailed ways many directions that future research may usefully take. We would like to conclude with some general observations and remarks on relevant trends in some of the contributory disciplines.

The very range of the material we have reviewed might give rise to the suspicion that politeness, construed in this broad way, subsumes just about every facet of the social world; and thence to the concern that there is no unitary field of enquiry here. Of course, every attempt at synthesis is open to such suspicions; we lay our case on the detailed evidence that these aspects of language use and our three main social parameters simply do cohere, and we point out that though broad in scope our perspective is in some ways narrow — for example, in the short shrift given to cultural variations, the minimization of factors other than our three social parameters and the reluctance to generalize from an act-based account to an account of style (all matters complained about by commentators).[28]

Rather than assemble a curio collection, we believe we happen to have stumbled on (not without prior guides of course) an area where many orthogonal aspects of social life converge in a set of crucial preoccupations in social interaction. We hope that the interdisciplinary interest in politeness will promote further work in general on social interaction. Our framework attempts to tie together phenomena of quite different kinds, from parameters of social structure to the linguistic details of message construction, each the preserve of various disciplines. But the integration is possible, if indeed it is, just because there is one domain where all these factors are instantiated, namely social interaction. Since the groundbreaking work of Goffman, Garfinkel and other early workers, there have been of course signal advances in the study of this crucial domain, but it remains the Cinderella of the social sciences, despite its good claims to methodological priority (see e.g. Giddens 1984; Heritage 1984b; Schegloff, in press). We believe that work on the fundamentals of interactional systematics will continue to reveal the importance of politeness considerations in one of two ways: either the systems under investigation will be directly addressed to issues of politeness, or, more often, they will constitute the medium through which politeness is expressed. Social interaction is remarkable for its emergent properties which transcend the characteristics of the individuals that jointly produce it; this emergent character is not something for which our current theoretical models are well equipped. Workers in artificial intelligence have already detected a paradigm clash between 'cognitivism' and 'interactionism', and noted the failure of the former paradigm to account for interactional organization (see e.g. Bateman 1985; Suchman, in press); our own account suffers from the same overdose of 'cognitivism'. Work on interaction as a system thus remains a fundamental research priority, and the area from which improved conceptualizations of politeness are most likely to emerge.

However, it is only when we have achieved a good understanding of systems of interaction in a reasonable number of unrelated languages and cultures that we would find ourselves in a position to do this fundamental reconceptualization from a cross-cultural perspective. Here one naturally looks to anthropology. However, at present, there are only a handful of researchers actively engaged in the study of verbal interaction in societies outside Western cultural dominance; and of those, few have native cultural competence. We simply do not know, for example, the extent to which conversational organization is universal, although preliminary findings point to extensive parallels. The search for universals in language usage should be a major research objective: without such knowledge, the claims of cultural peculiarities in language use cannot be properly assessed, while with it the possibility of functional accounts of universal linguistic properties arises.

Meanwhile, we may hope to receive from anthropologists further intensive studies of how politeness is thought of in particular societies, i.e. folk theories of 'face', deference and demeanour. As we have pointed out above (*2.2.1), our universal claims constrain but do not determine what we would expect native concepts in this area to be. It would be worth testing these hypothetical constraints, but beyond that much might be learnt by attending directly to folk formulations, seeing to what extent they correspond to behaviour, and how cultural elaborations in this area fit cultural preoccupations in other areas.

Turning now to linguistics, and in particular to linguistic theories of

48

language usage, it is worth noting that the role of politeness in theories of pragmatics is undergoing change. When we first wrote, the major justification for the bifurcation of the theory of meaning into semantics and pragmatics was the basic Gricean observation that what is 'said' is typically only a part of what is 'meant', the proposition expressed by the former providing a basis for the calculation of the latter. In this perspective, *indirection*, together with related kinds of mismatch between the said and the unsaid, is a central phenomenon, and has received much technical attention. But why does the phenomenon exist at all? It was that motivational question that our politeness theory was specifically designed to answer. For some theorists, Leech (1983) for example, politeness still plays this central explanatory role in pragmatics. However, others think that the relation between what is 'said' and what is pragmatically calculated is really very much more complicated — for the proposition that we express by an utterance is itself determined only very partially by what is 'said': it takes pragmatic principles, for example, to fix the reference of referring expressions (Sperber and Wilson 1986; Levinson, in press). Thus, on this view, pragmatics enters the arena twice: once to fix the proposition expressed by what is 'said', the second time to calculate the indirect or contextual implications of the proposition expressed. Politeness will still be seen to play a central role in the second kind of calculation, though perhaps only a negligible role in the first kind (but euphemisms, honorifics, etc., may provide interesting exceptions). While research effort is diverted to understanding the pragmatic processes involved in determining the proposition expressed by an utterance, issues of politeness are likely temporarily to lose the limelight even though they surely deserve a good part of the stage.

In sociolinguistics, one development that we confidently expect is a change of stress away from concern with linguistic indicators of social origin and identity (as in the influential Labovian paradigm) towards a greater concern with the linguistic expression of social relationships (Brown and Levinson 1979). Of course the two concerns are linked, as stressed in 'accommodation theory' (Giles 1980, 1984; Trudgill 1981; Street and Giles 1982; Coupland 1980), and this has been underscored by Bell's (1984) re-analysis of the Labovian concept of 'style': he shows that sociolinguistic variables are tied more fundamentally to social relationships than to self-monitoring (or 'formality' conceived of as degree of attention to speech). There is already some evidence that these sociolinguistic variables perform discourse functions (Labov and Fanshel 1977), and it is therefore possible that these phonological and morphological variants vary with the kind of speech action being done — in short are FTA sensitive. In any case, a change of stress towards an interactional sociolinguistics

(Gumperz 1982a, b) promises signal advances, for all the social motivations for patterns of language use must be at least mediated through the 'playing out' of social relationships in interaction.

Such a development in sociolinguistics would have the merit of connecting issues in language use directly to matters at the heart of social theory. We may conclude by reminding the reader of the particular importance that Goffman attributed to the behaviours that we have collected under the rubric of politeness, namely as indicative of essential aspects of human nature and its social construction:

> If persons have a universal human nature, they themselves are not to be looked to for an explanation of it. One must look rather to the fact that societies everywhere, if they are to be societies, must mobilize their members as self-regulating participants in social encounters. . . . .
>
> Universal human nature is not a very human thing. By acquiring it, the person becomes a kind of construct, built up not from inner psychic propensities but from moral rules that are impressed upon him from without. . . . . The general capacity to be bound by moral rules may well belong to the individual, but the particular set of rules which transforms him into a human being derives from requirements established in the ritual organization of social encounters. (Goffman, 1967:44-5)

Notes

1 Since the first appearance of this work we have had the benefit of comments from too many people to acknowledge individually here, but we must single out Pascal Boyer, David Good, Rachael Harris, Geoffrey Leech, Ruven Ogien, Marion Owen, Ben Slugoski, Ivo Strecker, Jenny Thomas and David Zeitlin for supplying thoughts and material specifically for this introduction. The many relevant papers given at the International Pragmatics Conference at Viareggio (see Papi and Verschueren, in press) were also a useful stimulus. We must especially thank Esther Goody, whose editorial skills got the first issue of this work into print and who encouraged this reissue. We dedicate this work to the memory of Erving Goffman, from whose ideas it directly stems, and from whose encouragement we took much succour, but specifically with this thought in mind — that without him, observational studies of social interaction would hardly exist today. That dedication pre-empts proper expression of two great debts: the one to Edmund Leach, who taught Levinson what little he understands of social theory (and much else besides), and the other to John Gumperz, who taught us both how to dare to mingle sociological and linguistic speculations, and who has played a special role in establishing a field of interactional sociolinguistics. Our earlier acknowledgements to the original essay stand of course unabated.

2 Other kinds of formal protocol that regulate potential conflicts, as in the courtroom, committee room or democratic assembly, may perhaps be usefully explored in this perspective; see, for example, Atkinson 1979; Atkinson and Drew 1979. For a striking example of the role of rituals of greeting in the avoidance of conflict, see Youssouf, Grimshaw and Bird 1976.

3 References to sections in the original essay are unasterisked; those to sections of this introduction are preceded by an asterisk.

4 The sense in which (at least some) Gricean principles might be said to be 'asocial' in contrast to politeness principles is nicely shown up by the contrast between human interaction and man–machine interaction — see Pateman 1982b; see also Good 1985.

5 Leech refers here to Bolinger's notion of a *second-instance proposition*, i.e. one that presumes that another is entertained in the context; see here also Sperber and Wilson's concept of an *echoic utterance* (1986:237ff).

6 This is another place where Leech unnecessarily proliferates maxims by positing a maxim of negative uninformativeness, even whilst noting that its effects are independently predicted (1983:100ff). See Horn 1978 for a Gricean account of negation.

7 Incidentially, Riley (1981) accuses us of an inappropriate Clause-witzian or zero-sum analysis of interactional strategy. It is true that

Goffman's perspective, with its emphasis on the 'virtual offence', and the consequent metaphors of 'threat', etc., might give that impression. But the diplomatic assumption of the 'virtual offence' is precisely designed to convert a potential zero-sum game into a non-zero-sum game or game of pure coordination (Schelling 1960, Schiffer 1972) to which we obliquely referred in 4.1. See also Heritage's (1981) response to Riley. Also relevant here is Labov and Fanshel's (1977:345–6) 'paradox of microanalysis' — interactional analyses 'exaggerate the aggressive character of verbal interaction' by separating what was done from how it was done; yet they concede that 'mitigating devices do indeed mitigate conflict'. Cf. Leech (1983:113): 'the function of the Tact maxim is a negative one: it is a means of avoiding conflict'.

8   We are here primarily defending the cross-cultural relevance of the Gricean perspective; we deal below with the potentially separate issue of whether politeness can reasonably be held to be based on universal principles. Incidentally, the perspective of the individual actor we adopt can retrospectively be seen to be part of a general trend in social science theorizing (see Ortner 1984).

9   Since we made the appeal in 8.1.1 below for more linguistic work on social pressures on linguistic structure, much has appeared under the rubric of *functionalist* approaches to linguistics. Insofar as there is a unitary approach here at all, it is marked by an emphasis (which only non-specialists would think unexceptionable) on the precon-ditions a language must meet to be effective as an instrument of communication (see e.g. Givon 1979; Foley and Van Valin 1983; Leech 1983:Ch. 3). However, approaches that emphasize the social functions of language still remain relatively undeveloped. For example, Van Valin (1980), reviewing the Stanford universals volumes (Greenberg et al. 1978), notes that of all that work only Ferguson 1978, exploring crosslinguistic generalizations about baby talk, falls into that category; see also Silverstein 1979.

10   We must once again thank Dr E. Annamalai for his help here with the Tamil. We should also mention, for the record, (*pace* one reviewer), that one of the authors is a native speaker of British English, the other of American English.

11   See for example, Benedict (1946:Ch. 8) on Japanese concepts of '*giri* to one's name', or Brown (1979:Ch. 2) on Tzeltal sensitivity to slurs on female sexual morality and the showdowns they invoke.

12   For example, there is a considerable literature on the 'honour and shame' complex of Mediterranean societies, see e.g. Peristiany 1965, Pitt-Rivers 1977; for connections to linguistic politeness, see e.g. Harris 1984. Incidentally, it is as well to remember that 'folk-models' in this domain can be, like all ideology, considerably out of line with actual practice, and therefore such models cannot them-selves offer direct confirmation or refutation of theories, like our own, concerned primarily with practice.

13   Goffman (1967) in pursuing the metaphor of 'face' refers to this

study and to Mauss's (1966:38) reference to the Kwakiutl use of the same metaphor. Goffman's essay remains the essential introduction to these concepts.

14   We are grateful to Ruven Ogien and Rachael Harris for persuading us of the importance of these points. Ogien appeals for more attention to folk terms, like *tactful, polite, delicate, considerate,* etc., and the semantic field they delineate.

15   See though, in *1.1 above, our reservations about the proliferation of politeness maxims. Here we may add that such a framework in fact presupposes the core concepts of face we (and others) have developed, as the notions that integrate modesty, generosity, agreement, etc., within a single conceptual field of 'politeness'.

16   It may, for example, cause problems in quantifying strategies in an attempt to measure degrees of conveyed politeness (see Shimanoff 1977, for example, which we discuss below).

17   We cannot attempt an exhaustive bibliography here; useful bibliographical leads will be found in Head 1978, Levinson 1978, Wenger 1982, the references in the text below, and in addition, by area: for Australia, Haviland 1979a, b; for Amerindia, Hill and Hill 1979, Lefebvre 1979, Miller 1980, Mannheim 1982; for China, Scotton and Wanjin 1983, Fang and Hen 1983; for India, Bean 1978, Mehotra 1981, Levinson 1982, Carter 1984; for Japan, Ide 1982, 1983, Ide et al. 1986, Harada 1976, Mackie 1983, Neustupný 1978, Ogino 1986, Shibamoto 1985; for Java, Silverstein 1979, Smith-Hefner 1981; for the Middle East, Jahangiri 1980, Alrabaa 1985.

18   For example, there is some further crosslinguistic evidence now for the use of 'we-inclusive' as a polite pronoun of address, noted for Tamil in Table 3 below: see Lefebvre 1979 and Mannheim 1982 for Quechua, Duranti 1981 for Samoan.

19   There are a number of recent reviews of this area; see, for example, Kramer, Thorne and Henley 1978, Philips 1980, Kramarae 1981, McConnell-Ginet 1983. Recent books include Butturff and Epstein 1978; Eakins and Eakins 1978; Orasanu, Slater and Adler 1979; McConnell-Ginet, Borker and Furman 1980; Vetterling-Braggin 1981; Thorne et al. 1983; Smith 1985; Philips, Steele and Tanz, in press.

20   This last point has often been ignored in the eager search for sex differences in speech, and might well account for some of the inability to find them (e.g. Brouwer, Gerritsen and de Haan 1979). Speech in contexts where gender is salient, for example in cross-sex interaction between potentially sexually accessible interlocutors, or same-sex interaction in gender-specific tasks, would be promising areas to focus on (see Hogg 1985). Stereotypes, as portrayed in soap-operas and the like, need to be contrasted with realities (see e.g. Shibamoto 1985 and in press on Japanese women's speech; cf. e.g. Leech 1983:136–7.

21   To exemplify: if a male A addresses a female B from a higher-status group, another female C, of the same status group as male A, might

be expected to be more polite than A to B because she would be of relatively lower status due to the contribution of gender; but on the other hand B and C sharing gender may perceive less social distance, with the net result that A and B do not use perceptibly different levels of politeness to C.

22　See Schegloff, in press, however, for a critique of this work, including the observation that in the White House transcripts it appears that President Nixon tended to yield the floor to his subordinates, indicating power/status isn't necessarily directly related to interruptions. See also Lycan 1977.

23　For example, there are now empirical studies of gender styles (e.g. Brown 1979, 1980 for Tzeltal, Ide 1982, 1983, 1986 and Shibamoto 1985 for Japanese, Maltz and Borker 1982, Tannen 1982, 1984a, and papers in Philips, Steele and Tanz, in press), which relate the styles carefully to ethnographic conditions in an open-minded way.

24　Compare here Schegloff's (n.d.) observation of a perennial tendency for 'innocent' utterances to be interpreted as complaints.

25　Meanwhile, see e.g. Moerman 1977 and in press; Brown 1979; Irvine 1981; Harris 1984; Schieffelin 1979 and in press; Ochs 1984 and in press b; Bayraktaroglu, in preparation; Haviland, in preparation; for analysis of conversation in non-Indo-European languages that specifically addresses some of these issues.

26　See especially Gibbs 1979, Fraser 1980, Stubbs 1983, Holmes 1984.

27　One perspective of special relevance is concerned with the sociolinguistic description of style; see e.g. Tannen 1984a and references therein.

28　See e.g. Mathiot 1982, Slugoski 1985, Scollon and Scollon 1981:171, respectively. This paragraph is prompted by apposite remarks by Ruven Ogien.

1.00 INTRODUCTION

1.1 Prologue

This paper has a broad sweep, and a diversity of motives. It will help here at the beginning to extract and formulate our major aims. The foremost aim is simply to describe and account for what is in the light of current theory a most remarkable phenomenon. This is the extraordinary parallelism in the linguistic minutiae of the utterances with which persons choose to express themselves in quite unrelated languages and cultures. The convergence is remarkable because, on the face of it, the usages are irrational: the convergence is in the particular *divergences* from some highly rational maximally efficient mode of communication (as, for example, outlined by Grice 1967, 1975). We isolate a motive — politeness, very broadly and specially defined — and then claim, paradoxically enough, that the only satisfactory explanatory scheme will include a heavy dash of rationalism. The bulk of the paper provides evidence of the parallelisms, and demonstrates their rational sources.

But why concern ourselves with this? Is this not a problem for ethology or psychology? We confess to underlying motives of a different sort. We believe that patterns of message construction, or 'ways of putting things', or simply language usage, are part of the very stuff that social relationships are made of (or, as some would prefer, crucial parts of the expressions of social relations). Discovering the principles of language usage may be largely coincident with discovering the principles out of which social relationships, in their interactional aspect, are constructed: dimensions by which individuals manage to relate to others in particular ways. But what we present here is the tool, rather than its sociological application.[2] It is a tool for describing, in some much more precise but nevertheless simple way, a phenomenon that has been a persistent interest of anthropologists: the quality of social relationships. And since the tool is here presented with an explanatory account, we hope that its cross-cultural applicability may have more than purely descriptive status.

Another point of immediate sociological relevance is methodological: anthropologists routinely make inferences about the nature of social relationships by observations of their interactional quality. They do this unreflectingly, on the basis of implicit assumptions about universal principles of face-to-face interaction. When made explicit these amount to principles like those here described. Until sociological methodology is explicit, descriptions will have an uncertain status and must be taken on the assumption that other observers so placed would similarly observe.

It is against the background of these broad sociological aims, then, that the overt goals of this paper should be read. Returning to the overt, our subsidiary aims (or, at least, points we wish to emphasize) are these:

(i) We identify some principles of a universal yet 'social' sort, and in so
    doing provide a possible social candidate for deep functional pres-
    sures on the shape of grammars in general.

(ii) We wish to provide an antidote to the undervaluation in the socio-
     logical sciences of the complexity of human planning. The wonders
     explored in cognitive psychology, linguistics, or artificial intelligence
     have no counterparts in social theory (outside perhaps of some
     schools of cognitive anthropology, and ethnomethodology). Here
     we merely scratch, in a groping way, the surface of one area of
     interaction, and we wish to draw the attention of social scientists
     to the richness and complexity of the assumptions and inferences
     upon the basis of which humans understand and cooperate with one
     another. Consequently, we wish to demonstrate the role of rationa-
     lity, and its mutual assumption by participants, in the derivation of
     inferences beyond the initial significance of words, tone, and gesture.
     It is our belief that only a rational or logical use of strategies pro-
     vides a unitary explanation of such diverse kinesic, prosodic, and
     linguistic usages.

(iii) Hence we identify message construction (the cross-level structure of
      the total significance of interactional acts) as the proper datum of
      the analysis of strategic language use. And since we see interaction
      as at once (a) the expression of social relationships and (b) crucially
      built out of strategic language use, we identify strategic message
      construction as the key locus of the interface of language and
      society. But to understand sociological aspects of language use one
      must first explore its systematics, as we do in this paper. Socio-
      linguistics (to coin a slogan) ought to be applied pragmatics. And to
      show that the slogan can be made a programme is one of our aims.

(iv) A final goal, perhaps largely unnecessary nowadays, is to rebut the
     once-fashionable doctrine of cultural relativity in the field of inter-
     action. Weston La Barre (1972), for instance, catalogues endless
     superficial differences in gesture as evidence of relativism in that
     sphere. We hope to show that superficial diversities can emerge from
     underlying universal principles and are satisfactorily accounted for
     only in relation to them.

1.2 The problem

Our initial problem derives from the observation that, across cultures, the
nature of the transaction being conducted in a verbal interchange is often

56

evident as much in the manner in which it is done as in any overt performative acts. In other words, one recognizes what people are doing in verbal exchanges (e.g. requesting, offering, criticizing, complaining, suggesting) not so much by what they overtly claim to be doing as in the fine linguistic detail of their utterances (together with kinesic clues). For instance, it is rarely that people actually say things like 'I hereby request . . .'; and yet as soon as one hears things like 'Look, I'm terribly sorry to bother you, would it be awfully inconvenient if . . .' one knows perfectly well what sort of interactional fix one is in. Or again, even if one doesn't know the language, on seeing one person approach another with the kinesics of unusual deference (not expectable simply by virtue of the statuses of the pair) and speak to him with hesitations, *umms* and *ahhs* and the like, we have a strong clue that he is making a request or doing something that he considers (or considers that the other will consider) imposing.

As we began to formulate an account for our initial problem, we saw that it suggested a solution to some further problems. For instance, it is observable that in many languages (in circumstances where social structures permit such distinctions), when formulating a small request one will tend to use language that stresses in-group membership and social similarity (as in the inclusive 'we' of 'Let's have another cookie then' or 'Give us a dime').[3] When making a request that is somewhat bigger, one uses the language of formal politeness (the conventionalized indirect speech acts, hedges, apologies for intrusion, etc.). And finally, when making the sort of request that it is doubtful one should make at all, one tends to use indirect expressions (implicatures). The same holds, *mutatis mutandis,* for criticisms, offers, complaints, and many other types of verbal act. What these related problems seem to share is a strategic orientation to participants' 'face', the kernel element in folk notions of politeness.

Our overall problem, then, is this: What sort of assumptions and what sort of reasoning are utilized by participants to produce such universal strategies of verbal interaction? We want to account for the observed cross-cultural similarities in the abstract principles which underlie polite usage. We hope, further, that a formal model that accounts for these cross-cultural similarities will also provide a reference model for culturally specific usages: that is, it promises to provide us with an ethnographic tool of great precision for investigating the quality of social relations in any society.

1.3 Method

This is an essay not in analysis, but in constructivism.[4] We attempt to account for some systematic aspects of language usage by constructing, tongue in cheek, a Model Person. All our Model Person (MP) consists in is a wilful fluent speaker of a natural language, further endowed with two special properties — rationality and face. By 'rationality' we mean something very specific — the availability to our MP of a precisely definable mode of reasoning from ends to the means that will achieve those ends. By 'face' we mean something quite specific again: our MP is endowed with two particular wants — roughly, the want to be unimpeded and the want to be approved of in certain respects.

With this cardboard figure we then begin to play: How would such a being use language? In particular, caught between the want to satisfy another MP's face wants and the want to say things that infringe those wants, what would our rational face-endowed being do? By a strange coincidence we find that a dyadic model of two cooperating MPs (potentially with an audience) accounts for just those peculiar cross-cultural regularities in language usage that we have introduced above as our problem. We can show this by deriving linguistic strategies as *means* satisfying communicative and face-oriented *ends*, in a strictly formal system of rational 'practical reasoning'.

In carrying out this programme we lay ourselves open to the attack that we are here inappropriately reviving the economic homunculus, since our predictive model is essentially built on the assumption of rational agents with certain properties. However, there is intended no claim that 'rational face-bearing agents' are all or always what actual humans are, but simply that these are assumptions that make the most sense of the data, and are assumptions that all interacting humans know that they will be expected to orient to. A stronger point is this: it can be demonstrated that in order to derive the kind of inferences from what is said that speakers can be shown to draw, such assumptions simply have to be made. This is a technical point first made by Grice (1967, 1975) when discussing 'conversational implicature' and substantiated by work in linguistics since. If A says 'What time is it?', and B replies '(Well) the postman's been already', then A assumes that what B said was rationally oriented to what A said, and hence A derives from B's utterance the inference that it is, say, past 11 a.m. This kind of inference is what we refer to throughout as 'conversational implicature' (c.i.). The whole exchange is heard as coherent only on the assumption that B intended to cooperate, and rationally chose a means that would achieve his cooperative end. So in language usage, at any rate, it is demonstrable that such rational assumptions are in fact made.

But our hope is not merely to factor out the lowest common denominators in some aspects of language usage. We hope that our MP will provide a reference model for the description of culture-specific styles of verbal interaction; we hope in fact by this means to be able to characterize to some extent the 'ethos' of a culture or subculture, and that most ephemeral of ethnographic observations, the affective quality of social relationships.

Note that we shall be attempting here a reduction of some good, solid, Durkheimian social facts — some norms of language usage — to the outcome of the rational choices of individuals. The chances are that if you actually ask a speaker why he said 'You couldn't by any chance tell me the time, could you?' rather than 'Tell me the time', he'll say he is conforming to conventional expectations of politeness. But although, as Lewis has argued (1969), conventions can themselves be overwhelming reasons for doing things (as anthropologists have usually assumed),[5] there can be, and perhaps often are, rational bases for conventions. The observations below include, we claim, examples of such rationally based conventions.

We consider that if the predictions made by our model are borne out by the data drawn from usage in a small sample of unrelated cultures and languages, strong support may be inferred for the original assumptions. Our data consist in first-hand tape-recorded usage for three languages: English (from both sides of the Atlantic); Tzeltal, a Mayan language spoken in the community of Tenejapa in Chiapas, Mexico; and South Indian Tamil from a village in the Coimbatore District of Tamilnadu. This is supplemented by examples drawn from our native-speaker intuitions for English, and by elicited data for Tzeltal and Tamil. Occasional examples are drawn from secondhand sources for Malagasy, Japanese, and other languages. We believe it is legitimate to project from a careful three-way experiment in three unrelated cultures to hypotheses about universals in verbal interaction because, as will become evident, the degree of detail in convergence lies far beyond the realm of chance.

Model Person (MP)

2.00 SUMMARIZED ARGUMENT

We outline the argument here, to keep it from getting lost in the detailed explanations and definitions that follow. Concepts defined in the next section are in bold type. 'S' stands for 'speaker' and 'H' for 'addressee' throughout the paper; in this outline, S and H are MPs. Among MPs, it is mutual knowledge[6] that for all MPs:

(i)   All MPs have **positive face** and **negative face,** and all MPs are **rational agents** — i.e. choose means that will satisfy their ends.

59

(ii)   Given that face consists in a set of wants satisfiable only by the actions (including expressions of wants) of others, it will in general be to the mutual interest of two MPs to maintain each other's face. So S will want to maintain H's face, unless he can get H to maintain S's without recompense, by coercion, trickery, etc.

(iii) Some acts intrinsically threaten face; these 'face-threatening acts' will be referred to henceforth as **FTAs**.

(iv)   Unless S's want to do an FTA with maximum efficiency (defined as **bald on record**) is greater than S's want to preserve H's (or S's) face to any degree, then S will want to minimize the face threat of the FTA.

(v)   Given the following set of strategies, the more an act threatens S's or H's face, the more S will want to choose a higher-numbered strategy; this by virtue of the fact that these strategies afford payoffs of increasingly minimized risk:

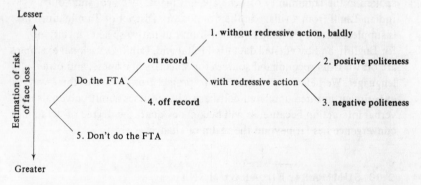

(vi)   Since i–v are mutually known to all MPs, our MP will not choose a strategy less risky than necessary, as this may be seen as an indication that the FTA is more threatening than it actually is.

3.00 THE ARGUMENT: INTUITIVE BASES AND DERIVATIVE DEFINITIONS

3.1 Assumptions: Properties of interactants

We make the following assumptions: that all competent adult members of a society[7] have (and know each other to have)

(i)   'face', the public self-image that every member wants to claim for himself, consisting in two related aspects:

   (a)   negative face:[8] the basic claim to territories, personal preserves, rights to non-distraction — i.e. to freedom of action and freedom from imposition

   (b)   positive face: the positive consistent self-image or 'personality' (crucially including the desire that this self-image be appreciated and approved of) claimed by interactants

(ii)   certain rational capacities, in particular consistent modes of reasoning from ends to the means that will achieve those ends.

3.1.1 Face. Our notion of 'face' is derived from that of Goffman (1967) and from the English folk term, which ties face up with notions of being embarrassed or humiliated, or 'losing face'. Thus face is something that is emotionally invested, and that can be lost, maintained, or enhanced, and must be constantly attended to in interaction. In general, people cooperate (and assume each other's cooperation) in maintaining face in interaction, such cooperation being based on the mutual vulnerability of face. That is, normally everyone's face depends on everyone else's being maintained, and since people can be expected to defend their faces if threatened, and in defending their own to threaten others' faces, it is in general in every participant's best interest to maintain each others' face, that is to act in ways that assure the other participants that the agent is heedful of the assumptions concerning face given under (i) above. (Just what this heedfulness consists in is the subject of this paper.)

Furthermore, while the content of face will differ in different cultures (what the exact limits are to personal territories, and what the publicly relevant content of personality consists in), we are assuming that the mutual knowledge of members' public self-image or face, and the social necessity to orient oneself to it in interaction, are universal.

3.1.2 Face as wants. It would have been possible to treat the respect for face as norms or values subscribed to by members of a society (as perhaps most anthropologists would assume). Instead, we treat the aspects of face as basic wants, which every member knows every other member desires, and which in general it is in the interests of every member to partially satisfy. In other words, we take in Weberian terms the more strongly rational *zweckrational* model of individual action, because the *wert-rational* model (which would treat face respect as an unquestionable value or norm) fails to account for the fact that face respect is not an unequivocal right. In particular, a mere bow to face acts like a diplomatic declaration of good intentions; it is not in general required that an actor fully satisfy another's face wants. Secondly, face can be, and routinely is, ignored, not just in cases of social breakdown (affrontery) but also in cases of urgent cooperation, or in the interests of efficiency.[9]

Therefore, the components of face given above in section 3.1 may be restated as follows. We define:

> **negative face:** the want of every 'competent adult member' that his actions be unimpeded by others.
> **positive face:** the want of every member that his wants be desirable to at least some others.

Negative face, with its derivative politeness of non-imposition, is familiar as the formal politeness that the notion 'politeness' immediately conjures up. But positive face, and its derivative forms of positive politeness, are less obvious. The reduction of a person's public self-image or personality to a want that one's wants be desirable to at least some others can be justified in this way. The most salient aspect of a person's personality in interaction is what that personality requires of other interactants — in particular, it includes the desire to be ratified, understood, approved of, liked or admired. The next step is to represent this desire as the want to have one's goals thought of as desirable. In the special sense of 'wanting' that we develop, we can then arrive at positive face as here defined. To give this some intuitive flesh, consider an example. Mrs B is a fervent gardener. Much of her time and effort are expended on her roses. She is proud of her roses, and she likes others to admire them. She is gratified when visitors say 'What lovely roses; I wish ours looked like that! How do you do it?', implying that they want just what she has wanted and achieved.

Our definition of positive face is adequate only if certain interpretations are borne in mind. First of all, the wants that a member wants others to find desirable may actually have been satisfied; that is, they may now be past wants represented by present achievements or possessions. Also, the wants may be for non-material as well as material things: for values (love, liberty, piety), or for actions (like going to the opera or to the races, or playing tennis).

In addition, on the view that the objects of desire are propositions like 'I have beautiful roses', natural-language expressions of wanting often leave the subject and predicate unspecified, as in 'I want an ice cream cone.' This leaves an ambiguity in our formula for some agent A's face want: A wants some B to want his wants, but is B desired to want 'B has an ice-cream cone' or 'A has an ice cream cone' or 'Everyone eats ice cream cones'? The answer seems to be that in different circumstances each of the different interpretations may be reasonable. For instance, if a male admires a female's apparel it would be a natural interpretation that he wanted her apparel for her, rather than for himself.[10]

A third point is that, in general, persons want their goals, possessions, and achievements to be thought desirable not just by anyone, but by some particular others especially relevant to the particular goals, etc. (For instance, I may want my literary style to be admired by writers, my roses by gardeners, my clothes by friends, my hair by a lover.) These others constitute a collection of sets (extensionally or intensionally defined) each linked to a set of goals.

So our formula is to be interpreted in the light of this (grossly over-simplified) example:

H wants some persons (namely a_1, a_2, a_3 ...) to want the corresponding set of H's wants (w_1, w_2, w_3 ...).

Let a_1 = set of all the classes of persons in H's social world.

a_2 = set of all the persons in H's social strata.

a_3 = H's spouse.

Let w_1 = H has a beautiful front garden; H is responsible and law-abiding.

w_2 = H has a powerful motorbike and a leather jacket.

w_3 = H is happy, healthy, wealthy, and wise.

These particular facts are obviously highly culture-specific, group-specific, and ultimately idiosyncratic. Nevertheless there do exist (in general) well-defined areas of common ground between any two persons of a society. If they are strangers it may be reduced to an assumption of common interest in good weather or other such safe topics; if they are close friends it may extend to a close identity of interests and desires. Still, however well-defined these areas are, to *assume* that (say) I am in the set of persons who will please you by commenting on your clothes is to make an extremely vulnerable assumption, one that may cause affront. It is largely because of this that attention to positive face in a society is often highly restricted.

3.1.3 Rationality. We here define 'rationality' as the application of a specific mode of reasoning — what Aristotle (1969) called 'practical reasoning' — which guarantees inferences from ends or goals to means that will satisfy those ends. Just as standard logics have a consequence relation that will take us from one proposition to another while preserving truth, a system of practical reasoning must allow one to pass from ends to means and further means while preserving the 'satisfactoriness' of those means (Kenny 1966).

The sorts of inferences one wants a system of practical reasoning to capture are things like:

(1) Vote!

(Vote for Wilson!) or (Vote for Heath!)

That is, if I want to, or ought to, or have been ordered to, vote, then to satisfy that want or command, I ought to vote for Wilson, or Heath, or anybody for that matter.

Or again, take Aristotle's 'practical syllogism', which in standard logic would follow the fallacious form of 'affirming the consequent':

(2) This man is to be heated.

If I rub him, he'll be heated.

Ergo, let me rub him.

These have a curious relation to standard logical inferences, for:

(3) John voted

John voted for Wilson

is certainly not necessarily true, but the inverse:

(4) John voted for Wilson

John voted

64

is certainly true. This prompted a suggestion of Kenny's that a *means* to an *end* should be considered satisfactory only if, when the proposition ~suggestion~ describing the means is true, the proposition describing the end is true. It turns out that based on this interpretation of practical-reasoning consequence, a decidable formal system with a semantic interpretation can be constructed, and Aristotle's intuitions can be cast into a rigorous mould which we dub 'Kenny logic'. (For more details, see section 4.00 below, and Atlas and Levinson 1973.)

A further aspect of rational behaviour seems to be the ability to weigh up different means to an end, and choose the one that most satisfies the desired goals. This can be captured by a 'fuzzy' version of Kenny logic, with an added preference operator (as discussed in 4.2 below). This will treat all preferences as rational ones, and exclude extrinsically weighted wants or Kantian imperatives — for our purposes a perfectly feasible move.

While our formal system accounts for much of the content of the intuitive notion of rationality, the latter does seem to include some notion of maximization, or minimum-cost assessment in the choice of means to an end. For example, if I want a drink of water, and I could use the tap in this room or the tap in the bathroom or the tap in the garden, it would surely be 'irrational' to trot out into the garden unnecessarily (provided that I have no secret want to be in the garden, etc.). If this is so, we can capture it by defining a perennial desire of MPs, in general, not to waste effort to no avail.

relating to the essential nature of a thing.

3.2 Intrinsic FTAs

Given these assumptions of the universality of face and rationality, it is intuitively the case that certain kinds of acts intrinsically threaten face, namely those acts that by their nature run contrary to the face wants of the addressee and/or of the speaker. By 'act' we have in mind what is intended to be done by a verbal or non-verbal communication, just as one or more 'speech acts' can be assigned to an utterance.[11]

3.2.1 First distinction: Kinds of face threatened. We may make a first
distinction between acts that threaten negative face and those that threaten positive face.

Those acts that primarily threaten the addressee's (H's) negative-face want, by indicating (potentially) that the speaker (S) does not intend to avoid impeding H's freedom of action, include:

(i)   Those acts that predicate some future act A of H, and in so doing put some pressure on H to do (or refrain from doing) the act A:

65

(a) orders and requests (S indicates that he wants H to do, or refrain from doing, some act A)

(b) suggestions, advice (S indicates that he thinks H ought to (perhaps) do some act A)

(c) remindings (S indicates that H should remember to do some A)

(d) threats, warnings, dares (S indicates that he − or someone, or something − will instigate sanctions against H unless he does A)

(ii) Those acts that predicate some positive future act of S toward H, and in so doing put some pressure on H to accept or reject them, and possibly to incur a debt:

(a) offers (S indicates that he wants H to commit himself to whether or not he wants S to do some act for H, with H thereby incurring a possible debt)

(b) promises (S commits himself to a future act for H's benefit)

(iii) Those acts that predicate some desire of S toward H or H's goods, giving H reason to think that he may have to take action to protect the object of S's desire, or give it to S:

(a) compliments, expressions of envy or admiration (S indicates that he likes or would like something of H's)

(b) expressions of strong (negative) emotions toward H − e.g. hatred, anger, lust (S indicates possible motivation for harming H or H's goods)

Those acts that threaten the positive-face want, by indicating (potentially) that the speaker does not care about the addressee's feelings, wants, etc. − that in some important respect he doesn't want H's wants − include:

(i) Those that show that S has a negative evaluation of some aspect of H's positive face:

(a) expressions of disapproval, criticism, contempt or ridicule, complaints and reprimands, accusations, insults (S indicates that he doesn't like/want one or more of H's wants, acts, personal characteristics, goods, beliefs or values)

(b) contradictions or disagreements, challenges (S indicates that he thinks H is wrong or misguided or unreasonable about some issue, such wrongness being associated with disapproval)

(ii) Those that show that S doesn't care about (or is indifferent to) H's positive face:

(a) expressions of violent (out-of-control) emotions (S gives H possible reason to fear him or be embarrassed by him)

(b) irreverence, mention of taboo topics, including those that are inappropriate in the context (S indicates that he doesn't value H's values and doesn't fear H's fears)

(c) bringing of bad news about H, or good news (boasting) about S (S indicates that he is willing to cause distress to H, and/or doesn't care about H's feelings)

(d) raising of dangerously emotional or divisive topics, e.g. politics, race, religion, women's liberation (S raises the possibility or likelihood of face-threatening acts (such as the above) occurring; i.e., S creates a dangerous-to-face atmosphere)

(e) blatant non-cooperation in an activity — e.g. disruptively interrupting H's talk, making non-sequiturs or showing non-attention (S indicates that he doesn't care about H's negative- or positive-face wants)

(f) use of address terms and other status-marked identifications in initial encounters (S may misidentify H in an offensive or embarrassing way, intentionally or accidentally)

Note that there is an overlap in this classification of FTAs, because some FTAs intrinsically threaten both negative and positive face (e.g. complaints, interruptions, threats, strong expressions of emotion, requests for personal information).

3.2.2 Second distinction: Threats to H's face versus threats to S's.

Secondly, we may distinguish between acts that primarily threaten *H's* face (as in the above list) and those that threaten primarily *S's* face. To the extent that S and H are cooperating to maintain face, the latter FTAs also potentially threaten H's face. FTAs that are threatening to S include:[12]

(i) Those that offend S's negative face:

(a) expressing thanks (S accepts a debt, humbles his own face)

(b) acceptance of H's thanks or H's apology (S may feel constrained to minimize H's debt or transgression, as in 'It was nothing, don't mention it.')

(c) excuses (S indicates that he thinks he had good reason to do, or fail to do, an act which H has just criticized; this may constitute in turn a criticism of H, or at least cause a confrontation between H's view of things and S's view)

(d) acceptance of offers (S is constrained to accept a debt, and to encroach upon H's negative face)

(e) responses to H's *faux pas* (if S visibly notices a prior *faux pas*, he may cause embarrassment to H; if he pretends not to, he may be discomfited himself)

    (f)   unwilling promises and offers (S commits himself to some
          future action although he doesn't want to; therefore, if his
          unwillingness shows, he may also offend H's positive face)

(ii) Those that directly damage S's positive face:[13]

    (a)   apologies (S indicates that he regrets doing a prior FTA,
         thereby damaging his own face to some degree — especially
         if the apology is at the same time a confession with H learning
         about the transgression through it, and the FTA thus conveys
         bad news)

    (b)   acceptance of a compliment (S may feel constrained to deni-
         grate the object of H's prior compliment, thus damaging his
         own face; or he may feel constrained to compliment H in
         turn)

    (c)   breakdown of physical control over body, bodily leakage,
         stumbling or falling down, etc.

    (d)   self-humiliation, shuffling or cowering, acting stupid, self-
         contradicting

    (e)   confessions, admissions of guilt or responsibility — e.g. for
         having done or not done an act, or for ignorance of something
         that S is expected to know

    (f)   emotion leakage, non-control of laughter or tears

These two ways of classifying FTAs (by whether S's face or H's face is
mainly threatened, or by whether it is mainly positive face or negative
face that is at stake) give rise to a four-way grid which offers the possibility
of cross-classifying at least some of the above FTAs. However, such a cross-
classification has a complex relation to the ways in which FTAs are
handled.[14]

3.3 Strategies for doing FTAs

In the context of the mutual vulnerability of face, any rational agent will
seek to avoid these face-threatening acts, or will employ certain strategies
to minimize the threat. In other words, he will take into consideration
the relative weightings of (at least) three wants: (a) the want to communicate the content of the FTA x, (b) the want to be efficient or
urgent,[15] and (c) the want to maintain H's face to any degree. Unless (b)
is greater than (c), S will want to minimize the threat of his FTA.

    The possible sets of strategies may be schematized exhaustively as in
Fig. 1. In this schema, we have in mind the following definitions.

    An actor goes **on record** in doing an act A if it is clear to participants
what communicative intention led the actor to do A (i.e., there is just

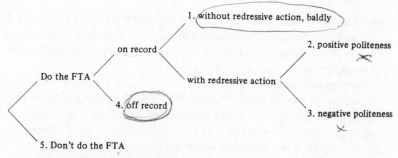

Fig. 1. Possible strategies for doing FTAs

one unambiguously attributable intention with which witnesses would concur). For instance, if I say 'I (hereby) promise to come tomorrow' and if participants would concur that, in saying that, I did unambiguously express the intention of committing myself to that future act, then in our terminology I went 'on record' as promising to do so.

In contrast, if an actor goes **off record** in doing A, then there is more than one unambiguously attributable intention so that the actor cannot be held to have committed himself to one particular intent. So, for instance, if I say 'Damn, I'm out of cash, I forgot to go to the bank today', I may be intending to get you to lend me some cash, but I cannot be held to have committed myself to that intent (as you would discover were you to challenge me with 'This is the seventeenth time you've asked me to lend you money'). Linguistic realizations of off-record strategies include metaphor and irony, rhetorical questions, understatement, tautologies, all kinds of hints as to what a speaker wants or means to communicate, without doing so directly, so that the meaning is to some degree negotiable.

Doing an act **baldly, without redress,** involves doing it in the most direct, clear, unambiguous and concise way possible (for example, for a request, saying 'Do X!'). This we shall identify roughly with following the specifications of Grice's Maxims of Cooperation (Grice 1967, 1975). Normally, an FTA will be done in this way only if the speaker does not fear retribution from the addressee, for example in circumstances where (a) S and H both tacitly agree that the relevance of face demands may be suspended in the interests of urgency or efficiency; (b) where the danger to H's face is *very* small, as in offers, requests, suggestions that are clearly in H's interest and do not require great sacrifices of S (e.g., 'Come in' or 'Do sit down'); and (c) where S is vastly superior in power to H, or can enlist audience support to destroy H's face without losing his own.

By **redressive action** we mean action that 'gives face' to the addressee, that is, that attempts to counteract the potential face damage of the FTA by doing it in such a way, or with such modifications or additions, that indicate clearly that no such face threat is intended or desired, and that S in general recognizes H's face wants and himself wants them to be achieved. Such redressive action takes one of two forms, depending on which aspect of face (negative or positive) is being stressed.

Positive politeness is oriented toward the positive face of H, the positive self-image that he claims for himself. Positive politeness is approach-based; it 'anoints' the face of the addressee by indicating that in some respects, S wants H's wants (e.g. by treating him as a member of an in-group, a friend, a person whose wants and personality traits are known and liked). The potential face threat of an act is minimized in this case by the assurance that in general S wants at least some of H's wants; for example, that S considers H to be in important respects 'the same' as he, with in-group rights and duties and expectations of reciprocity, or by the implication that S likes H so that the FTA doesn't mean a negative evaluation in general of H's face.

Negative politeness, on the other hand, is oriented mainly toward partially satisfying (redressing) H's negative face, his basic want to maintain claims of territory and self-determination. Negative politeness, thus, is essentially avoidance-based, and realizations of negative-politeness strategies consist in assurances that the speaker recognizes and respects the addressee's negative-face wants and will not (or will only minimally) interfere with the addressee's freedom of action. Hence negative politeness is characterized by self-effacement, formality and restraint, with attention to very restricted aspects of H's self-image, centring on his want to be unimpeded. Face-threatening acts are redressed with apologies for interfering or transgressing, with linguistic and non-linguistic deference, with hedges on the illocutionary force of the act, with impersonalizing mechanisms (such as passives) that distance S and H from the act, and with other softening mechanisms that give the addressee an 'out', a face-saving line of escape, permitting him to feel that his response is not coerced.

There is a natural tension in negative politeness, however, between (a) the desire to go on record as a prerequisite to being seen to pay face, and (b) the desire to go off record to avoid imposing. A compromise is reached in **conventionalized indirectness**, for whatever the indirect mechanism used to do an FTA, once fully conventionalized as a way of doing that FTA it is no longer off record. Thus many indirect requests, for example, are fully conventionalized in English so that they are on record (e.g., 'Can you pass the salt?' would be read as a request by all participants; there is no longer a viable alternative interpretation of the utterance except in very special circumstances). And between any two (or more) individuals, any utterance may become conventionalized and therefore on record, as is the case with passwords and codes.

70

A purely conventional 'out' works as redressive action in negative politeness because it pays a token bow to the negative-face wants of the addressee. That is, the fact that the speaker bothers to phrase his FTA in a conventionally indirect way shows that he is aware of and honours the negative-face wants of H.

3.4 Factors influencing the choice of strategies

We have outlined the five possible strategic choices for dealing with FTAs in section 3.3 above. In this section we argue that any rational agent will tend to choose the same genus of strategy under the same conditions — that is, make the same moves as any other would make under the circumstances. This is by virtue of the fact that the particular strategies intrinsically afford certain payoffs or advantages, and the relevant circumstances are those in which one of these payoffs would be more advantageous than any other.

We consider these in turn — first the intrinsic payoffs and then the relevant circumstances — and then relate the two.

3.4.1 The payoffs: *a priori* considerations. Here we present a fairly complete list of the payoffs associated with each of the strategies, derived on *a priori* grounds.

By going *on record*, a speaker can potentially get any of the following advantages: he can enlist public pressure against the addressee or in support of himself; he can get credit for honesty, for indicating that he trusts the addressee; he can get credit for outspokenness, avoiding the danger of being seen to be a manipulator; he can avoid the danger of being misunderstood; and he can have the opportunity to pay back in face whatever he potentially takes away by the FTA.

By going *off record*, on the other hand, a speaker can profit in the following ways: he can get credit for being tactful, non-coercive; he can run less risk of his act entering the 'gossip biography' that others keep of him; and he can avoid responsibility for the potentially face-damaging interpretation. Furthermore, he can give (non-overtly) the addressee an opportunity to be seen to care for S (and thus he can test H's feelings towards him). In this latter case, if H chooses to pick up and respond to the potentially threatening interpretation of the act, he can give a 'gift' to the original speaker. Thus, if I say 'It's hot in here' and you say 'Oh, I'll open the window then!', you may get credit for being generous and cooperative, and I avoid the potential threat of ordering you around.

For going on record with *positive politeness*, a speaker can minimize the face-threatening aspects of an act by assuring the addressee that S considers himself to be 'of the same kind', that he likes him and wants his wants. Thus a criticism, with the assertion of mutual friendship, may lose much of its sting — indeed, in the assumption of a friendly context it often becomes a game (cf. Labov 1972a) and possibly even a compliment (as between opposite-sexed teenagers). Another possible payoff is that S can avoid or minimize the debt implications of FTAs such as requests and offers, either by referring (indirectly) to the reciprocity and on-going relationship between the addressee and himself (as in the reference to a pseudo prior agreement with *then* in 'How about a cookie, then') or by including the addressee and himself equally as participants in or as benefitors from the request or offer (for example, with an inclusive 'we', as in 'Let's get on with dinner' from the husband glued to the TV).

For going on record with *negative politeness,* a speaker can benefit in the following ways: he can pay respect, deference, to the addressee in return for the FTA, and can thereby avoid incurring (or can thereby lessen) a future debt; he can maintain social distance, and avoid the threat (or the potential face loss) of advancing familiarity towards the addressee; he can give a real 'out' to the addressee (for example, with a request or an offer, by making it clear that he doesn't really expect H to say 'Yes' unless he wants to, thereby minimizing the mutual face loss incurred if H has to say 'No'); and he can give conventional 'outs' to the addressee as opposed to real 'outs', that is, pretend to offer an escape route without really doing so, thereby indicating that he has the other person's face wants in mind.

Finally, the payoff for the fifth strategic choice, 'Don't do the FTA', is simply that S avoids offending H at all with this particular FTA. Of course S also fails to achieve his desired communication, and as there are naturally no interesting linguistic reflexes of this last-ditch strategy, we will ignore it in our discussion henceforth.

For our purposes, these payoffs may be simplified to the following summary:

On-record payoffs:

    (a)   clarity, perspicuousness

    (b)   demonstrable non-manipulativeness

Bald-on-record (non-redressed) payoff:

    efficiency (S can claim that other things are more important than face, or that the act is not an FTA at all)

Plus-redress payoff: S has the opportunity to give face

    (a)   positive politeness — to satisfy H's positive face, in some respect

(b)   negative politeness — to satisfy H's negative face, to some degree

Off-record payoffs:

(a)   S can satisfy negative face to a degree greater than that afforded by the negative-politeness strategy

(b)   S can avoid the inescapable accountability, the responsibility for his action, that on-record strategies entail.

When they are considered in this order, we can already see that on *a priori* grounds there is a pattern of circumstances in which the payoffs would be most advantageous: roughly, the more dangerous the particular FTA x is, in S's assessment, the more he will tend to choose the higher-numbered strategy. Running through the individual payoffs we see why this would be so.

The use of the first strategy (on record, minus redress) leaves S responsible without any means to minimize the FTA x. The use of redressive action affords S the opportunity to placate H by partially satisfying some of his perennial desires. The use of the second strategy (positive redressive action) allows S to satisfy a wide range of these perennial desires of H's (not necessarily directly related to x), while the use of the third (negative redressive action) allows S to satisfy to some extent H's want to be left unimpeded — the want that is directly infringed by x. By indicating reluctance to impinge on H, S implies that if the matter had been less pressing S would never have disturbed H (and will not do so for future matters that are not so pressing). Finally, the fourth strategy (off record) affords S the opportunity of evading responsibility altogether (by claiming, if challenged, that the interpretation of x as an FTA is wrong), and simultaneously allows S to avoid actually *imposing* the FTA x on H, since H himself must choose to interpret x as an FTA rather than as some more trivial remark.

Note that positive politeness precedes negative politeness in the continuum of FTA 'danger' for the following reasons. Positive politeness redresses by means of fulfilling H's want that some others should want some particular desires of his. To pursue this strategy S must make the assumption that he is a member of the set of these others; the efficacy of his redress is totally vulnerable to H's concurrence in this assumption. Negative politeness, on the other hand, is addressed to a generalized desire for freedom of action; in paying H in this currency, S makes no vulnerable assumptions and does no redressive action that is not immediately *relevant* to the imposition that x imposes (thus leaving himself invulnerable to charges of irrelevant flattery, etc.).[16]

Why then, given the danger associated with FTAs, do actors not take out the maximum insurance policy and always choose the off-record strategy? There must be some factors in the circumstances or the payoffs that cause a tension in the opposite direction from the pull that FTA danger exerts. One of these is a purely practical functional pressure: the off-record strategy leads to ambiguities and unclarities, while redressive action takes time, foresight, and effort. But another seems to be the inherent tension between an actor's negative-face wants and his positive-face wants, for the latter include both the former and (typically) contrary wants. Thus I can want simultaneously both to be undisturbed and to be shown tokens of admiration, care, regard, etc. — opposing wants that I will resolve (say) by in general wanting to be not imposed upon, but in some circumstances wanting some particular persons' expressions of regard, care, etc. For reasons discussed above it is safer to assume that H prefers his peace and self-determination than that he prefers your expressions of regard, unless you are certain of the contrary. But most importantly, since the availability of the strategies and the nature of face and practical reasoning are mutual knowledge to participants, they will have expectations of certain estimates of face risk for particular FTAs in particular circumstances. If an actor uses a strategy appropriate to a high risk for an FTA of less risk, others will assume the FTA was greater than in fact it was, while it is S's intention to *minimize* rather than overestimate the threat to H's face. Hence in general no actor will use a strategy for an FTA that affords more opportunity for face-risk minimization than is actually required to retain H's cooperation.

Thus the set of discrete payoffs can be lined up against a continuum of opposing forces that describes the circumstances in which each strategy would be most advantageous. We can sum up this section diagrammatically, as in Fig. 2.

3.4.2 The circumstances: Sociological variables. In this section we argue that the assessment of the seriousness of an FTA (that is, the calculations that members actually seem to make) involves the following factors in many and perhaps all cultures:

(i)   the 'social distance' (D) of S and H (a symmetric relation)
(ii) the relative 'power' (P) of S and H (an asymmetric relation)
(iii) the absolute ranking (R) of impositions in the particular culture.

An immediate clarification is in order. We are interested in D, P, and R only to the extent that the actors think it is mutual knowledge between them that these variables have some particular values. Thus these are not intended as *sociologists'* ratings of *actual* power, distance, etc., but only

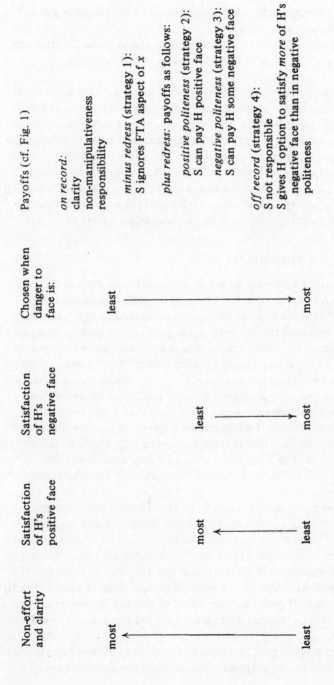

Fig. 2. *A priori* factors influencing strategy selection

as *actors*' assumptions of such ratings, assumed to be mutually assumed, at least within certain limits.

Our argument here has an empirical basis, and we make the argument in as strong a form as our ethnographic data will allow.[17]

3.4.2.1 Computing the weightiness of an FTA.

For each FTA, the seriousness or weightiness of a particular FTA x is compounded of both risk to S's face and risk to H's face, in a proportion relative to the nature of the FTA. Thus apologies and confessions are essentially threats to S's face (as we have seen), and advice and orders are basically threats to H's face, while requests and offers are likely to threaten the face of both participants. However, the way in which the seriousness of a particular FTA is weighed seems to be neutral as to whether it is S's or H's face that is threatened, or in what proportion. So let us say that the weightiness of an FTA is calculated thus:

$$W_x = D(S,H) + P(H,S) + R_x$$

where W_x is the numerical value that measures the weightiness of the FTA x, $D(S,H)$ is the value that measures the social distance between S and H, $P(H,S)$ is a measure of the power that H has over S, and R_x is a value that measures the degree to which the FTA x is rated an imposition in that culture. We assume that each of these values can be measured on a scale of 1 to n, where n is some small number.[18] Our formula assumes that the function that assigns a value to W_x on the basis of the three social parameters does so on a simple summative basis. Such an assumption seems to work surprisingly well, but we allow that in fact some more complex composition of values may be involved. In any case, the function must capture the fact that all three dimensions P, D, and R contribute to the seriousness of an FTA, and thus to a determination of the level of politeness with which, other things being equal, an FTA will be communicated.

First, we must clarify our intent. By D and P we intend very general pan-cultural social dimensions which nevertheless probably have 'emic' correlates.[19] We are not here interested in what factors are compounded to estimate these complex parameters; such factors are certainly culture-specific. For instance, $P(H,S)$ may be assessed as being great because H is eloquent and influential, or is a prince, a witch, a thug, or a priest; $D(S,H)$ as great because H speaks another dialect or language, or lives in the next valley, or is not a kinsman. More specifically, we can describe these factors as follows.

D is a symmetric social dimension of similarity/difference within which S and H stand for the purposes of this act. In many cases (but not all), it is based on an assessment of the frequency of interaction and the kinds of material or non-material goods (including face) exchanged between S and H (or parties representing S or H, or for whom S and H are representatives). An important part of the assessment of D will usually be measures of social distance based on stable social attributes. The reflex of social closeness is, generally, the reciprocal giving and receiving of positive face.

P is an asymmetric social dimension of relative power, roughly in Weber's sense. That is, P(H,S) is the degree to which H can impose his own plans and his own self-evaluation (face) at the expense of S's plans and self-evaluation. In general there are two sources of P, either of which may be authorized or unauthorized — material control (over economic distribution and physical force) and metaphysical control (over the actions of others, by virtue of metaphysical forces subscribed to by those others). In most cases an individual's power is drawn from both these sources, or is thought to overlap them. The reflex of a great P differential is perhaps archetypally 'deference', as discussed below.

R is a culturally and situationally defined ranking of impositions by the degree to which they are considered to interfere with an agent's wants of self-determination or of approval (his negative- and positive-face wants). In general there are probably two such scales or ranks that are emically identifiable for negative-face FTAs: a ranking of impositions in proportion to the expenditure (a) of *services* (including the provision of time) and (b) of *goods* (including non-material goods like information, as well as the expression of regard and other face payments). These intra-culturally defined costings of impositions on an individual's preserve are in general constant only in their rank order from one situation to another. However, even the rank order is subject to a set of operations that shuffles the impositions according to whether actors have specific rights or obligations to perform the act, whether they have specific reasons (ritual or physical) for not performing them, and whether actors are known to actually *enjoy* being imposed upon in some way.[20]

So an outline of the rankings of negative-face impositions for a particular domain of FTAs in a particular culture involves a complex description like the following:

(i) (a) rank order of impositions requiring services
     (b) rank order of impositions requiring goods

(ii) Functions on (i):
     (a) the lessening of certain impositions on a given actor determined by the obligation (legally, morally, by virtue of employment, etc.) to do the act A; and also by the enjoyment that the actor gets out of performing the required act

(b) the increasing of certain impositions determined by reasons why the actor *shouldn't* do them, and reasons why the actor *couldn't* (easily) do them

For FTAs against positive face, the ranking involves an assessment of the amount of 'pain' given to H's face, based on the discrepancy between H's own desired self-image and that presented (blatantly or tacitly) in the FTA. There will be cultural rankings of aspects of positive face (for example, 'success', 'niceness', 'beauty', 'generosity'), which can be re-ranked in particular circumstances, just as can negative-face rankings. And there are personal (idiosyncratic) functions on these rankings; some people object to certain kinds of FTAs more than others. A person who is skilled at assessing such rankings, and the circumstances in which they vary, is considered to be graced with 'tact', 'charm', or 'poise'.

In the argument below we associate with each of these variables, D, P, and R, a value from 1 to *n* assigned by an actor in particular circumstances. No special substantial claim is intended; the valuation simply represents the way in which (for instance) as S's power over H increases, the weightiness of the FTA diminishes.[21] One interesting side effect of this numerical representation is that it can describe these intuitive facts: the threshold value of risk which triggers the choice of another strategy is a constant, independent of the way in which the value is composed and assessed. Thus one goes off record where an imposition is small but relative S–H distance and H's power are great, and also where H is an intimate equal of S's but the imposition is very great.

3.4.2.2 Context-dependence of P, D, and R. Our social dimensions P, D and R can be viewed in various ways. Taking P as an extended example, we could argue that individuals are assigned an absolute value on this dimension that measures the power that each individual has relative to all others. Thus a bank manager might be given a high rating, and a lowly worker a low one. But when the worker pulls a gun, or sits on a jury trying the manager, or represents his union, the power may be reversed. To save the view that there are absolute (context-free) assignments to P, we would then have to allow for contextual reclassifications that adjust the assignments in certain circumstances.

A more plausible view would be that P is a value attached not to individuals at all, but to roles or role-sets. Thus in the role-set manager/ employee, or parent/child, asymmetrical power is built in. Then we would have to allow that there are role-sets like gangster/victim, in order to handle the way in which individuals can find the relative P values that they normally expect inverted by circumstances. But do all kinds of naked power come clothed in role-sets? If so, the notion of social role must be watered down. There is, moreover, another problem with this view. Individuals acquire sets of roles, and high P values in one role do carry over into the conduct of another. When a new President is elected, his old friends may still be friends, but they are unlikely to retain the old equality.

A third view would be that stable social valuations, whether of individuals or of roles, are only one element that enters into the assessment of P. Other situational sources of power may contribute to or adjust or entirely override such stable social valuations. Momentary weaknesses in bargaining power, strength of character, or alliances may all play a role in the assessment of P.

It is the last view that seems to us most adequate, even if it is the least definite suggestion. And we shall assume that situational factors enter into the values for P, D, and R, so that the values assessed hold only for S and H in a particular context, and for a particular FTA. Let us just illustrate the kinds of ways in which each of our social dimensions is context-relative in this sense.

Taking first the distance variable, note that two American strangers who would treat one another with great circumspection and formality in a chance encounter in the streets of New York City might well embrace each other with all the excesses of positive politeness if they were to meet in the Hindu Kush. A possible explanation of this familiar phenomenon is that wherever one is, all members of the local social universe must be assigned places across the entire scale of social distance. So in New York the strangers are assigned high D values, but in the Hindu Kush the even stranger natives displace the American visitors towards each other on the dimension of social distance.

The context-relativeness of relative power P is demonstrable in the following case. A man from a lowly caste in South India who approaches a Brahman requiring ritual services will treat him with great deference. When the Brahman comes to visit the low-caste man in the latter's capacity as a government official, it will be the Brahman who adopts the deferent or even servile attitude (Beck 1972:159, nn.34, 35). Compare too the switch in deference in Europe when one speaker passes from his own field of expertise into the other speaker's field. In these cases, P values seem to change as the roles of supplicant/specialist and expert/learner are switched.

Some of the special ways in which the ranking of impositions can be contextually inverted have been mentioned. But even where the rank order is maintained, impositions can still situationally vary in value; to ask for a dollar is generally to ask for more than to ask for a dime, yet to ask for a dime just outside a telephone booth is less than to ask for a dime for no apparent reason in the middle of the street. Thus the perceived situational reasonableness of the request enters into an assessment of its R value.

3.4.2.3 P, D, and R as independent variables.

It might be appropriate to be able to demonstrate that our P, D, and R factors are all relevant and independent, and are the only relevant ones used by actors to assess the danger of FTAs. But our claim is not that they are the *only* relevant factors, but simply that they *subsume* all others (status, authority, occupation, ethnic identity, friendship, situational factors, etc.) that have a principled effect on such assessments. However, we can illustrate their independence and relevance by the following examples, with reference to our formula and to the claim that W_x provides the speaker with the major reason for choosing among the five sets of politeness strategies.

Considering first the D variable, we can take two cases where P and R are constant and have small values in the estimate of S — in other words, where the relative power of S and H is more or less equal, and the imposition is not great. Such small impositions are found, for example, in requests for 'free goods', those things and services (like a match, or telling the time, or giving directions) which all members of the public may reasonably demand from one another. With P and R held constant and small, only the expression of D varies in the following two sentences:

(1)   Excuse me, would you by any chance have the time?

(2)   Got the time, mate?

Our intuitions are that (1) would be used where (in S's perception) S and H were distant (strangers from different parts, say), and (2) where S and H were close (either known to each other, or perceptibly 'similar' in social terms). D, then, is the only variable in our formula that changes from (1) to (2), and in doing so lessens W_x which provides the motive for the particular linguistic encoding of the FTA.

Turning to the P variable, suppose D and R are held constant and have small values (e.g. if S and H know each other by sight, and the imposition is a request for free goods):

(3)   Excuse me sir, would it be all right if I smoke?

(4)   Mind if I smoke?

Our intuitions are that (3) might be said by an employee to his boss, while (4) might be said by the boss to the employee in the same situation. Here, then, P is the only variable that changes from (3) to (4) (more exactly, P of H over S), and this again lessens W_x which provides S with the reasons for his choice between (3) and (4) for his linguistic encoding.

That R is also independently variable can be similarly demonstrated.

Suppose P is small and D is great (S and H are strangers, for example), and P and D are held constant. Then compare:

(5) Look, I'm terribly sorry to bother you but would there be any chance of your lending me just enough money to get a railway ticket to get home? I must have dropped my purse and I just don't know what to do.

(6) Hey, got change for a quarter?

Both might be said at a railway station by a frustrated traveller to a stranger, but our intuitions are that S in saying (5) considers the FTA to be much more serious than the FTA done in (6). The only variable is R, and it must be because R_x is lower in (6) that the language appropriate to a low W_x is employed there. Our conclusion is that in the ranking of impositions in Anglo-American culture, asking for a substantial amount of money without recompense is much more of an imposition than a request to search in one's pockets for change. In each case above, the first option (examples 1, 3, and 5) is a linguistic realization of the negative-politeness strategy, and the second (2, 4, and 6) is a realization of the positive-politeness strategy.

3.4.2.4. Ambiguity and disambiguation as evidence for P, D, and R.
One major argument that we use to demonstrate that our formula must be at least a partially accurate representation of cognitive process is as follows. Parameters like P, D, R must have some cognitive validity, since they are the basis of a wide range of 'exploitations' discussed in section 6.1 below. Consider the following facts. Our formula is a means of compounding the factors that make an FTA dangerous into a single index of risk, W_x. W_x is then a motive for the choice of one of the strategies 1–5 in Fig. 1 (p. 69) rather than any other. Hence the choice of strategy will in general 'encode' the estimated danger of the FTA; this is why one receives with considerable apprehension phrases like:

(7) I'm awfully sorry to bother you, and I wouldn't but I'm in an awful fix, so I wondered if by any chance . . .

But if our representation of the factors underlying the assessment of W_x is correct, such phrases do not display *which* variable (D, relative P, or R) is primarily responsible for the weight of x. In other words, the formula, in compounding the variables into a single index, makes the sources of the final assessment ambiguous. This is a fundamental fact to which the exploitations described in section 6.1, and also the display of deference discussed in 5.4, are primarily addressed.

Taking deference to be the humbling of the self or the 'raising' of the other — that is, claims about the value of P(H,S) — we can see that it may perform the function of disambiguating which factor was most important in the assessment of W_x. For suppose the choice of negative politeness (strategy 3) or off record (strategy 4) 'encodes' a weighty W_x: then if S asserts that H is relatively much more powerful than S, he indicates that W_x was assessed crucially on values of P, hence that R_x is probably small (since a bigger value would send S to strategy 5, 'Don't do the FTA at all'). Some markers of deference, then, ought to ease the apprehension of the addressee when he hears a sentence like example (7) above.

In terms of our first observation that W_x is compounded of the risk of x to H's face and the risk of x to S's face, if S indicates that H's relative power is greater than his, he claims that W_x is primarily a risk to himself rather than to H. Note then that phrases like (7) above are likely to be prologues to awful impositions only where D and relative P are mutually known to be fairly small, leaving only R_x to account for the high W_x. The low D and P values may be assumed, or in the case of D may be claimed by means of familiar usages like:

(8) $\left\{ \begin{array}{l} \text{Look,} \\ \text{Hey,} \\ \text{My God,} \end{array} \right\}$ Harry, I'm awfully sorry to bother you . . .

(9) Look, Harry, you're a friend, so . . .

while high P values and low R values can be claimed by usages like:

(10) Excuse me, $\left\{ \begin{array}{l} \text{Sir,} \\ \text{Officer,} \\ \text{Your Excellency,} \end{array} \right\}$ I'm sorry to bother you but I

wonder if you could just possibly do me a small favour . . .

These examples show that factors like P, D, and R are involved in the calculation of W_x, and since that calculation compounds them and the chosen strategy does not directly reflect them, there would be motivation for their values to be directly claimed.

Again, consider threatening suggestions or warnings like (11), (12), and (13) below, in the light of our claim that W_x is compounded of risk to H's face and risk to S's face:

(11) It's no skin off my teeth, but I think you might want to take a look at what your son is up to in the gooseberry patch.
(12) I don't care, but I think maybe you ought to be more careful when you park your car next to mine in future.

Since the initial phrases deny any risk to the speaker's face, and the strategy chosen is off record, W_x is high but can only be due to risk to H.

Hence this sort of FTA may be designed to cause considerable consternation to the addressee. And a threat like (13) again refers to the factors D, P, and R, claiming small D with an initial address phrase, and small R with words like *little* and *just*, and thus leaving only a very high relative P of S over H — and not vice versa — to account for the choice of an off-record strategy:

(13) Look sonny, it might not be advisable to just go pushing your little fingers into this little pie.

3.4.3 The integration of assessment of payoffs and weighting of risk in the choice of strategies.

We here explain why, as W_x increases, a rational agent would tend to choose to use the higher-numbered strategies. Fig. 2 (section 3.4.1 above) summarizes the circumstances in which each strategy would be most appropriately employed on *a priori* grounds. As the FTA danger increases, the higher-numbered strategies serve best to minimize face risk. Immediately we can see why the observed factor W_x would correlate with the choice of strategies, for W_x is an estimate of risk.

We can now relate the *a priori* and the sociological facts. Any MP with the properties we have attributed to him (the ability to use practical reasoning from wants to means that will satisfy those wants, and the retention of the specific wants called 'face') would employ the strategies in the circumstances in which the payoffs of each one were most appropriate (i.e. would most satisfy his face wants) — in fact, as in Fig. 2.

Now, if it is empirically the case that FTA danger is assessed by estimating P, D, and R values, then our MP would take the least possible risk with 'strangers' (high D values) and 'dominant members' (high P(H,S) values) when making serious impositions (high R_x values).

Our MP would not do all FTAs with the strategy of *least* risk because it costs more in effort and loss of clarity, because he may wish to satisfy the other perennial desire of H's — for positive face — but most importantly because choice of the least risky strategy may indicate to H that the FTA is more threatening than it actually is, since it would imply an excessively high rating of P or D or R, or some combination.

In short, our original assumptions that define our MP as a 'rational agent with face' *predict* that rational face-bearing agents will choose ways of doing face-threatening acts that minimize those threats, hence will choose a higher-numbered strategy as the threat increases. This neatly fits the observational ethnographic fact that as risk estimated in terms of *social* variables increases, a similar choice of strategies can be observed.

Because some such weak universal sociological generalizations appear to be viable (that the danger of an FTA is assessed in terms of factors like P, D, R), and because our MP is a reasonable approximation to universal assumptions, we can account for the fact that an observer in a foreign culture, on seeing a speaker and addressee interact, feels that S is (say) not a close friend of H's (or thinks that H is more powerful than S, or thinks x is a big imposition) purely from observing the linguistics of S's FTA. This observation may be made in Chiapas, in Tamilnad, or in California.

4.00 ON THE NATURE OF THE MODEL

4.1 Remarks on alternative models

One way of thinking about our enterprise is this: we are attempting a description, in a very limited area, of the principles that lie behind the construction of social behaviour. There can be no doubt that one reason that social theory has never come to ground level is the notable lack of a satisfactory theory of action. The major social theorists (for instance Durkheim, Parsons, Weber), and indeed analytical philosophers, have only made crude attempts at the analysis of the single act. Only cognitive anthropologists (inspired initially by Miller, Galanter and Pribram 1960), cognitive psychologists, and workers in artificial intelligence (e.g. in Schank and Colby 1973) have looked at actions in the context of hierarchical plans which may specify sequences of actions. But how does one generate plans? How does one mentally check their validity? What kinds of reasoning lie behind them? These are questions which, compared to the study devoted to deductive reasoning, have received scant attention since Aristotle (but see for instance Körner 1974). Above all, a satisfactory account of action in an interactional setting has been grossly neglected, despite evidence that very special properties of coordination arise in such settings (Grice 1971, 1975; Lewis 1969; Schelling 1960). Indeed, here our own analysis must be found wanting, dominated as it is by the act-by-act analysis of contemporary philosophy and linguistics; we try to make amends in section 6.3.

It is in this context, then, that we propose a general schema for deriving actions from goals. It is tempting to capitalize on the fascination that anthropologists have found in the new linguistics, with its talk of rule-bound creativity, its explicit goals and precise methods. Part of the glamour probably derives from a misunderstanding of the linguist's concept 'generative', which non-linguists (aided by Chomsky's own invocation of Humboldtian and Goethean parallels) have tended to construe more in the image of the dynamo than in the intended quasi-mathematical sense (of precise and explicit description: Bach 1973:27). Unlike transformational generative grammar, the system we present in fact finds both senses of 'generative' applicable. It is a formal system that has closer parallels in deductive logic, with its axioms and rules of inference, than in transformational grammar. Given a set of goals (parallel to the premises of a deductive argument) and rules of inference (parallel but distinct from rules of deductive inference), one can derive in this system *means* that will achieve those goals. The system that produces these inferences could be said to be generative in an uninteresting but similar way to transformational grammar. But in addition, an element of the image of the dynamo is indeed appropriate, for the goals, the things desired, are what constrain the inferences made (just as the premises in a deductive argument do). It is a system driven by intentions and (more remotely) motives. The output of the system is not then parallel to the output of a generative grammar (the well-formed sentences of a language) so much as to a model of the process from thought to sentence. Such a system is much more appropriate for sociological applications than weak metaphors drawn from transformational grammar. It has indeed very general applications.[22]

A short note is in order on our use of the word 'strategy'. We do not mean to imply that what we dub 'strategies' are necessarily conscious. For the most part they do not seem to be, but when interactional mistakes occur, or actors try to manipulate others, they may very well emerge into awareness. And they are open to introspection, at least in part. But the general unconscious nature of such strategies raises fundamental methodological problems that we simply skirt. We cannot pretend to have any special insight into what is probably the biggest single stumbling block to theory throughout the social sciences: the nature of the unconscious and preconscious where all the most important determinants of action seem to lie.[23] We continue to use the word 'strategy', despite its connotations of conscious deliberation, because we can think of no other word that will imply a rational element while covering both (a) innovative plans of action, which may still be (but need not be) unconscious, and (b) routines — that is, previously constructed plans whose original rational origin is still preserved in their construction, despite their present automatic application as ready-made programmes.

Let us now briefly turn to possible alternatives to the explanation of the cross-cultural parallels that we present. One such alternative might in fact be phrased in terms of norms or rules. This is the way that, for instance, workers in the 'ethnography of speaking' have talked about precisely similar kinds of fact: patterns of speaking whose description cross-cuts the levels of a grammar. Even intraculturally there are problems, for the kinds of norms envisaged by such workers are extremely specific, in some cases being strict applications of (possibly recursive) rules specifying ritual formulae (as for example in Irvine 1974). But this will not produce the flexible and indefinitely productive strategic usage we here describe, unless the norms are as abstract as our face wants (or at least our four major strategies) and are related to behaviour by the same practical reasoning. However, this possibility has no attraction in a cross-cultural perspective. For norms, being specific to particular social populations, have a severely limited explanatory role in comparative (cross-cultural) research. Moreover, as has been persuasively argued by Lewis (1969), conventions — and therefore also norms — may have rational origins. This suggests that the notion 'norm' may not have the utility as a sociological primitive that it has usually been accorded.

Elementary though this point is, it is worth emphasizing because there is a tendency, especially among linguists, to think of pragmatic (language-usage) principles as *rules* (as in for example the treatment of Grice's Maxims by R. Lakoff (1973a, 1974a, 1975)). But to posit highly specific and diverse universal rules is to invent a problem to be explained, rather than to explain it.

The Scylla to the normative Charybdis is the presumption of highly detailed innate predispositions of a specific sort. The problem with such a whole-hearted ethological approach is that the parallels observed across cultures are not formal but functional in nature, and yet the functions are rationally linked to form; what is done by high pitch in one culture may be done by indirect uses of language in another. Moreover, the details of linguistic and kinesic realizations of our politeness strategies are so specific, so rationally constructed and non-arbitrary, that the degree and nature of the preprogramming would be absurd. For instance, there would have to be an innate predisposition to use the 'polite subjunctive' in just those circumstances where it is (apparently optionally) employed — and this disposition would not hold for speakers of a language not having such a subjunctival option. There may indeed be a handful of preprogrammed signals (deference kinesics, for example) in the enormous open-ended inventory of means for realizing politeness strategies, but their ethological explanation will not explain the rest. We can allow that at the abstract level of face wants we may be dealing with ethological primitives (indeed, we have no other explanation there), but any more detailed suggestion seems untenable.

A middle way is to allow that rational adjustments to various simple constraints (the face wants), presumably of an ethological origin, can produce extraordinarily elaborate and detailed parallelisms. These may then become normatively stabilized within cultures. And this is the tack we take.

4.2 Toward a formalization

Our model posits a rational being with certain wants which characterize face. We then ask how such a being would act in respect to such wants.

In this section we show that this question can be given a formal characterization which would provide precise answers to it. Then we can see if the predicted answers fit the facts.

As indicated in the discussion of rationality in section 3.1.3 above, we need a formal characterization of desirability reasoning. First we take the notion of *desiring* or *wanting* something, or being in a position where one *ought* to do something, and limit it to a relativized version, as in:

(1)   If I want to get to London by 10.00, then I $\left\{ \begin{array}{l} \text{want to} \\ \text{ought to} \\ \text{should} \\ \text{must} \\ \text{have to} \end{array} \right\}$ catch the 6.06 train.

That is, I want to get the 6.06 relative to wanting to get to London by 10.00. We exclude here the sense of 'want' as pure longing, or the sense of 'ought' as pure moral injunction (although the distinction between the practical and the moral 'ought' is certainly an analytical philosopher's distinction; natural languages seem never to make it,[24] and natural societies have an investment in seeing that it is not made). Following Kenny, we represent sentences like the antecedent and consequent of example (1) as 'fiats', propositions with an external 'optative mood' indicator F.

We then define a logical system — 'Kenny logic' — of practical reasoning which attempts to capture the intuitive consequence relation expressed in the 'If ... then ...' of (1). Borrowing an idea from Kenny (1966), we define a notion of relative 'satisfactoriness':

> A fiat F(a) is satisfactory relative to a set G of desires $\{F(g_1), F(g_2) \ldots F(g_n)\}$ if and only if, whenever a is true, $(g_1,$ and $g_2 \ldots$ and $g_n)$ is true.

For example, the desire that I eat a pork pie is (wholly) satisfactory relative to my goal desire that I satisfy my hunger *iff*, whenever I eat a pork pie, 'my hunger is satisfied' is true. We then define a rule of inference, 'relativised Kenny implications':

The inference $\dfrac{F(a)}{F(b)}$K is valid *iff*, whenever F(a) is satisfactory relative to G, F(b) is satisfactory relative to G.

Hence one may check a Kenny inference by means of standard logical apparatus — for example, where G′ is the set of phrastics or propositions of every member of the set of Goal Wants G, and ⊢ is an assertoric mood indicator, then:

Given: $\dfrac{F(p)}{\dfrac{\vdash(q \supset p)}{F(q)}}$ then: $p \supset G'$ ought to be valid, (which of course $\dfrac{q \supset p}{q \supset G'}$

it is by the 'hypothetical syllogism').

If we define 'satisfaction' such that a fiat F(a) is satisfied if *a* is true, it can easily be seen that the 'logic of satisfactoriness is the mirror image of the logic of satisfaction'. As Kenny stipulated:

If F(a) ⊢ F(b) in the logic of satisfaction,
then F(b) ⊢$_K$ F(a) in the logic of satisfactoriness.

This will secure apparently inverted inferences like:

(2) $\dfrac{\text{Vote!}}{\text{Vote for Wilson!}}$

and the validity of 'affirming the consequent', a fallacious syllogism in ordinary sentential logic.

Around these central ideas we can build a semantically interpreted formal system,[25] whose syntax is simply an extension of the language of standard sentential logic with an additional sentence operator F and an additional set of starred sentential connectives. To this language we then provide a semantics: a truth valuation relative to a point of view *i* that assigns one of two truth values to each assertoric sentence in the language, and for every fiat in the language a satisfaction valuation *and* a satisfactoriness valuation, both relative to a point of view *i*. The trick is then to include, among the indices that constitute *i*, a set of goal-fiats G$_i$ relative to which the plan-fiat may be evaluated as satisfactory or unsatisfactory. By this means we obtain a system that has been proved to be decidable[26] and defines a proper consequence relation that meets the requirements of transitivity, reflexivity, and monotonicity.

The formalization we propose also captures two further features of

88

natural practical deliberation: its 'defeasibility', and its 'ampliativeness'. An inference like:

(3)   I want a million dollars
      If I murder my uncle, I'll inherit a million dollars
      ───
      Ergo, let me murder my uncle

or:

(4)   I want a drink
      ─────────────────────────────
      So I want this poisonous drink

may seem counter-intuitive. Of course they are so only in the context of wants that usually don't have to be spelled out, like 'I don't want to kill anyone' and 'I want to go on living'. By the addition of such wants explicitly as premises or goal-fiats, the arguments in (3) and (4) become invalid in Kenny logic too. Hence the defeasibility, or context-dependentness, of natural practical reasoning is captured by relativized Kenny implication. This makes Kenny logic a natural tool for the explanation of Gricean conversational implicature.

Secondly, Kenny logic is ampliative; that is, a conclusion in a Kenny-logic inference may be more informative than its premise, as in the 'Vote!' – 'Vote for Wilson!' example, or in:

(5)   I want that cup
      ─────────────────────────
      I want that cup and saucer

For this reason, unless the goal-fiats exclude this possibility, Kenny logic will churn out an indefinite number of means that will achieve an end.

As Grice has pointed out (1973), desirability reasoning shares these properties of defeasibility and ampliativeness with inductive inference. His conclusion is that practical inference has more to do with probabilistic reasoning than with deductive inference; our conclusion, however, is that if this is so, this divergence from deduction is still characterizable in a system (Kenny logic) that is essentially parasitic on deductive reasoning.

But Grice had in mind what he calls a 'weighted desirability reasoning', a species of practical inference that chooses, from among different means, that one which will most completely satisfy a given end. For instance, given that I want a pint of beer, I will prefer half a pint to a quarter. That is, practical deliberation is often concerned with *partial* satisfactoriness, *partial* satisfaction, and the 'maximization' of satisfactoriness. Many of the inferences that we intuitively describe in this paper are of this sort.

We need, then, a verson of Grice's weighted desirability reasoning. First we exclude from consideration 'extrinsic' weighting – that is, a desirability

value that is Kantian or moral or absolute, which has nothing t[...]
the extent to which the want would satisfy some superordinate[...]
Intrinsic weighting, then, consists in the degree to which a su[...]
want would satisfy a superordinate one. Given the fact that sa[...]
ness in Kenny logic is defined in relation to truth, if we want [...]
satisfactoriness we will need degrees of truth. To logicians the[...]
'degrees of truth' is a conceptual confusion, but G. Lakoff (1[...]
building on some ideas of Zadeh's, has shown that some analogue at lcast
is required to deal with natural-language data, and has proposed ways of
constructing a 'fuzzy logic' that will handle degrees of truth. Lakoff
further reports an idea of Dana Scott's that captures degrees of truth in
terms of an ordered set of classical (two-valued) valuations, and hence
reconciles the natural-language facts with logical purity.

So, given a fuzzy propositional logic, we can define a fuzzy Kenny logic,
by allowing any number in the real interval 0–1 to be a satisfactoriness
valuation, and the satisfactoriness of a fiat a relative to b to be dependent
on the degree to which, when a is true, the propositions in G are true. We
then define a preference operator, Pr, which given two or more fiats will
select the fiat which has the highest satisfactoriness value in relation to
the goal-fiats. Thus a fuzzy Kenny logic with a satisfactoriness-maximizing
preference operator should constitute a viable version of Grice's weighted
desirability reasoning.

With this apparatus it ought to be possible to cast our argument (as
summarized in section 2.00 above) into a formal mould. Here an intuitive
outline will suffice.

Our formalization of the argument would proceed very approximately
along the following lines. We treat the problem of the selection of face-
saving strategies as a complex practical inference with a sequence of simple
inferences or steps. We take our two face wants as goal-fiats for our ego-MP
(the speaker S) and enter them together with the desire to perform some
particular FTA as the ends to whose satisfaction all the reasoning is
addressed.

As a first step we derive S's wish to fulfil H's face wants to some
degree, as a rational means to secure H's cooperation, either in respect of
face maintenance or some joint activity or both. (There may of course be
other more desirable means, such as coercion.) So we have then a derivative want of S's to minimize the FTA.

S must then decide to what extent he wishes to minimize the FTA,
bearing in mind any wants (like the desire for clarity or urgency, or the
desire to not be seen to think the FTA greater than he estimates it is) that
might lead him to desire little minimization. He rationally decides this by
choosing a strategy that yields opportunities of minimization proportional

.... (or extra-
...ans that will satisfy his strategic end. Each strategy provides
...ally a range of degrees of politeness (or face-risk minimization), so
S will bear in mind the degree of face threat in choosing appropriate
linguistic realizations and in constructing and compounding verbal
minimizing expressions.

5.00 REALIZATIONS OF POLITENESS STRATEGIES IN LANGUAGE

5.1 Introduction

We have claimed that a face-bearing rational agent will tend to utilize the
FTA-minimizing strategies according to a rational assessment of the face
risk to participants. He would behave thus by virtue of practical reasoning,
the inference of the best means to satisfy stated ends.

We now claim that what links these strategies to their verbal expressions
is exactly the same kind of means–ends reasoning. For example, suppose
our Model Person has chosen the strategy of negative politeness: recall that
negative politeness consists in doing the FTA on record, with redressive
action directed to the addressee's perennial want to not be imposed upon.
Then our MP must unambiguously express the FTA, and choose between
a set of appropriate ways that would partially satisfy that negative-face
want of the addressee's; that is, he must do so if he intends to rationally
satisfy *his* desire to achieve the end we have labelled negative politeness.
He may choose more than one such means of redressive action, as long as
those chosen are consistent, and the effort expended not out of proportion
to the face risk attending the FTA.

Such redressive action need not of course be verbal. In order to partially
satisfy your want to have your wants desired, I may indicate my understanding of them by bringing you a gift appropriate to them. (Stereotypical
gifts – the box of chocolates, the bunch of flowers – are addressed to the
'safe' wants that may be assumed to be shared.) In order to satisfy your
want to not be imposed upon, I may humble myself kinesically (e.g. body
still and shoulders bent in English culture; a bow in Japan), thereby indicating my respect for your preserve, my powerlessness to compel you to
act, my reluctance to impinge (and perhaps my wish to satisfy your desire
for power). I may go off record in confronting you with a face-threatening
imposition by simply pointing at the evidence of your misdeeds (e.g. an

realizations', we have in mind also the broader communicative spectrum including paralinguistic and kinesic detail. But the apparatus for describing language is so much better developed that we organize our description around the linguistic categories. Nevertheless, it is interesting that many aspects of non-linguistic communicative behaviour can be naturally accommodated in the same scheme.

In what follows we rely heavily on three charts – Figs. 3, 4, and 6 – that summarize the derivation of the strategies we discuss. Some important clarifications of these now follow. We provide a chart for each of the super-strategies of positive politeness, negative politeness, and off record. On the left-hand side of each chart is entered the chosen super-strategy as a desire or end of the speaker's; connected to this desire by divergent arrows are the means that would (at least partially) achieve this end. In many cases these means are no more than more specific wants – i.e. consequent desires – and themselves have arrows leading to means that will achieve them. In this way we arrive at more and more specific wants, finally arriving at the linguistic means that will satisfy (to some extent) all the wants connected to them by the arrows. Thus, in moving from left to right on the charts, we move from higher-order or super-strategies to lower- and lower-order strategies.

Strategies, then, form hierarchies of strategies that will achieve higher-order goals. Where necessary we refer to the four highest-level strategies (bald on record, positive politeness, negative politeness, and off record) as 'super-strategies', to the strategies that emanate from these as 'higher-order strategies', and to the final choice of linguistic means to realize the highest goals as 'output strategies' (identified in the text thus: BE VAGUE). In general, however, we use the word 'strategy' to refer to a plan at any of these levels, relying on the context to make clear which hierarchical level we are talking about.

Each arrow on the charts is a representation of a practical-reasoning consequence relation, in most cases a partial-satisfactoriness version of a Kenny implication relation. Hence more than one path may be followed simultaneously, provided that they are not incompatible wants or means (or, if so, that there is some reasonable compromise). Thus our charts *are not decision trees or flow diagrams*, but are merely convenient representations of the grouping of wants by specificity, and the practical-reasoning consequence relations holding between them.

A further feature of the charts is that there is on occasion convergence from more than one want to a single means of satisfying them all: that is, there may be multiple motivation for any one genre of linguistic realization. So *we do not claim that the wants in the charts are the only motivation for using these linguistic means.* Indeed, there are very general social motivations for using various techniques of positive politeness and negative politeness; they operate, respectively, as a kind of social accelerator and social brake for decreasing or increasing social distance in relationships, regardless of FTAs. And a variety of aims other than face maintenance may stimulate the use of the off-record strategy — for example the want to be poetic, or to avoid responsibility (as in the evasions of a servant or the vagueness of a Delphic oracle), or to play with language.

Before plunging into the detailed examples, we may note that there are two general aspects of the use of linguistic means to serve politeness functions which we may deal with here, as they hold equally for all strategies. First, it appears that selection of a set of strategic wants to be realized by linguistic means may also involve the *organization* and *ordering* of the expression of these wants, so that (1) may be more polite than (2):

(1)   If you don't mind me asking, where did you get that dress?
(2)   Where did you get that dress, if you don't mind me asking?

and (3) more polite than (4):

(3)   Goodness, aren't your roses beautiful! I was just coming by to borrow a cup of flour.
(4)   I was just coming by to borrow a cup of flour. Goodness, aren't your roses beautiful!

Presumably, the processes involved here have to do with topicalization and focus, and we shall have relatively little to say about this in what follows.

The second general observation about the outputs of all the strategies is this. In general, the more *effort* S expends in face-maintaining linguistic behaviour, the more S communicates his sincere desire that H's face wants be satisfied (for negative face, the more he communicates his desire to impinge on H to the least possible extent; for positive face, the more he communicates his care for H and H's face). He may achieve this effort simply by compounding the branching means to achieve wants, or by elaborate realizations of particular means, or both. For negative politeness, for example, he may, with enormous syntactic complexity, a profusion of conjoined sentences and adverbial clauses, do all these: apologize, express reluctance, give deference, and belittle his own incapacities — 'I'm terribly sorry to bother you with a thing like this and in normal circumstances I wouldn't dream of it, since I know you're very busy, but I'm simply unable to do it myself, so . . .' Similarly, effort put into the effusions of positive politeness, or into the intricately built-up hints of off-record strategies, communicates sincere desire to satisfy H's face wants (unless, of course, the effort is marked as being sarcastic or ironic). Such expenditures of effort seem to be intimately linked to polite usages across many cultures. Their extent and degree are rough indications of the importance that face wants and other attendant wants are afforded in any culture.

One final general point is in order. We phrase the discussion below in the general terms of rational language *usage*. But the motivations that lie behind such usages are powerful enough to pass deep into language *structure*. In section 8.1 we draw together examples of how the encoding of the strategies addressed to such wants can become part of the grammar: as lexicalizations (*sorry, sir*), as transformations (passivization, ellipsis, dubitative inflections, nominalization), and as phonetic (including pro-sodic) modifications (high pitch, hesitation phenomena, creaky voice). There we make the argument in a strong form: in general the abundance of syntactic and lexical apparatus in a grammar seems undermotivated by either systemic or cognitive distinctions and psychological processing factors. The other motivation is, grossly, social, and includes processes like face-risk minimization.

In the following sections we take up each of the four super-strategies for doing FTAs. For the bald-on-record strategy we simply outline the uses to which bald-on-record utterances are put, since all the outputs are the same: follow Grice's Maxims. After each chart summarizing the linguistic strategies for positive politeness, negative politeness, and off record, there follows a set of examples; these are instances of the classes of linguistic expressions indicated on the right-hand side of each chart, and the strategy numbers cross-identify the outputs of the chart and the associated examples. Each set of examples is introduced with some theoretical discussion tracing its derivation in the chart; we then illustrate initially with instances drawn from English usage, following with close parallels drawn from Tamil and Tzeltal, the languages that constitute the basis of our three-way experiment. When possible we also add examples from additional languages and cultures.

5.2 Bald on record

For our purposes, we can treat the bald-on-record strategy as speaking in conformity with Grice's Maxims (Grice 1975). These Maxims are an intuitive characterization of conversational principles that would constitute guidelines for achieving maximally efficient communication. They may be stated briefly as follows:

> Maxim of Quality: Be non-spurious (speak the truth, be sincere).
> Maxims of Quantity: (a) Don't say less than is required.
> (b) Don't say more than is required.
> Maxim of Relevance: Be relevant.
> Maxim of Manner: Be perspicuous; avoid ambiguity and obscurity.

These Maxims define for us the basic set of assumptions underlying every talk exchange. But this does not imply that utterances in general, or even reasonably frequently, must meet these conditions, as critics of Grice have sometimes thought. Indeed, the majority of natural conversations do not proceed in such a brusque fashion at all. The whole thrust of this paper is that one powerful and pervasive motive for *not* talking Maxim-wise is the desire to give some attention to face. (No doubt many other motives exist as well; the want to avoid responsibility emerged as one in our field-work.) Politeness is then a major source of deviation from such rational efficiency, and is communicated precisely by that deviation. But even in such departures from the Maxims, they remain in operation at a deeper level. It is only because they are still assumed to be in operation that addressees are forced to do the inferential work that establishes the underlying intended message and the (polite or other) source of the departure — in short, to find an implicature, i.e. an inference generated by precisely this assumption. Otherwise the polite strategies catalogued in the succeeding sections would simply be heard as mumbo-jumbo. There is a basic assumption in talk that there is underlying method in the madness.[27]

The prime reason for bald-on-record usage may be stated simply: in general, whenever S wants to do the FTA with maximum efficiency *more than* he wants to satisfy H's face, even to any degree, he will choose the bald-on-record strategy. There are, however, different kinds of bald-on-record usage in different circumstances, because S can have different motives for his want to do the FTA with maximum efficiency. These fall into two classes: those where the face threat is not minimized, where face is ignored or is irrelevant; and those where in doing the FTA baldly on record, S minimizes face threats by implication. Direct imperatives stand out as clear examples of bald-on-record usage, and we concentrate on them in the examples that follow.[28] (A more detailed discussion of English imperative usages can be found in Bolinger 1967.)

5.2.1 Cases of non-minimization of the face threat.

Where maximum efficiency is very important, and this is mutually known to both S and H, no face redress is necessary. In cases of great urgency or desperation, redress would actually decrease the communicated urgency. For example:

(1)   Help! (compare the non-urgent 'Please help me, if you would be so kind')
(2)   Watch out!
(3)   Your pants are on fire!
(4)   Give me just one more week! (to pay the rent)

In Tzeltal we find equivalent urgent imperatives:

(5)   ma ša?čik' ?a?k'ab!
      Don't burn your hand!

And similarly in Tamil:

(6)   eRu! eRu! periya paampu!
      Get up, get up! (There's a) big snake!

Where S speaks *as if* maximum efficiency were very important,[29] he provides metaphorical urgency for emphasis. Good examples of this are found in attention-getters used in conversation:

(7)   Listen, I've got an idea.
(8)   Hear me out: ...
(9)   Look, the point is this: ...

The verb 'look' in Tzeltal (as in Tamil, too) is used in precisely the same way, for emphasis in making a rhetorical point:

(10) ?ila?wil, ?ay ?ek lek stohol ta me ba¢'il melel, yu?un ...
      Look, it's good if that's really the case, because ...

This metaphorical urgency perhaps explains why orders and entreaties (or begging), which have inverted assumptions about the relative status of S and H, both seem to occur in many languages with the same superficial syntax — namely, imperatives. Thus beggars in India make direct demands like:

(11) kaacu kuTu.
      Give money.

So also in English one uses imperatives in formulaic entreaties:

(12) $\left\{ \begin{array}{l} \text{Excuse} \\ \text{Forgive} \\ \text{Pardon} \end{array} \right\}$ me.

(13) Accept my thanks.

Similarly in Tzeltal:

(14) pasben perdon.
      Forgive me. (lit.: 'Make forgiveness for me')

And this is perhaps also the source of certain metaphorical 'entreaties':

(15) Send me a postcard.
(16) Don't forget us!

where S speaks as if imploring H to care for S, thereby stressing his high valuation of H's friendship.

Another motivation for bald-on-record (non-redressed) FTAs is found in cases of channel noise, or where communication difficulties exert pressure to speak with maximum efficiency. This can be seen, for example, when S is calling across a distance:

(17) Come home right now!

or talking on the telephone with a bad connection:

(18) I need another £1000.

Again, where the focus of interaction is task-oriented, face redress may be felt to be irrelevant, as in:

(19) Lend me a hand here.
(20) Give me the nails.
(21) That's wrong; the gap should be bigger.

Such task-orientation probably accounts for the paradigmatic form of instructions and recipes:

(22) Open other end.
(23) Add three cups of flour and stir vigorously.

Another set of cases where non-redress occurs is where S's want to satisfy H's face is small, either because S is powerful and does not fear retaliation or non-cooperation from H:

(24) Bring me wine, Jeeves.
(25) In future, you must add the soda áfter the whisky.

or because S wants to be rude, or doesn't care about maintaining face. A good example of socially acceptable rudeness comes in teasing or joking. For example, in Tzeltal when teasing the baby one may say:

(26) ʔok'an. ʔilinan.
      Cry. Get angry.

without risk of offending.

A third set of cases where non-minimization is likely occurs where doing the FTA is primarily in H's interest. Then *in doing* the FTA, S conveys that he does care about H (and therefore about H's positive face), so that no redress is required. Thus sympathetic advice or warnings may be baldly on record:

(27) Careful! He's a dangerous man. (warning H against someone who could threaten him)

(28) Your slip is showing.

(29) Your wig is askew; let me fix it for you.

(30) Your headlights are on!

Comforting advice may similarly be non-redressed, as in the Tzeltal:

(31) ma ša⁷ mel ⁷a⁷wo⁷tan.
Don't be sad.

And granting permission for something that H has requested may likewise be baldly on record, as in English:

(32) Yes, you may go.

or in Tzeltal:

(33) yakuk. la⁷ čuka tey ⁷a.
OK. Come tie it there. (i.e. your bull in my field)

These usages (of imperatives for actions directly in H's interest) give rise to a host of cliché farewell formulae, as in the English 'advice' delivered to those departing on a trip:

(34) $\begin{Bmatrix} \text{Take care of} \\ \text{Treat} \\ \text{Enjoy} \end{Bmatrix}$ yourself, be good, have fun.

(35) Don't take any wooden nickels.

The Tzeltal farewell formulae are directly comparable:

(36) ¢ahta me bel.
Take care of yourself. (lit.: 'Choose your way')

(37) ma ba št'ušahat.
Don't fall down.

(38) k'un k'un šbenat bel.
Go slowly, carefully.

5.2.2 Cases of FTA-oriented bald-on-record usage. The above, the standard uses of bald on record, are usages where other demands (at least metaphorically) override face concerns. But another use of bald on record is actually oriented to face. This nicely illustrates the way in which respect for face involves mutual orientation, so that each participant attempts to foresee what the other participant is attempting to foresee. For in certain circumstances it is reasonable for S to assume that H will be especially preoccupied with H's potential infringements of S's preserve. In these circumstances it is polite, in a broad sense, for S to alleviate H's anxieties by pre-emptively inviting H to impinge on S's preserve.

Three areas where one would expect such pre-emptive invitations to occur in all languages are these: (i) welcomings (or post-greetings), where S insists that H may impose on his negative face; (ii) farewells, where S insists that H may transgress on his positive face by taking his leave; (iii) offers, where S insists that H may impose on S's negative face.

These three functional categories are all potential FTAs: there is a risk that H may not wish to receive such invitations. Where this risk is great, we would expect some other strategy than bald on record to be utilized. Thus S will not say 'Come in' to persons who are clearly more important than he and are clearly in a hurry. But we would predict that where such risk is small, these pre-emptive invitations will always and in all languages be delivered baldly on record. The reason for this is clear: if H is reluctant to impinge, he will be the less reluctant the firmer the invitation is. So, provided that no other face wants are infringed, the firmer the invitation, the more polite it is.

The classic example of such invitations is perhaps 'Come in', which is a bald-on-record imperative in many languages:

(39) English: Come in, don't hesitate, I'm not busy.
(40) Tzeltal: ⁊očan.
             Enter.
(41) Tamil: vaa.
           Come in.

Greetings and farewells, and in general rituals of beginning or terminating encounters, often contain such bald-on-record commands. In Tzeltal we have:

(42) la⁊. (response to a greeting hail)
       Come.
(43) ban. (farewell)
       Go.
(44) naklan. (offer to visitor)
       Sit down.
(45) solan. (trail greeting)
       Pass.

In Tamil (as in English) we find:

(46) ukkaaru.
     Sit down.
(47) pooy vaa.
     Come again. (lit.: Go and come)

Gillian Sankoff informs us (personal comm.) that in Buang, a Melanesian language spoken in New Guinea, leave-taking always involves the person who is staying behind providing an on-record specification of what both parties are to do. For example:

(48) ke m'do, g'na.
     I am staying, you (singular) go.

Similar usage is applied in *Tok Pisin* (New Guinea pidgin English), where the stayer says:

(49) Orait, mi stap, yu go.
     All right, I'm staying, you are going.

Other examples of bald-on-record imperatives include offers, as in English:

(50) (You must) have some more cake.[30]
(51) Don't bother, I'll clean it up.
(52) Leave it to me.

Similarly, in Tzeltal offers are often baldly on record:

(53) hi¢'an tal. la? we?an.
     Pull (your chair) up. Come eat.

And the Tzeltal imperative:

(54) poka?a?k'ab.
     Wash your hands.

accompanied by the holding-out of a water-basin, constitutes a standard offer of a meal. Equally, in Tamil one says to a guest:

(55) caappiTTu.
     Eat!

in offering a meal.

   Other cases of bald-on-record imperatives seem to be addressed to H's reluctance to transgress on S's positive face (as contrasted with the above, which are aimed at forestalling H's reluctance to impinge on S's negative face). For example, in:

(56) Don't worry about me.
(57) Don't let me keep you.

S communicates essentially 'Feel free to get on with your business and don't worry about offending me.' And in:

(58) Don't mind the mess.

S communicates something like, 'Don't worry that I will mind you seeing me (or my preserve) in such a mess; I won't.'

Note that only sometimes is the 'urgency' expressed by such face-oriented bald-on-record usages totally unredressed. Often it may be emphasized by positive-politeness hedges:

(59) Dó come in, I insist, really!
(60) Dó go first.

Or it may be softened by negative-politeness respect terms, or by *please*:

(61) Please come in, (sir).

5.3 Positive politeness

Positive politeness is redress directed to the addressee's positive face, his perennial desire that his wants (or the actions/acquisitions/values resulting from them) should be thought of as desirable. Redress consists in partially satisfying that desire by communicating that one's own wants (or some of them) are in some respects similar to the addressee's wants.[31]

Unlike negative politeness, positive politeness is not necessarily redressive of the particular face want infringed by the FTA; that is, whereas in negative politeness the sphere of relevant redress is restricted to the imposition itself, in positive politeness the sphere of redress is widened to the appreciation of alter's wants in general or to the expression of similarity between ego's and alter's wants. As the outputs charted in Fig. 3 illustrate, the linguistic realizations of positive politeness are in many respects simply representative of the normal linguistic behaviour between intimates, where interest and approval of each other's personality, presuppositions indicating shared wants and shared knowledge, implicit claims to reciprocity of obligations or to reflexivity of wants, etc. are routinely exchanged. Perhaps the only feature that distinguishes positive-politeness redress from normal everyday intimate language behaviour is an element of exaggeration; this serves as a marker of the face-redress aspect of positive-politeness expression, by indicating that even if S can't with total sincerity say 'I want your wants', he can at least sincerely indicate 'I want your positive face to be satisfied.' Thus the element of insincerity in exaggerated expressions of

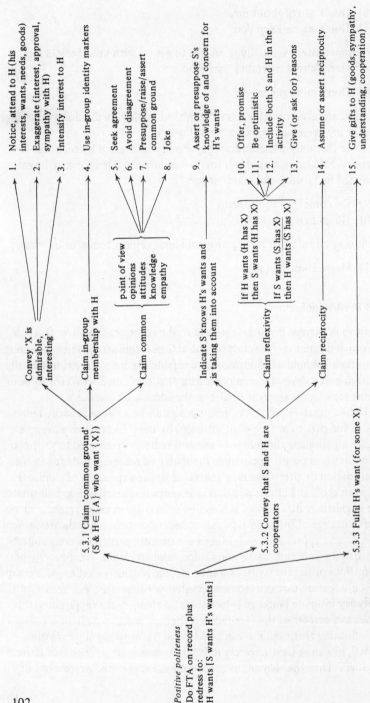

Fig. 3. Chart of strategies: Positive politeness

Positive politeness
Do FTA on record plus
redress to:
H wants [S wants H's wants]

5.3.1 Claim 'common ground'
(S & H ∈ {A} who want {X})

5.3.2 Convey that S and H are
cooperators

5.3.3 Fulfil H's want (for some X)

Convey 'X is
admirable,
interesting'

Claim in-group
membership with H

Claim common
ground

Indicate S knows H's wants and
is taking them into account

Claim reflexivity

Claim reciprocity

Give gifts to H (for some X)

1. Notice, attend to H (his
    interests, wants, needs, goods)
2. Exaggerate (interest, approval,
    sympathy with H)
3. Intensify interest to H

4. Use in-group identity markers

5. Seek agreement
6. Avoid disagreement
7. Presuppose/raise/assert
    common ground
8. Joke

9. Assert or presuppose S's
    knowledge of and concern for
    H's wants

10. Offer, promise
11. Be optimistic
12. Include both S and H in the
    activity
13. Give (or ask for) reasons

14. Assume or assert reciprocity

15. Give gifts to H (goods, sympathy,
    understanding, cooperation)

point of view
opinions
attitudes
knowledge
empathy

If H wants {H has X}
then S wants {H has X}

If S wants {S has X}
then H wants {S has X}

approval or interest ('How absolutely marvellous! I simply can't imagine how you manage to keep your roses so exquisite, Mrs B!') is compensated for by the implication that the speaker really sincerely wants Mrs B's positive face to be enhanced.

It is precisely this association with intimate language usage that gives the linguistics of positive politeness its redressive force. Positive-politeness utterances are used as a kind of metaphorical extension of intimacy, to imply common ground or sharing of wants to a limited extent even between strangers who perceive themselves, for the purposes of the interaction, as somehow similar. For the same reason, positive-politeness techniques are usable not only for FTA redress, but in general as a kind of social accelerator, where S, in using them, indicates that he wants to 'come closer' to H.

5.3.1 Claim common ground. The strategies of positive politeness involve three broad mechanisms, labelled 5.3.1–5.3.3 on the chart (Fig. 3). Those of the first type involve S claiming 'common ground' with H, by indicating that S and H both belong to some set of persons who share specific wants, including goals and values. Three ways of making this claim are these: S may convey that some want (goal, or desired object) of H's is admirable or interesting to S too; or he may stress common membership in a group or category, thus emphasizing that both S and H belong to some set of persons who share some wants; finally, S can claim common perspective with H without necessarily referring to in-group membership. The outputs of these three methods of stressing common ground give us positive-politeness strategies 1–8, which we now examine in turn.

Strategy 1: Notice, attend to H (his interests, wants, needs, goods)

In general, this output suggests that S should take notice of aspects of H's condition (noticeable changes, remarkable possessions, anything which looks as though H would want S to notice and approve of it). Examples used as FTA redress include, in English:

(1) Goodness, you cut your hair! (. . .) By the way, I came to borrow some flour.
(2) You must be hungry, it's a long time since breakfast. How about some lunch?
(3) What a beautiful vase this is! Where did it come from?

In Tzeltal, similar examples serve the same function:

(4) lom lek ʔaʔk'uʔ, $\begin{cases} \text{banti manoh?} \\ \text{haʔat ʔaʔpasoh?} \end{cases}$

Your blouse is very good, $\left\{ \begin{array}{l} \text{where was it bought?} \\ \text{did you make it yourself?} \end{array} \right\}$

And similarly, in Tamil:

(5) ookoo! putu pooTToo pooTTiinkalaa?
     Ah! You've got a new photo (on your wall), eh?

or of a newly painted house:

(6) oo! nallaa irukkiratu!
     Oh! it's very nice!

Another aspect of the NOTICE output is that when H makes an FTA against himself (a breakdown of body control, or any *faux pas*), S should 'notice' it and indicate that he's not embarrassed by it. (By contrast, in negative politeness S should always ignore H's *faux pas*.) He can do this by a joke, or teasing H about his penchant for *faux pas*:

(7) English: God you're farty tonight!
(8) Tzeltal: lom s¢'isnah! ('very much his fartiness!')

or by including S himself as part of the act (cf. positive-politeness strategies numbered 4 and 7 below):

(9) *We* ate too many beans tonight, didn't *we*!

Similarly, if H's nose is running, a positively polite thing for S to do is to offer H a tissue, or comfort for having a cold, rather than ignoring it as in negative politeness.

Strategy 2: Exaggerate (interest, approval, sympathy with H)

This is often done with exaggerated intonation, stress, and other aspects of prosodics, as well as with intensifying modifiers, as in the English:

(10) What a fantástic gárden you have!
(11) Yes, isn't it just ghástly the way it always seems to rain just when you've hung your laundry out!

(12) How absolutely $\left\{ \begin{array}{l} \text{márvellous} \\ \text{extraórdinary} \\ \text{dévastating} \\ \text{incrédible} \end{array} \right\}$!

Similarly, in Tamil, positive-politeness exaggerations abound:

(13) viiTu payankaramaa kaTTirukkiraar.

lit.: He built the house terrifyingly. (conversationally implicates
(c.i.): he built it amazingly lavishly; he really splashed out)

(14) peN lakshanamaa irukkiratu.
      The girl's (as beautiful as) Lakshmi.
      (c.i.: she has grace and beauty; this is a typical comment on a bride)

or:

(15) peN avaLavo lakshanamaa irukkumnnu naan nennekkavee
      ille: aRakaana irukkiratu.
      I never thought a girl could be so Lakshmi-like: she's beautiful. (a
      woman reports on the bride at a recent marriage)

(16) ciile rompa aRakaana irukkiratu; on-ooTiya nerattukku itu kaTTinaa,
      pramaatamaa irukku!
      That sari is very beautiful; for your colouring it's outstanding!

(17) anta kalyanattle payankaramaa kuuTTam ekaccakamaa iruntatu!
      At that marriage there was a terrifyingly excessive crowd! (said in
      admiration)

Tamil has some special intensifying devices much used in such circumstances: one of these is a set of conventional sound symbolisms, followed by
the quotative particle. Thus *jumm-nnu* means 'exquisite', 'perfect'. Another
device is reduplication: *periya periya kuTumpattile* (lit.: 'in a big big
family'), which emphasizes (and in this case pluralizes), conveying: 'in
many really *big* families . . .' The two devices work together to produce
forms like *jilajilu-nnu* ('very chilly'), *paLapaLa-nnu* ('very shiny'),
jum:majumm-nnu ('really exquisite').[32]

   In Tzeltal the exaggeration in positive politeness is quite remarkable,
even to an observer who doesn't know a word of the language. (One
American visitor observed that the women, talking to one another, sounded
as if they were 'acting in a play', their emotional expression was so drama-
tized.) A rough tonal contour is all we can do to non-technically characterize this on paper. For example:

(18) k'an me ta yuč'oh to yilel. yalel ?ihk'al štun to bal yilel.

      wozol naniš shol ?a, štaytun naniš sne ?a, ho?pol naniš ?a!

This is the speech of a woman describing the disreputable appearance of
her drunken husband to a church crowd, eliciting their sympathy with

heightened pitch (of outrage), exaggerated stress and rhythmicity, and exaggerated intonation contours. A rough translation: 'He loóked as íf he was stíll drúnk; he looked incrédibly dírty, reálly úncómbed haír, reálly cróoked clóthes, reálly his bélt hálf-tíed!'

Interestingly enough, the intonation and prosodics of sympathy or commiseration are very similar in English and Tzeltal; elsewhere we have outlined an argument for the universal bases for the semantics of prosodic usage (Brown and Levinson 1974).

The exaggerative or emphatic use of words or particles, illustrated in the above examples, is another feature of this positive-politeness output. For English, they include expressions like *for sure, really, exactly, absolutely*; in Tzeltal the particles *nanič* ('really'), *č'i, č'e* (exclamatory' particle), *melel* ('truly'), *naš* ('exactly', 'just so'), and others serve the same function (see the discussion under 'Hedges' in section 5.4.2).

Strategy 3: Intensify interest to H

Another way for S to communicate to H that he shares some of his wants is to intensify the interest of his own (S's) contributions to the conversation, by 'making a good story'. This may be done by using the 'vivid present', for example; this is a common feature of positive-politeness conversations, as it pulls H right into the middle of the events being discussed, metaphorically at any rate, thereby increasing their intrinsic interest to him. For example:

(19) I come down the stairs, and what do you think I see? — a huge mess all over the place, the phone's off the hook and clothes are scattered all over . . .

Sometimes this can involve switching back and forth between past and present tenses, as in the following passage where the speaker is relating her family's reactions to a past event:

(20) Black I like. I used to wear it more than I do now, I very rarely wear it now. I wore a black jumper, and when I wear it my Mum says 'Ah', she said. But Len likes it, he thinks it looks ever so nice and quite a few people do. But when my Mum sees it she said, 'Oh it's not your colour, you're more for pinks and blues.'

Similar vacillation occurs in Tamil:

(21) neettu raattri anta kaTekku pooneen. avaan-kiTTe saamaanam vaankureen. nallaa irukkiraanee. nallaa peecuraan. inikki avaan cettupooy-taan keeTTu rompa aaccaariyam irukkutee.

'Yesterday night I went to that shop. I buy some thi
He's all right, isn't he? He speaks nicely. Today I he[a]
dead and gone and I was very surprised.'

Such use of the vivid present, especially in reported conver
phrases as *naan appaTiyenkireen* ('and I says this . . .'), were felt by Tamil
informants to be female traits, and especially associated with the unedu-
cated and the low-statused. Similar stereotypes exist in our own culture;
it is the way 'charwomen' tend to be portrayed on British television. Why
such similar social distributions of similar strategies exist is an important
question (we make some suggestions in section 7.2).

The use of directly quoted speech rather than indirect reported speech
is another feature of this strategy, as is the use of tag questions or expressions that draw H as a participant into the conversation, such as 'you
know?', 'see what I mean?', 'isn't it?'.

A related technique is to exaggerate facts, to overstate:

(22) There were a *million* people in the Co-op tonight!
(23) I've *never* seen such a row!
(24) You *always* do the dishes! I'll do them this time.
(25) I'll be done in *one second*. (half a sec', half a mo')

The exaggeration in these cases may redress an FTA simply by stressing
the sincerity of S's good intentions, but there also seems to be an element
of attempting to increase the interest of the conversational contributions
by expressing them dramatically.

Strategy 4: Use in-group identity markers

By using any of the innumerable ways to convey in-group membership,
S can implicitly claim the common ground with H that is carried by that
definition of the group. These include in-group usages of address forms,
of language or dialect, of jargon or slang, and of ellipsis.

Address forms. In many languages (for reasons discussed below) the second-
person plural pronoun of address doubles as an honorific form to singular
respected or distant alters. Such usages are called T/V systems, after the
French *tu* and *vous* (see Brown and Gilman 1960). In such languages, the
use of a T (singular non-honorific pronoun) to a non-familiar alter can
claim solidarity.

Other address forms used to convey such in-group membership include
generic names and terms of address like *Mac, mate, buddy, pal, honey,
dear, duckie, luv, babe, Mom, blondie, brother, sister, cutie, sweetheart,*

ᴐ, *fellas*. In Tzeltal, an equivalent among males is *kere* ('boy'); and in Tamil, *tampi* (lit. 'younger brother') and *vaattiyaar* ('teacher') are used. Diminutives and endearments (as in some of the above examples, or in English by adding *-ie* to the addressee's name) have a similar function of claiming in-group solidarity.

Such forms may be used to soften FTAs:

(26) Here mate, I was keeping that seat for a friend of mine . . .

(27) Help me with this bag here, will you $\left\{ \begin{array}{l} \text{luv} \\ \text{son} \\ \text{pal} \end{array} \right\}$?

Using such in-group kinds of address forms with imperatives, as in (27), or in:

(28) Come here, $\left\{ \begin{array}{l} \text{mate} \\ \text{honey} \\ \text{buddy} \end{array} \right\}$.

indicates that S considers the relative P (power, status difference) between himself and the addressee to be small, thus softening the imperative by indicating that it isn't a power-backed command. Thus even when used to children, it turns a command into a request:

(29) Bring me your dirty clothes to wash, $\left\{ \begin{array}{l} \text{honey} \\ \text{darling} \\ \text{Johnny} \end{array} \right\}$.

The same softening use of address forms appears in Tzeltal:

(30) ¢'usa kala ti⁷nail *kan¢il.*
Shut my little door, *my girl.*

And in Tamil, *tampi* ('younger brother') is used to soften FTAs:

(31) periya visaysham! kaacu veeNum. *tampi* naan veLLakovilukku
pookaNum. naaLekeki taareen.

Big news! I need cash. *Younger brother*, I've got to go to Vellakovil.
I'll give it back tomorrow.

Other fictive Tamil kin terms are also used, mostly on the basis of persistent cross-caste relations of a traditional kind (see Beck 1972:120; Levinson 1977); these too are probably more likely to occur in accompanying an FTA. Among friends, where the use of *tampi* standardly occurs, an element of joking is likely to creep in, due no doubt to the fact that in an Indian setting friendship is compounded of elements of conjunction and disjunction (cross-caste, cross-familial ties), as Radcliffe-Brown would put it. Friends then behave as if each were the younger brother of the other, using what are normally power-laden or abusive address forms such as *-ppaa* (a contracted form of 'father', like the American English *Pop*), used standardly to inferiors, or *-Taa* or *raa*, and *Teey*, attention-getters with sharp power connotations. These forms are then used jokingly to soften FTAs. Thus a Tamil parallel to (28) is:

(32) pattu ruupaay kuT*uraa*. enekku veeNum.
      Give us 10 rupees, *sonny*. I need it.

Also, the English word *brother* and *vaattiyaar* ('teacher') are used as generic address terms (like *Mate* in English) in urban relationships in South India.

In some languages, the use of diminutives or endearments may extend beyond their function as address terms. In Tzeltal, for example, the particle *ala*, 'a little', is often sprinkled liberally throughout a positively polite conversation and seems then to function simply as an overall endearment for the topic of the conversation. It serves, in this case, as a marker of small talk, where the subject of talk is not as important as the fact of carrying on a conversation that is amply loaded with such markers of emotional agreement. Take, for example, this excerpt from the beginning of a conversation, where A has come to visit B:

(33) A: '. . . ?ay binti ya k*ala* pas šane,' šon yu?un, 'nail to hoy ta koral
         k*ala* mut.'

         'There's something else I'll a-little do,' I said, 'first I'll put my-little chickens in an enclosure.'

      B: la wan ?a?hoy ta koral ?a?w*ala* mut!

         You perhaps put your-little chickens in an enclosure!

      A: la. ha?in ya slo?laben k*ala* k'al.

         I did. It's because they eat my-little cornfield up for (if I don't confine them, that is).

      B: ya slo? ta me yaš ?*ala* č'iiše.

         They eat (it) if it a-little grows up (big enough).

      A: ?*ala* lawaltikiš!

         It's a-little grown already!

Here the subject of the diminutivizing ?*ala* moves from what A is going to do, to her chickens, to her cornfield, to the size to which the corn grows; clearly the function of ?*ala* here is to stress the emotional bond between A and B engaging in this conversation, rather than as a literal description of A's actions, corn, chickens, etc. (See section 5.4.2, p. 157, for other examples of the use of ?*ala*.)

109

G. Sankoff observes (personal comm.) that there is an analogous word in Buang, *d'ke*, 'a bit, a little', which is sprinkled throughout positively polite conversations in a similar way to the Tzeltal *ʔala*.

Use of in-group language or dialect. The phenomenon of *code-switching* involves any switch from one language or dialect to another in communities where the linguistic repertoire includes two or more such codes. In some cases, situations of *diglossia* (Ferguson 1964), the switch is between two varieties or dialects of a language, one of which is considered 'high' and prestigious, the other 'low' and domestic. Other cases simply involve switching from one language to another, in bilingual or multilingual communities.

In situations where code-switching occurs, we may expect a switch into the code associated with in-group and domestic values to be a potential way of encoding positive politeness when redress is required by an FTA (a resource nicely paralleled by a switch from the V to the T pronoun in languages with T/V systems). Thus Gumperz (1970:135) describes some examples of code-switching among California Chicanos, where a switch from English into Spanish marks personal involvement or embarrassment, while English is used for making general and detached statements. Our analysis of this would suggest that in this case Spanish is used for positive politeness, English for negative politeness. There is also evidence from Black English, that the Black dialect (NNE) may be switched into for emphasis, or to show speaker involvement (stressing the 'we'), while Standard English is used to stress detachment (stressing the 'they') (Gumperz 1970:137). And similarly in switching from standard (Bokmål) into local (Ranamål) dialects in Norway (Blom and Gumperz 1972), one finds 'metaphorical' switches for local topics, and presumably also for emotion-laden and FTA-relevant utterances.

On the other hand, switches into a code associated with external relations may, amongst other things, signal an FTA accompanied with negative politeness (nicely paralleled by a switch from a T to a V pronoun). Or it may simply signal a withdrawal of positive politeness and its associated emotional support, as in the following case from a Puerto Rican community in Jersey City, where the speaker encodes anger and firmness by switching from Spanish into English (Gumperz 1975; cf. 1970:132):

(34) Mother's first call: ven acá, ven acá.
                      Come here, come here.

    Mother's exasperated second call: Come here, you.

This is comparable to the switch within English, from nickname to full name (Gumperz 1970:133):

(35) First call: Come here, Johnny.
Second call: John Henry Smith, you come here right away.

Another type of code-switching phenomenon is the switch in English into a spurious dialect, or a dialect not normally used by S or H, to soften an FTA or turn it into a joke — for example, making a complaint in a fake Cockney accent or Alfred E. Neumann-style nasal twang.

Use of jargon or slang. Related to the use of an in-group language or dialect is the use of in-group terminology. By referring to an object with a slang term, S may evoke all the shared associations and attitudes that he and H both have toward that object; this then may be used as FTA redress. For example, use of brand names in a request may stress that S and H share an (in-group) reliance on the required object:

(36) Got any Winstons?
(37) I came to borrow some Allinsons if you've got any.

And just as in British English one uses:

(38) Lend us two *quid* then, wouldja mate?

and in American English:

(39) Lend us two *bucks* then, wouldja Mac?

so in village Tamil:

(40) nammukku reNTu $\left\{ \begin{array}{l} maan \\ kappal \end{array} \right\}$ kuTu.

Give us (incl.) two $\left\{ \begin{array}{l} \text{deer.} \\ \text{ships.} \end{array} \right\}$

(a 'deer' = a five-rupee note, a 'ship' = a ten-rupee note, after the engraved design)

Contraction and ellipsis. Because of the reliance on shared mutual knowledge to make ellipsis comprehensible, there is an inevitable association between the use of ellipsis and the existence of in-group shared knowledge. For example, in order for the utterance 'Nails' to be interpretable, S and H must share some knowledge about the context that makes the utterance understandable (for example that S and H are cooperating in building a house and S has the hammer in his hand). It is perhaps for this reason that the use of ellipsis and contraction is associated with positive politeness, and therefore the presence of ellipsis may mark an utterance as being positively polite. Even the use of conventionally indirect requests, normally a feature of negative politeness, if marked by ellipsis crosses over into positive politeness:

(41) Mind if I smoke?
(42) Got any spare cash?
(43) How about a drink?

(We discuss this in more detail in section 8.1 below.)

Note also that, in English at any rate, many nicknames are simply contracted forms of the full name — for example, Liz, Jenny, Joe, Tom, Sam. It seems that to contract is to endear, perhaps because of the association with smallness, perhaps partly because of the contrast with negative politeness where one tries to *increase* the metaphorical size of H.

Strategy 5: Seek agreement

Safe topics. Another characteristic way of claiming common ground with H is to seek ways in which it is possible to agree with him. The raising of 'safe topics' allows S to stress his agreement with H and therefore to satisfy H's desire to be 'right', or to be corroborated in his opinions. The weather is a safe topic for virtually everyone, as is the beauty of gardens, the incompetence of bureaucracies (to those outside of them, at least), and the irritations of having to wait in line. The more S knows about H, the more close to home will be the safe topics he can pursue with H — so, for example, on one of our tapes a group of young Black athletes in a Berkeley, California, gym swap stories about gory accidents they have experienced and revel in the agreement thus generated (also satisfying positive-politeness outputs 2, 3, 4, 7 and 8 to a marked degree at the same time). Such rapport-inspiring topics are commonly raised as a way of doing the FTA of initiating an encounter with a stranger. And in many cultures, the FTA of making a request is normally preceded by an interim of small talk on safe topics (in Tenejapa and in Tamilnad it is usually about crops, or weather, or illness, or current local happenings), as a way of reassuring H that you didn't come simply to exploit him by making a request, but have an interest in general in maintaining a relationship with him.

Another aspect of seeking agreement involves looking for those aspects of topics on which it is possible to agree and sticking to them. So, for example, if your neighbour comes home with a new car and you think it hideously huge and pollution-producing, you might still be able to say sincerely: 'Isn't your new car a beautiful colour!'

Repetition. Agreement may also be stressed by *repeating* part or all of what the preceding speaker has said, in a conversation. In addition to demonstrating that one has heard correctly what was said (satisfying output 1: NOTICE, ATTEND TO H), repeating is used to stress emotional agreement with the utterance (or to stress interest and surprise). For example:

(44) A: John went to London this weekend!
     B: To Lóndon!

(45) A: I had a flat tyre on the way home.
     B: Oh God, a flat tyre!

This process is highly conventionalized in Tzeltal, so that for example, if it is possible to answer a question by repeating part of it, rather than simply by 'yes' or 'no', the answer will repeat:

(46) A: *baht* bal ta k'išin k'inal?
        Did she go to hot country?
     B: *baht*.
        She went.

Often such repeats go back and forth for several conversational turns; so that nuances of surprise, approval, or disapproval or simply emphatic assertion may be revelled in:

(47) A: ... tey ʔa toktael stukel ʔa bi?
        ... there he is, at work alone, is he?
     B: tey ʔay stukel ʔa.
        There he is alone.
     A: tey ʔay.
        There he is.
     B: tey.
        There.
     A: tey.
        There.

And there are a number of Tzeltal particles (see under 'Hedges' in section 5.4.2 below) that function to indicate emphatic agreement; whenever someone is telling a story or relating an incident, there has to be someone to take the respondent role and utter brief agreements after each sentence or two (just as in English the addressee often utters 'yes', 'uhuh', 'really!?', as someone tells a story).

Strategy 6: Avoid disagreement

Token agreement. The desire to agree or appear to agree with H leads also to mechanisms for pretending to agree, instances of 'token' agreement. Sacks (1973) has collected numerous examples in English of the remarkable degree to which speakers may go in twisting their utterances so as to appear to agree or to hide disagreement — to respond to a preceding utterance with 'Yes, but . . .' in effect, rather than a blatant 'No'. To draw on Sacks's American data (1973), the 'Rule of Agreement' yields examples like the following (where B is a response to A, in each case):

(48) A: That's where you live, Florida?
      B: That's where I was born.

(49) A: Can you hear me?
      B: Barely.

(50) A: You hate your Mom and Dad.
      B: Oh, sometimes.

(51) A: So is this permanent?
      B: Yeh, it's 'permanent' — permanent until I get married again.

(52) A: Have you got friends?
      B: I have friends. So-called friends. I had friends. Let me put it that way.

(53) A: And they haven't heard a word, huh?
      B: Not a word. Not at all. Except Mrs H. maybe.

We found similar 'preference for agreement' in our data on British English:

(54) A: What is she, small?
      B: Yes, yes, she's small, smallish, um, not really small but certainly not very big.

A parallel strategy is involved in the 'Rule of Contiguity' (Sacks 1973), which states that answers should follow questions but are displaced to soften disagreement, as in the following:

(55) A: Yuh comin down early?
      B: Well I got a lot of things to do. I don't know. It won't be too early.

(56) A: It left her quite permanently damaged I suppose.
      B: Apparently. Uh, he's still hopeful.

Albert (1972) reports the same phenomenon for the Burundi, where the second speaker says, in effect, 'Yes, I definitely agree with the first speaker', and then carries on to state his own opinion which may be completely contrary to that of the first speaker.

Note also that irony may be used as a way of superficially agreeing with the preceding utterance (see examples in section 5.5, Off record).

Pseudo-agreement. Another example of apparent or pseudo-agreement is found in English in the use of *then* as a conclusory marker, an indication that the speaker is drawing a conclusion to a line of reasoning carried out cooperatively with the addressee. This may refer to a genuine prior agreement; for example:

(57) I'll meet you in front of the theatre just before 8.0, then.

where *then* points to a conclusion of an actual agreement between S and H. English *so* works in a similar way:

(58) So when are you coming to see us?

But *then* and *so* are often used where there is in fact no prior agreement; by pointing to a *fake* prior agreement they call upon the cooperative agreement associations, as in:

(59) I'll be seeing you then.
(60) Take this radio off my hands for 5 quid then?

Example (60) was the speaker's first utterance as he walked up to an acquaintance; *then* in this case, by referring to a fake prior agreement, pressured the addressee to accept the request/offer.

What looks like exactly the same phenomenon occurs in Tzeltal with the particle *ȼ'in*, which has no identifiable literal meaning but appears to function just like the conclusory *then* in English, for real *or* fake conclusions to prior agreements. For example, in taking leave (as in (59) above) one standardly says:

(61) hk'opon hbatik ȼ'in.
    We'll be talking together then.

or in implying a request for help:

(62) mančuk hal ȼ'in hnae?
    My house would be OK then? (i.e., if I left for a few minutes)

where S conveys a request for H to keep an eye on her house as though H had already offered. Other Tzeltal examples are cited under negative politeness particles, p. 148.

Tamil *appuram* ('then') appears to work in precisely comparable ways. For example:

(63) appuram naam pooyTTu vaareenka.
    I'll be seeing you then.

White lies. A further output of the positive politeness desire to avoid disagreement is the social 'white lie', where S, when confronted with the necessity to state an opinion, wants to lie ('Yes I do like your new hat!')

115

rather than damage H's positive face. In Tzeltal one conventionally avoids a confrontation when refusing a request by lying, pretending there are reasons why one cannot comply. For example, in response to a request to borrow a radio:

(64) eh mastak. lahemiš sbaterias.
      Oh I can't. The batteries are dead.

Both S and H may know that this is not true, but H's face is saved by not having his request refused point-blank.

Hedging opinions. Alternatively, S may choose to be vague about his own opinions, so as not to be seen to disagree. We have seen that one positive-politeness output (strategy 2) leads S to exaggerate, and this is often manifested by choosing words at the extremes of the relevant value scale. Thus words like the following may abound in positively polite talk:

marvellous	appalling
fantastic	ghastly
extraordinary	devastating
wonderful	outrageous
delightful	despicable
ravishing	revolting
divine	ridiculous
incredible (good)	incredible (bad)

as well as intensifying modifers such as *absolutely*, *completely*, and the like. Now clearly, choosing strategy 2 and using such extremes to characterize one's opinions is risky, in light of the desire to agree — that is, risky unless S is certain of H's opinion on the subject.

For this reason, one characteristic device in positive politeness is to hedge these extremes, so as to make one's own opinion safely vague. Normally hedges are a feature of negative politeness, and we discuss them below in more detail in that connection, but some hedges can have this positive-politeness function as well, most notably (in English): *sort of, kind of, like, in a way*. For example:

(65) I really sort of $\left\{ \begin{array}{l} \text{think} \\ \text{hope} \\ \text{wonder} \end{array} \right\}$ . . .

(66) It's really beautiful, in a way.

(67) I kind of want Florin to win the race, since I've bet on him.

(68) I don't know, like I think people have a right to their own opinions.
      (Californian English)

116

(69) Ah, the weather's bad like. (Welsh English)

These hedges may be used to soften FTAs of suggesting or criticizing or complaining, by blurring the speaker's intent:

(70) You really sort of botched it, didn't you?
(71) You really should sort of try harder.
(72) You really are sort of a loner, aren't you?
(73) A: What's the matter?

B: Well my husband $\left\{\begin{array}{l}\text{sort of, never dóes anything, you know } \ldots \\ \text{is always sort of át me, you know } \ldots\end{array}\right\}$

The hedges in these sentences serve to avoid a precise communication of S's attitude. Perhaps this derives from the fact that these hedges also function as markers of metaphors, as in:

(74) That knife sort of 'chews' bread.

That is, expressions like *sort of* in FTAs may mark the word that they modify as being a metaphor of some sort, leaving it up to the addressee to figure out how to interpret it. So the use of these hedges assumes some degree of common ground between S and H, in that S calls upon H to use his common knowledge to interpret S's attitude. (See related discussion under strategy 7 below.)

In Tzeltal, some particles may be used to the same effect, in particular *niwan, mak, ʔala,* and the subjunctive *-uk*:

(75) haʔ niš ¢'in mak.

That's just it, then, $\left\{\begin{array}{l}\text{maybe.}\\ \text{sort of.}\end{array}\right\}$

(76) melel niwan.
True maybe.

(77) ya hk'an ʔala pešuk.
I want sort of a peso's worth.

Strategy 7: Presuppose/raise/assert common ground

Gossip, small talk. The value of S's spending time and effort on being with H, as a mark of friendship or interest in him, gives rise to the strategy of redressing an FTA by talking for a while about unrelated topics. S can thereby stress his general interest in H, and indicate that he hasn't come to see H simply to do the FTA (e.g. a request), even though his intent to do it may be made obvious by his having brought a gift. This strategy for softening requests — at least, requests for favours — is commonly used in

Tenejapa, and probably in all kinship-based societies. Furthermore, in discussing general shared interests with H, S has ample opportunity to stress the common ground he shares with H — common concerns, and common attitudes towards interesting events.

Point-of-view operations. Nearly all sentences in natural languages encode point of view by means of *deixis*. Deixis has to do with the ways in which sentences are anchored to certain aspects of their contexts of utterance, including the role of participants in the speech event and their spatio-temporal and social location. For example, the pronoun 'I' normally refers to the participant who has the role of speaker, while 'now' refers to a time that includes the time of utterance, and 'there' refers to a place more distant from the speaker than that indicated by 'here' — and so on.

Fillmore (1971b, 1974, 1975) has developed a set of distinctions that characterize the ways in which sentences are deictically anchored in this way, and we rely heavily on his suggestions throughout this section. It seems a safe hypothesis that the normal unmarked deictic centre is the one where the speaker is the central person, the time of speaking (or 'coding time') is the central time, and the place where the speaker is at coding time is the central place. Thus the sentence 'John came to London' encodes that John's motion was towards the speaker, as indicated by the verb 'to come', and that the event took place prior to the time of speaking, as indicated by the past tense. (Actually, there are other interpretations, but they are strictly limited.) That is to say, temporal and spatial descriptions are here understood relative to the time and place of speaking, the central reference point. These central locations provide the unmarked anchorage point, from which all other usages are departures which take their meaning by reference to this basic anchorage point.

However, the fact is that many utterances have deictic centrings that are not this one. We call such departures 'point-of-view operations', since what they achieve are things like these: S speaks as if coding time (i.e., the central time) were located in a past event; or S speaks as if the central place were the hearer's location rather than the speaker's; or S speaks as if the central person were the hearer. Such operations or metaphors serve many purposes — stylistic, as in the 'vivid present'; conceptual, as in the hedge on certainty in sentences like 'That rustling will be a chipmunk' (cf. R. Lakoff 1970); and others.

They also perform basic politeness functions (as Fillmore (1971b) predicted), especially by switching into the addressee's point of view. Thus Fillmore notes (1975) that in a Mexican Indian language, when being deferential, instead of the normal 'I am *here*, you are *there*', one says 'I am *there*, you are *here*'. In other words, 'here' now means the place where the addressee is. Such methods of 'taking the role of the other' are basic politeness phenomena, so we discuss them in some detail. Those that are characteristic of positive politeness, that attempt to bring together or merge the points of view of speaker and addressee, are described here. Those that serve to 'distance' the speaker from the addressee are described below under negative-politeness strategy 7 (pp. 204-6). Here, then, are some examples of possible departures from the normal usage, used as techniques for *reducing* the distance between S's and H's points of view.

Personal-centre switch: S to H. This is where S speaks as if H were S, or H's knowledge were equal to S's knowledge. An example is the use of tag questions with falling intonation in some local dialects of British English:

(78) I had a really hard time learning to drive, didn't I.

where H couldn't possibly know, having just met S; or when giving directions to a stranger, unfamiliar with the town:

(79) It's at the far end of the street, the last house on the left, isn't it.

The Tamil tag *alla* has the same properties:

(80) en paNam elaam poocc alla.
      All my money's gone, hasn't it.

And the Tzeltal particle *bi* ('what') is used similarly:

(81) ya niš mel ko^ʔtan ¢'in ^ʔa *bi*.
      I just am sad then, aren't I.

Another form of personal-centre switch is seen in cases where, in giving empathy, one asserts what only H can know:

(82) A: Oh this cut hurts awfully, Mum.
      B: Yes dear, it hurts terribly, I know.

The personal-centre switch in this case can be carried in prosodics as well: both A's and B's utterances could be expressed with 'creaky voice' (very low pitch and a constricted glottis), where the prosodics of giving comfort is the same as (or a metaphor for) the prosodics of asking for sympathy. Furthermore, one can merge the 'I' and the 'you' into an inclusive 'we', although it is only H who is really being referred to:

(83) OK now, let's stop the chatter and get on with our little essays.
(84) Oh dear, we've lost our little ball, haven't we, Johnny?
(85) Now, have we taken our medicine? (doctor to patient)

In Tamil, in certain dialects, instead of 'my house', 'my father', 'my car', etc. or the 'our (exclusive) house' of higher-caste dialects, we find 'our (inclusive) house' (*namma viiTu*) used extensively as a positive-politeness form.

Another form of this point-of-view 'flip' is found in the use of *you know* in English; where H couldn't possibly 'know', this parallels the use of tag questions in (78) and (79) above:

(86) I really had a hard time learning to drive, you know.

When *you know* is scattered through a story, it may not claim that H's knowledge of the particular details to which it is attached is equivalent to S's, but rather claims H's knowledge of that *kind* of situation in general:

(87) I'm just walkin' down the street, ya know, and I damn near get run over by this *huge* Cadillac that comes roarin' by, ya know, like he owns the world, and I'm so scared, ya know I just about die. . . .

In Tzeltal there exists a comparable usage of 'ya know', in the form *ya?wa?y* ('you know/see/understand/feel'). This is often scattered throughout a story to draw the hearer into it, as in English, and even more extreme cases of flip occur. In fact, where English speakers would exclaim 'I see!', Tzeltal speakers say *ah wa?y!*, or 'Ah, *you* see' meaning '*I* understand!' It is thus used (with or without emphatic particles) to express emphatic agreement or understanding:

(88) wa?y naš kati ¢'in č'i!
'You' (*I*) see, exactly really then to be sure!

Or it is used to encourage H to follow the emotional trend of a complaining story:

(89) ha? lah hič la spasik *ta?wa?ye*; ya lah stihikon ta čukel te ?ahwalil, lom bayel lah la s¢e?la *ta?wa?y* bi ya yal te maestro.

Thus it is, they say, that they do, *you know* (lit.: 'in your knowing'); they say the chief will jail me, they say they really laughed a lot, *you know*, at what the teacher said.

Or it may simply be used to jog H's memory as to the details and relationships in a story — asking him to fill in the gaps, to make the appropriate associations:

(90) '. . . yaš batik ¢'in', šyut lah *ta?wa?y* sbankil *ta?wa?y* ?ih¢'inal winike.
'We'll go, then' he urged it-is-said *you see,* the older-brother *you see* of the younger man.[33]

Time switch. The use of the 'vivid present', a tense shift from past to present tense, seems in English to be a distinctly positive-politeness device:

(91) And Martha *says* to Bill, 'Oh Heavens', and I *says* . . .

(92) John *says* he really loves your roses.

Actually, this is a specific way of doing speech acts via a messenger, as in:

(93) John *says* do you want to come too?

And as illustrated in our discussion of strategy 3, the vivid present functions to increase the immediacy and therefore the interest of a story.

Place switch. The use of proximal rather than distal demonstratives (*here, this*, rather than *there, that*), where either proximal or distal would be acceptable, seems to convey increased involvement or empathy:

(94) (on saying goodbye): $\left\{ \begin{array}{c} \text{This} \\ \text{?That} \end{array} \right\}$ was a lovely party.

(95) (in reference): $\left\{ \begin{array}{c} \text{This} \\ \text{Here} \end{array} \right\}$ is a man I could trust.

    (versus): $\left\{ \begin{array}{c} \text{That} \\ \text{There} \end{array} \right\}$ is a man I could trust.

(96) This guy came up to me and . . . (versus 'There was a guy who . . .')

These spatial metaphors of closeness have their FTA uses, both impolite:

(97) (Look) Here! How dare you! Get out of the refrigerator!

and polite:

(98) Here! You must come in and have some tea.

Another aspect of this occurs in the use of verbs of movement to and from — that is, in English, *take* versus *bring,* or *go* versus *come* (see Fillmore 1972, 1975). English seems to encode a basic positive-politeness 'taking the role of the other' point of view in the usage of *come*. Whereas in Japanese, for example, a child would answer Mother's call to table with 'I'm going' (Fillmore 1972), in English (and intra-familial Tamil, and Tzeltal) such a summons must be answered with 'I'm coming'. This makes the use of *come* in English rather complex, encoding either movement toward the present speaker's or the present hearer's present locus. But there are further complications still, metaphorical extensions whereby the deictic spatial centre is located outside both S and H, as in these examples (where both S and H are removed from the goal of movement):

(99) $\left\{ \begin{array}{c} \text{Come} \\ \text{Go} \end{array} \right\}$ and meet me at my favourite restaurant in Conduit Street.

(100)   Oh, you're acting in *Othello* tomorrow night, are you? – I'll
$\begin{Bmatrix} \text{come} \\ \text{go} \end{Bmatrix}$ and watch you from the gallery.

In both sentences the use of *come* is licensed by an association of S or H
with a place (S in (99); H in (100)); and in both cases the use of *go* would
be a distancing device, in (100) a very rude or non-courteous one.

For similar reasons, *come* often has a participatory connotation, where
go would be distancing:

(101) Do you want to $\begin{Bmatrix} \text{come} \\ \text{go} \end{Bmatrix}$ with me to the movies?

So in these cases where the deictic opposition between *come* and *go* is
neutralized (i.e. where both are licensed by the situation), to use *come* is
to convey participation and cooperation, to use *go* is to convey distance
and less participation.

Avoidance of adjustment of reports to H's point of view. Where S is trying
to stress common ground that he shares with H, we would expect him to
make only the minimal adjustment in point of view when reporting; that
is, we would expect him to assume that H's point of view is his, or his is
H's. Hence we would expect a preference for direct quotes with uninter-
preted referring expressions, names, and so on, even where this may result
in loss of clarity.

The use of direct quoted speech in English is associated by stereotype
with the working class – along with the use of names and references without explanation. (See discussion below under 'Ethos', section 7.2.1.) In
Tzeltal and in Tamil, direct quoted speech is very generally used as a
positive-politeness technique.

Presupposition manipulations. We use the word 'presuppose' loosely in
this sense: S presupposes something when he presumes that it is mutually
taken for granted (but see Stalnaker 1972 for a tighter definition along
the same lines). The manipulation of such presuppositions where something is *not* really mutually assumed to be the case, but S speaks *as if* it
were mutually assumed, can be turned to positive-face redress, as illustrated in the following four sets of examples.

Presuppose knowledge of H's wants and attitudes. Negative questions,
which presume 'yes' as an answer, are widely used as a way to indicate
that S knows H's wants, tastes, habits, etc., and thus partially to redress
the imposition of FTAs. For example, for offers:

(102) Wouldn't you like a drink?

(103) Don't you want some dinner now?

or for opinions:

(104) Don't you think it's marvellous!?
(105) Isn't it a beautiful day!

Similarly, in Tzeltal, in offering food to household members:

(106) ma ya?we wah me??   or ma ya?wuč ?ek tat?
    Won't you eat, Mother?   Won't you drink too, Father?

or in response to a request for permission to stay in town alone:

(107) ma bal ya?mel ?a?wo?tan hilel mak.
    Won't you get sad by yourself?

In Latin, the use of *nonne* in questions presumes a 'yes' answer in a similar way, and presumably would have been available for this positive-politeness function.

Presuppose H's values are the same as S's values. The use of scalar predicates such as 'tall' assumes that S and H share the criteria for placing people (or things) on this scale. As G. Lakoff points out (1972), a man is in the set of 'tall men' according to his degree of tallness, which depends on his height relative to all the other men with whom he is being compared. So Lakoff assigns 'absolutely tall' only to a man 6 ft 3 in. tall, but a Mayan Indian would assign 'tall' to a man of 5 ft 10 in. Even more relative are value judgements on scales like good–bad, beautiful–ugly, interesting–boring; not only is the mapping of the criterion on to the predicate contextually relative, but the criteria themselves are relative.

Thus the preference for extremes on value scales that is a feature of positive politeness (see strategies 2 and 6 above) derives part of its impact from the tacit claim that S and H have the same values with respect to the relevant predicate, the same definition of what the scale is, of what constitutes beauty or goodness.

The sequencing of statements conjoined with *and* or *but* also may reveal shared values, and may be used to stress them (see R. Lakoff, 1971a), as any cursory examination of gossip will amply illustrate.

Presuppose familiarity in S-H relationship. The use of familiar address forms like *honey* or *darling* presupposes (in some analyses, at any rate) that the addressee is 'familiar'. The use of generic familiar address forms to strangers (e.g., *Mac, mate, buddy, luv,* etc.) may therefore soften or redress the threat of FTAs (see illustrations above, under strategy 4).

But in addition to presupposing such familiarity, it may also be explicitly asserted as FTA redress:

(108) Look, you're a pal of mine, so how about . . .

Presuppose H's knowledge. The use of any term presupposes (in some senses) that the referents are known to the addressee. Thus the use of in-group codes — language, dialect, jargon, local terminology — assumes that H understands and shares the associations of that code. This assumption may be exploited as a positive-politeness device:

(109) Well I was watching *High Life* last night and . . .
(110) Harry took me to the movies the other day.

Where the addressee doesn't know that there is a TV programme called *High Life,* or that S has a boyfriend called Harry, S's assumption that H does know these things may operate as an expression of good intentions, indicating that S assumes that S and H share common ground.

So also the use of pronouns where the referent has not been made explicit is typical of positive politeness:

(111) How about letting me have one of *those*! (sniffing appreciatively at the smell of cookies wafting in)
(112) Oh, *this* is lovely! (on walking into a house)

S may also assert H's knowledge (concerning S's needs, for example) as FTA redress:

(113) Look, you know I've got this test coming up, well how about lending me your *Encyclopaedia Britannica*?

Strategy 8: Joke

Since jokes are based on mutual shared background knowledge and values, jokes may be used to stress that shared background or those shared values. Joking is a basic positive-politeness technique, for putting H 'at ease' — for example in response to a *faux pas* of H's, S may joke (see strategy 1, above). Or a joke may minimize an FTA of requesting, as in:

(114) OK if I tackle those cookies now?
(115) How about lending me this old heap of junk? (H's new Cadillac)

Jokes may be used as an exploitation of politeness strategies as well, in attempts to redefine the size of the FTA. We discuss this in section 6.1 below.

124

5.3.2 Convey that S and H are cooperators.

Our second major class of positive-politeness strategies charted in Fig. 3 derives from the want to convey that the speaker and the addressee are cooperatively involved in the relevant activity. If S and H are cooperating, then they share goals in some domain, and thus to convey that they are cooperators can serve to redress H's positive-face want.

This cooperation may be stressed by S's indicating his knowledge of and sensitivity to H's wants, as in output strategy 9. It may be done by claiming some kind of reflexivity between S's and H's wants — either that S wants what H wants for H, or (by a point-of-view flip) that H wants what S wants for himself. These manipulations give us output strategies 10, 11, 12, and 13. Thirdly, S may convey his cooperation with H by indicating that he believes reciprocity to be prevailing between H and himself, that they are somehow locked into a state of mutual helping. Strategy 14 is derived from this means.

Strategy 9: *Assert or presuppose S's knowledge of and concern for H's wants*

One way of indicating that S and H are cooperators, and thus potentially to put pressure on H to cooperate with S, is to assert or imply knowledge of H's wants and willingness to fit one's own wants in with them. The negative questions discussed above may sometimes function in this way, as may utterances like the following:

(116) Look, I know you want the car back by 5.0, so should(n't) I go to town now? (request)

(117) I know you can't bear parties, but this one will really be good — do come! (request/offer)

(118) I know you love roses but the florist didn't have any more, so I brought you geraniums instead. (offer + apology)

Strategy 10: *Offer, promise*

In order to redress the potential threat of some FTAs, S may choose to stress his cooperation with H in another way. He may, that is, claim that (within a certain sphere of relevance) whatever H wants, S wants *for* him and will help to obtain. Offers and promises are the natural outcome of choosing this strategy; even if they are false ('I'll drop by sometime next week') they demonstrate S's good intentions in satisfying H's positive-face wants.

Strategy 11: Be optimistic

The other side of the coin, the point-of-view flip that is associated with the cooperative strategy, is for S to assume that H wants S's wants for S (or for S and H) and will help him to obtain them. That is, for S to be so presumptuous as to assume H will cooperate with him may carry a tacit commitment for S to cooperate with H as well, or at least a tacit claim that H will cooperate with S because it will be in their mutual shared interest. An utterance like (119) makes such a claim:

(119) Wait a minute, you haven't brushed your hair! (as husband goes out of the door)

The wife wants the husband to brush his hair before appearing in public; by expressing this want in terms that assume he (H) wants it too (even though he may well not care), she puts pressure on him to cooperate with her wants.

Presumptuous or 'optimistic' expressions of FTAs are one outcome of this strategy (and constitute perhaps the most dramatic difference between positive-politeness and negative-politeness ways of doing FTAs). For example:

(120) You'll lend me your lawnmower for the weekend, $\left\{ \begin{array}{l} \text{I hope.} \\ \text{won't you.} \\ \text{I imagine.} \end{array} \right\}$

(121) I've come to borrow a cup of flour.

(122) Look, I'm sure you won't mind if I $\left\{ \begin{array}{l} \text{borrow your typewriter.} \\ \text{point out that your flies are} \\ \quad \text{undone.} \\ \text{remind you to do the dishes} \\ \quad \text{tonight.} \end{array} \right\}$

(123) I'll just help myself to a cookie then – thanks!

Similarly in Tamil, to a very close friend, one can say:

(124) onka vaNTi kuTukkiriinka, illeyaa?
    You'll lend me your bike, right?

(125) koncam uppu vaankalaam-nnu vanteen.
    I've come to get a little salt.

Such optimistic expressions of FTAs seem to work by minimizing the size of the face threat – W_x – implying that it's nothing to ask (or offer, etc.) or that the cooperation between S and H means that such small things can be taken for granted. This minimization may be literally stated with expressions like *a little, a bit, for a second.* And the presumptuousness may be partially softened with a token tag, as in:

(126) I'm borrowing your scissors for a sec — OK?
(127) You don't have any objections to me helping myself to a bit of cake, do you?
(128) I just dropped by for a minute to invite you all for tea tomorrow — you will come, won't you?

Strategy 12: Include both S and H in the activity

By using an inclusive 'we' form, when S really means 'you' or 'me', he can call upon the cooperative assumptions and thereby redress FTAs. Noting that *let's* in English is an inclusive 'we' form, common examples are:

(129) Let's have a cookie, then. (i.e. *me*)
(130) Let's get on with dinner, eh? (i.e. *you*)
(131) Let's stop for a bite. (i.e. *I* want a bite, so let's stop)
(132) Give us a break. (i.e. *me*)

Similarly in Tamil, a man can invite a female visitor to eat in the following way, although decorum forbids that he should actually eat with her:

(133) naama caappiTTalaamaa?
      Shall we (inclusive) eat?

In Tzeltal the inclusive 'we' form is often used to soften requests, as if pretending that H wants the object or action requested as well:

(134) hk'antik ʔaʔwala ʔa¢'am ʔa.
      We (inclusive) want your little salt.
(135) hmahantik ʔaʔk'uʔ.
      We (inclusive) borrow your blouse.

And equally to soften offers, pretending that S is as eager as H to have the action performed:

(136) ya h¢'ustik ʔin nae, meʔtik. yašʔoč tal ʔik'.
      We (inclusive) will shut the door, ma'am. The wind's coming in.
(137) ya hp'istik ta lok'el.
      We (inclusive) will go fetch it. (i.e. '*I* will')

This last example seems to be used to stress the cooperativeness of S's action, implying 'I will do it for our benefit.' Similarly, in English, a

127

sweet-shop lady might say, when asked if she has any chocolate gingers:

(138) Let's just go into the back room and see if we have any.

and then trundle back alone, but for the common good.

Strategy 13: Give (or ask for) reasons

Another aspect of including H in the activity is for S to give reasons as to why he wants what he wants. By including H thus in his practical reasoning, and assuming reflexivity (H wants S's wants), H is thereby led to see the reasonableness of S's FTA (or so S hopes). In other words, giving reasons is a way of implying 'I can help you' or 'you can help me', and, assuming cooperation, a way of showing what help is needed — as example (136) above illustrates.

This fact leads to pressure to go off record, to test H and see if he is cooperative; if he is likely to be, the context may be enough to push the off-record reason into an on-record request or offer. Thus indirect suggestions which demand rather than give reasons are a conventionalized positive-politeness form, in English:

(139) Why not lend me your cottage for the weekend?
(140) Why don't we go to the seashore!
(141) Why don't I help you with that suitcase.

and in Tzeltal:

(142) bistuk ma ša?wak'betik bel hmahantik ?a?son?
      Why don't you lend us (inclusive) your record-player? (lit.: What good is it that you don't . . .)
(143) bi yu?un ma?yuk yaš?atinat?
      Why don't you bathe at all?

and in Tamil:

(144) nammukku een kankayam pooka kuuTaate?
      Why shouldn't we go to Kangayam? (conveying 'Let's go!')

These work by demanding reasons 'why not?', and assuming (via optimism) that if there are no good reasons why H shouldn't or can't cooperate, he will. Similarly, for past actions, if H is asked to give reasons why he did or didn't do something, and he has no good reasons, the FTA of criticizing may thereby be accomplished:

(145) Why didn't you do the dishes?!

Equally, in Tzeltal:

(146) bi yuʔun ma laʔwil, laʔwes te k'aʔpale?
       Why didn't you watch, as you burned your field? (complaining that
       the fire encroached on S's field)

Strategy 14: Assume or assert reciprocity

The existence of cooperation between S and H may also be claimed or
urged by giving evidence of reciprocal rights or obligations obtaining
between S and H. Thus S may say, in effect, 'I'll do X for you if you do
Y for me', or 'I did X for you last week, so you do Y for me this week'
(or vice versa). By pointing to the reciprocal right (or habit) of doing
FTAs to each other, S may soften his FTA by negating the debt aspect
and/or the face-threatening aspect of speech acts such as criticisms and
complaints.

5.3.3 Fulfil H's want for some X. Our last positive-politeness strategy
involves S deciding to redress H's face directly by fulfilling some of H's
wants, thereby indicating that he (S) wants H's wants *for H*, in some
particular respects.

Strategy 15: Give gifts to H (goods, sympathy, understanding, cooperation)

Finally, S may satisfy H's positive-face want (that S want H's wants, to
some degree) by actually satisfying some of H's wants. Hence we have
the classic positive-politeness action of gift-giving, not only tangible gifts
(which demonstrate that S knows some of H's wants and wants them to
be fulfilled), but human-relations wants such as those illustrated in many
of the outputs considered above — the wants to be liked, admired, cared
about, understood, listened to, and so on.

5.4 Negative politeness

Negative politeness is redressive action addressed to the addressee's negative face: his want to have his freedom of action unhindered and his attention unimpeded. It is the heart of respect behaviour, just as positive
politeness is the kernel of 'familiar' and 'joking' behaviour. Negative
politeness corresponds to Durkheim's 'negative rites', rituals of avoidance.
Where positive politeness is free-ranging, negative politeness is specific and
focused; it performs the function of minimizing the particular imposition
that the FTA unavoidably effects. When we think of politeness in Western

cultures, it is negative-politeness behaviour that springs to mind. In our culture, negative politeness is the most elaborate and the most conventionalized set of linguistic strategies for FTA redress; it is the stuff that fills the etiquette books (but not exclusively — positive politeness gets some attention[34]). Its linguistic realizations — conventional indirectnesses, hedges on illocutionary force, polite pessimism (about the success of requests, etc.), the emphasis on H's relative power — are very familiar and need no introduction.

We should, however, stress that the wants outlined in Fig. 4 are not the only motivations a speaker may have for using the linguistic realizations characteristic of negative politeness. The outputs are all forms useful in general for social 'distancing' (just as positive-politeness realizations are forms for minimizing social distance); they are therefore likely to be used whenever a speaker wants to put a social brake on to the course of his interaction.

5.4.1 Be direct. Once one has chosen the super-strategy of negative politeness, one seeks means to achieve it. Negative politeness enjoins both on-record delivery and redress of an FTA. Now the simplest way to construct an on-record message is to convey it directly, as in bald-on-record usages. However, it turns out that this clashes with the need for redress attuned to H's negative face, so in fact one does not issue negatively polite FTAs completely directly.

Nevertheless, intuition tells one that there is an element in formal politeness that sometimes directs one to minimize the imposition by coming rapidly to the point, avoiding the further imposition of prolixity and obscurity. Indeed, R. Lakoff has suggested (1973a) that this is the most important feature of politeness. In this we cannot agree with her, yet it is true that in certain circumstances — bothering important persons for favours, for instance — this is an important element. So although the desire to go on record provides a pressure towards directness and forthrightness, it is a desire that never issues in bald-on-record talk. For the other aspect of negative politeness intervenes, the need for negative-face redress, and some compromise is reached in the hybrid strategy of conventional indirectness.

Figure 4 shows the clash between these two wants, that is, the want to BE DIRECT stemming from DO FTA ON RECORD, and the want to BE INDIRECT that derives from DON'T COERCE H. A weighted desirability reasoning should be able to provide, as a consequence to two equal conflicting wants, a compromise means of partially satisfying them both, providing that is practically possible. The following discussion of negative-politeness output strategy 1 develops this mechanism in detail.

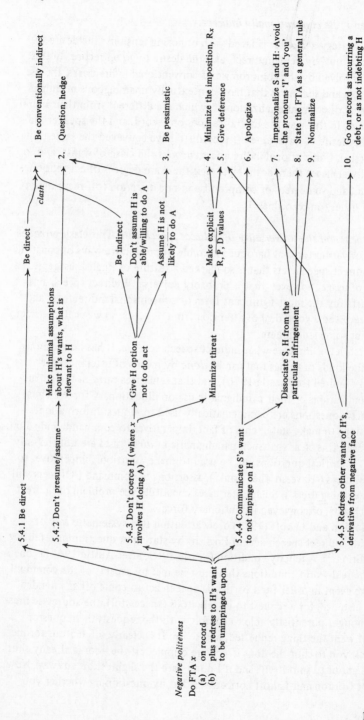

Fig. 4. Chart of strategies: Negative politeness

Negative politeness

Do FTA x
  (a) on record
  (b) plus redress to H's want
      to be unimpinged upon

5.4.1 Be direct

5.4.2 Don't presume/assume

5.4.3 Don't coerce H (where x involves H doing A)

5.4.4 Communicate S's want to not impinge on H

5.4.5 Redress other wants of H's, derivative from negative face

Make minimal assumptions about H's wants, what is relevant to H

Give H option not to do act

Minimize threat

Communicate S's want to not impinge on H

Dissociate S, H from the particular infringement

Redress other wants of H's, derivative from negative face

Be direct

Be conventionally indirect

clash

Be indirect

Don't assume H is able/willing to do A

Assume H is not likely to do A

Make explicit R, P, D values

1. Be conventionally indirect

2. Question, hedge

3. Be pessimistic

4. Minimize the imposition, R$_x$

5. Give deference

6. Apologize

7. Impersonalize S and H: Avoid the pronouns 'I' and 'you'

8. State the FTA as a general rule

9. Nominalize

10. Go on record as incurring a debt, or as not indebting H

131

Strategy 1: Be conventionally indirect

In this strategy a speaker is faced with opposing tensions: the desire to give H an 'out' by being indirect, and the desire to go on record. In this case it is solved by the compromise of conventional indirectness, the use of phrases and sentences that have contextually unambiguous meanings (by virtue of conventionalization)[35] which are different from their literal meanings. In this way the utterance goes on record, and the speaker indicates his desire to have gone off record (to have conveyed the same thing indirectly). Conventional indirectness *encodes* the clash of wants, and so partially achieves them both. Note that there are degrees of conventionalization, and so degrees of compromise in one direction (off-recordness) or the other (on-recordness).

Politeness and the universality of indirect speech acts. This clash provides the motivation for that baroque ensemble of productive ways of constructing indirect speech acts that is so marked a feature of English usage; it is a form of usage, however, that is probably universal. Indirect speech acts are certainly the most significant form of conventional indirectness and have received a good deal of attention from linguists, so we shall consider them at some length here.

First, let us indicate what indirect speech acts are. It has been claimed that the kinds of things that can be *done* by means of utterances are strictly limited (see Searle 1976), and that sentences carry in their structure indications of their paradigmatic use or 'illocutionary force'. Thus syntactic questions are paradigmatically used to request information, assertions to make statements of fact, imperatives to command, and so on. However, it is clear that such paradigmatic or *direct* uses are not the only ones: rhetorical questions can be used to make assertions, imperatives to make offers ('Have another drink'), assertions to command ('Officers will wear evening dress'). Such other cases constitute the problem of indirect speech acts, or conveyed illocutionary force.

Gordon and Lakoff (1971) drew attention to a systematic way of making indirect speech acts in English: by stating or questioning a felicity condition.[36] A felicity condition (Searle 1969, after Austin 1962) is one of the real-world conditions that must be met by aspects of the communicative event in order for a particular speech act to come off as intended. For instance, for a request to be felicitous (successful), the addressee must be thought potentially able to comply with the request, the requestor must want the thing requested, and so on. It is clearly infelicitous for me to ask you to shut the door if you are crippled, if the door is already shut or is about to shut itself, and if I don't care the slightest bit anyway. Now, what Gordon and Lakoff noticed was that by questioning whether you can shut the door ('Can you shut the door?') or by asserting that I want you to shut it ('I'd like you to shut the door') and so on, one can construct readily understandable indirect speech acts. In many contexts these are conventionalized to the extent that there can be no doubt about what is meant — that is, they are on-record expressions. In fact, those that have a propositional content identical with that of the act they indirectly perform may be syntactically marked so that they cannot have their literal meanings or direct illocutionary force. Such transformations sensitive to conveyed meanings include the insertion of sentence-internal *please* in:

(1)   Can you please pass the salt?

which can only be an indirect request (and not conceivably a question about the addressee's potential abilities). Another transformation that rules out the literal meaning and forces an indirect-speech-act reading is that which converts (2) to (3) by the deletion of the auxiliary and tense markers (as noted by Gordon and Lakoff 1971):

(2)   Why are you painting your house purple?
(3)   Why paint your house purple?

Example (2) could be either an innocent question provoked by curiosity (the literal reading) or a critical challenge (a conveyed indirect reading). But after the deletion of tense and auxiliary, (3) can only be a critical challenge. Similarly, the insertion of exclamatory expressions (or exclamatory stress and intonation) pushes the challenge over to on-recordness:

(4)   Why $\begin{Bmatrix} \text{for God's sake} \\ \text{in the world} \\ \text{in Christ's name} \\ \text{the hell} \end{Bmatrix}$ are you painting your house purple?!

Such grammatical reflexes of indirect speech acts are further discussed in section 8.1.

The motivation for such expressions as a class is, we claim, the speaker's want to communicate his desire to be indirect even though in fact the utterance goes on record. Even where the literal interpretation is not blocked by the application of a transformation, such expressions in English are so idiomatic and conventionalized that it needs fairly bizarre circumstances to render:

(1')   Can you pass the salt?

a viable request for information. But this is a matter of degree dependent on whether expectations about the nature of the activity in which the utterance is embedded makes (say) a request reading probable, as (5) and (6) illustrate:

(5) Can you play the piano? (in the presence/absence of a piano)

(6) Can you do advanced calculus? (when speaker is/isn't doing a home-work assignment)

Any indirectness — that is, any communicative behaviour, verbal or non-verbal, that conveys something more than or different from what it literally means — which in context could not be defended as ambiguous between literal and conveyed meaning(s), and therefore provides no line of escape to the speaker or the hearer, would serve the same purpose as the more idiomatic expressions. For instance:

(7) I need a comb.

or

(8) I'm looking for a comb.

said to a shopkeeper, is on record as a request even without any final *please* or *if I may*, although these additions would make a request reading unavoidable in any situation. So in addition to the more conventionalized indirect speech acts considered here, other ways of satisfying the wants to simultaneously go on record and be indirect are catalogued in the section on off-record strategies; to slip up into negative politeness, these must simply be used in a context where they are unambiguously on record. The point here is that 'on record' and 'off record' are categories that do not precisely coincide with categories of linguistic forms, but only with linguistic forms in context.

But if the clash of wants (BE DIRECT versus BE INDIRECT) provides a motive for the existence of a *class* of conventionalized or idiomatic indirect speech acts, further politeness motives lie behind which individual indirect expressions are so conventionalized. We can say (loosely) that speech acts standardly presuppose their felicity conditions. Hence to question, or to assert doubt about, such a precondition on a speech act is (a) to indicate that S does not presume that the precondition is in fact met, where such a presumption may be rude, and/or (b) to provide H with a line of escape through denial that the precondition is met. In short, indirect speech acts function as *hedges* on illocutionary force, in a sense to be explained below. Clearly, *which* precondition is questioned or doubted is highly relevant to whether the form is indeed polite, and to what degree, in a particular context. Some empirical work (Sinclair 1976) shows that actual usage of forms based on different preconditions is extremely systematic.

Looking just at the indirect speech acts which are expressed by the assertion or questioning of their felicity conditions, we can make some generalizations about their relative politeness. But first note that

Gordon and Lakoff are mistaken in claiming (1971) that the assertion of a hearer-based felicity condition (one that predicates something of H) would be unusable as an indirect request. Thus:

(9)   You could perhaps pass the salt.

is fine as a request, not even overly curt if said with courteous intonation. Although it might be claimed that (9) is a suggestion, not a request, (10) is definitely a request:

(10)   You couldn't possibly $\left\{ \begin{array}{l} \text{pass the salt,} \\ \text{tell me the time,} \end{array} \right\}$ please.

On the other hand, the questioning of a speaker-based sincerity condition is clearly unusable as a request, for obvious reasons:

(11)   Do I want you to pass the salt?

although this might perhaps be a prelude to a request.

With this restriction, the constraints on conventional indirect requests appear to have to do largely with politeness; that is, the expressions must satisfy some of the wants which appear in our charts of strategies (Figs. 3, 4, and 6). For requests, only the forms represented by the following schema are polite (and hence are reasonably likely to be heard as requests between status equals):

felicity condition + $\left\{ \begin{array}{l} \text{question}^{37} \pm \text{subjunctive} \pm \text{possibility operator} \pm \\ \textit{please} \\ \text{assertion} + \text{negation} \pm \text{subjunctive} \pm \text{possibility} \\ \text{operator} \pm \text{tag} \pm \textit{please} \end{array} \right\}$

This predicts the following distribution between polite and rude indirect requests (where r = rude, P = polite, and * = non-grammatical):

Questioned:

(12) ^{P}Can you pass the salt?
(13) ^{P}Could you pass the salt?
(14) ^{P}Could you possibly pass the salt (please)?
(15) ^{r}Couldn't you (possibly) pass the salt? (This, however, is OK if it is a suggestion, that is, if it is in H's interest)
(16)   *Couldn't you (possibly) pass the salt, could you?

Asserted:

(17) ^{r}You can pass the salt. (with *please* = a very peremptory request)
(18) $^{?r}$You could pass the salt. (with *please* = a slightly presumptuous request)
(19)   You couldn't pass the salt. (This can't be a request, unless some possibility notion is added as well, as in (21))

(20) ?*You couldn't pass the salt please. (OK, however, if a tag is added,
Could you?, or a question is intonationally or kinesically conveyed —
e.g. with raised eyebrows)

(21) ^{P}You couldn't $\left\{ \begin{array}{l} \text{possibly} \\ \text{by any chance} \\ \text{I suppose} \\ \text{perhaps} \end{array} \right\}$ pass the salt (please), (could you?)

In short, it looks as if the asserted forms need to be negated, and in addition to have at least a tag or a possibility expression (or a hedge on the
illocutionary force, as in *I suppose*), and, from the point of view of politeness, preferably both.

These facts could be predicted from Fig. 4, which includes the following
derivative wants:

> BE PESSIMISTIC (assume H is unlikely to be willing/able to do any
> acts predicated of him)
> QUESTION, HEDGE (don't assume H is able/willing to do any acts
> predicated of him)

Here the speaker chooses one of two courses. Either he wants to definitely
convey the assumption that H is unlikely to do the act A, and so he
asserts it, or he wants to convey that he is unsure whether H can do A,
and so he questions it. The strategies are mutually exclusive, because if S
questions the improbability of H's doing A, he wouldn't be assuming it.

Most of these ways of making indirect speech acts appear to be universal,
or at least independently developed in many languages (contrary to
Sadock 1974). Looking just at indirect speech acts based on felicity conditions, and at indirect requests in particular, we can produce a table of
correspondences in English, Tamil and Tzeltal, as illustrated in Table 1.[38]
These devices are productive; on the basis of these felicity conditions it is
possible to construct open-ended lists of sentences that express them.
These would correspond in Tamil, Tzeltal and English, except where the
idiosyncrasies of the language provide no adequate translations.[39] Our
table holds also for Malagasy (E. O. Keenan and E. L. Keenan, personal
comm.).

However, a cross-linguistic survey is by no means as simple as appears
from such a table. In the first place, indirect speech acts are not restricted
to those based on Searle's felicity conditions; hints of various less direct
sorts proliferate empirically and are theoretically indefinite in number.
Secondly, not all the items in the table are equally conventional or idiomatic in the language. Thirdly, the set of idiomatic or commonly used
expressions is not necessarily equivalent to a third important set: those

Table 11. Indirect speech acts classified by felicity conditions

English	Tamil	Tzeltal
Propositional content condition (H will do A)		
Will you shut the door?	(__)* racam (__) pooTuriinkaLaa? 'Are you serving the soup?'	ya bal ʔaʔφ'us tiʔnail? 'Are you shutting the door?'
Are you shutting the door?		
Won't you shut the door?	(__) racam (__) pooTa maaTTiinkaLaa? { 'Aren't you serving / Won't you serve } the soup?'	ma bal yaʔφ'usben tiʔnail? 'Won't you shut the door for me?'
Aren't you shutting the door?		
Preparatory conditions		
(i) H is able to do A		
Can you shut the door?	(__) racam pooTalaamee? 'Can you serve the soup?'	ya bal stak yaʔφ'us tiʔnail? 'Can you shut the door?'
Are you able to shut the door?	(__) racam pooTa muTiyamaa? 'Are you able to serve the soup?'	ya bal šhu ʔaʔwuʔun ya ʔpasben čohak'? 'Are you able to make me a net bag?'
(ii) Any objects requested exist		
Is there any salt?	(__) racam (__) irukkaa? 'Is there any soup?'	ʔay to bal čʔum? 'Is there still any squash?'
(iii) The action desired has not already been done		
Did you shut the door?	racam (__) innum pooTaleyee? 'Isn't the soup already served?'	ma bal laʔφ'us tiʔnail? 'Didn't you shut the door?'
Didn't you shut the door?		la bal ʔaʔφ'usiš tiʔnail? 'Did you shut the door?'
Sincerity condition (S wants H to do A)		
I want you to do A	racam (__) (pooTa) veeNum. 'I want (you to serve) the soup.'	ya hk'an yaʔφ'us tiʔnail. 'I want you to shut the door.'

* The blanks indicate slots where the Tamil equivalent of sentence-internal *please* insertion can occur, as discussed below (pp. 139–40).

forms which allow syntactic marking of their indirect illocutionary force.

These problems are worth reviewing in detail, because in some recent work it has been implied on the basis of some slender evidence that principles lying behind the construction of indirect speech acts are not in fact universal (Sadock 1972, 1974; Green 1975a), whereas it is important for our thesis that they are. But the facts are somewhat involved. Readers not interested in these specialist details may like to skip to where we pick up the main argument on p. 142.

Turning to the first problem, the class of viable hints for any particular communicative intent is likely to correspond closely with the members of the set of practical-reasoning premises that underlie the actor's decision to convey his intent. Thus statements of motives ('I need the salt') or of the situation that provided the motives ('This soup is a bit bland') are likely to be viable hints.[40] In addition, practical-reasoning premises will include preconditions on the success of the act; for example, that the things requested are thought to exist, that the hearer can (or might be able to) do the things requested, that the act required has not already been done and will not automatically be done, and so on. The set of practical-reasoning premises is considerably larger than, but includes, the set of felicity conditions on speech acts identified by Searle (1969, 1975), which have no privileged status as far as we can see.[41]

Turning to the second problem, only a subset of indirect speech acts are idiomatic in a language or rather in a population, this being an area of considerable subcultural difference. (There are quite marked differences, for instance, in Tamil, between rural peasant usage and urban middle-class usage.) One is tempted to identify the set of idiomatic indirect speech acts with those most frequently used, where habitual use predisposes members of a population to jump directly to the conclusion of a practical-reasoning argument without passing through the full inferential process. However, though this may be true for some forms on their way to achieving (or having achieved) full idiom status, it seems that in general idiomatic indirect speech acts are an indefinitely large set selected from the class of viable hints by the following, largely social, principles:

(i)   Certain cultural taboos or touchy areas are avoided.
(ii)   Particular presuppositions, connotations, or ambiguities of lexical items (especially modals) which are inappropriate to face redress in general, or infringe the particular cultural taboos in (i), are avoided.
(iii) Particular status relations in a society may rule out some otherwise viable hints. For instance 'Would you mind doing A?' is unlikely to have any idiomatic function as an indirect speech act in social relations dominated by power. If S is powerful, he doesn't care if H does mind; if S is dominated, then it is presumptuous to assume

that H might not mind, and even if he didn't, his not minding would not provide him with any motive to do A.

(iv) Hierarchies of politeness, based on principles of the sort described on pp. 135-6 and 142-4, will select the more idiomatic indirect forms from amongst the more polite ones, since the major motivation for being indirect at all is politeness.

On the whole, indirect speech acts *do* translate across quite unrelated languages and cultures, but where they do not, the translation gaps are due either to particular linguistic gaps or to social filters of this nature. The lack of a highly idiomatic translation of 'Can you do A?' in Tamil, with the force of a request, is an instance of this, which we examine as an example in another context on pp. 175-6.

Let us turn now to the third problem, the fact that the set of idiomatic indirect speech acts does not necessarily coincide with the forms which allow the syntactic marking of their indirect illocutionary force. It is on the basis of the mistaken identifications of the set of *possible* indirect speech acts with the set of *idiomatic* indirect speech acts and with the set of *syntactically marked* indirect speech acts that Sadock (1974:90-5) is led to claim that indirect speech acts are not predictable across languages but are rather a matter of idiosyncratic idioms in particular grammars. He claims, for instance (*ibid.*: 78,90), that unlike (22), (23) is not a possible indirect speech act of requesting:

(22) Can you post this letter for me?
(23) Are you able to post this letter for me?

But this is clearly false; indeed, with outputs from our other strategies encoded, (23) can be as idiomatic as (22):

(23') Are you by any chance able to post this letter for me?

There is, it is true, a difference between (22) and (23), in that (22) allows the insertion of sentence-internal *please* as a force disambiguator. But this syntactic marking of indirect force does not coincide with any simple set of highly idiomatic indirect requests, as (24) and (25) illustrate:

(24) Let me ask you to please close the door.
(25) I hope that you'll please close the door.

Another case is provided by the Tamil equivalent of sentence-internal *please* insertion — *koncam* insertion. As both adjective and adverb, *koncam* means literally 'a little', but it can easily be shown that it occurs in circumstances where it cannot have its literal meaning, as below:

(26) inta paattiratt-le   neriya   *koncam* teeva paTutu
     this vessel-in   much   a little need is felt

   This plate needs much more $\left\{ \begin{array}{l} \text{please.} \\ \text{*a little.} \end{array} \right\}$

In fact, *koncam* functions as an adverb on the highest performative verb, where its literal meaning seems to carry over naturally as a hedge on illocutionary force: 'I request you a little' and so on.[42]

Now, *koncam* can be inserted in all the Tamil examples in Table 1, in the slots marked (__). Just like English *please*, it makes these sentences irretrievably into requests. But it also occurs in forms like 'Can you do A' which are not very idiomatic in Tamil at all (see p. 175). Thus the set of syntactically marked indirect speech acts is not identical with the set of idiomatic ones in Tamil either.

We may conclude from this digression into detail that a cross-linguistic analysis of indirect speech acts is not methodologically a simple enterprise. Nevertheless, all the evidence we have confirms that the underlying principles are the same across languages and cultures. Nothing can convey this better than a simple list of common idiomatic indirect forms in a language unrelated to English, so we offer Table 2 as a sample of indirect request forms from Tzeltal usage in addition to those cited in Table 1.

Note that many of these indirect requests are quite presumptuous, because they assume (to a greater or lesser degree) that the act requested

Table 2. *Indirect requests in Tzeltal*

English	Tzeltal
You did not do A.	ma laʔ¢'us tiʔnail. not (past tense) you shut the door
You are not (perhaps) doing A for me.	ma (wan) yaʔ¢'usben tiʔnail. not (perhaps) you (present tense) shut the door for me.
Do you want to do A?	ya bal ʔaʔk'an yaʔ¢'us tiʔnail? Do you want to shut the door?
Don't you (perhaps) want to do A? (c.i. a suggestion)	ma (wan) yaʔk'an yaʔweʔ wah? Don't you (perhaps) want to eat tortillas?
You $\left\{ \begin{array}{l} \text{do A} \\ \text{are doing A} \end{array} \right\}$ (an instruction)	yaʔ¢ak ʔini, yaʔnit ʔini. You grab here, you pull here.
A isn't done.	ma ba ¢'usul tiʔnail. The door isn't shut.

Table 2 — *continued*

English	Tzeltal
Isn't A (perhaps) done?	ma $\begin{Bmatrix} bal \\ wan \end{Bmatrix}$ ¢'usul ti?nail? $\begin{Bmatrix} \text{Is the door not shut?} \\ \text{The door isn't perhaps shut?} \end{Bmatrix}$
Is there permission to do A?	?ay bal permiso yaš baon ta č'iwič? Is there permission I go to market?
Can I do A? (request for permission)	ya bal stak yaš baon? Can I go?
There isn't $\begin{Bmatrix} any \\ much \end{Bmatrix}$ X.	ma?yuk $\begin{Bmatrix} bayel \\ ?ala \end{Bmatrix}$?a¢'am. There isn't much/any salt. (c.i. Fetch some)
There is a lot of X. (something bad but remediable)	?ay lom bayel čail. There's a lot of smoke. (in appropriate circumstances, c.i. Open the door)
It isn't sufficiently $\begin{Bmatrix} salty. \\ warm. \\ done. \\ (etc.) \end{Bmatrix}$	ma ba či?. It isn't salty. (c.i. Bring the salt)
It still lacks taste.	?ay to sk'an yael. It's lacking in taste. (c.i. Bring the salt)
OK, you are helping me do A.	yakuk ya?koltaon ta k'ut ?išim. OK you help me in shelling corn. (c.i. Please do)
I'll do A. (offer conveying a request)	ya h¢ak tal ?a¢'am ho?on htukel. I'll go bring some salt myself. (c.i. request for permission to get salt)
It's good if you do A.	ha? lek me yaš baat ta lum. It's good if you go to town. (c.i. Please do so)
What would you $\begin{Bmatrix} say \\ think \end{Bmatrix}$ if I were to do A?	bi ya?wut ta me ya hpas ?ini? What'd you say if I did this? (c.i. Is this OK with you?)

should in fact be done. The last eleven examples are so presumptuous that they would probably only be done in a positive-politeness context, but any of them may be made less presumptuous — more tentative — by the Tzeltal deferent high pitch or by the addition of hedging particles (as discussed in the next section).

We have argued in this section that indirect speech acts have as their prime *raison d'être* the politeness functions they perform. We went on to argue that their internal structure is best accounted for as conforming with the demands of particular politeness strategies. And finally we took pains to establish that indirect speech acts are universal and for the most part are probably constructed in essentially similar ways in all languages. We may suggest, then, that the universality of indirect speech acts follows from the basic service they perform with respect to universal strategies of politeness.

Degrees of politeness in the expression of indirect speech acts. So far, beyond the categorization 'polite/impolite' we have not properly investigated what makes some conventionally indirect expressions slightly more or less polite than others. One cannot always make simple generalizations across speech acts; for example, polite offers are often bald-on-record imperatives. Moreover, although one's intuitions are clear that, say, (27) is more polite than (28):

(27) I don't suppose I could possibly ask you for a cup of flour, could I?
(28) I'd like to borrow a cup of flour if I may.

one has to be cautious in generalizing across contexts — (27) might well be standoffish if said to a very close friend (or even ironic, from an officer to a cook in the army). The point is that where participants mutually know that the speaker's assessments of the social dimensions D, P, and R have certain specific values, then any variation from the expectable W_x (as encoded in strategy choice) will generally be assumed to communicate (perceived) changes in D or P. So any generalizations about the relative politeness of expressions will only hold where W_x is held constant and at a value where (say) the speaker is trying to be as negatively polite as possible.

In just such a context, where S is trying to be maximally negatively polite, we might get the following intuitive ordering of polite requests (from most to least):

(29) There wouldn't I suppose be any chance of your being able to lend me your car for just a few minutes, would there?
(30) Could you possibly by any chance lend me your car for just a few minutes?

142

(31) Would you have any objections to my borrowing your car for a while?

(32) I'd like to borrow your car, if you wouldn't mind.

(33) May I borrow your car please?

(34) Lend me your car.

What are the general principles involved in such ratings? One seems to be a principle mentioned in section 5.1: the more *effort* a speaker expends in face-preserving work, the more he will be seen as trying to satisfy H's face wants. This being so, the greater the number of compatible outputs charted in Fig. 4 that S utilizes, the more he may be judged as trying to at least appear polite. So some simple compounding of hedges and indirectness, particles, and so on, increases the relative politeness of expressions.

Another general principle one would predict on the basis of our theory is that those strategic choices which most satisfy the end or want to which they stand as means will be preferred (in the above special contexts) over other strategies that satisfy the end to a lesser degree. This should predict that the BE PESSIMISTIC strategy would be preferred to the QUESTION, HEDGE strategy, where they are incompatible. This would partially explain the preference for (29) over (30) above.

For an illustration of some more specific principles we may turn to the following intuitive ranking (obtained from native speakers) of indirect requests for a cigarette in Tamil:

(35) sikaraTT koNTuvantirukka maaTTiinkaLee?
    You wouldn't have brought any cigarettes, would you?

(36) onka-kiTTe oru sikaraTT irukkum $\left\{\begin{array}{l} \text{-aa} \\ \text{-ee} \\ \text{-le} \end{array}\right\}$?

Would there be a cigarette on you?

(37) oru sikaraTT irukkum $\left\{\begin{array}{l} \text{-aa} \\ \text{-ee} \\ \text{-le} \end{array}\right\}$?

Would there be a cigarette?

(38) onka-kiTTee oru sikaraTT irukk $\left\{\begin{array}{l} \text{-aa} \\ \text{-ee} \\ \text{-le} \end{array}\right\}$?

Is there a cigarette on you?

(39) oru sikaraTT irukk $\left\{\begin{array}{l} \text{-aa} \\ \text{-ee} \\ \text{-le} \end{array}\right\}$?

Is there a cigarette?

(40) niinka oru sikaraTT veccirukkiinkaL $\left\{ \begin{array}{c} \text{-aa} \\ \text{-ee} \end{array} \right\}$?

Are you producing a cigarette?

(41) sikaraTT iruntaa, kuTunka.
If there's a cigarette, you (V) give (me one).

(42) sikaraTT kuTunka.
You (V) give a cigarette.

(43) sikaraTT kuTu.
You (T) give a cigarette.

These are ordered in decreasing order of politeness; and within each set of options bracketed together, the order is likewise in decreasing order of politeness. The principles that underlie this ordering have for the most part already been considered: (35) is almost off record, and combines polite subjunctive and negative realizations of the strategy of pessimism. (36) retains the indirectness, now in an idiomatic conventionalized form, together with the 'subjunctive' aspect given by the use of the Tamil 'future' tense (see p. 174). The optional final elements in (36)–(40) are ranked as they are because they are questioning suffixes ordered by the degree to which they express a strong question force (-aa most strongly, -le least). The deletion from (37) of the *onka-kiTTee* ('on you') present in (36) makes the expressed doubt about H's cigarette-carrying more general, and in an Indian context could carry unwelcome implications of importunity. (Replacing *onka* (you V) with *on* (you T) would further lessen the politeness of (36).) (38) lacks the subjunctive force of the future tense, so realizes fewer strategies than (37); again the deletion of *onka-kiTTee* in (39) carries possibly rude imputations. (40) is a presumptuous (but not unidiomatic) indirect request, presupposing that H does have a cigarette. (41) is a direct request hedged with an 'if' clause which suspends that very presupposition (that H does have a cigarette). (42) is an unhedged direct request with deferential V-pronominal agreement, while (43) lacks even that element of politeness.

5.4.2 Don't presume/assume. Whereas the desire to be direct derives from the aspect of negative politeness that specifies on-record delivery of the FTA, all other negative-politeness strategies derive from the second specification that redress be given to H's negative face. Here we examine one way in which such redress can be given – by carefully avoiding presuming or assuming that anything involved in the FTA is desired or believed by H. This will include avoiding presumptions about H, his wants, what is relevant or interesting or worthy of his attention – that is, keeping ritual distance from H.

144

This gives us negative-politeness strategy 2, which enjoins the speaker to question or hedge such assumptions. As Fig. 4 shows, however, this strategy is given further motivation by wants stemming from the third class of derivative wants — DON'T COERCE H — and in particular from the subordinate want — DON'T ASSUME H IS/ABLE/WILLING TO DO A, an act required of him by the FTA. Thus here, as in strategy 1, we find multiple motivation for the same strategic output. The discussion below should clarify the ways in which this works.

Strategy 2: Question, hedge

Our second output in Fig. 4 derives from the want not to presume and the want not to coerce H. We have dealt with questions above, in discussing conventional indirectness. Here we turn our attention to hedges.

In the literature, a 'hedge' is a particle, word, or phrase that modifies the degree of membership of a predicate or noun phrase in a set; it says of that membership that it is *partial*, or true only in certain respects, or that it is *more* true and complete than perhaps might be expected (note that this latter sense is an extension of the colloquial sense of 'hedge'). For example:

(44) A swing is *sort of* a toy.
(45) Bill is a *regular* fish.
(46) John is a *true* friend.
(47) I *rather* think it's hopeless.
(48) I'm *pretty* sure I've read that book before.
(49) You're *quite* right.
(50) This paper is not *technically* social anthropology.

G. Lakoff, who drew attention to the theoretical importance of the phenomenon, also reports R. Lakoff's observation that certain usages convey hedged performatives — that is, they modify the force of a speech act (G. Lakoff 1972:213):

(51) I $\begin{Bmatrix} \text{suppose} \\ \text{guess} \\ \text{think} \end{Bmatrix}$ that Harry is coming.

(52) Won't you open the door? (which could be glossed as 'I hedgedly request that you open the door')

Now, the thrust of our argument is that ordinary communicative intentions are often potential threats to cooperative interaction. Communicative intentions are regulated and encoded in speech acts, and if one looks at the conditions on the felicitous use of speech acts, the sources of threat became clear. For to ask someone to do something is to presuppose that they can and are willing to do it, and have not already done it; to promise to do something is to admit that one hasn't already done it, to assume that the addressee wants it done and would prefer you to do it – and so on, as we argued in the discussion of indirect speech acts above. Consequently, to hedge these assumptions – that is, to avoid commitment to them– is a primary and fundamental method of disarming routine interactional threats; we discuss these hedges on illocutionary force in the first section below. In an exactly parallel way, conversational principles are the source of strong background assumptions about cooperation, informativeness, truthfulness, relevance, and clarity, which on many occasions need to be softened for reasons of face. Here too, hedges are the most immediate tool for the job, and we discuss such hedges on Grice's Maxims in the succeeding section. Then we consider briefly certain hedges addressed directly to politeness strategies, and finally hedges encoded in prosodic and kinesic usages.

In what follows it should be borne in mind that the semantic operation of hedging can be achieved in indefinite numbers of surface forms; we merely give examples of what is in general a productive linguistic device. Secondly, many of the devices illustrated are not restricted to negative-politeness usage, or even to politeness usages at all: the Watergate transcripts (*New York Times* 1973, 1974) contain a formidable array of hedges designed to limit criminal culpability. Once again we see that there may be many different motivations for the choice of a linguistic means of expression. Certain kinds of hedges were discussed briefly under positive-politeness strategies (pp.116–17); here we delve into hedges in more detail, because of the elaborate use to which they are put in negative politeness.

Hedges on illocutionary force. It is performative hedges in particular that are the most important linguistic means of satisfying the speaker's want, DON'T ASSUME H IS ABLE/WILLING TO DO A (and, to some extent, the want to MAKE MINIMAL ASSUMPTIONS ABOUT H'S WANTS). Such hedges may be analysed as adverbs on (often deleted) performative verbs that represent the illocutionary force of the sentence (see, for example, Davison 1973, 1975; and for related discussions Corum 1974, Fraser 1975).

Hedges encoded in particles. In some languages there are particles which encode such hedges in linguistic structure. They often constitute among the most commonly used words in a language, but are typically omitted from dictionaries and given little theoretical attention. As an example,

146

R. Lakoff (1972, following Uyeno 1971) describes how the Japanese particle *ne* suspends the sincerity condition on assertions, the preparatory condition of coerciveness on orders, and the essential condition on questions – operations that are syntactically done in English with tags or with expressions like *I wonder*:

(53) It was amazing, wasn't it!

(54) $\begin{Bmatrix} \text{Do me a favour,} \\ \text{Take this out,} \end{Bmatrix}$ will you?

(55) I wonder if (you know whether) John went out.

In addition, as Schubiger has illustrated (1972), hedging that is done in English by intonation is done in other languages – here specifically German – by particles.

In some languages, performative hedges are encoded in words or particles which may also hedge propositional content. In assertions this distinction – as to whether the hedge is on performative force or on propositional content – may have little conceptual importance, as in the two readings, (57) and (58), of (56):

(56) He *really* did run that way.
(57) I tell you *sincerely,* he ran that way.
(58) I tell you he *certainly* ran that way.

But a 'certainly' reading is ruled out in (59):

(59) Réally, he probably ran that way.

This example illustrates that adverbs on higher performatives may be lowered into an embedded position in their complement sentences; hence the ambiguity as to what is being modified.

Tzeltal, like Japanese, has many such particles which hedge illocutionary force. The Tzeltal hedging particles and expressions are listed below, along with examples and rough English counterparts. The particles and corresponding glosses are in italics. We have divided them into *strengtheners* (those that mainly act as emphatic hedges, 'exactly' or 'precisely' or 'emphatically') and *weakeners* (those that soften or tentativize what they modify); no clear literal meaning exists for most of these, but in one way or another they all indicate something about the speaker's commitment toward what he is saying, and in so doing modify the illocutionary force.

The following examples illustrate the uses of some Tzeltal strengthening particles:

č'e or *č'i* – exclamatory or emphatic particle:

(60) wokolok *č'i*
Do please!

(61) ʔobolbahan *č'i*
Do help (me)!

(62) eh, haʔ *č'e*
Oh, so it is, *to be sure!* (emphatic agreement with preceding utterance)

(All these are very polite: for example, as responses to a guest's offer to shut the door.)

¢'in – 'then', in conclusion, as a result (not 'then' in the time sense):

(63) yakuk, wayan *¢'in.*
OK, sleep (here) *then.* (permission granting, after deliberation)

(64) ʔay niš ʔala teb *¢'in,* peru ma to ba ya htiʔbe yoʔtan *¢'in* to.
There is just a little bit (of bull to sell) *I concede, then,* but *then* it's not ready to be eaten.

With *č'i, ¢'in* marks an emphatic polite finalizer:

(65) hk'opon hbatik *¢'in č'i.*
So we'll be talking together (soon) *then, for sure!* (polite farewell)

(66) weʔa me *¢'in č'i.*
Do eat, then! (polite offer)

(67) yakuk *¢'in č'i.*
OK *then!* (polite acceptance of offer or command)

but it may be simply very exclamatory:

(68) ʔila me *¢'in č'i!* ma šaʔčik' ʔaʔweh *¢'in!*
Look out *then!* Don't burn your mouth *then!* (mother to child)

naš – 'only', 'just', 'exactly so', 'truly' (Quality Maxim emphasizer):

(69) haʔ *naš.*
That's *just* it.   (strengthens agreement

(70) hič *naš.*   with preceding utterance)
Thus, *precisely.*

As a modifier of propositional content, *naš* means 'just', 'merely', 'only just':

(71) haʔ *naš* ya smil tuluk' htat.
It is *only* my father who kills turkeys.

And sometimes it is ambiguous between modifying the performative and modifying the proposition:

(72) haʔ *naš* ya hmel koʔtan yuʔun ¢'in.
It's *just* that I'm sad because of it then. (ambiguous between 'I *sincerely* say that I'm sad' and 'I'm *simply* sad . . .')

This ambiguity may be eliminated by the addition of a weakening particle, as in:

(73) haʔ naš ya smel yoʔtan *mak.*
It's just that he's sad, *I guess.*

naniš – 'really', 'sincerely':

(74) hič *naniš* me kiname, ma sk'an sč'un hk'op.
Thus *really* is my wife; she doesn't want to obey me.
(75) ya *naniš* stak ya šbaʔ¢'us ʔa.
You *really* can go shut it (the door). (= 'I sincerely say . . .', as in a polite request from hostess to guest)
(76) lek *naniš* te weʔelil.
The food is *really* good. (='I sincerely assure you . . .', e.g. as a response to hostess who has denigrated her food offer to the guest)

niš – 'just exactly so, just merely':

(77) meru melel *niš* ʔa!
That's *just* really true!
(78) hič *niš* ʔa me kiname, p'ih me kiname.
That's *just* how my wife is; she's clever, my wife.

Sometimes *niš* acts as a weakener rather than a strengthener:

(79) ʔay *niš* ʔala teb ¢'in.
There is *just* (*merely*) a little bit, then.
(80) ʔak'a *niš* kiltik.
Just let us see it.
(81) tal kilat ta me telomat *niše.*
I've come to see you, *just* to see if you're well.

-iš – 'completely, fully': this is normally a verb-aspect suffix indicating past action completed:

(82) la bal ʔaʔlilin*iš.*

Did you $\begin{cases} \text{clean it } completely? \\ finish \text{ cleaning it?} \end{cases}$

149

(83) bahtiš!
He has gone, *completely*!

But it may be used as a kind of 'for sure' strengthener:

(84) yuʔwan yaš lok'atiš yaʔwaʔy.

You mean you are $\left\{\begin{array}{l} definitely \\ really \end{array}\right\}$ leaving.

(85) hič bal te yaš nuphunatiš sok te winike?
Is it true that you are marrying the man *for sure*?

(86) mamališ te winike.
He is an old man, *to be sure*, that man.

melel – 'true', 'really': acts as a sincerity hedge:

(87) *melel* haʔ lek tey naš yašʔainon hoʔtik, *melel* muk'ul parahe
yilel ta baʔayon hoʔtik.
Really, it's good (if) we just stay there, *really*, ours is a big village.

(88) ma me štun ta me yaʔwak'ik tey ʔa te sna maestro tey ʔa,
melel ma me štun.
It's no good if you put the teacher's house there, *really* it's no good.

(89) *melel* te hoʔone, ma hk'an.
Really, as for me, I don't want it.

These rhetorical assurances of sincerity proliferate in any long argument (especially in public speaking by men), along with two others that derive from Spanish, *puru* and *meru*:

(90) *meru melel* ya kil!
That's *really* true, (as) I see it!

(91) *melel* lom bol te promotor, *puru* baȼ'ilk'op ya yak' ta nopel, *puru*
lom bolik.
The teacher (is) *really* stupid, he teaches $\left\{\begin{array}{l} only \\ purely \end{array}\right\}$ Tzeltal,

$\left\{\begin{array}{l} only \\ purely \\ completely \end{array}\right\}$ very stupid.

Here the first *puru* modifies the propositional content, the second one

150

illocutionary force. Similarly, *baȼ'il* ('true', 'genuine') may strengthen *melel*:

(92) *baȼ'il* melel bal?

Is that $\left\{\begin{array}{l} really \\ genuinely \end{array}\right\}$ true?

(93) ma ba *baȼ'il* melel ʔa baht, slot niwan.
It's not *really* true that he went; it's a lie maybe.

bun – 'boy!' 'sure!' 'extremely so' (from Spanish *buen*): speaker vouches for the extremeness ('I really declare . . .'):

(94) *bun* lek ʔayatis ta yalel yaʔwil.
You *sure* are completely lucky, ya know.

(95) lom spas k'op, *bun* lom šcukawan, te maestro.
He fights very much, *boy does he ever* jail people a lot, that teacher.

solel – 'really', 'I declare emphatically' (I really declare . . .):

(96) *solel* čahp to kaʔy!
It's *really* bad I think! (God, is it bad!)

(97) *solel* bayel ta č'oh yaloh hwiš.
Really, a lot of times my sister has fallen down.

kati – exclamatory particle, indicates speaker's surprise or emphasis:

(98) waʔy *kati*!   (or) waʔy naš *kati*!
You see! (i.e. Oh, I see!)   I see, *exactly*!

(99) bi lah *kati* yuʔun ȼ'in, ʔoč šan ta yakubeli?
Why *in the world*, then, has he gone and got drunk again?

(100) $\left\{\begin{array}{l} hič \\ huʔuk \\ haʔ \end{array}\right\}$ *kati*!

$\left\{\begin{array}{l} Thus \\ No \\ It\ is \end{array}\right\}$ *to be sure!* (agreeing emphatically with the preceding utterance)

(101) yaʔ kati ȼ'uʔ waleʔ.
You *surely* (will) have some sugarcane. (positively polite offer)

The following are some usages of Tzeltal weakening particles:

bi – 'what' – can be used as a tag question at the end of a statement, or to suspend the hearer-knowledge felicity condition in a question:

(102) ah, ma niš mač'a baʔay ʔa ȼ'i *bi*.
So there was just no one there then, *eh*?

(103) baht ta ?ihk'al ?a *bi*?

He went in the dark, *did he*?

(104) mač'a mene ȼ'i *bi*?

Who is that one, *do you suppose*?

č'ah – implies 'OK', 'all right' – a concession with a finalizing note; seems to soften commands in casual speech:

(105) pasa? *č'ah*.

All right, do it.

(106) ?ak'be lah ?a?*č'ah* ?ala moeluk.

OK, give him, she says, the little bit (of land) up the hill.

(107) tey hič s*č'ah* ?a.

Well OK there. (agrees to a request)

It may also soften farewells:

(108) ban me s*č'ah*.

Go, *OK*.

(109) lakon me s*č'ah*.

Well goodbye.

(110) hk'opon hbatik s*č'ah*.

We'll be talking to each other, *OK*.

lah – quotative particle 'it is said' (speaker avoids responsibility for believing in the truth of the utterance):

(111) ?ay *lah* čamel ta lum.

There is, *it is said*, sickness in town. ('They say there's sickness in town')

(112) ?ay *lah* pulemal ta nameh.

There was, *it is said*, a flood long ago. (disavowing the speaker's responsibility in story-telling)

(113) lihk *lah* sk'ahk'al.

He/she said he got angry. (used in indirect reporting of speech)

But it may also be used to distance the speaker from a command, by indicating (truly, or as a pretence) that it is a third-party command:

(114) ?ila? čohak'. ban *lah*.

Here is your net bag. Go, $\begin{Bmatrix} \textit{it is said.} \\ \textit{she said.} \end{Bmatrix}$ (i.e. 'Go, I was told to tell you')

(115) pasa *lah* ?a?č'ah.

OK, do it, $\begin{Bmatrix} \textit{it is said,} \\ \textit{he/she said,} \end{Bmatrix}$ (i.e., permission-granting under pretence of persuasion)

(116) ya *lah* bal šbaht ta č'iwič te ʔač'iše?

Is she, $\left\{\begin{array}{l}\textit{it is said,}\\ \textit{she said,}\end{array}\right\}$ going to market? (third-person request for permission: c.i. 'May she go to market?')

mati – 'perhaps', 'I wonder' – is a tentativizer which seems often to indicate the presence of an implicature; it can turn a statement into a question, or a request, or an invitation, or it can suspend the hearer-based felicity condition on questions (that H knows the answer). For example:

(117) ʔay *mati* šbaon ta hobele.

$\left\{\begin{array}{l}\textit{Perhaps}\\ \textit{I wonder if}\\ \textit{I'm thinking}\end{array}\right\}$ I'll go to San Cristóbal. (possibly c.i. 'Will you come too?')

(118) ʔay *mati* yaš ba kil k'ine.

$\left\{\begin{array}{l}\textit{Perhaps I'll}\\ \textit{I may}\end{array}\right\}$ go see the fiesta.

(119) ya *mati* šbaon škal ʔeke?

I say, I *wonder if* I'll be going too? (c.i. a request, 'May I?')

(120) yuʔ *mati* lok'eme.

Because he has left, $\left\{\begin{array}{l}\textit{maybe?}\\ \textit{could it be?}\\ \textit{I suppose?}\end{array}\right\}$

(121) hič bal yašʔilin yuʔ ya hnop baȼ'ilk'op ʔek? hič *matie*?

Thus is it that he's angry because I'm learning Tzeltal too?

$\left\{\begin{array}{l}\textit{Is it thus, I wonder?}\\ \textit{Could that be it?}\end{array}\right\}$

me – 'if', possibility marker – is the normal word for 'if', but is also used to soften commands, perhaps by including a notion of possibility or 'if' in the command, turning it into a polite suggestion:

(122) laʔ *me*.   e.g. laʔ*me* weʔokotik.
    Come here (*if*).   Come (*if you want to*) eat.
                           laʔ*me* ta wayal.
                           Come (*if you want to*) to bed.
                           laʔ*me* ta pašeal.
                           Come (*if you like*) for a walk.

(123) weʔa *me* wahe, nohesa *me*ʔaʔč'uht.

Eat (*if*) some tortillas, fill (*if*) your stomach. (polite offer)

It may also be used to soften farewells:

(124) lakon *me* me?.
      Goodbye (*if*), mother. ('I take my leave, *if I may.*')

The addition of *me* can turn the syntax of assertion into a (gentle) command, perhaps in the hearer's interest:

(125) štalat *me* ¢'in.
      You come (*if*) then. ('Come.')
(126) ma *me* ša?mel ?a?wo?tan.
      Not *if* you (should) be sad. ('Don't be sad.')
(127) ma *me* ša?čik' ?a?k'ab.
      Not *if* you burn your hand. ('Don't burn your hand.')

It may also be used to soften a presumption:

(128) tal *me* hk'oponat šan.
      I've come *if I may* to speak with you again.
(129) tal *me* kilat hwayuk.
      I've come *if I may* to spend a night, as it were.

mak – dubitative particle, 'perhaps', 'I guess', 'I suppose' – suspends the felicity condition on assertions that the speaker knows what he says to be true. In some cases this seems simply to turn a statement into a question (replacing the normal question particle, *bal*):

(130) ya mel ?a?wo?tan *mak*.

      You are sad $\left\{ \begin{array}{l} ? \\ I\ guess? \end{array} \right\}$

(131) *mak* ya?¢'u? wale?.
      Q you have some sugarcane. (offer, as in 'Will you have some sugarcane?')

But it may be used in sentences that have another question particle, and here it usually carries the additional connotation that the speaker or the addressee has some idea of the answer:

(132) *mak* bi?ora yaš baat ta hobel?
      Q   when you go to San Cristóbal.
      When *do you suppose* you're going to San Cristóbal?

(133) yaš baat ta č'iwič pahel *mak*.
      You are going to market tomorrow, *I suppose.*

Thus it may make a rhetorical question:

(134) *mak* ba ho?tik ya kak'betik snop ho?tik.
Where *do you suppose* we do teach them?! (c.i. Nowhere)

(135) *mak* bi yu?un me ma šp'ihube me sluse?
Q   why   if not she-gets-clever   that Lucy.
Why *do you suppose* that Lucy doesn't wisen up?

Without a question particle *mak* simply indicates that S is inferring that his statement is true, and does not know it to be certain, as in B's reply to A in (136):

(136) A: binti la yak'?
What did he give?

B: ha?in tak'in *mak*.
It was money, *I guess*. (inferring answer)

Sometimes *mak* is used to soften the over-extravagant emphasis of the strengthening particles, taking back with one hand what is given with the other (it is therefore useful for understatement and irony; see examples in section 5.5 below):

(137) melel naniš *mak*.
It's really true *perhaps*.

(138) ha? niš ¢'in *mak*.
That's just it then, *perhaps*.

(139) ya niš hmel ko?tantik yu?un ¢'in *mak*.
I'm just sad because of it then, *I guess*.

(140) ha? hič snopoh ku?untik ta melel ho?tik ¢'in *mak*.
It's thus that they learn from us for sure then, *I suppose*.

(141) puersa k'ešlal ¢'in mak!
For sure, really, she's embarrassed then, *I bet*.

niwan (or simply *wan*) suspends the sincerity condition, so that S is not claiming to be doing the speech act he appears to be doing, or does not take responsibility for the truth of his assertion. It may be used for accepting a compliment:

(142) A: t'uhbil ?a?hol!
Your hair is beautiful!

B: eh, t'uhbil *wan*.
Oh, *perhaps* it is beautiful.

for minimizing a price:

(143) A: hayeb stohol?
　　　How much does it cost?

　　B: ?ala ho?lahuneb *niwan.*
　　　A little 15 pesos *I suppose.*

or

(144) B: maškil. ha? *niwan* hič te bit'il ya yalik yantik winiketik.
　　　I don't know. *Perhaps* just thus what other men say. (i.e. the price)

in response to a delicate question (such as 'Are you really getting married?'):

(145) yak *niwan* ta me ?ay ya?wa?yohe.
　　　Yes, *I suppose so*, if so you have heard.

in offering:

(146) ya? *niwan* ¢'u? wale?.
　　　Perhaps you (will) have some sugarcane.

as a noncommittal response to an inquiry about buying something:

(147) A: ('I've come to ask you how much rent I pay for that bit of land I'm borrowing from you.')

　　B: ah, ya *wan* ?a?hohk'obeiš slok'ol.
　　　Oh, so you are asking about its rent, *eh.*

and in softening presumptuous statements (such as those that predicate something of H):

(148) ma *wan* la?¢'us hilel ti?nail ¢'in č'i?
　　　Might you not have left the door shut then?!

(149) ?ay *niwan* ?ay la ka?y ta ?a?yeh, ?ay škohtle yu?un ši ?a?k'olal.
　　　There is *perhaps*, so I heard, there is one chicken of theirs, said the gossip about you. (or more loosely translated: 'I heard by the grapevine that you might have a chicken to sell.')

škal — explicit performative, 'I say', 'shall we say?' — with questions, seems to suspend the preparatory condition that the addressee knows the answer; with assertions, that the speaker believes his statement to be true:

(150) mač'a *škal?*
　　　Who, *do you suppose?*

(151) bi yu?un *škal?*
　　　Why, *do you suppose?*

(152) ma wan nakaluk *škal.*
　　　He perhaps might not be home, *I suppose.*

(153) ya mati šbaon škal ʔeke?

Perhaps I'll go too, $\begin{Bmatrix} \textit{I say?} \\ \textit{do you think I could?} \\ \textit{shall we say?} \end{Bmatrix}$

Finally, there are two particle-like phenomena — the word ʔala and the 'subjunctive' suffix -uk — which do not really modify performative force but which have related hedging functions.

ala — diminutivizing adjective or adverb, 'a little', 'a bit', 'sort of', 'a mere', 'cute little':

(154) ya hk'an *kala* k'inal, ya hpas *kala* na.
I want my *bit* of land, to make my *little* house (there). (e.g. a son asking his father for his share of land)

(155) ya niwan šba kaʔy ʔala kurso ta hobel.
I'm maybe going to go take a *little* course in San Cristóbal. (e.g. as used by a daughter to her mother, to ask permission)

(156) haʔa tal hohk'obet te bit'il ya hlok' te ʔala k'inal hpas.
It's that I've come to ask you how much to pay you for that *little bit of* land I'm renting (from you).

(157) hič ʔala ʔočanik ȼ'in.
Thus, *sort of* go on in then. (granting permission to borrow house)

(158) haʔin ya *kala* htiʔ hoʔtik ʔeki.
It's that we're *sort of* going to eat it ourselves. (as a refusal to sell a chicken)

(159) yaš ʔala yakubon hoʔtikike.

We are $\begin{Bmatrix} \textit{sort of} \\ \textit{a little bit} \\ \textit{merely} \end{Bmatrix}$ getting drunk.

(160) yaš ʔala ben.
She walks *adorably* (said of a baby or a puppy, for example).

-uk, -ok — subjunctive suffix, 'as it were', 'sort of' (speaker can use this to deny responsibility for the truth of the utterance, and can make statements as though they were 'contrary to fact', or more vague than they really are):

(161) ya hk'an ʔala peš*uk*.

I want $\begin{Bmatrix} \textit{sort of} \text{ a peso's worth.} \\ \text{a peso's worth, } \textit{more or less.} \end{Bmatrix}$

(162) tal me kilat hway*uk*.

I've come to see you for $\begin{Bmatrix} \textit{what might} \text{ be a night.} \\ \text{a night } \textit{or so.} \end{Bmatrix}$

157

(163) A: ya lah bal šbaht ta č'iwič', te ʔač'iše?

　　　Is she (she says) going to market? . . . (asking permission for third
　　　　party)

　　B: ʔa bahtuk ta binti ya šba sle.

$$\left\{\begin{array}{l}\text{She } \textit{might} \text{ go} \\ \text{Let her } \textit{perhaps} \text{ go}\end{array}\right\}\text{ for whatever she's looking for.}$$

This subjunctive is also used to minimize a transgression of H's, and thus
minimize his shame at apologizing:

(164) A: la hmal čenek'. ya bal ʔaʔpas perdon?

　　　I spilled the beans. Will you forgive me?

$$\text{B:}\left\{\begin{array}{l}\text{lahuk. ('So you } \textit{may} \text{ have, } \textit{as it were}') \\ \text{maluk. ('Spilled, } \textit{as it were}') \\ \text{yakuk. ('OK' c.i. I forgive you — lit. 'yes, } \textit{as it were}')\end{array}\right\}$$

It is noteworthy that the word for 'please' in Tzeltal has this same subjunctive ending: wokolok (lit.: 'difficult, as it were'). So do many of the most
common words:

> mančuk — OK, it's all right
> yakuk — OK, I agree
> huʔuk — no
> maʔyuk — none, nothing
> haʔuk — so it may be
> baʔayuk — wherever
> biluk — whatever
> hičuk — thus it may be; so let it be; as if it were so
> teyuk — there, as it were; so let it be there

— a tribute, perhaps, to the Tzeltal desire to be noncommittal. A few more
examples of this are:

(165) ma wan nakaluk škal.

$$\left\{\begin{array}{l}\text{Perhaps he isn't home } \textit{as it were}, \text{ I say.} \\ \text{He perhaps } \textit{might} \text{ not be home, I suppose.}\end{array}\right\}$$

(166) čikan ta me ya snop yuʔun kastila, ma hwentauk.

　　　So what if she learns Spanish from it, it's *sort of* nothing to me. (c.i.
　　　　'I could care less')

(167) ma la wan ʔayuk yaʔɓon ʔaʔmutik.

$$\text{You}\left\{\begin{array}{l}\text{don't } \textit{perhaps} \\ \textit{might} \text{ not}\end{array}\right\}\text{have any chickens to sell, it is said. (third-}$$
$$\text{party request)}$$

(168) ʔalben ʔa te slus ʔa taluk.

　　　Tell Lucy for me, she *might* come. (c.i. She should come)

158

As the Tzeltal examples above illustrate, some of the Tzeltal particles are usable either as performative hedges or as propositional-content modifiers (e.g. *naniš, melel, naš, niwan, mak, me*), but some have apparently no use except as performative hedges: *č'ah, č'e/č'i, kati, mati, ¢'in, solel, lah, škal*.[43]

Tzeltal, then, is very rich in particle hedges. In Tamil there are also a number of particles which have no immediately obvious literal meaning (for informants or linguists) and which function amongst other things as hedges on illocutionary force. A partial list of force-'weakeners' would include particles like *-ee, -oo, -aam*, and tag-question particles like *illeyaa* and *le*; while force-'strengtheners' include *taan* and some special uses of other particles. Here we examine just three, and explore the way they work. And since the translation of these particles into Indian English is quite revealing, we give some such usages.[44]

Apart from special uses — for instance, as a sentence conjunction that glosses roughly as 'but' — the particle *-oo* has a basic speculative function. Thus (where italics mark the particle and its gloss):

(169) appaa vanturavaar-*oo*.
    I wonder if father is coming.

might be said by a frightened boy to himself as he looks through his father's desk. Similarly one can reflect aloud:

(170) naaLekki pooveen-*oo*.
    I wonder whether I'll (be able to) go tomorrow.

This speculative sense extends naturally to a dubitative sense:

(171) naan cencatu tapp-*oo*.
    Maybe what I did was wrong.

and thence to a concessive sense with FTA uses, best illustrated by an exchange:

(172) A: avaan varalle.
        He didn't come.

    B: avaan taan vantaan!
        He did come!

    A: avaan vantaan-*oo*.
        Well maybe he did come *then*.

All of these senses of *-oo* seem to be illocutionary-force modifiers.
    Another particle, *-ee*, apart from acting as an adverbializer, has a number

159

of related but distinct functions. Perhaps the core element is a contrary-to-expectation sense,[45] which can be glossed as 'even', as in:

(173) avaan-*ee* varalle.
    Even he didn't come (although at least he was expected).
    Indian English: He *himself* didn't come.

From this one moves fairly naturally to an emphatic-negation sense in negative sentences, where *-ee* functions like a quantifier, glossable as 'not at all', 'not one':

(174) naan appaTiyee collav-*ee* ille.
    I didn't say that *at all.*
(175) innum puctankaL-*ee* varalle.
    Not one of the books has come.

Also from the contrary-to-expectation sense one moves naturally to a commiserative usage which softens the FTA of conveying bad news, and which we can gloss as 'I'm afraid', 'I'm sorry':

(176) avaar pooyTTaar-*ee*.
    He's left, *I'm afraid.*

This may also be related to an ancient sorrow-indicating particle *-ee*, glossable as 'alas!', still existent in frozen expressions like *aTa paavum-ee*, 'alas, alack'. With some ingenuity we might also relate the contrary-to-expectation sense to a reflexive sense of *-ee*, as in:

(177) naan-*ee* colreen.
    I *myself* will tell (it).

ambiguous (as in English) between the senses 'I rather than you' and 'I in person'.

But perhaps the most important use of *-ee* is as a tag-question-like particle. Tamil does not make the same sharp distinction that English makes between 'real' questions and tagged assertions, either syntactically or semantically. We can line up at least four particles in descending order of question force:

    -aa: full question particle (comparable to an English yes/no question)
    -ee: slightly less questioning
    -le: still less questioning (approximately comparable to English tag questions)
    -illeyaa: even less questioning

(We have a similar cline of illocutionary force in English from orders, through requests, to suggestions.) A natural context for the tag sense of

-ee would be the exchange in (178), which contrasts with that in (172) above:

(178) A: avaan vantaan.
      He came.
    B: avaantaan varalle!
      He didn't come!
    A: avaan vantaan-ee.
      (*I think*) he came, *didn't he?*

We may use the example to illustrate the FTA usages of tag *-ee*, for if B were A's boss, A might typically use *-ee* here to politely weaken a statement he in fact knows to be true. A can thus gently disagree. This tag usage is clearly an illocutionary-force modifier, and is related to the other usages of *-ee* by the fact that to express that a proposition is contrary to what S thought is (or may be) implicitly to question that the proposition is the case.

A third Tamil particle of interest is *taan*. Again there are multiple senses or usages, but a central function is to pick out a member of a set to the exclusion of other members. Thus:

(179) ivaan-*taan* naan connavaan.
      This man (*and not anyone else*) is the one I mentioned.
(180) nii connaa*taan*, naan pooreen.
      Only if you say so, will I go.
(181) nii enna connaalum, nii cencatu tappu*taan*.
      Whatever you say, what you did was wrong *and nothing else.*
      (Indian English: What you did was wrong *only.*)

Interestingly, exactly as with English *just* and *quite*, there are implicatures of a quite opposite kind:

(182) nallaataan iruntatu.
      It was *quite* good (but I have reservations).
(183) avaan nallavan *taan*.
      He's a good guy, *certainly, but . . .*

Such reversals of meaning are discussed below in section 8.1, but their FTA function as indirect versions (and hence softeners) of criticisms is clear.

A third important sense of *taan* is concessive. Here *taan* stresses S's acceptance of some proposition which either was expressed before or is part of participants' mutual knowledge. It translates roughly as 'I admit, but' or 'to be sure, but', as in:

(184) aNNan*taan* kuTikaaran, tampiayaavatu paTiccu munneettrukku vara
      kuuTaataa?

The elder brother is a drunkard, *to be sure, but* shouldn't the
younger brother at least have studied and come up in the world?

The particle *taan*, then, has a basic emphatic-restriction sense and
underlines the precision of the point made. It spells out and reinforces the
standard implicatures generated under Grice's Maxims of Quality and Quantity, that what is said is true and is exactly as informative as required.
From there it extends by implicature to two FTA usages, one in which
criticisms are mollified by indirect delivery (as in (182) and (183)), and
another in which disagreements are mollified by prior concessions (as in
(184)).

Adverbial-clause hedges. There are numerous expressions in English, paralleled perhaps in other languages by particles (as can be seen in some of
the above Tzeltal examples), that hedge illocutionary force:

(185) That's just how it is,
$$\left\{ \begin{array}{l} \text{in fact.} \\ \text{in a way.} \\ \text{in a sense.} \\ \text{as it were.} \\ \text{in all probability.} \\ \text{I shouldn't be surprised.} \\ \text{it seems to me.} \\ \text{don't you agree.} \end{array} \right\}$$

'If' clauses are another very productive source in English. Heringer has
noted (1972) that felicity conditions may be suspended by putting them
in 'if' clauses (excluding those that predicate mental states of the speaker,
as the starred form indicates);

(186) Close the window,
$$\left\{ \begin{array}{l} \text{if you can.} \\ \text{if it closes.} \\ \text{if it isn't already closed.} \\ \text{if you want.} \\ \text{*if I want you to. (but note} \\ \text{that this is OK if S might} \\ \text{later ask H to do it)} \end{array} \right\}$$

Heringer also proposes two felicity conditions of 'deference' and 'politeness': that the speaker presupposes that he has the permission of the

162

addressee to do the volitional acts predicated in the speech act, and that the addressee will not mind doing them. These are to account for:

(187) Would you close the window,
$$\left\{ \begin{array}{l} \text{if I may ask you?} \\ \text{if you'll forgive my asking?} \\ \text{if you want to help me?} \\ \text{if you don't mind?} \end{array} \right\}$$

There are quasi-paraphrases of these with 'or not' phrases (an equivalence one would expect if natural language 'if–then' is logically equivalent to 'or–not', as material implication is equivalent to 'or–not'):

(188) Close the window, or can't you?

(189) Would you close the window, or do you mind?

Parallels hold across the board in English, for all speech acts. For instance:

(190)
$$\left\{ \begin{array}{l} \text{If you'll allow me,} \\ \text{If we're all ready,} \end{array} \right\} \text{ I declare the meeting open.}$$

(191) I'll take you all out to dinner if you'll let me.

Note that just as felicity conditions can be seen as particularizations of Grice's Maxims to specific communicative intentions (i.e. to speech acts; see Levinson 1973), so Heringer's deference conditions can be seen as particularizations of face-preserving principles such as those charted in Fig. 4.

Our data on other languages are feeble here. Probably one can do the same things in any language that has well-defined 'if' clauses. In fact, in Tamil such 'if' clauses as hedges on requests constitute perhaps the standard way of doing on-record polite requests, as in:

(192) koncam paNam iruntaa, kuTunka.
    If you have a little money, give (i.e. lend) it.

(193) muTincaa, koncam paNam kuTunka.
    If you can, give some money.

But 'if' clauses don't seem to be especially idiomatic in Tzeltal as they are in Tamil and English. The following are all usable, but not particularly common:

(194) ša?ham ?in ti?naili,
    Open this door,
$$\left\{ \begin{array}{l} \text{ta me ya stak. (if you can)} \\ \text{ta me ya?k'an. (if you want)} \\ \text{ta me ya šham. (if it opens)} \\ \text{ta me ma ba hambil. (if it isn't already open)} \end{array} \right\}$$

Note also the rather surprising example cited above in another connection: in response to a friend's question, 'Is it true you are really getting married?', a girl answers:

(195) yak niwan ta me yuʔun ʔay ʔaʔwaʔyohe.
Yes, perhaps, if so you've heard.

And the use of *me* as a softener in commands is perhaps an implicit 'if'-clause hedge, turning commands into suggestions or tentative requests (see examples under *me*, pp. 153–4 above).

Hedges addressed to Grice's Maxims. The speaker's want to avoid presuming may be partially satisfied by not assuming that H wants to co-operate (in Grice's sense: 1967, ch.3), or by not assuming that S's assessment of what would be a contribution to the cooperative enterprise of talking is the same as H's. The communication of these non-presumptions (or presumptions) may be made by a set of hedges oriented to Grice's cooperative dimensions: non-spuriousness (Quality); saying neither more nor less than is cooperatively necessary (Quantity); being 'to the point' (Relevance); and being perspicuous, neither vague nor ambiguous (Manner).

Since these are the dimensions which, when applied to the communicative intentions underlying speech acts, yield felicity conditions − e.g., the Quality Maxim provides sincerity conditions, the Relevance Maxim provides preparatory conditions − there will be some overlap here with the hedges on illocutionary force discussed above.

These hedges emphasize that the cooperative condition is met, or serve notice that it may not have been met, or question whether it has been met.

Examples for English, Tamil and Tzeltal follow (many Tzeltal cases have already been discussed as particles above). See Baker 1975 for additional English examples.

Quality hedges may suggest that the speaker is not taking full responsibility for the truth of his utterance. For example:

There is some evidence to the effect that . . .
To the best of my recollection . . .

$$I \begin{Bmatrix} \text{think} \ldots \\ \text{believe} \ldots \\ \text{assume} \ldots \end{Bmatrix}$$

Or alternatively they may stress S's commitment to the truth of his utterance:

With complete honesty I can say . . .

I absolutely $\left\{\begin{array}{l}\text{deny}\\\text{promise}\\\text{believe}\end{array}\right\}$ that . . .

Or they may disclaim the assumption that the point of S's assertion is to inform H:

As you know . . .
As is well known . . .
As you and I both know . . .

The following examples are taken from McCord's testimony in the Watergate hearings (*New York Times* 1973):

As I remember it,

My best recollection $\left\{\begin{array}{l}\text{would have been } . . .\\\text{is } . . .\end{array}\right\}$

. . . you might say . . .
(so) I would say . . .
As I recall . . .
I can explain a partial answer to that . . .
Quite candidly, quite frankly, this is exactly my motivation, my reason, the basic motivation of mine for being involved (p. 163).

Examples from Tamil are comparable:

(196) Nixon keTTikaarantaan-*nnu vacci kuvoom.*
Nixon is a clever guy, *let's suppose.*
(197) avaan vantaan *pool(e) irukku.*
It seems that he came.
(198) maRe peyum *nnu tooNatu.*
It appears that it'll rain.
(199) nii etoo conna *maatiri* iruntatu.
It seemed that you said something.
(200) avaar naaLekki varraar-*aam.*
They say that he'll come tomorrow.

Note that the particle *-aam* (as in (200)) is standardly used in newspapers to implicate doubt about the truth of the prior proposition. Example (200) is paralleled in Tzeltal by the particle *lah* ('it is said'), as illustrated above (pp. 152-3). Other Tzeltal locutions with the same effect are *ya ka?y* ('so I hear'), *ta sk'olal* ('in words'), or *ta?yeh* ('in your words') – as in the English expression *Word has it that* . . .

To return to Tamil, there are also hedge uses of tense modals and auxiliaries. Tamil has no lexical item equivalent to English *perhaps.* Instead,

as Quality hedges we have degrees of probability expressed in increasing
doubt in this way:

(201) varraan (present tense) 'He's (definitely) coming.'
     varuvaan (future)   'He will (probably) come.'
     varalaam (modal)   'He may come.'
     vantaalum varuvaan   'He just may come.'
     vantaalum varalaam   'He just might come.'

The last two forms are literally tautologies ('If he comes, he will/may
come'), but carry the conventional implicatures of the English glosses.
Similar hedges on Quality are performed by the auxiliary *iru* ('to be'),
with different tenses:

(202) tiruTan pooTTe oTiccaan. (simple past)
     The thief broke the lock (for sure: I saw it).

     turuTan pooTTe oTiccirukkaan. (past participle + *iru* + present)
     The thief broke the lock (I can infer).

     tiruTan pooTTe oTicciruppaan. (past participle + *iru* + future)
     The thief broke the lock (I wildly conjecture).

A standard way of hedging an explicit performative, as in:

(203) avaar varra maaTTaan *enkireen*.
     I tell you he won't come.

is therefore to put the 'explicit performative' in the future:

(204) avaar varra maaTTaan *enpeen*.
     I would (literally, 'will') *say* he won't come.

There are also Quality-emphasizing adverbs on explicit or deleted performatives: *uNmeeyaa, nejamaa, saltyamaa* ('truthfully', 'honestly'); *kaTavul
saachiyaa* ('by the witness of God'); *nyaayamaa* ('in justice', 'truthfully').

Turning to Quantity hedges, we find archetypal examples in these
English expressions, which give notice that not as much or not as precise
information is provided as might be expected:

     roughly
     more or less
     approximately
     give or take a few
     or so
     I should think
     I can't tell you any more than that it's . . .
     to some extent
     all in all

in short
basically
so to speak

We also get expressions with clear politeness functions, like *I'll just say*, as in:

(205) I'll just say he's not easy to get on with. (cf. Cogen and Herrmann 1975)

and *well*, as in the following exchange (cf. R. Lakoff 1973b):

(206) A: How far is it?
B: *Well*, it's too far to walk.

and *you know* and *I mean* (cf. Goldberg 1982), as in:

(207) I mean, ya know, it's a long way.

Comparable examples from Tamil include the following:

(208) *kiTTa-taTTa* ippaTi-taan connaar.
Roughly, this is what he said.
(209) avaan pattu ruupai-*oo ennamoo* kuTuttaan.
He gave *some* ten rupees, *more or less*.

This is standardly used to soften the FTA of conveying bad news, where it conveys commiseration:

(210) avaan varalle*yoo ennamoo*.
I'm sorry, he didn't come.

Tamil has some specific rules for producing 'echo-words' by partial reduplication; these have the effect of making the set of referents vague. Thus:

(211) maaTu-*kiiTu* $\left\{ \begin{array}{l} \text{vaarum} \\ \text{*vantatu} \end{array} \right\}$

cow-(*echo-word*) $\left\{ \begin{array}{l} \text{will come} \\ \text{*came} \end{array} \right\}$ ('A cow or something will come in

(if you leave the gate open . . .)')

The tense restrictions follow from the semantics; the definite connotations of the simple past are not consistent with the 'etcetera' quality of the echo-word hedge.

The Tamil word *etoo* (lit.: 'something', a noun) has hedge uses conveying 'so-so', 'somewhat', where it behaves syntactically as an adjective or adverb:

(212) ava *etoo* aRakaa irukkaa.

She's *somewhat* beautiful.

(213) A: eppaTi irukkiinka?

How are you?

B: *etoo* irukkeen.

I'm *so-so.*

(214) *etoo* paTikkiraan.

He's studying *something or other.* (c.i. there's nothing special to say about it, and anyway I don't approve)

The last two both illustrate FTA usage (implicated admissions and criticisms). Again in its adverbial sense (contrast here *etaavatu*, 'something') another FTA usage of *etoo* is in acceptance of offers:

(215) A: evaLavo kuuLi veeNum?

How much pay do you need?

B: *etoo* kuTunka.

Give *somewhat.* (c.i. give what you think fit)

There is also a strengthening hedge, *cummaa*, which means 'just, exactly, and nothing else', and serves to cancel possible Quantity implicatures. Thus with the verb 'to give' it means 'to give free' (*cummaa kuTu*); with the verb 'to be' it means 'to just be (quiet)' or 'to be idle' (*cummaa iru*). It has classic FTA functions in situations like the following (only the relevant turn is given in Tamil):

(216) A_1: When are you going to Delhi?

B_1: Wednesday, why?

A_2: *cummaa keeTTeen.*

I just asked.

(A and B continue talking)

A_3: By the way, if you can get some cheese in Delhi, I'd be very grateful.

Such displacement of requests is polite because early topic slots are reserved for the expression of an unmotivated friendliness, but by routine usage *cummaa* often announces a forthcoming request or other FTA.

Another Quantity-'strengthening' hedge is the phrase *collapoonaa* (lit.: 'if you go to say') as a sentence conjunction. Thus:

(217) varuvaan, *collapoonaa*, naaLekki-taan varraan.

He'll come, *as a matter of fact* he's coming tomorrow.

Turning now to Relevance hedges, we note that because of the sensitivity of topic changes as impositions on H's face, such changes are often done off record. For example, President Nixon, apologizing for a temporary change of topic, says: 'We've got to run the government too' (*New York Times* 1974). Hedges that mark the change, and perhaps partially apologize for it, include:

$$\text{This may not be} \left\{ \begin{array}{l} \text{relevant,} \\ \text{appropriate,} \\ \text{timely,} \end{array} \right\} \text{but} \ldots$$

Now is probably the time to say . . .
I might mention at this point . . .

$$\text{Since} \left\{ \begin{array}{l} \text{I've been wondering} \\ \text{it's been on my mind} \end{array} \right\} \cdots$$

$$\left\{ \begin{array}{l} \text{Sorry,} \\ \text{Hey,} \\ \text{Oh,} \end{array} \right\} \text{I've just thought} \ldots$$

By the way . . .
Oh I know . . .
Anyway . . . (cf. R. Lakoff 1973b; Sacks 1973)

$$\text{While I} \left\{ \begin{array}{l} \text{remember} \\ \text{think of it,} \end{array} \right\} \cdots$$

$$\text{Expletives: Oh} \left\{ \begin{array}{l} \text{God} \\ \text{Christ} \\ \text{Lord} \\ \text{damn} \end{array} \right\} \text{(I've just remembered)} \ldots$$

Excuse me if I mention this while I'm thinking of it . . .
All right, now . . .

The use of *now* interacts with the use of tense deixis, *now* making a claim for relevance (because it is a proximal deictic marker, like *here*) and past tense hedging a bit on the relevance:

Now, I was wondering if . . .

Also under this rubric fall hedges on whether the point or purpose of the speech act is in fact relevant. Examples for assertions:

(218) If the door's locked, I have a key.
(219) I don't know whether you're interested, but . . .
(220) John went to a movie, in case you want to know.
(221) If you ask me where your bandages are, they're on the chair.

for replies to questions:

(222) Yes, $\left\{\begin{array}{l}\text{since you ask.}\\\text{if you care to know.}\end{array}\right\}$

for questions:

(223) Did John go to the movies, $\left\{\begin{array}{l}\text{do}\\\text{would}\end{array}\right\}$ you know?

for commissives:

(224) I'll definitely do it, if you want.

for expressives:

(225) I'm sorry, if you want to know my feelings.
(226) I'm furious, if you care to inquire about my feelings on the matter.

for declaratives:

(227) $\left\{\begin{array}{l}\text{If you'll allow me,}\\\text{If we all agree, then,}\end{array}\right\}$ I declare the meeting adjourned.

And there are clauses that modify the performative verb by giving *reasons* why the speaker made the utterance, making thus an implicit claim to being relevant (cf. Davison 1973):

(228) John's home, since his car's outside.
(229) Do you have any wire, since my exhaust's fallen off?
(230) Would you like to borrow my coat, since it's snowing outside?
(231) Do you have any flour to spare, because I've just run out?

In Tamil, *atu cari* is a turn-initial phrase (lit.: 'That is OK/good') which claims the partial irrelevance of the prior turn. It functions much like 'That may be so, but . . .' or 'OK, yes, but . . .' in English.

Tamil *connaapoole* (lit.: 'as was said') ties the present utterance back to a distantly prior one, or else to the immediately prior one when it glosses as 'Yes, that's true', as in:

(232) A: Gopal can't get the job because he's over thirty, isn't he.
　　　 B: *connaapoole*, avaan ennekku munnaalee perantavaanlee?
　　　 Yes, that's true, he was born before me wasn't he?

And Tamil *paarkka poonnaa* (literally 'if we go to see') functions as a relevance hedge, as illustrated by:

(233) *paarkka poonnaa* nii anke poonatee tappu.
　　　 Come to think of it, even your going there was wrong.

Various other phrases act as relevance-emphasizers in Tamil: *intaanka* (literally a donatory deictic term similar to '*voilà!*' in French) often glosses as 'Wait, look here', and *atule paaru* as 'look here' (lit.: 'look in this').

Finally, some common Manner hedges include:

if you see what $\left\{\begin{array}{l}\text{I'm getting at.}\\ \text{I'm driving at.}\\ \text{I mean.}\end{array}\right\}$

to be succinct
in a nutshell
not to beat about the bush . . .
you see
What I meant was . . .
More clearly . . .
To put it more simply . . .
Now, to be absolutely clear, I want . . .

Not unrelated are these expressions that query whether H is following S's discourse adequately:

yeah?
got it?
OK?
you with me?
is that clear?
see?

and Tzeltal *waʔy* ('you see?') and Tamil *alle* ('eh?').

Such Maxim hedges as those we have been discussing (and many others as well) are used with great frequency in ordinary talk. They have in many cases straightforward politeness applications. For example, Quality hedges that weaken S's commitment may redress advice or criticisms ('I think perhaps you should . . .'), while those that strengthen are useful for making promises ('I absolutely promise to . . .'). Quantity hedges may be used to redress complaints or requests ('Could you make this copy more or less final?'). Relevance hedges are useful ways of redressing offers or suggestions ('This may be misplaced, but would you consider . . .'). And Manner hedges can be used to redress all kinds of FTAs — for example, insults ('You're not exactly thrifty, if you see what I mean').

Hedges addressed to politeness strategies. In addition to the hedges on the Maxims with their FTA uses, there are some which, while they may be derived from Maxim hedges, function directly as notices of violations of face wants. Such are, for example, *frankly, to be honest, I hate to have to say this, but* . . . (which preface criticisms or bad news), phrases like *if I do say so myself* (which are tagged onto brags), and phrases like *I must say* (which occur with both types of FTA). Essentially these seem to signify that what is said on record might more properly have been said off record, or not at all.

Prosodic and kinesic hedges. Perhaps most of the verbal hedges can be replaced by (or emphasized by) prosodic or kinesic means of indicating tentativeness or emphasis. The raised eyebrow, the earnest frown, the *umms* and *ahhs* and hesitations that indicate the speaker's attitude toward what he is saying, are often the most salient clue to the presence of an FTA, even cross-culturally. In Tzeltal, there is a highly conventionalized use of high pitch or falsetto, which marks polite or formal interchanges, operating as a kind of giant hedge on everything that is said. (Elsewhere (Brown and Levinson 1974) we have argued for the universal association between high pitch and tentativeness.) Use of it seems to release the speaker from responsibility for believing the truth of what he utters, so that the presence of this falsetto in an otherwise normal conversation may well mark the presence of a social lie. Indeed, one of the most common expressions in Tzeltal is *maškil!* ('I don't know') uttered with very high and trailing-off pitch; it is equivalent to English *Who knows?* with hands thrown up and eyes raised to the heavens as if to invoke the gods in support of the speaker's total ignorance and innocence.

5.4.3 Don't coerce H. Another class of ways of redressing H's negative-face want is used when the proposed FTA involves predicating an act of H – for example, when requesting his aid, or offering him something which requires his accepting. For such FTAs, negative-face redress may be made by avoiding coercing H's response, and this may be done on the one hand by explicitly giving him the option *not* to do the act A. This higher-order strategy then produces the subordinate want to BE INDIRECT, which in clashing with BE DIRECT gives us output strategy 1. It also produces the subordinate want DON'T ASSUME H IS WILLING/ABLE TO DO A, which motivates output strategy 2, as we have seen. And it produces a third strategy which involves S assuming H is *not* likely to do A, thereby making it easy for H to opt out; this yields output strategy 3, BE PESSI-MISTIC.

On the other hand, avoiding coercion of H may take the form of attempting to minimize the threat of coercion by clarifying S's view of the P, D, and R values. Thus he may claim R_x is small (and hence the coercion is small), giving output strategy 4. He may also claim that H's relative P is great (hence implying that S is powerless to coerce H), giving output strategy 5, GIVE DEFERENCE. This last strategy is further motivated by the derivation of wants discussed in section 5.4.5 below.

Strategy 3: Be pessimistic

This strategy gives redress to H's negative face by explicitly expressing doubt that the conditions for the appropriateness of S's speech act obtain. We have already discussed some of the ways in which this want may be realized: namely, doing indirect requests with assertions of felicity conditions which have had a negated probability operator inserted (as in 'You couldn't possibly/by any chance lend me your lawnmower'). The use of the subjunctive in English seems also to be related to the satisfaction of this want:

$$(234) \quad \left\{ \begin{array}{l} \text{Could} \\ \text{Would} \\ \text{Might} \end{array} \right\} \text{ you do X?}$$

in contrast to:

$$(235) \quad \left\{ \begin{array}{l} \text{Can} \\ \text{Will} \\ \text{May (not a request)} \end{array} \right\} \text{you do X?}$$

However, (236) is not likely to be a request (though it might function as a dare):

(236) Could you jump over that five-foot fence?

What it asks is, in some hypothetical world related to this one, *can* you do so. Quite what the 'alternativeness relation' is in this case is only implicated; perhaps the missing specifying 'if' clause is 'if you tried', or 'if you were in top form' or 'in your youth' or 'not wearing your city clothes', or 'if there weren't a pigsty on the other side'. Similarly, in the sentences in (234), the relation of the hypothetical world in which the sentences in (235) hold is only implicated; the specifying 'if' clause might be: 'if I were to ask you'/'if it were desperate'/'without putting yourself out' (and Searle 1975:79 suggests 'if you please'/'if you will'). But in any case it is not assumed that the hypothetical world is close to this one, and this partially satisfies the injunction BE PESSIMISTIC.

The same use of the subjunctive is found in Tzeltal, encoded by the verbal suffix *-uk* (glossable as 'as it were'); this is frequently used for purely face-preserving motives:

(237) tal me kilat hway*uk*.
   I've come (if I may) to see you for what might be a night.

(238) la?me we?okotik.
   Come that we *might* eat.

(Other examples are discussed above under 'Hedges', pp. 157-8.) R. Lakoff (1972) has argued that Latin has a comparable use of the subjunctive, which is paralleled in other languages by the dubitative (expressed in English with forms like *I guess*). And Gregersen (1974:51) observes that the subjunctive is used to form polite imperatives in a number of African languages.

   Tamil has a 'subjunctive' and counter-factual aspect formed with the auxiliary verb *iru*, as in (239):

(239) inke paNam koNTuvantiruppiinka.
   Here you would have brought money.

The negation of (239) is:

(240) inke paNam koNTuvantirukaa maaTTiinkaLee?
   Here you wouldn't have brought money, would you?

which is a readily interpretable way to make a request for a loan, functioning just like English 'You wouldn't have brought any money here, would you?'.[46]

   Another relevant linguistic resource Tamil offers here is the use of the future tense, which has a strong aspectual component implying uncertainty. Thus:

(241) onka-kiTTee sikaraTT irukkaa?
   Is there a cigarette on you?

is relatively rude (or at least familiar) because the present-tense suffix gives rise to the implicature that it is likely that H has a cigarette. In contrast, (242) with future-tense suffix avoids this implicature and is consequently considerably more polite:

(242) onka-kiTTee sikaraTT irukkumaa?
   Will there be a cigarette on you?

It translates more closely as 'Would you (rather than 'will you') have a cigarette?' This is a very common idiomatic form for indirect speech acts in Tamil.

   Other encodings of polite pessimism in English are found in negative usages like:

(243) I don't $\left\{ \begin{array}{l} \text{imagine} \\ \text{suppose} \end{array} \right\}$ there'd be any $\left\{ \begin{array}{l} \text{chance} \\ \text{possibility} \\ \text{hope} \end{array} \right\}$ of you . . .

(244) You don't have any manila envelopes, do you by any chance?

and in the use of pessimistic hedges:

(245) *Perhaps* you'd care $\left\{\begin{array}{l}\text{to help me.}\\\text{for a lift.}\end{array}\right\}$

Numerous Tzeltal examples of pessimistic hedges have been given above (pp. 151–8). It is also normal when asking a favour in Tzeltal, to assume an unhelpful or uncooperative response, hedged often with high pitch:

(246) maʔyuk yaʔčonben ʔič.

   You wouldn't sell me any chilis.

(247) maʔyuk ʔaʔwala ʔič.

   You wouldn't have any chilis (to sell).

(248) Visitor: ma lah wan ʔayuk yaʔčon ʔaʔmutik. ya lah sk'an ya sman maestro.

   You wouldn't perhaps sell your chicken, it was said. The teacher wants to buy one, he said.

   Host: maʔyuk. haʔin ya kala tiʔ hoʔtik ʔeki.

   There is none, as it were. We're just going to eat it ourselves.

   Visitor: ʔayuk lah šaʔta kohtoke. maʔyuk mač'a ya sčon šan yantik.

   There might be sort of one you could find, he said. No one else has any to sell.

We have, then, three important realizations of the strategy BE PESSI-MISTIC: the use of the negative (with a tag), the use of the subjunctive, and the use of remote-possibility markers. This strategy, then, together with the strategy QUESTION, HEDGE underlies the schema for the construction of polite indirect speech acts on p. 135.

In Tamil, exactly similar usages exist, although they are used in slightly more restricted ways. For instance, in Tamil indirect requests it seems that the circumstances should not be such that it is absolutely obvious that the action requested can be performed. That is to say that the Tamil equivalents of 'You couldn't by any chance pass the salt, could you?' would be interactionally bizarre, as the examples below will make clear. The use of polite negatives is complicated by the large array of subtly different modes of negation on the one hand, and diverse tag-like particles on the other, and finally their complex interaction. For instance:

(249) onka-kiTTee sikaraTT ille-le?

   With you there's no cigarette, is there?

is idiomatic as an indirect request, but:

(250) onka-kiTTee sikaraTT irukkaatu, illeyaa?
    With you there will-not (habitually) be a cigarette, will there?

would hardly ever be heard as a request. The reason is instructive: the use
of this particular negative inflection in (250) presupposes that H doesn't
habitually have cigarettes; but in that case S wouldn't ask. But since S
does ask, the question presupposes that it *is* reasonable to assume that H
may have cigarettes. The clash between the two assumptions generates
the Gricean implicature that H does not usually *lend* his cigarettes; hence
the sentence is unbearably rude. And it is *because* it is rude that it is not
readily heard as an indirect request. This seems to be confirmed by the
fact that when the clash between the two assumptions is contextually
removed, the form becomes a viable indirect request. Thus:

(251) inke onka-kiTTee sikaraTT irukkaatule?
    Here with you there won't be a cigarette, will there?

(with the same negative inflection) is quite usable because the inclusion
of 'here' removes the general assumption of habitual non-cigarette-
carrying and restricts it to the present location; hence (251) will be particularly natural in a temple or otherwise unlikely place. Similarly:

(252) inta cameyum (maaca kaTeci) onka-kiTTee paNam irukkaatule?
    Now (at the end of the month) you will not have any money, will
    you?

with or without the material in brackets will be quite usable between
monthly-paid clerics just at the end of the month.

   These details are important because they show that it is not through
any failure of universal face assumptions or rationality that certain close
equivalents of English expressions fail to operate in a general way in some
other language. On the contrary, it is precisely these principles together
with the nuances of the language's semantics that on a finer-grain analysis
predict the failure of equivalence.

Strategy 4: Minimize the imposition, R_x

As mentioned in section 3.4.2 above, the choice of a strategy encodes the
perceived danger of the FTA – i.e. W_x – but it does not of itself indicate
which of the social factors, D, P, or R, is most responsible in determining
the value W_x. One way of defusing the FTA is to indicate that R_x, the
intrinsic seriousness of the imposition, is not in itself great, leaving only
D and P as possible weighty factors. So indirectly this may pay H deference.

In English this is achieved by expressions like:

(253) I *just* want to ask you if $\left\{\begin{array}{l}\text{I can borrow}\\ \text{you could lend me}\end{array}\right\}$ a $\left\{\begin{array}{l}\text{tiny bit of}\\ \text{little}\\ \text{single sheet of}\end{array}\right\}$ paper.

(254) I *just* dropped by for a minute to ask if you . . .

Here, *just* conveys both its literal meaning of 'exactly', 'only', which narrowly delimits the extent of the FTA, and its conventional implicature 'merely'. Exactly the same usage is common in Tzeltal with the particle *naš*, as in:

(255) haʔ naš talukon kilat ʔahk'uk.
       It's just that I've come as it were to see you for sort of a moment.
(256) haʔ naš ya hk'an hohk'obet ʔaʔwala ʔič.
       It's just that I want to ask you (to sell) a bit of chili.

Again, in (253) the euphemism 'borrow' (for 'take and consume') minimizes the imposition. Compare other substitutions:

(257) Could I have a *taste* (c.i. slice) of that cake?
(258) Just a second. (c.i. a few minutes)[47]

In Arabic, Indian, and Mexican cultures, a sentence like:

(259) Come again *tomorrow* and I'll have it fixed.

is likely to mean 'in a few days', said with no less sincerity than I might say (258). Not all euphemisms, of course, serve this purpose; most simply avoid confrontation with taboo topics.

Returning to (253) above, another range of expressions that minimize R_x are expressions like: *a tiny little bit, a sip, a taste, a drop, a smidgen, a little, a bit.* (Note that in a number of languages – Tamil and Malagasy, for instance – the word for 'a little' functions like English *please*.) Comparable forms are much used in Tzeltal (with *ʔala*) and in Tamil too; a South Indian beggar is likely to say:

(260) *oru* paise koncam kuTunka caami.
       One cent give (a little), oh saint.

but would be outraged to be given less than ten. Compare Tzeltal:

(261) ya hk'an *ʔala* pešuk.
       I want *a little* peso's worth, as it were.
(262) hmahantik ʔaʔbohč *ʔala* ʔahk'uk.
       I/we borrow your gourd for *a little* moment or so.

The Tzeltal *?ala* can be used to minimize one's own actions or goods, or those of the addressee:

(263) hič *?ala* *?*očanik ¢'in.

   Thus *just* go on in. (offer to lend S's house in town)

(264) Asking price: ha?a tal hohk'obet te bit'il ya hlok' te *?ala* k'inal hpas.

   It's that I've come to ask you how much to pay for that *bit of* land I'm borrowing.

(265) Telling price: ma?yuk, *?ala* ho?lahuneb niwan.

   Nothing, *just a little* 15 pesos perhaps.

(266) Reproach: ma?yuk lom yaš tal *?a?wala* *?*ilotik *?*ek ¢'in.

   Not at all much you come to see us *a bit* then!

(267) (Visitor queries whether his sister is at home; his mother answers 'No, why', and he responds):

   ma?yuk, ya naš hk'an, wokol k'opta, *?*ay, ¢'isben *yala* hun *kala* č'in kerem, *?*ay lah ha¢em *yala* hun.

   Nothing, I just want, to please ask her, (if she'd) sew up for me my *little* son's *little* book, he says his *little* book is ripped.

These examples also illustrate the custom (common in English as well as in Tzeltal) of preceding an FTA with a disclaimer: 'Nothing', or 'It's nothing'.

The need on occasion to disambiguate the major determinant of the seriousness of an FTA explains why these expressions (which suggest that P or D is great, rather than R_x) are polite, although one might at first sight expect they would be rude, since they minimize (say) a favour asked.

Strategy 5: Give deference

There are two sides to the coin in the realization of deference: one in which S humbles and abases himself, and another where S raises H (pays him positive face of a particular kind, namely that which satisfies H's want to be treated as superior). In both cases what is conveyed is that H is of higher social status than S. By conveying directly the perception of a high P differential, deference serves to defuse potential face-threatening acts by indicating that the addressee's rights to relative immunity from imposition are recognized — and moreover that S is certainly not in a position to coerce H's compliance in any way. Where, as occasionally happens, reciprocal deference occurs, what is conveyed is a mutual respect based on a high D value, but this seems to be an exploitation of the asymmetrical use of deference to convey an asymmetrical social ranking. In any case, rights to immunity are emphasized here too. That deference has this double-sided nature (either the raising of the other or the lowering of oneself) is clearly shown by the honorific systems of many languages which have both 'deferential' and 'humiliative' forms. To illustrate the more alien humiliative mode, in the Urdu of Delhi Muslims the respectful way of inviting someone to your house is to say something that glosses as 'Please bring your ennobling presence to the hut of this dustlike person sometime'; while forms glossing as 'slave' and 'government' do duty as first- and second-person pronouns respectively (Jain 1969:84–5). (For such humble forms in Ponape, see Garvin and Reisenberg 1952; for Japanese, see section 8.1 below, and references there.)

Deference phenomena represent perhaps the most conspicuous intrusions of social factors into language structure, in the form of honorifics. By 'honorifics' in an extended sense we understand direct grammatical encodings of relative social status between participants, or between participants and persons or things referred to in the communicative event. Some descriptions of exotic languages indicate very pervasive invasion (see Geertz 1960 for Javanese, O'Neill 1966 for Japanese, Martin 1964 for Japanese and Korean). One kind of honorific, the use of plural pronouns to singular addressees, has a world-wide distribution in unrelated languages; we analyse this usage as derived from the strategy of impersonalization and deal with it below. In general, honorifics derive from frozen outputs of politeness strategies — as we argue in detail in section 8.1 — where these directly or indirectly convey a status differential between speaker and addressee or referent. Where they indirectly convey such a status differential, as T/V pronouns do via the general strategy of pluralizing in order to impersonalize, they are discussed under the output of Fig. 4 which provides their rational origin.

Unfortunately, there is no wide survey of, nor any descriptive apparatus or theory developed for, the honorific systems of the world's languages.[48] Even language-internal descriptions in the most-studied cases are fragmentary and confused. We offer here a few theoretical remarks and some speculations based on our understanding of the available evidence in the hope that more systematic work in this important area can be provoked. We confine ourselves to just those cases where the encoded social information is primarily of relative status on a hierarchical social dimension (our P), but there are many cases where social categories (like sex, or group membership) are encoded directly and relative hierarchy only (if at all) indirectly (see, for example, Haas 1964; Dixon 1972:5–6).

Fillmore (1975) has suggested that honorifics are properly considered part of the deictic system of a language. Just as the meaning of *here* and *come* are anchored by reference to the spatial properties of the communicative event, so *vous* and *Professor Fillmore* are anchored by reference to the social properties of participants in the event. This suggestion has two merits. On the one hand it gives some structure to the possible distinctions among kinds of honorifics — for example, it predicts distinctions like 'gestural' versus 'symbolic' usages of deictic terms in the social sphere.[49] Secondly it suggests limitations to the variety of honorifics; every kind must be anchored to some particular aspect of the speech event — speaker, addressee, other participants or overhearers, setting, and so on.

Comrie (1976) argues that there are three main types of honorific, categorizable in terms of the axes on which the systems are built:

> the speaker–addressee axis: the relation of speaker to hearer (addressee honorifics)
>
> the speaker–referent axis: the relation of speaker to things or persons referred to (referent honorifics)
>
> the speaker–bystander axis: the relation of speaker (or hearer) to 'bystanders' or overhearers (bystander honorifics)

Noting that traditional descriptions have confused addressee and referent honorifics, Comrie cites the speech levels of Japanese and Javanese as examples of addressee honorifics. (To these we may add Korean and Madurese: see Martin 1964 and Stevens 1965 and references therein.) The so-called 'honorifics' of the same languages are examples of referent honorifics, and Dyirbal 'mother-in-law' language (a code used in the hearing of certain 'taboo' relatives) is a case of bystander honorifics (Dixon 1972:32 and passim). More surprisingly, Comrie points out that the familiar T/V pronoun alternation in European languages is in fact a case of referent honorifics, and not addressee honorifics as might be supposed. For in these European T/V systems, as in all systems based on the speaker–referent axis, it is not possible to express respect to H without *reference* to him or her, in contrast to the South Asian 'speech levels' mentioned above. The distinction is neatly exemplified in Tamil, where the plurality of the T/V distinction carries over into third-person pronouns, *avaanka* ('they') being used to refer respectfully to him or (especially) her. It carries over as well into the first person, with the use of the 'royal' *we*. Thus plurality signifies respect throughout the pronominal paradigm of reference (as will be discussed below). In contrast, there is one particle, *-nka*, which occurs freely attached to the constituents of a sentence, and which signifies respect to the addressee only, not to any referents (i.e., it involves the speaker–addressee axis), regardless of its location(s) in the sentence. This particle is probably an emancipated token of the standard plural marker, which is normally bound as a suffix on plural noun phrases or their agreeing predicates.

We have, then, five points of reference, with connecting axes as

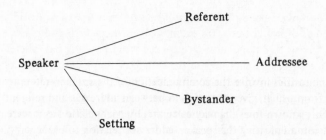

Fig. 5. Honorific axes

schematized in Figure 5. We add the Speaker–Setting axis because it seems probable that diglossic levels (Ferguson 1964) essentially communicate just such a socially deictic relation between speakers and situations – or, perhaps better, between social roles assumed by speaker and audience, as partially conditioned by setting and activity type (see Blom and Gumperz 1972 for a model of this type).

While T/V systems as referent honorifics give respect directly to H, other referent honorifics can provide inferences that indirectly give respect to the addressee. In English the second member of pairs like Snuggs/Dr Snuggs, eat/dine, man/gentleman, give/bestow, bit/piece, book/volume and so on encode greater respect to the person, activity or thing. By using these referent honorifics about something associated with H, one gives respect to H:

(268) We look forward very much to $\left\{ \begin{matrix} \text{dining} \\ \text{eating} \end{matrix} \right\}$ with you.

(269) The library wishes to extend its thanks for your careful selection of $\left\{ \begin{matrix} \text{volumes} \\ \text{books} \end{matrix} \right\}$ from your uncle $\left\{ \begin{matrix} \text{Dr Snuggs's} \\ \text{Snuggs's} \end{matrix} \right\}$ bequest.

We would expect, then, that referent honorifics would be sensitive to in-group membership; and such is the case in Japanese. For example, a salesman in a Japanese store addressing a customer cannot refer to the manager (his employer) with honorifics (Yamanashi 1974:765), for such honorifics are reserved for out-group members (here non-members of the firm). There are also inbuilt group references in the Japanese verbs of giving and receiving (Kuno 1973:ch.9).

What seems to be involved here is this. As schematized in the following diagram:

referent honorifics involve the communication of the speaker–referent
relation, from which, given the relation between addressee and referent
(presumably known to H), H may calculate, by triangulation as it were,
what S is communicating the speaker–addressee relation to be. Where the
referent is directly associated with H (e.g. his house, his possessions, his
kin), this will be simple; where the referent is directly associated with S,
again the inference will be straightforward, though humbling rather than
raising the referent will be appropriate. In either case, the appropriate
raising or lowering of the referent by using an honorific or dishonorific
label (e.g. 'your palace', 'my hovel') can serve to give deference to H. It is
this inferential process that introduces great complexity into the use of
reference terms for persons (which are extraordinarily diverse and elaborated in most languages partly for this reason); it is one element, but only
one, in the complex process that ethnomethodologists call 'formulation'
(Schegloff 1972a). Indeed, a moment's reflection on English reference
terms for persons will show that they participate in all four of the relationships diagrammed above. (Further remarks on the grammatical encoding of
deference will be found in section 8.1 below.)

Probably all languages encode deference in generalized forms of address
for strangers, unfamiliars, etc. These may be borrowed from kinship terms,
as in Tamil *appaa* or *ayaa* ('father'); and in Tzeltal *tat* or *ta* ('father'),
meʔnin ('elderly woman', deriving from 'mother'), and *bankilal* ('elder
brother'). In English, they originally had aristocratic connotations: *Sir,
Madam, Lady*. Hitherto the basic assumption in the study of such address
forms has generally been that their usage presupposes certain social attributes of their referents, and that they can be viewed as properly applied
only to some specific human 'denotata'. In other words, they have been
considered on the whole to be automatic reflexes or signals of predeter-
mined social standing.[50] Our data, however, show that they are typically
strategically used to soften FTAs, by indicating the absence of risk to the
addressee. The following are illustrations of the sensitivity to FTAs of
these supposedly socially prescribed usages.

Consider the use of English *sir*, for example in a railway carriage where
S and H are both well-dressed adult males. (271) is not usually an appropriate response to (270), unlike (272):

(270) Would you $\begin{Bmatrix} \text{like} \\ \text{care for} \end{Bmatrix}$ a sandwich?

182

$$(271) \left\{ \begin{array}{l} \text{Yes,} \\ \text{Thank you,} \end{array} \right\} \text{sir.}$$

$$(272) \text{ (Oh) (yes) } \left\{ \begin{array}{l} \text{please.} \\ \text{thank you.} \end{array} \right\}$$

Nor is (274) a very likely answer to (273) (unless *sir* is ironic or the addressee is obviously very grand):

(273) I'm sorry.
(274) That's all right, sir.

Now suppose one of our travellers confronts the other:

(275) Did you move my luggage?
(276) Yes, sir, I thought perhaps you wouldn't mind and . . .

In this heavy FTA context, *sir* seems fine. Similarly, in (277):

(277) Excuse me, sir, but would you mind if I close the window?

sir seems natural, but not in (278):

(278) Goodness, sir, that sunset is amazing.

Of course, if the speaker is much younger and in the army or was educated in certain old-fashioned institutions, such usages may occur, but in general, *sir* in English (especially American English) is only appropriate where the speaker is performing an FTA.

The same is true of the use of titles and names as address forms outside of greetings, hails, attention-gainers. For instance, in the Watergate tapes (*New York Times* 1974) Petersen addresses Nixon as 'Mr President' on just a few occasions, but these are systematically distributed. Apart from greetings and farewells there are two major uses: where Petersen wishes to convey to Nixon a sincere assurance:

(279) Mr President, if I thought you were trying to protect someone
I would have walked out. (p. 680)

and where Petersen is doing an FTA. For instance, they initiate interruptions (pp. 775, 679), suggestions (p. 677), the admission of bad news (p. 679, 695):

(280) Well, Mr President, if I could only put your mind at ease . . . (p. 680)

touchy probes:

(281) Mr President, what would you do if we filed indictment against Mr
Magruder? (p. 680)

and as finals to advice:

(282) I don't think you ought to do that, Mr President. (p. 688)

Such usages are also typical in legal proceedings, the title and name accompanying questions that are intended to nail the defendant, for instance, rather than small clarifications of fact.

In fact, the classic cases of the encoding of social status in linguistic structure also turn out to be FTA-sensitive. Take for example the T/V pronoun distinction. In Tamil the T pronoun is occasionally switched to V, more often V to 'super-V', to indicate FTAs. However, switching from *nii* (T) to *niinka* (V) in FTAs is likely to occur only when the social relationship is in any case borderline *vis-á-vis* T or V usage. For instance, E. Annamalai tells us (personal comm.) that in radio plays a middle-class boy to a gardener and a washerman will stick solidly to T, to a postman to V; but to an office messenger may well switch from T to V for FTAs.[51] In Russian one gets FTA-sensitive switches in both directions; Friedrich's data indicate the T-to-V switch in offers and rebukes (1972:279) and the reverse switch (V to T) to encode sympathy (*ibid.*:283).

Other cases of the encoding of social status in linguistic structure may also be FTA-sensitive. Bilingual code-switching is a case in point: for example, Ervin-Tripp (1972:232) mentions Spanish-Guarani switches in requests (see also Gumperz 1975). In Tamil, the single purely addressee honorific (the particle *-nka*) also participates in such FTA-provoked switches. Thus a child who usually used the T pronoun (and no *-nka*) to his grandmother, when rebuked used *-nka* to her:

(283) Grandmother: een?
                   Why (did you do it)?
    Child: illii*nka*
          No (I didn't) + honorific

And the Tamil address terms mentioned above are FTA-sensitive as well, in at least two ways. For instance, in one recorded episode, a low-caste man asked indirectly for his daughter's wages from a high-caste landlord. Having been talking about other things, he introduced the FTA-loaded topic using the very prestigious title *esamaanka* ('Lord') to initiate the FTA:

(284) *esamaanka* appara anta puLLe veele paNa(m) inke iruntaa, cantekki
      (i)ppiTiyee pooreenunka.

    Lord, then, if that girl's wages are here, I'm on my way to market.

This is similar to the use of *Mr President* in (281) above: the title is the appropriate one to use if a title is to be used at all. But the decision to use one is apparently determined by the introduction of an FTA.

Another kind of FTA-sensitivity is represented by an actual switch from a less respectful mode of address used in unmarked circumstances to a more honorific form used to introduce an FTA. Thus one informant (Barber caste) volunteered that he switches from caste titles to the very honorific title *caami* ('Lord-God'), most appropriately used only to Brahmans, to make requests of any of his higher-caste clients. The same title was used in a recorded case by a high-caste woman to a powerful member of her own caste in a desperate plea. She was requesting, off record, aid against an employer casting her out of hearth and home:

(285) poo nnu naanka pompaLe enkiink *caami* poovoom?
If they say 'go', where will us women go, oh *Lord-God*?

The usage within a caste of a term loaded with such a status differential actually caused comment amongst the audience.

The same sorts of processes seem to hold for the selection of kinship terms (rather than zero address) in Tamil and in Tzeltal. (See also Brown and Ford 1964 for address-term usage in English.)

However, deference phenomena are by no means limited to social factors encoded in language structure; they are also freely expressed in language usage. Take for example the humbling of one's self, one's capacities and possessions — this is done in English by sentences like the following, used when serving a meal:

(286) It's $\left\{ \begin{array}{l} \text{not much,} \\ \text{not elaborate,} \end{array} \right\}$ I'm afraid, but $\left\{ \begin{array}{l} \text{it'll fill our stomachs.} \\ \text{it's protein.} \end{array} \right\}$

in giving a present:

(287) It's not much, it's just a little thing I picked up for a song in a bargain basement sale in Macy's last week, I thought maybe you could use it.

in asking for help:

(288) I think I must be absolutely stupid but I simply can't understand this map.

in accepting congratulations:

(289) Gosh, I was sure I flunked that exam!

Some cultures go to great lengths along these lines; the Japanese host, for example, traditionally belittles himself and his tea and his house

(Benedict 1946). In Tzeltal a person presenting a reciprocal gift or token payment may say things like:

(290) ma bal ʔayuk yaʔhip ta ʔak'al ʔala tiʔbal?
You wouldn't throw a little (gift of) meat to the ground?

and the offeree may make a token refusal of the meat by belittling *his* offer or gift to which the above was a response:

(291) huʔuk. bištuk ʔaʔwuʔun, maštuniš te hnae.
No. What good is it to you, my house (that you are going to borrow) is completely worthless.

Other ways of indicating deference include conveying that your wants are more important than mine, and hence become mine, as in the Tamil stock phrase in response to a suggestion:

(292) etanaalum, cari.
Whatever you say, fine.

or the English:

(293) Just as you like.

Or one can just behave incompetently and make a fool of oneself. In societies all over the world members of dominated groups or lower strata express deference to dominant members by bumbling, by the kinesics, prosodics and language of slow-wittedness or buffoonery. One of the characteristic behaviour patterns of women in many societies is their 'deferent' self-humbling in front of men, with lowered eyes, shy or embarrassed silence, and kinesic self-effacement. And Albert records this kind of behaviour, including buffoonery, for the Bahutu when interacting with their 'caste' superiors the Batutsi in Central Africa (1972:83); remarks to the same effect may be found in most ethnographies of Indian villages (e.g. Berreman 1963). Detailed analysis of tapes from our Tamil village shows that strategies for this mode of self-humbling are highly developed by low-caste (Harijan) speakers, but are only used to high-caste persons in positions of considerable power. For instance, in front of a landlord, a Harijan when reprimanded may giggle like an English child; when given instructions he may appear slow to comprehend; when speaking he may mumble and speak in unfinished sentences as if shy to express foolish thoughts; and when walking he may shuffle along. All this contrasts sharply with the same man bargaining with less powerful but still high-caste persons, and there can be no doubt that this bumbling is a strategically selected style.

Whatever the social status of the speaker may be, however, a show of hesitation (merging reluctance and incompetence) may accompany many FTAs — for example, the use of 'uh' in English:

(294) I think you should, uh, attend to your flies.

which can be accompanied or replaced by hesitant prosodics. The Tzeltal high pitch/falsetto also seems to be 'naturally' self-humbling; it is noteworthy that the women's version of high pitch is much higher than is the men's, and it is used much more liberally by women.

5.4.4 Communicate S's want to not impinge on H. One way to partially satisfy H's negative-face demands is to indicate that S is aware of them and taking them into account in his decision to communicate the FTA. He thus communicates that any infringement of H's territory is recognized as such and is not undertaken lightly.

There are two basic ways that this can be done. The first is to straightforwardly APOLOGIZE for the infringement — our output strategy 6, which involves recognizing the impingement and making amends for it. The other, less obvious, is to implicitly convey a reluctance on the part of S to impose on H. This can be done by dissociating either S or H or both from the FTA. By implication, then, S conveys that it is not his own wish to impose on H but someone else's, or that it is not on H in particular but on some people in general that this imposition must be made. Because S bothers to dissociate himself or H from the FTA, and to suggest that he is not responsible or H not alone involved, S conversationally implicates that he is reluctant to impinge.

This dissociation can be achieved in a variety of ways: by making it unclear or generalizing who the agent of the FTA actually is, by being vague or non-designatory about who H is, by phrasing the FTA itself as a general principle rather than a volitional act done by S, and by de-stressing the act of imposing by nominalizing the expression of the FTA. These then give us negative-politeness output strategies 7 through 9.

Strategy 6: Apologize

By apologizing for doing an FTA, the speaker can indicate his reluctance to impinge on H's negative face and thereby partially redress that impingement. The deferential use of hesitation and bumbliness discussed above is one way of showing this reluctance, but there are many expressions in common use that have the same effect. There are (at least) four ways to communicate regret or reluctance to do an FTA.

Admit the impingement. S can simply admit that he is impinging on H's face, with expressions like:

(295) I'm sure you must be very busy, but . . .
(296) I know this is a bore, but . . .
(297) I'd like to ask you a big favour:
(298) I hope this isn't going to bother you *too* much:

In Tzeltal, a bald-on-record admission of an impingement is the standard way of apologizing. Thus an assertion like:

(299) la htek'bet ?a?wakan.
   I stepped on your foot.

accompanied with hesitant prosodics and kinesics, serves to apologize for having done so, and no word for 'I'm sorry' exists in common usage. Similarly, a self-humbling remark may constitute the apology, as in:

(300) lom bolobon me?tik, ma ba hk'oponat.
   I'm very stupid, Mother, I didn't greet you.

Indicate reluctance. Secondly, S can attempt to show that he is reluctant to impinge on H with the use of hedges (discussed above) or by means of expressions such as the following:

(301) I normally wouldn't ask you this, but . . .
(302) Look, I've probably come to the wrong person, but . . .

(303) I don't want to $\left\{ \begin{array}{l} \text{bother} \\ \text{interrupt} \end{array} \right\}$ you, but . . .

(304) I hate to $\left\{ \begin{array}{l} \text{intrude,} \\ \text{impose,} \end{array} \right\}$ but . . .

(305) I'm terribly embarrassed to have to admit . . .
(306) I hesitate to trouble you, but . . .
(307) You've never bothered me, I know, but . . .
(308) I hope you don't mind me saying this, but . . .

In Tzeltal, a piling-up of hedges, hesitations, and preliminary forewarnings of transgression indicates such reluctance, as in the following FTA of confessing an (accidental) misdeed:

(309) tal kilbet, ya bal ?a?pasben perdon, binti ya?wuton ya?tik yu?un la hčik'bet ?a?k'inal.

   I've come to see you, will you forgive me, what will you say now, because I've burned your field.

Give overwhelming reasons. Thirdly, S can claim that he has compelling reasons for doing the FTA (for example, his own incapacity), thereby implying that normally he wouldn't dream of infringing H's negative face:

(310) I can think of nobody else who could ...

(311) I simply can't manage to ...

(312) I'm absolutely lost ...

(313) I can't understand a word of this language; do you know where the American Express office is?

(314) Can you possibly help me with this, $\left\{ \begin{array}{l} \text{because I can't manage it.} \\ \text{because there's no one else} \\ \text{I could ask.} \end{array} \right\}$

In Tzeltal – as in Tamil as well – such reasons accompany all requests except the most routine, and may in fact make an indirect request clearly on record, as in the Tzeltal:

(315) maʔyuk šaʔwak' hmahantik ʔaʔwala ʔakil, ... yuʔun ma stak ba sweʔiš kala wakaš.

You wouldn't lend me ('us') your little pasture ... because there's absolutely nowhere my little bull can feed.

And they may also operate as thanks, as in this acceptance of an offer to lend land:

(316) yakuk. ta me yaʔnaʔbekon yobolil hbae, maʔyuk banti stak ba hmahan k'inal.

OK, if you realize I'm in a bad way. There's nowhere (else) that I can borrow land.

Beg forgiveness. Finally, S may beg H's forgiveness, or at least ask for 'acquittal' – that is, that H should cancel the debt implicit in the FTA:

(317) Excuse me, but ...

(318) I'm sorry to bother you ...

(319) $\left\{ \begin{array}{l} \text{I hope you'll} \\ \text{Please} \\ \text{Would you} \end{array} \right\}$ forgive me if ...

(320) I beg your indulgence ...

That the Tzeltal bald-on-record acknowledgement of transgressions is really a request for such acquittal (even if this is not explicitly asked for) is shown by the customary polite replies to them, which minimize the imposition. For example:

(321) A: la hmal čenek'.
   I spilled the beans.

   B: yakuk. maluk. ma hwenta.
   OK. Spilled, as it were. It doesn't matter to me.

In Tamil one may beg forgiveness (though not as freely as in English requests) with the phrase *mannikkaNum* ('you should/must forgive me'), but by far the most common way to beg forgiveness for some minor affront is to use the kinesic gesture of prayer and supplication (a bow with hands together in prayer, or a reduced version) used to deities.

The Tzeltal word for 'thank you' encodes the notion of reluctance literally – *wokolˀaˀwal* ('difficult your words') – as does the expression for requesting – *wokol k'opta* ('difficult speaking'). Japanese apparently has an expression for 'thank you' that is directly comparable, translatable as 'oh, it is difficult'. The Tzeltal word for 'please' is also derived from the notion of difficulty – *wokolok* ('difficult as it were'). And the expression for 'not at all' or 'you're welcome' denies the necessity for reluctance by denying the difficulty – *maˀyuk wokol* ('nothing at all difficult'). These are prime examples, then, of FTA-sensitivity entering into linguistic structure.

Strategy 7: Impersonalize S and H

One way of indicating that S doesn't want to impinge on H is to phrase the FTA as if the agent were other than S, or at least possibly not S or not S alone, and the addressee were other than H, or only inclusive of H. This results in a variety of ways of avoiding the pronouns 'I' and 'you'.

Performatives. This avoidance of the 'I' and 'you' pronouns may be such a basic desire that it helps to explain the very general loss of overt reference to the subject and indirect object of the highest performative verb. In general in languages, forms like:

(322) I tell you that it is so.
(323) I ask you to do this for me.

are conversationally unusual, in contrast to the more expectable:

(324) It is so.
(325) Do this for me.

Of course in formal speeches explicit performatives are often retained as a rhetorical device (as E. O. Keenan (personal comm.) reports for Malagasy, for example).

Imperatives. In the direct expression of one of the most intrinsically face-threatening speech acts — commanding — most languages omit the 'you' of the subject of the complement of the performative. In English, (327) is marked as aggressively rude, compared to (326) (which is itself too rude to occur in most normal social situations):

(326) Take that out!
(327) You take that out!

So also in Tamil:

(328) kuTunka.
Give (it).
(329) niinka kuTunka.[52]
You give (it).

and in Tzeltal:

(330) ban.
Go.
(331) ha?at, ban.
You, go.

'You' in Tzeltal is normally a verbal affix which *cannot* occur with the imperative affix, and is here a special emphatic free form of the pronoun (*ha?at*), which makes the command extremely rude.

Note too that in a great many languages the imperative inflection does not encode person (and often not number either), where other inflections do.

Impersonal verbs. In many languages, agent deletion is allowed not only in imperatives but also in other verb forms that encode acts which are intrinsically FTAs. Thus, in Tamil, the modals of necessity and obligation are dative verbs which, after the optional deletion of dative agents, leave no person- or number-encoding in their inflections:

(332) (onkalukku) veeNTi irukku
(To you) it is obligatory to . . .
(333) (onkalukku) aavasiyum
(To you) it is necessary that . . .

The glosses indicate optional cognates in English (also in Spanish — *es necessario*), which are obligatory in French:

(334) Il faut que . . .
It is necessary that . . .

In English as well, verbs taking dative agents are often used with that agent deleted:

(335) It $\left\{\begin{array}{l}\text{appears} \\ \text{seems}\end{array}\right\}$ (to me) that ...

(336) It looks (to me) like ...

(337) It would be desirable (for me) ...

and although some 'semantic naturalness' might be claimed for verbs taking such dative agents, the existence of near paraphrases with nominative agents (e.g., (338) for (337)) makes this dubious:

(338) I would like ...

In short, we would predict that in languages with dative-agent deletion (but restrictions on nominative-agent deletion) and person–number coding in inflection, among the verbs which take such agents will be those that intrinsically might threaten face: namely, modals of obligation, verbs of wanting and desiring (especially in cultures where notions of envy and witchcraft are pervasive), predicates of emotional and extreme physical states. In languages like Tamil and Tzeltal which have no true passive, this will be especially likely. If this is not the case in a particular language, we would at least expect verbs expressing such concepts to allow impersonal phrasing.

One such impersonalizing technique has already been illustrated – the omission of person and number inflections in verbs. In Tamil, even when a modal is not a dative verb, it generally fails to encode person and number in the verbal affix:

(339) (nii) ceyya muTiyum.
      (You) can do it.
(340) (nii) ceyyalaam.
      (You may) do it.
(341) (nii) ceyyaNum.[53]
      (You) should do it.

where the pronoun can be deleted without leaving traces in verbal agreement.

In Tzeltal, the ability modals *tak* and *hu?* are likewise agent-deleting verbs inflectable only in the third-person singular (unmarked) present tense, and the 'you' or 'I' in the following verb is often deleted. For example:

(342) ma stak (ya?) pas mene.
      It is not possible (you) do that.

(343) ma šhuʔ spasel.

    not able its doing. (c.i. 'I am not able to do it')

Thus *ma šhuʔ* figures in a conventionalized self-complaint equivalent to the English 'I got out of bed on the wrong side today':

(344) ma šhuʔ k'inal.

    not able the land

The Tzeltal verb *k'an* ('to want') may also be used as an impersonal modal, meaning 'it needs'. For example to convey an impersonalized indirect request one can say:

(345) sk'an to tebuk ʔa¢'am.

    It still wants (i.e. it needs) a bit of salt.

(346) ta slamalam niwan hulel ya sk'an.

    On its binding perhaps it wants (needs) mending.

The notable absence in Tzeltal of other lexicalized modals for 'must', 'may', 'ought', 'permit', and so on is probably due to their off-record conveyance by particles or circumlocutions motivated by face considerations. Thus for example, 'ought' may be conveyed by *lek ta me* . . . ('it is good if . . .').

In addition to verbs that necessarily take dative agents (deleted or undeleted), other verbs may allow 'stative phrasing' (Annamalai's term). Thus one can say in English:

(347) It broke.

instead of

(348) I broke it.

This option is much used in Tamil, indeed to such an extent that to say the equivalent of (348) (*oTecceen*) rather than the equivalent of (347) (*oTencupooccu*) is to implicate, for instance, intentional breakage. Thus the normal way to announce that one has made soup would be:

(349) campare veccirukku.

    Soup is made.

and to say instead:

(350) (naan) campare veccirukkeen.

    I have made soup.

is to implicate that one has taken a personal interest in it, that it is some special soup. This preference for impersonality is aided by the existence and widespread use of the stativizing (third-person neuter) forms of the auxiliary-like verbs *aacci, irucci, poocci*. (For further details, see Schiffman 1971:II,32ff). What is interesting is that these impersonalizations are used especially in FTAs. Thus one gets exchanges like:

(351) A: een leeTT?
        Why (are you) late?
      B: taym aay irucci saar.
        The time arrived, sir.

and apologies or admissions like:

(352) puttakam kiLinciruccu poocci.
      The book went and tore.

Passive and circumstantial voices. The passive coupled with a rule of agent deletion is perhaps the means *par excellence* in English of avoiding reference to persons involved in FTAs. It may be used to remove direct reference to the speaker, as in the following pairs:

(353) I regret that
      It is regretted that
(354) I would appreciate if
      It would be appreciated if
(355) I expect
      It is expected

or to the hearer, as in:

(356) if you can
      if it is possible

Or, by means of a further deletion rule for dative noun phrases, the passive may be used to remove reference to *both* S and H, as in:

(357) Further details should have been sent (to us by you).
(358) That letter must be typed immediately (by you for me).

English also has the 'get' passive (R. Lakoff 1971b), as in:

(359) I got delayed; I'm sorry.

here used to avoid the blaming of explicit others (including oneself). Similarly in Tzeltal, where there is no true passive, the same defocussing (and, optionally, deletion) of the subject (without, however, necessarily foregrounding the object) may be achieved by the use of the verb *ič'* ('to receive') and a verbal noun:

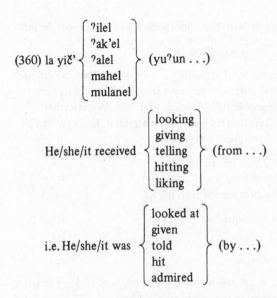

(360) la yič'
{ ʔilel
ʔak'el
ʔalel
mahel
mulanel }
(yuʔun . . .)

He/she/it received
{ looking
giving
telling
hitting
liking }
(from . . .)

i.e. He/she/it was
{ looked at
given
told
hit
admired }
(by . . .)

Such 'passives' tend to be used in potential FTA situations, as for example:

(361) haʔ to melel ya niš yič' kuyel ta yal ʔalal ʔa.

And she really just was thought (lit.: 'received mistaken belief')
to be pregnant.

The same is true for another passive-like construction with the verb *ta*
('to encounter'), as in:

(362) staik tal ʔuȼ'inel ʔa.

They encountered pestering on the way here. (i.e. 'they got
pestered')

But some languages make these resources in English and Tzeltal appear
pale by comparison. Malagasy and most Polynesian languages have a
'circumstantial voice', in addition to a passive,[54] which takes an underlying oblique case (e.g., instrumental, locative, benefactive) and promotes
it to a surface subject (E. L. Keenan 1972:4).[55] The same sort of thing
can be done in English by more clumsy means; compare the following
sentences:

(363) You beat that child with a stick. (active)
(364) That child was beaten by you with a stick. (passive)
(365) A stick was used by you to beat that child. (equivalent to circumstantial)

This would allow the expression of an FTA of accusation to avoid direct confrontation by deletion of both the underlying agent and object, as in:

(366) A stick was used. That is going too far.

The Malagasy three-voice distinction holds for imperatives, too, where such deletions would tend to be especially relevant socially. The 'passive imperative' has functional equivalents in English with certain somewhat stilted or archaic expressions (in this example, material in brackets can be deleted, leaving agent and recipient ambiguous):

(367) Let it be done $\left\{ \begin{array}{l} \text{(by you for me to him).} \\ \text{(by me for you).} \\ \text{(by him for them to her).} \end{array} \right\}$

Tamil has the similar but colloquial:

(368) ceyyaTTum.
Let it be done.

which, when questioned, is one of the most polite ways of making an offer, and when asserted, of accepting the offer, as in (369):

(369) irukkaTTum.
Let it be.

These facts reinforce the natural interpretation of dative-agent verbs and passive and circumstantial voices (perhaps within a case-grammar framework) as a single basic set of phenomena to do with operations taking an underlying agent (which would normally be realized as a surface subject) and demoting it to another superficial case location. With some dative-agent verbs this would be obligatory (as in English *It occurs to me* and the Tamil examples above). At the same time, some other noun phrase would be promoted, or a dummy introduced (like the 'it' in 'it seems'), to take the place of the superficial subject. The social motivation would be basically the same for all cases, which would explain the stylistic homogeneity of phrases like 'It would be desirable (for me)', 'It would be appreciated (by me)', and 'It seems (to me)' as they occur in English business letters.

We suggest that at least part of the motivation for such superficial case-shunting operations in language is the social pressure to bring some crucial noun phrases (especially those that refer to S, H, their kin, their actions, their belongings, etc.) into syntactic positions where they can be deleted. To a lesser extent, the same pressure would motivate the same rules in order to achieve defocusing rather than deletion.

It is striking that the Malagasy language, embedded in a culture where there are quite remarkable norms of non-confrontation (E. O. Keenan 1974b) and where the avoidance of 'I' and 'you' pronouns goes even further than in the best English business usage (E. O. Keenan, personal comm.), should have developed a set of syntactic tools for the job.

Replacement of the pronouns 'I' and 'you' by indefinites. Many languages have some standardized impersonal versions of pronouns which may serve FTA purposes to good effect, as in English:

(370) One shouldn't do things like that.

rather than:

(371) You shouldn't do things like that.
(372) One might think . . .

rather than:

(373) $\begin{Bmatrix} \text{You} \\ \text{I} \end{Bmatrix}$ might think . . .

and:

(374) $\begin{Bmatrix} \text{I-can't-guess-who} \\ \text{Some one (I know)} \end{Bmatrix}$ finished the cookies.

rather than:

(375) You finished the cookies.

Note also the indefiniteness of:

(376) OK, $\begin{Bmatrix} \text{folks,} \\ \text{you guys,} \\ \text{you all,} \end{Bmatrix}$ let's get on with it.

In Tzeltal the same function is performed by *mač'a* ('someone'), as in:

(377) ʔay bal mač'a ʔay sk'uʔ ya hmahan . . .

Is there someone who would have a blouse I could borrow . . . ?
(c.i. 'Would you or your sisters or mother lend me a blouse?')

In languages which allow subject deletion since they encode person and number in most verbs, the same effect can be obtained by simply omitting the subject pronouns, with those exceptional verbs that lack such inflections (typically modals, as discussed above). Thus Tamil:

(378) pookalaamaa?

May (one) go? (i.e. May $\begin{Bmatrix} \text{I} \\ \text{we} \\ \text{etc.} \end{Bmatrix}$ go?)

can be a polite suggestion that you and I do something. The use of such verbs, with deleted pronouns, is then the standard way of doing in Tamil what impersonal 'one' does in English:

(379) atu colla muTiyaatu.
      That (one) can't say.

Note that the introduction of 'one' for 'you' or 'I' also has a significant point-of-view effect of distancing. Thus 'one' takes third-person (rather than first- or second-person) verbal inflections. American and British English seem to diverge a little here: in some American English usage *one* is anaphorically pronominalized (obligatorily?) to *he*:

(380) One just goes along as best he can.

This is not normal in British English, which prefers:

(381) One just goes along as best one can.

And only American English permits:

(382) Wherever *one* goes in Europe, *you* hear bullfinches.

The generalization seems to be that in British English the impersonalized point of view is more consistently insisted upon, at least with respect to *one* (an observation which is consistent with other observations about British/American cultural style).

Pluralization of the 'you' and 'I' pronouns. It seems to be very general in unrelated languages and cultures that the 'you' (plural) pronoun, when used to refer to a single addressee, is understood as indicating deference (P) or distance (D) (see Brown and Gilman 1960). Particular cultural explanations for T/V systems will not do in the face of this widespread distribution, the extent of which has perhaps not been appreciated. In addition to the cases described by Brown and Gilman (1960) for French, German, Spanish and Italian, Friedrich (1972) provides data for Russian; Comrie (1975) for other Slavic languages and for Greek; Laberge (1977) for Canadian French; Slobin (1963) for Yiddish; Hollos (1976) for Hungarian; Paulston (1975) for Swedish; Neustupný (1968) for Czech; Jain (1969) for Hindi; Lefebvre (1975) for Quechua; Levinson (1977) for Tamil; Thorne (1975–6) for Welsh; and Gregerson (1974) for many African languages. An explanation in terms of rational exploitation (or implicature) and the social motives for it seems called for.

Our theory provides a number of possible motives for the phenomenon. On the one hand 'you' (plural) provides a conventional 'out' for the hearer (as R. Lakoff 1973a has observed). That is, since it does not *literally* single out the addressee, it is *as if* the speaker were giving H the option to interpret it as applying to him rather than, say, to his companions. The fact that by conventionalization it no longer really does give H that out does not render it useless. Rather, it conveys the *desire* of the speaker to render H that tribute, while fulfilling the practical needs of clarity and on-record talk. In other words, 'you' (plural) can be understood as motivated by exactly the same wants that we use above to account for conventional indirectness.

A second possible motive is this: in kinship-based societies in particular, but in all societies where a person's social status is fundamentally linked to membership in a group, to treat persons as representatives of a group rather than as relatively powerless individuals would be to refer to their social standing and the backing that they derive from their group. In some societies, of course, the individual's social standing is so much derived from group membership that for one to take the life of a member of another group leads to indiscriminate retaliation on *any* member of the slayer's group, without preference for the slayer himself. In such social settings, persons are always representatives, and the motivation for a plural 'you' of deference or distance would be the same as for the plural of the 'we' of corporations and corporations sole.

These motives would be little more than speculative origins for stabilized T/V systems, were it not for the fact that one can find existing systems where no stabilized pronominal honorifics exist but where plurality in pronouns is productively and strategically used to satisfy just such motives. E. O. Keenan (1974a:69–74), for instance, describes how in Malagasy plural pronouns are used both to avoid the singling out of persons in reference, and to embed persons referred to in the groups to which they belong — facts that seem to support both of the possible motives above as plausible sources for more stabilized T/V systems.

Tamil, too, provides clear cases of the motivation for respectful plurality deriving from the treatment of the individual as a member of a corporate group. Nouns which refer to groups or to group property (including group members) seldom take singular pronouns. Thus 'my father' is rendered *enka appaa,* meaning 'our (exclusive) father'. (The form *namma appaa*, meaning 'our (inclusive) father', would be a positive-politeness option.) 'My home town' is *enka uuru*, 'our (exclusive) place'; and reference to a small boy's father while addressing the boy would use the 'your' (plural) form *onka appaa*, even though the boy himself would be addressed with the T pronoun. (Similarly, the boy's house would be *onka viiTu*, 'your (plural) house'.) Likewise, in referring to the same boy's father while talking to someone else, the expression would be *avaanka appaa* ('their father').[56]

Continuous pressure from these two motives is reflected in language history. In Tamil the original singular second-person pronoun was *nii*, with plural *niir*. This latter became used as an honorific, so a second plural morph was added to reintroduce the singular/plural dimension. But this new plural *niirkal* became inevitably used as an honorific also, and the *niir* form fell out of frequent usage as being second-best on the politeness scale. The colloquial system now has *nii, niinka*, with the latter ambiguous between 'you' + plural and 'you' + respect. What this illustrates is that it is not for lack of an honorific form that the plural becomes used as a singular; Tamil rejected a possible three-element system. It is the *plurality* itself that is the 'honorific' feature.[57]

The pressures that underlie the use of plural second-person pronouns as honorifics do not stop at second-person pronouns. They operate in other spheres as well; thus Garvin and Reisenberg (1952:205) report the use of plural titles of address (and plural third-person pronouns) to Ponapean royalty. Returning to Tamil pronouns, we find that plurality as a marker of respect in fact pervades the whole pronominal paradigm. Thus just as 'you' (plural) yields respect to the hearer, so 'they/their' for 'he/his' or 'she/hers' expresses respect in Tamil:

(383) motal mantiri *avaanka* mantirikal ooTa poor*aanka*.
The Prime Minister *they go* accompanied by ministers.[58]

In addition, 'we' can serve for 'I' (respected). Thus in all three persons, plural pronouns can be used to give respect to singular referents. But the facts are more complicated than this; not only number but also person can be switched, and within these person switches plurality still conveys respect. Table 3 displays the full range of usage in one Tamil village for singular referents. For each such referent, there are sets of alternates which are arranged (from top to bottom) in increasing order of respect, and speakers must choose their pronouns from this set on purely social grounds. Clearly, to account for the sex and person switches some additional principles are required. These are as follows.

The third-person singular neuter *atu* is used − often just encoded in verbal agreement − to avoid the disrespectful singular pronouns *naan* ('I'), *nii* ('you'), *avaan* ('he'), *ava* ('she'). Thus, to find an intermediate level between *ava* and *avaanka*, one uses *atu*:

(384) ammaa collutu
Mother says (third-person neuter verbal agreement)

or simply:

(385) atu collutu
it says (c.i. Mother says)

Table 3. *Person–number switches in Tamil pronoun usage*

Actual singular referent	Forms used	Literal meaning
Speaker	naan	'I'
	atu ‡	'it'
	naanka	'we' (exclusive)
	naam	'we' (inclusive)
Addressee	nii	'you' (singular)
	atu	'it'
	niir ‡	archaic 'you' (plural); now 'you' (singular) with connotations of respectful equality
	niinka	'you' (plural)
	naam	'we' (inclusive)
	taanka ‡	'themselves'
Third person: male	avaan	'he' (singular)
	atu	'it'
	avaar	archaic 'they', now 'he' (singular) plus respect
	avaanka/aviika	'they'
Third person: female	ava	'she' (singular)
	atu	'it'
	avaanka/aviika	'they'

‡ relatively rare usage

Of course it is not simply that *atu* is used just to avoid both respect and disrespect; it also inherently impersonalizes and thus fulfils the same strategy as pluralization in a different way. (This 'neutral honorific' is thought to be growing in usage, perhaps in response to social changes. See Annamalai and Ramanujan n.d.)

The other third-person form which can be used to refer to addressees, *taankaL*, probably has a different source. A similar use of 'they' for 'you' (respected) is found in German, Spanish, Ponapean, and other languages. These usages presumably derive from the same source as the use of referent titles in address, as in:

(386) Would His Highness prefer tea in the pink or the lavender room?

Caste (and other) titles are used in this way in Tamil villages. Here the underlying principle seems to be the distancing afforded by speaking to the addressee as if the speaker (or the hearer) were not present. The principle is then presumably a predictable output of the strategic point-of-view operations discussed below (pp. 204–6), which together with the principle of respectful plurality explains the use of 'they' or 'themselves' as a doubly honorific 'you'.

A further principle is required to explain the use of *naam* (inclusive 'we') as 'you' (super-honorific). In village usage this is the pronoun used by lower-status persons to higher-caste persons, especially in FTAs (when switching from *niinka* typically occurs). In such a dyad, the higher-status person is likely to refer to himself with the 'royal "we"' – that is, with *naam*. So the use of the same pronoun to refer to the same referent by a different (lower-rank) speaker could be seen as a dramatic point-of-view operation in which the inferior adopts the superior's point of view. Another possible source is the idiom of ownership: the master owns his servants, and they 'possess' him as their master. So to address him as 'you and I' is to convey the absorption of the inferior in the superior's domain. Interestingly, further cases of the usage of 'we' (inclusive) for 'you' (honorific) have been reported from Quechua (Lefebvre 1975) and from Malagasy (E. O. Keenan 1974a, and as discussed below).

These additional principles, themselves also outputs of negative-politeness strategies, will account for the person switches cited in Table 3. And our respectful-plurality principle will handle the number switches within each person, in Tamil and other languages. Thus in addition to the widespread use of V pronouns to singular addressees, there is also the widespread phenomenon of 'we' used to indicate 'I' + powerful. Apart from the royal 'we' which most of us don't experience, there is the episcopal 'we' and the business 'we'. There may be two distinct sources here. One is the 'we' that expresses the nature of the 'corporation sole' or the jural accompaniments of high office – 'we' as office and incumbent and predecessors. Then there is also the 'we' of the group, with roots precisely analogous to the second source of 'you' (plural) discussed above: a reminder that I do not stand alone. The business 'we' perhaps attempts to draw on both sources of connotations of power, as in the English:

(387) We cannot $\left\{ \begin{array}{l} \text{accept responsibility.} \\ \text{trace your cheque.} \end{array} \right\}$

(388) We regret to inform you . . .

(389) We feel obliged to warn you that . . .

(390) We at Lockheed are not excessively concerned.

In Tamil it is disrespectful to oneself and shows overweening pride to say 'my family', 'my mother', or even 'my car', either in their presence or in reference. Here as we have seen we have an enjoined group 'we' that reflects the ideals of the solidary extended family, either as a powerful group behind the speaker (exclusive 'we'), or as a partnership (inclusive 'we').

In languages where there is an exclusive/inclusive 'we' distinction, a whole new dimension enters. The English institutional *we* is exclusive, of course, but exclusive 'we' in Tamil has to be carefully used. In positive-politeness situations, inclusive 'we' is most appropriate; one speaks as if everything were shared between members. Thus for instance between equals a speaker may refer to his wife as *namma sarasu* ('our (inclusive) Sarasu'), and a polite invitation to supper would take the form:

(391) vaanka, namma viiTTlee caappiTalaam.
     Come, let's eat at our (inclusive) house.

And we have already seen how inclusive 'we' in Tzeltal is used in positively polite requests to suggest 'for our mutual benefit', although what is really meant is 'I' or 'you' (see p. 127 above).

But such an inclusive 'we' in other contexts may become the conventionalized polite form more appropriate to formal situations and negative politeness. In Malagasy, there is an avoidance of 'you', 'I', 'my', etc. in favour of 'our' (inclusive). E. O. Keenan (personal comm. and 1974a) suggests a scale of politeness for Malagasy pronouns as follows (as we understand it):

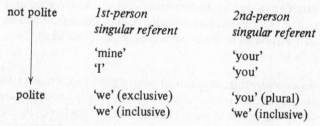

not polite	1st-person singular referent	2nd-person singular referent
↓	'mine' 'I'	'your' 'you'
polite	'we' (exclusive) 'we' (inclusive)	'you' (plural) 'we' (inclusive)

Presumably, syntax permitting, one chooses appropriately as one does an FTA.

Address terms as 'you' avoidance. Note the rudeness of 'you' as an address form in a hail or attention-getting phrase:

(392) Excuse me, $\begin{Bmatrix} \text{sir.} \\ \text{miss.} \\ ^r\text{you.} \end{Bmatrix}$

(393) Hey $\begin{Bmatrix} ^r\text{you.} \\ \text{Mac.} \\ \text{Mate.} \\ \text{Mister.} \end{Bmatrix}$

203

Just as 'you' (singular) gives H no 'out', nails him with an FTA, so the use of names may do likewise. In very many cultures one may not politely address people by name. In Malagasy, for example, an elaborate set of locutions has developed for avoiding the use of names both in reference and in address (E. O. Keenan 1974a). The common address form for persons in unfamiliar public contexts, for example, is *Ranona* ('Mr(s) Thing', i.e. 'Mr(s) So-and-so') (*ibid.*:79). Similarly, in Tamil only juniors or status or caste inferiors may ever be addressed by name, and to others the choice of name instead of a kin term or title would encode insult.[59] In Tzeltal, also, names are avoided in favour of kin terms.

Reference terms as 'I' avoidance. In the English of kings, his majesty might say:

(394) His Majesty is nót amused.

and in the English of presidents, Nixon does say (*New York Times* 1973:87):

(395) But the President should not become involved in any part of this case.

The root of this, of course, is the distinction between man and office, the communication of which underlies much of the ritual recorded in ethnographies. The speaker distances himself as an individual from acts he would rather have attributed to the duties and rights of the office.

Point-of-view distancing. In our discussion of positive-politeness strategy 7 in section 5.3, we referred to the potential exploitation of *deictic anchorage* to encode special points of view. The idea was that the basic unmarked anchorage is organized around the speaker and the place and time of his utterance. To organize sentences around some other central anchorage point could then, for instance, encode the speaker's identification with the addressee.

Here we turn to another set of potential exploitations: the use of point-of-view operations to *distance* S from H or from the particular FTA. One set of mechanisms involves manipulating the expression of tense to provide distancing in time. As the tense is switched from present into past, the speaker moves *as if* into the future, so he distances himself from the here and now. Hence we get negatively polite FTAs with increasingly remote past tenses, for requests:

(396) I $\begin{Bmatrix} \text{have been} \\ \text{was} \end{Bmatrix}$ wondering whether you could do me a little favour.

and for questions:

(397) I was kind of interested in knowing if . . .

Note that the present relevance of the present perfect form *have been* renders (396) less distant than the same sentence with *was*, and hence less negatively polite. Even more remote and therefore more polite are forms like:

(398) I $\left\{\begin{array}{l}\text{wondered whether}\\ \text{felt}\\ \text{hoped}\\ \text{thought}\end{array}\right\}$ I might ask you . . .

and still one more degree of remoteness can be gained by use of the unstressed auxiliary *did*, as in:

(399) I did wonder whether you might . . .

In Tamil one finds a similar use of the 'polite past':

(400) onka-kiTTee oNNu keekkaNum nnu rompa naaLaa nenneccu kiTTirunteen: . . .

    I had thought for many days that I wanted to ask something: . . .

which would function as a polite prelude to a big FTA.

The use of the recentring of deictic time to increase the politeness of indirect speech acts is yet another complexity to add to that difficult topic.

Deictic place switches can perform a comparable distancing function. Just as the use of proximal demonstratives etc. can convey empathy and involvement (see discussion above under positive-politeness strategy 7), so the use of distal markers can convey social distance, anger, or avoidance (cf. Fillmore 1975; R. Lakoff 1974b):

(401) Anger: Get *that* cat out of my house.
(402) Distance: *That* pub is a den of iniquity. (said when passing by)

(403) Could I borrow a tiny bit of $\left\{\begin{array}{l}\textit{that}\\ \text{this}\end{array}\right\}$ paper? (where either *this* or *that* is acceptable)

They may also convey emotional distance (from the source of distress), and thereby comfort:

(404) *There, there,* it'll be all right.

and may be used for the distancing of interactional termination:

(405) *There*, that's how it is . . .
(406) *There*, we'll be seeing each other.

Compare the Tzeltal:

(407) *tey*, hk'opon hbatik ¢'in.
There, we'll talk to each other (again) then.

and Tamil 'there' is used in the same way.

Adjustment of reports to H's point of view is one further form of S–H distancing, and is thus an expectable part of negative politeness. It is to be found in the preference for indirect reported speech in negative politeness. Consider:

(408) I'm sorry to bother you, but the Chancellor advised me to come and see you.

versus:

(409) I'm sorry to bother you, but the Chancellor said to me, 'Mr Jones, I'd go and see the Dean if I were you'.

Only (408) would be considered a sophisticated negatively polite way of initiating the FTA of introducing oneself and presenting a problem. In many languages there are a number of degrees of removal from actual quotation, and in general as the report becomes less 'quoty' and more 'gisty', the more the speaker commits himself to an interpretation of what was said, since he reports the speech act(s) done and makes reference unequivocal. In so doing, he avoids presuming that S and H share the point of view and the common set of background assumptions which they would have to share in order to derive the same interpretation from the direct quote. He also incidentally avoids giving social information about himself or others (as is given in 409) that is irrelevant in a negative-politeness context.

Strategy 8: State the FTA as a general rule

One way of dissociating S and H from the particular imposition in the FTA, and hence a way of communicating that S doesn't want to impinge but is merely forced to by circumstances, is to state the FTA as an instance of some general social rule, regulation, or obligation. So we get pronoun avoidance by means of the first items rather than the second in pairs of sentences like the following:

(410) (a) Passengers will please refrain from flushing toilets on the train.
(b) You will please refrain from flushing toilets on the train.

(411) (a) International regulations require that the fuselage be sprayed with DDT.
(b) I am going to spray you with DDT to follow international regulations.

Similar examples proliferate in airline-ese.

Corporate groups and corporations act like individuals in this respect (as in others):

(412) The committee requests the President . . .

(413) The United States expresses regrets over the occurrence of the incident.

Similarly, the imposition itself may be represented as merely a case of a general obligation. We have on tape many utterances like (414) used by middle-class teachers in California (and see Torode 1974; also middle-class family usage in Bernstein 1971):

(414) We don't sit on tables, we sit on chairs, Johnny.

This claims that the speaker is not imposing, but rather is merely drawing attention to the existence of a rule of not-sitting-on-tables which is independent of both S and H. Compare:

(415) I'm sorry, but late-comers cannot be seated till the next interval.

This very general phenomenon merges, of course, into indirectness; see our discussion of off-record strategy 13 in section 5.5 below.

Strategy 9: Nominalize[60]

Ross (1972) has suggested that rather than the age-old grammarian's syntactic categories of noun, verb, adjective, etc., the facts of syntax suggest a continuum from verb through adjective to noun (in linguistic terminology, a 'category squish'). This corresponds to a continuum from syntactic volatility to syntactic inertness.

Quite unexpectedly, we noticed that in English, degrees of negative politeness (or at least formality) run hand in hand with degrees of nouniness (see Ross 1973); that is, formality is associated with the noun end of the continuum. Consider the following sets:

(416) (a) You performed well on the examinations and we were favourably impressed.
    (b) Your performing well on the examinations impressed us favourably.
    (c) Your good performance on the examinations impressed us favourably.

Here (c) seems more formal, more like a business letter than (b), and (b) more than (a). Version (a) seems very much a spoken sentence, (c) very much a written one. So as we nominalize the subject, so the sentence gets more 'formal'. Now, try degrees of nominalization in the verb phrase of the same sentence:

(417) (a) ... and that impressed us favourably,
    (b) ... was impressive to us.
    (c) ... made a favourable impression on us.

That gives us, with combinations, a nine-tiered hierarchy of formality for a large set of sentences with very similar meaning.

    Not only subjects and predicates but complements as well have such degrees of formality corresponding to degrees of nouniness:

(418) I am surprised $\begin{cases} \text{that you failed to reply.} \\ \text{at } \begin{Bmatrix} \text{you} \\ \text{your} \end{Bmatrix} \text{ failing to reply.} \\ \text{at your failure to reply.} \end{cases}$

Interestingly, passives seem to have roughly adjectival status:

(419) (a) We urgently request your cooperation.
    (b) Your cooperation is urgently requested.
    (c) An urgent request is made for your cooperation.

Thus we get the hierarchy of formality of familiar phrases like these:

(420) (a) I am pleased to be able to inform you ...
    (b) It is $\begin{cases} \text{pleasing (to me)} \\ \text{pleasant} \\ \text{my pleasure} \end{cases}$ to be able to inform you ...

or:

(421) (a) We regret that we cannot ...
    (b) It is $\begin{cases} \text{regretted} \\ \text{regrettable} \end{cases}$ that we cannot ...
    (c) It is our regret that we cannot ...

Why should this be?

    Intuitively, the more nouny an expression, the more removed an actor is from doing or feeling or being something; instead of the predicate being something attributed to an actor, the actor becomes an attribute (e.g. adjective) of the action. As far as FTAs are concerned, with the progressive removal of the active 'doing' part of an expression, the less dangerous it seems to be — it is not *objects* that are dangerous, it is their trajectories.[61]

    Is this a purely English phenomenon, a convention about the construction (say) of business letters? Apparently not: colloquial Tamil (not a written language) has somewhat similar degrees of nouniness associated with the minimization of face threats. Examples are provided by the use of verbal nouns to replace finite verbs, as in the paired examples below:

(422) (a) nii poo! ('you go!')
       (b) nii pooratu (lit.: 'your going': understood as 'you should go')
(423) (a) ite yaar connaanka? ('who said this?')
       (b) ite yaar connatu (lit.: 'whose saying of this': understood as 'who said this?')
(424) (a) ate nii ceyyu ('you do it!')
       (b) ate nii ceyratu (lit.: 'your doing it': understood as 'you should do it')

The second member of each pair is a verbal noun (Annamalai and Ramanujan n.d.), and substituting it for the finite verb avoids such a direct confrontation. Thus the command in (424b) is considerably softened, almost to the level of a polite suggestion, which could be more directly expressed as *nii ceyyalaamee* ('you may do it, why don't you?').

5.4.5 Redress other wants of H's. A final higher-order strategy of negative politeness consists in offering partial compensation for the face threat in the FTA by redressing some particular other wants of H's. But these are not just any further wants, for negative politeness involves a focus on a narrow band of H's wants, a very narrow facet of his person. This of course is in contrast to positive politeness, where H's wants are actively attended to over a broad spectrum. Nevertheless, from the core want that negative politeness attends to — namely H's desire for territorial integrity and self-determination — other wants can be derived. For instance, if H is more powerful than S, then S will be likely to respect H's preserve; therefore H may be presumed to have the derivative want to be more powerful than S. Also, if S falls into H's debt (in the broad sense of having received some unrequited service), then S will fall — in a certain domain — into H's power, and again can be expected to treat H's preserve with more circumspection. Moreover, the more S is in H's debt, the more careful S may be presumed to be about avoiding falling further into debt. So for both reasons H may be presumed to want S to be in debt (in certain respects) to him, to some degree.

Two strategies naturally emerge from these two derivative wants attributable to H. The first is to give deference to H, indicating that he is respected and esteemed and felt to be superior. We thus derive another motive for giving deference — a strategy described above. The second is to acknowledge that in doing some FTA that imposes on H, one has incurred a debt, and perhaps added to already existing debts. This last yields negative-politeness strategy 10.

Strategy 10: Go on record as incurring a debt, or as not indebting H

S can redress an FTA by explicitly claiming his indebtedness to H, or by disclaiming any indebtedness of H, by means of expressions such as the following, for requests:

(425) I'd be eternally grateful if you would . . .
(426) I'll never be able to repay you if you . . .

and for offers:

(427) I could easily do it for you.
(428) It wouldn't be any trouble; I have to go right by there anyway.

Such redress is likely to have special force in cultures preoccupied with debt (such as the Japanese), but is probably relevant in any culture for doing large FTAs.

This form of redress is implicitly carried in the Tzeltal reference to 'difficulty' which is buried in the expressions for 'please' and 'thank you' (see above, p. 190). For example:

(429) wokolok ya?čahpanon tatik kunerol.
      Please ('difficult as it were') you settle this case for me, Mr President.
(430) tal me wokol k'optaat.
      I've come if I may to difficult-speak to you. (c.i. 'to ask you a favour')

By referring explicitly to the difficulty of H's complying (in 429), S implicitly puts himself in debt to H for causing him the difficulty. In (430) 'difficult' modifies 'speaking', implying that S finds it difficult to speak because he is about to impose heavily on H. In both cases the strategy is just the opposite of output strategy 4 discussed above (p. 176), where S tries to *minimize* the imposition.

In the same way, expressing thanks puts S on record in accepting a debt:

(431) wokola?wal hwe?tik ?a?wot.
      difficult your speech we (inclusive) eat your tortillas. (c.i. 'Thank you for feeding me')

Here the 'difficult' appears to involve a role switch: S says 'difficult *your* words' meaning '*I* thank you'. This implicit role switch embedded in the conventionalized expression for 'thank you' might perhaps be taken as evidence that Tzeltal members perceive FTAs such as thanking as 'difficult' for *both* S and H.

Other expressions also stress S's reliance on H, implicating a debt. For example, *?obolbahan*, 'help me', or 'pity me':

(432) wokolok ʔobolbahan hmahantik ʔaʔwe ʔa.
Please 'have pity on me' we (inclusive) borrow your mouth. (c.i.
'Please do me the favour of taking a message to someone')

This explains perhaps why *?obolbahan* can be emphasized with strengthening particles like *č'i*, although at first glance it would be rude for S to emphatically insist on H helping him. Rather, it stresses emphatically his dependence, his debt:

(433) ʔobolbahan č'i. hk'antik ʔaʔk'ab.
Do do me a favour! Lend us (inclusive) your hand.

But this is presumptuous enough to be usable only if S and H are socially close.

5.5 Off record

A communicative act is done off record if it is done in such a way that it is not possible to attribute only one clear communicative intention to the act. In other words, the actor leaves himself an 'out' by providing himself with a number of defensible interpretations; he cannot be held to have committed himself to just one particular interpretation of his act. Thus if a speaker wants to do an FTA, but wants to avoid the responsibility for doing it, he can do it off record and leave it up to the addressee to decide how to interpret it.

Such off-record utterances are essentially indirect uses of language: to construct an off-record utterance one says something that is either more general (contains less information in the sense that it rules out fewer possible states of affairs) or actually different from what one means (intends to be understood). In either case, H must make some inference to recover what was in fact intended.

The actual processes that lie behind the comprehension (and thus the production) of indirection in language are not well understood. We have already, in talking of indirect speech acts, illustrated the difficulties. Essentially, though, what is involved is a two-stage process:

(i)   A *trigger* serves notice to the addressee that some inference must be made.

(ii)   Some mode of *inference* derives what is meant (intended) from what is actually said, this last providing a sufficient *clue* for the inference.

A very plausible candidate for the trigger is some violation of a Gricean Maxim. But what kind of inference is involved is a matter of contention. G. Lakoff (1975) favours semantic entailment; Searle (1975) favours inductive reasoning; Atlas and Levinson (1973) favour practical reasoning, as used in this paper. Part of what is involved is what premises are actually made use of to make the inference. We believe that a crucial premise will be the reconstructed motive that led S to be indirect in the first place, and amongst such motives face preservation is perhaps the most important. The subject is too involved for discussion here, but is of prime importance; since there are grammatical correlates of implicature, what is at stake is whether a theory of language can ever be theoretically independent of a more general theory of communication that includes non-semantic types of inference. In addition, close inspection shows that the majority of ties across conversational turns are indirect and inferential, and this indicates that a full understanding of conversational organization will have to await an adequate account of indirect communication.

Leaving aside these issues, let us return to the notion 'off record'. This refers not simply to formal types of indirection but rather to such linguistic strategies *in context*. As will become clear, many of the classic off-record strategies — metaphor, irony, understatement, rhetorical questions, etc. — are very often actually on record when used, because the clues to their interpretation (the mutual knowledge of S and H in the context; the intonational, prosodic and kinesic clues to speaker's attitude; the clues derived from conversational sequencing) add up to only one really viable interpretation in the context. We have discussed one kind of 'on-record off-recordness' above in negative-politeness strategy 1: the use of conventionally indirect requests (and other speech acts), made (*inter alia*) by questioning or asserting the felicity conditions on the speech act of requesting. In English, and in some other languages, these have become so conventionalized as forms of requesting that they have even acquired (optional) syntactic markings of their indirect illocutionary force.

Whether any given utterance in context is off record or not may be tested by this question: Is there a viable response to a challenge of doing an FTA that avoids responsibility for a serious FTA (or at least for the challenged one)? The *degree* of off-recordness varies in relation to the viability of another interpretation (literal meaning *or* conveyed meaning) of the utterance, as meeting the Maxims in the context equally well. Given the vulnerability of mutual knowledge (the difficulty of 'knowing' what is inside anyone else's head), and the non-recoverability of intonational and kinesic clues, even fairly blatant indirectnesses may be defensible as innocent — a speaker could protest that he didn't mean an irony in a sarcastic way, for example. S and H could both go away from the interaction 'knowing' in their hearts that it really was sarcastic, but because face (as the word implies) is largely a matter of surface appearances, S may well get away with his FTA.

Because many off-record strategies are used in contexts that render their outputs in fact unambiguously on record, we have already touched upon many of the strategies in the sections above. Consequently, we can leave this section of the paper quite skeletal; but the strategies covered here are amongst the very most pervasive in all the social interactions we have studied.

We proceed now directly to a classification of some ways in which contextually ambiguous indirection is achieved. Fig. 6 classifies such off-record strategies, which are grouped first under the trigger which starts the inference rolling – the particular Gricean Maxim whose violation[62] serves notice that there is an inference to be made. Then, within each trigger type, we classify strategies by the kinds of clues that are presented by the speaker for the intended inferences to be derived from.

5.5.1 Invite conversational implicatures.

If a speaker wants to do an FTA, and chooses to do it indirectly, he must give H some hints and hope that H picks up on them and thereby interprets what S really means (intends) to say. The basic way to do this is to invite conversational implicatures by violating, in some way, the Gricean Maxims of efficient communication. H is left to ask himself 'Why did S say that that way?' and to hit upon an interpretation that makes the violation understandable. For example, if S says 'Hmm, it's pretty stuffy in here', he may implicate a request that H open the window. Such a conveyed intent is likely to be off record, and H can ignore the request with impunity (while, say, agreeing with the utterance).

Note that conversational implicatures are often dependent on the salient aspects of some particular context (that there is, for instance, a closed window in the example above). So when we indicate in the examples below that some utterance conversationally implicates some other sentence or proposition, we mean only that the utterance *could* so implicate given appropriate contextual cues.

Strategy 1: Give hints

If S says something that is not explicitly relevant, he invites H to search for an interpretation of the possible relevance. The basic mechanism here is a violation of the Maxim of Relevance. In this and the next two sections we consider three ways of utilizing this mechanism. The reader may follow the way in which we derive these strategies from the hierarchical structure in Fig. 6.

Many cases of truly indirect (off-record) speech acts are accomplished

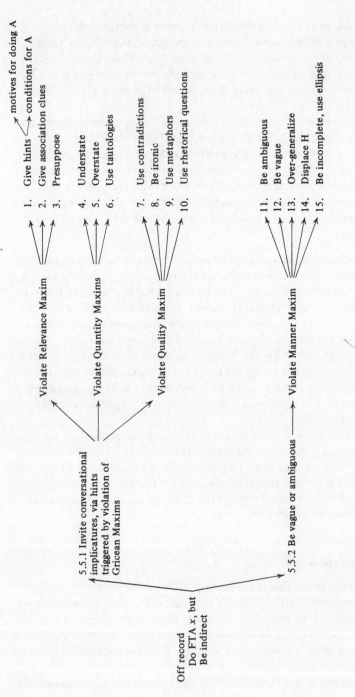

Fig. 6. Chart of strategies: Off record

by hints that consist in 'raising the issue of' some desired act A, for instance, by stating motives or reasons for doing A:

(1) It's cold in here. (c.i. Shut the window)
(2) I need some more nails to finish up this rabbit hutch. (c.i. Buy me some when you go to town)
(3) This soup's a bit bland. (c.i. Pass the salt)

(4) What a $\begin{cases} \text{hot day! (c.i. How about a drink?)} \\ \text{boring movie! (c.i. Let's leave)} \end{cases}$

Similarly, in Tamil:

(5) etoo paNam vaankinaa, paraville-ille?
     If some money is received, it wouldn't matter, would it?

provides a hint for a motive for lending money.

Hints may also be done by asserting or questioning the conditions for A (as in indirect requests); for example:

(6) That window isn't open.
(7) You didn't open the window when you came in.

(See additional examples in section 5.4.1, and especially Tables 1 and 2.)

Indeed, any steps in the practical reasoning leading to the want to do A and the ways to accomplish it may be used as hints, for all those FTAs that involve a response from H, as was discussed above in connection with indirect speech acts. But the construction of hints for other FTAs not requiring H to perform some act — for indirect criticisms, for instance — involves complex processes beyond the scope of this paper (and, indeed, beyond our present understanding).

Strategy 2: Give association clues

A related kind of implicature triggered by relevance violations is provided by mentioning something associated with the act required of H, either by precedent in S–H's experience or by mutual knowledge irrespective of their interactional experience. Thus the utterance:

(8) Oh God, I've got a headache again.

may be used to convey a request to borrow H's swimming suit, *if* S and H mutually know that they both have an association between S having a headache and S wanting to borrow H's swimsuit in order to swim off his headache. In a sense, association clues for indirect requests are nothing but more remote hints of practical-reasoning premises. What is special about them is that specific knowledge extrinsic to H's desired act is required to decode them. We would not expect here, then, the cross-cultural interpretability that direct hints of the type above seem in many cases to have. In Madagascar (E. O. Keenan 1974a and personal comm.), apparently most requests are done in this way, with a cumulative summing of associative hints, such as is indicated in the following glosses:

(9) My house isn't very far away . . . [intervening material] . . . There's the path that leads to my house. (c.i. Please come visit me)

(10) Are you going to market tomorrow? . . . There's a market tomorrow, I suppose. (c.i. Give me a ride there)

Such hints leave it up to H to offer, taking the responsibility for the FTA away from S.

In Tamil, too, this cumulative summing of hints is a much-used strategy. A detailed recounting of expenses, for example, may serve as an indirect request for a loan:

(11) paTuttavo neettu poRutukkum poocci. inta vaarom etoo celavukku aayirikku pattu ruupaay atiin kaaNoom.

Lying down (ill), the whole of yesterday was lost. This week there's ten rupees of expenses, and that too can't be seen.

and as an indirect refusal, as in (12) — which was the actual reply, later in the conversation, to the request in (11):

(12) celavukku inta camayam eppaTinnu nenecciinkoo? mooLavaaLeyoo kalyaaNam, vantatu, ancu ruupaa.

How do you think we are for expenses in this time? The marriage at mooLavaaLeyoo came, and that was five rupees.

Euphemisms for taboo topics are also presumably derived from implicatures of this kind (for example *WC, toilet, lavatory, bathroom, cloakroom, restroom, little girl's room,* etc.). As these become conventionalized there is constant pressure to create new euphemisms for truly taboo subjects, as by association the old euphemism becomes more and more polluted. Not all euphemisms are of this associative kind, however; some seem to be more strictly metaphorical (i.e. involve a transfer of secondary or incidental semantic 'features'), as in 'He fell asleep on the 15th September 1976' meaning 'He died on the 15th of September 1976'.

All our evidence indicates that euphemisms are a universal feature of language usage.

216

Strategy 3: Presuppose

A third set of clues to S's intent is related in a different way to the Relevance Maxim. An utterance can be almost wholly relevant in context, and yet violate the Relevance Maxim just at the level of its presuppositions. For instance, if S says:

(13) I washed the car again today.

he presupposes that he has done it before (e.g. last week) and therefore may implicate a criticism. The use of *again* forces H to search for the relevance of the presupposed prior event; if it is relevant only on the assumption that S and H are counting the times each does the task, and this in turn is relevant because S and H have agreed to share the task, then a criticism is implicated. With the addition of *yet* the critical implicature is forced:

(14) John's in the bathtub yet again.

Another way of presupposing is to use contrastive stress, which in conjunction with a contextual violation of the Relevance Maxim carries a criticism:

(15) Í don't go around boasting about mý achievements.
(16) It wasn't mé that did it.

Here the contrastive stress presupposes that *someone* does or did. This implicature is conveyed even more clearly with the addition of *at least*:

(17) At least Í don't go around boasting about mý achievements.

Strategy 4: Understate

In this and the following two strategies we consider how the addressee can be invited to make inferences by the speaker's violation of the Quantity Maxim. In a sense all conversational implicatures violate the Quantity Maxim ('Say as much as and no more than is required'), since by being indirect the speaker is inevitably saying something less than or something different from what he actually intends to convey. By saying less (that is, providing less information) than is required or by saying more than is required, S invites H to consider why. The social pressures against doing FTAs yield one set of interpretations.

Understatements are one way of generating implicatures by saying less than is required. Typical ways of constructing understatements are to choose a point on a scalar predicate (e.g. tall, good, nice) that is well below the point that actually describes the state of affairs, or to hedge a higher point which will implicate the (lower) actual state of affairs. The direction of the implicature (up or down the scale) in fact seems to depend not only on whether the value is a desirable attribute or not, but also on whether expressing such a value at the top or bottom of the scale is clamped down on by the FTA characteristics of the particular speech act. Thus a teenage girl might say 'He's all right' as an understated criticism implicating 'I think he's awful' *or* as an understated compliment implicating 'I think he's fabulous'. That is, in the case of a criticism, S avoids the lower points of the scale, and in the case of a compliment, or admission, S avoids the upper points.

Note that the necessity for background knowledge in order to interpret such informationally inadequate utterances means that, if they are contextually marked and therefore on record, they are essentially positive-politeness devices, stressing shared knowledge and/or shared values.

Here are some examples:

(18) A: What do you think of Harry?
     B: Nothing wrŏng with him. (c.i. I don't think he's very good)

(19) A: How do you like Josephine's new haircut?

    B: It's $\left\{ \begin{array}{l} \text{all right.} \\ \text{pretty nice.} \\ \text{OK.} \end{array} \right\}$ (c.i. I don't particularly like it)

(20) That house needs a touch of paint. (about a peeling slum, c.i. 'a *lot* of work')

(21) That car looks as if it might go! (about a flashy sports car, c.i. compliment)

(22) It's not half bad. (c.i. S thinks it's surprisingly good)

(23) She's some kind of idiot. (c.i. She's an idiot)

In addition, by hedging on the amount of some (good) attribute one may (without irony) implicate that one doesn't think it's good at all:

(24) That dress is quite nice.

(25) That's a rather good painting.

(26) $\left\{ \begin{array}{l} \text{John's hardly a genius.} \\ \text{That's hardly a Rembrandt.} \end{array} \right\}$ (where 'hardly' means 'only just', 'barely', c.i. 'Not at all')

and by hedging on the amount of some (potentially bad) attribute one may implicate that it's *very* bad; as in (23), and:

(27) That's somewhat amazing.

(28) I was pretty horrified.

218

Similarly, in Tamil,

(29) koncam cuTaa irukku.
It's a little hot. (c.i. It's too hot (to eat or drink))

In Tzeltal, the use of weakening particles such as *mak*, tacked onto an exclamatory emphatic statement, seem to make it even more exclamatory by virtue of the understatement thus produced:

(30) puersa k'ešlal ¢'in *mak*!
She's really embarrassed then *maybe*! (Compare English: I'm really *a bit* upset!)

(31) ha⁷ hič snopoh ku⁷untik ta melel ho⁷tik ¢'in *mak*.
It's thus that they (children) have learned from us really then, *maybe*!

Other examples in English include the understatement of accepting a compliment:

(32) A: What a marvellous place you have here.
B: Oh I don't know, it's a place.

the understatement of insults:

(33) Boswell: I do indeed come from Scotland, but I cannot help it . . .
Johnson: That, Sir, I find, is what a very great many of your countrymen cannot help.

and the understatement of accepting an offer:

(34) A: Have another drink.
B: I don't mind if I do.

Strategy 5: Overstate

If S says *more* than is necessary, thus violating the Quantity Maxim in another way, he may also convey implicatures. He may do this by the inverse of the understatement principle — that is, by exaggerating or choosing a point on a scale which is higher than the actual state of affairs. Here, however, the implicatures often lie far beyond what is said. For example:

(35) There were a million people in the Co-op tonight!

could convey an excuse for being late; and (36) could convey an apology for not getting in touch:

(36) I tried to call a hundred times, but there was never any answer.

while:

(37) You never do the washing up.
(38) Why are you always smoking?

could convey the relevant criticisms.

Furthermore, by the principle of 'the lady doth protest too much', if S wishes to convey an off-record sarcasm he might use overstatement as a trigger for the appropriate implicatures:

(39) Oh no, Mr Smith, we never meant to cause you any trouble. Nothing could have been further from our minds. I can't imagine how you could come to that conclusion. It's out of the question . . .

Strategy 6: Use tautologies

A third method of generating inferences by violations of the Quantity Maxim is to utter patent and necessary truths. By uttering a tautology, S encourages H to look for an informative interpretation of the non-informative utterance. It may be an excuse:

(40) War is war.
(41) Boys will be boys.

or a criticism:

(42) Your clothes belong where your clothes belong, my clothes belong where my clothes belong. Look upstairs!

In Tamil, tautologies serve similar functions, for example a refusal of a request:

(43) kuTukkamaaTTeennaa, kuTukkamaaTTeen.
     If I won't give it, I won't. (c.i. I mean it!)

or a complaint:

(44) rooTunnaa rooTu!
     If it's a road, it's a road! (c.i. Boy, what a terrible road!)

And a tautological statement like:

(45) amerikka amerikkataan.
     America is exactly America.

may be used to implicate disapproval (as when Jacqueline Kennedy married Onassis), or approval (as when Apollo landed on the moon). Tamil also has a conventionalized tautology which conveys the attitude 'to hell with X' (Schiffman 1971:30):

(46) avaar-aam avaaru.
     He they say is he. (c.i. 'Big deal him')

220

Similar implicatures are involved with statements that are blatantly obvious and non-informative. For example:

(47) You're men, why don't you do something about it?

addressed to men, via an assumption that men are the kind of creatures that *do* things, implicates that the addressees ought to do something to live up to their masculinity. A parallel example from Tzeltal illustrates the same point:

(48) bi ša?eš yael, *ha?eš ?ek winikeš*, bi yu?un ma ya stak hk'antik kah maestroetik li?eki?
What do you say, *you are men*, why can't we ask for our own teachers here too?

Strategy 7: Use contradictions

By violating the Quality Maxim ('Speak the truth, be sincere'), S forces H to find some implicature that preserves the Quality assumption which is perhaps the most basic principle of language usage. No one could even learn a language in a society where there was an assumption that no one told the truth (see Lewis 1969). It is presumably because this principle is so foundational that superficial violations of it provide the major figures of speech and many of the tools of rhetoric.

Contradictions, as well as the ironies, metaphors, and rhetorical questions considered in the following three sections, all involve violations of the Quality Maxim. By stating two things that contradict each other, S makes it appear that he *cannot* be telling the truth. He thus encourages H to look for an interpretation that reconciles the two contradictory propositions. For example:

(49) A: Are you upset about that?
B: Well, $\left\{ \begin{array}{l} \text{yes and no.} \\ \text{I am and I'm not.} \end{array} \right\}$

Such contradictions may convey a complaint or a criticism; for instance one might say of a drunken friend to a telephone caller:

(50) Well, John is here and he isn't here.

Strategy 8: Be ironic

By saying the *opposite* of what he means, again a violation of Quality, S can indirectly convey his intended meaning, if there are clues that his intended meaning is being conveyed indirectly. Such clues may be prosodic (e.g. nasality), kinesic (e.g. a smirk), or simply contextual:

(51) John's a real genius. (after John has just done twenty stupid things in a row)
(52) Lovely neighbourhood, eh? (in a slum)
(53) Beautiful weather, isn't it! (to postman drenched in rainstorm)

Irony may be combined with understatement:

(54) I think maybe John just might be a little bit of a genius.
(55) It's not as if I wárned you or anything. (c.i. I did, you know)
(56) This isn't exactly my idea of bliss.

Similar examples are common usage in Tzeltal:

(57) yuʔ ma sakubenuk ʔa hul čʼi.
It's not as if you came home pale or anything! (c.i. sympathy for illness: 'Boy are you pale!')
(58) yuʔun niwan ya hkʼan ya hta mul ya kaʔy.
Because perhaps I wánt to go looking for trouble. (c.i. Of course I don't!)
(59) mak yuʔwan hpʼeh naš snaik kʼoel škal ¢ʼin čʼi.
(Could it be) perhaps there's only one house there shall we say then! (c.i. Of course there are plenty of houses where she could work in Mexico City!)
(60) yuʔ ma ʔihkʼal čahpuk lah ta yalel ʔa ¢ʼi.
Because it's not really bad-as-it-were then. (c.i. It's really bad!)

In Tzeltal such ironies are often marked (and thus are on-record strategies), especially by particles that convey S's true feelings by indicating a contrary-to-fact statement (as in *-uk, niwan, ¢ʼin, ¢ʼin čʼi, ya kaʔy* in the above examples). And in English ironies they may be marked by similar hedges: *real, regular, just, exactly,* for example, or by exaggerated stress.

Strategy 9: Use metaphors

Metaphors are a further category of Quality violations, for metaphors are literally false. The use of metaphor is perhaps usually on record, but there is a possibility that exactly which of the connotations of the metaphor S intends may be off record. For example:

(61) Harry's a real fish. (c.i. He $\begin{cases} \text{drinks} \\ \text{swims} \\ \text{is slimy} \\ \text{is cold-blooded} \end{cases}$ like a fish)

In Tamil, one man criticized a kinsman (not a Jain) thus:

(62) avaar periyo ceTTu-TTu koRante.
       He's the son of a Jain household.

which, via associations of Jain wealth, implicates 'He's proud'. Indeed, metaphor is much used in Tamil to insult; for example:

(63) ote tinkaratuteen meeyinu.
       The main thing is that (he) 'eats kicks'. (c.i. Let him suffer)

Like irony, metaphors may be marked with hedging particles (*real, regular, sort of, as it were*) that make their metaphorical status explicit.

Some euphemisms proceed by metaphorical substitution, as in *sanitary engineer* for janitor, *home economists* for housewives; and in Tamil, *muuTitiruttuvaar cankam* ('hair-embellishers' union') for the lowly Barber caste, or *kaalani* ('colony') for *ceeri* (an outcaste hamlet). If such euphemisms proceed by the substitution of good things for bad, much verbal abuse derives from reversed metaphorical substitution, particularly the use of words for animals to apply to people (Leach 1964).

Strategy 10: Use rhetorical questions

To ask a question with no intention of obtaining an answer is to break a sincerity condition on questions — namely, that S wants H to provide him with the indicated information. This sincerity condition straightforwardly follows from the injunction 'Be sincere', i.e. the Quality Maxim. Questions that leave their answers hanging in the air, implicated, may be used to do FTAs — for example, excuses:

(64) How was I to know . . . ? (c.i. I wasn't)

or criticisms:

(65) How many times do I have to tell you . . . ? (c.i. Too many)
(66) What can I say? (c.i. Nothing, it's so bad)

In just the same way, in Tamil we find:

(67) ancu mailukku varra muTiyaataa?
       Can't you come five miles (to see us)? (c.i. Why haven't you come to visit?!)

Rhetorical questions are a frequent device in Tzeltal as well (often mixed with irony) for similar functions:

(68) yu? bal ho?on ?ay ba ya hta tak'in?

I suppose there's somewhere else I'll get money, eh? (c.i. Of course not)

(69) bi lah kati yu?un ȼ'i, ?oč šan ta yakubeli!

Why in the world did he go get drunk again? (c.i. No reason; plea for audience support)

(70) mak yu?un ya hmulantik k'abuel ?a — mak bit'il ša?wal!?

Is it that we líke being stared at — Q what can I say! (c.i. Of course we don't like being stared at!)

(71) bi yu?un yaš baate, yu? bal ma stak yaš hilat?

Why are you going, is it that you can't stay? (c.i. Of course you know you cán stay)

(72) bi yu?un niš ?ay ša?na? sȼ'isel ?ek ?a!

Just why would yóu know how to sew?! (c.i. Of course you wouldn't)

Sometimes the rhetorical nature of such questions is evidenced only in sequencing:

(73) A: mahtek ?a kilat, me telomatei.

I haven't seen you at all to see if you're well.

B: mak ban ya?wil ?a?ba?

Where would you have seen me? (c.i. Nowhere)

A: hu?uk.

No. (tying to B's implicature, not to the literal meaning)

(74) A: bi niš yaš ba hmulantik ?a.

Just what would we go wanting there? (c.i. Nothing)

B: binti ȼ'in. ma?yuk ba?ay bi stak mulanel ye ?ine.

What, then?! There's nothing there that could be wanted.

Words that help to force the rhetorical interpretation of questions (to push them on record) in English include *just, even, ever,* as in:

(75) Did he $\begin{cases} \text{even} \\ \text{ever} \end{cases}$ come to visit me once while I was in hospital?

(76) Just why would I have done that?

Similarly, in Tamil, rhetorical questions can be syntactically marked. (77) is ambiguous between a real request for information and a rhetorical question, but (78) is only rhetorical:

(77) naan eppaTi paakkireen?

How could I see?

(78) naan eppaTi paakkiratu?
How was there my seeing?

The Tamil particle *-taan* ('exactly so'), like English *just*, also forces a
rhetorical reading:

(79) yaarotaan tiiTTarle?
Just who didn't he scold?!

And in Tzeltal, disambiguation of rhetorical questions may be done by
certain combinations of particles, as in (69), where the exclamatory
particle *kati* forces the rhetorical interpretation.

5.5.2 Be vague or ambiguous: Violate the Manner Maxim. Rather than
inviting a particular implicature, S may choose to go off record by being
vague or ambiguous (that is, violating the Manner Maxim) in such a way
that his communicated intent remains ill-defined. As in the above cases, it
may be that the clues sum up to an utterance that is unambiguous in the
context; but by using what is technically indirectness, S will have given
a bow to H's face and therefore minimized the threat of the FTA. Here,
however, we are especially interested in the off-record usages of such
violations of Manner.

Below we discuss five methods of violating the Manner Maxim that
give rise to conversational implicatures that can convey FTAs off record.

Strategy 11: Be ambiguous

Purposeful ambiguity may be achieved through metaphor, since (as mentioned above) it is not always clear exactly which of the connotations of a
metaphor are intended to be invoked. Thus:

(80) John's a pretty $\begin{Bmatrix} \text{sharp} \\ \text{smooth} \end{Bmatrix}$ cookie.

could be either a compliment or an insult, depending on which of the
connotations of *sharp* or *smooth* are latched on to.

Other deliberate ambiguities, used in part for politeness reasons, are
illustrated by Grice (1975) and Weiser (1974).

Stretching the term 'ambiguity' to include the ambiguity between the
literal meaning of an utterance and any of its possible implicatures, we see
that every off-record strategy essentially exploits ambiguity in this wider
sense.

Strategy 12: Be vague

S may go off record with an FTA by being vague about who the object of the FTA is, or what the offence is — e.g., in criticisms:

(81) Looks like someone may have had too much to drink. (vague understatement)
(82) Perhaps someone did something naughty.

or in some euphemisms:

(83) I'm going $\left\{\begin{array}{l}\text{you-know-where.}\\\text{down the road for a bit. (c.i. to the local pub)}\end{array}\right\}$

Strategy 13: Over-generalize

Rule instantiation may leave the object of the FTA vaguely off record:

(84) The lawn has got to be mown.
(85) If that door is shut completely, it sticks.
(86) Mature people sometimes help do the dishes.

H then has the choice of deciding whether the general rule applies to him, in this case.

Similarly for the use of proverbs, although their implicatures may be conventionalized to the extent of being on record:

(87) People who live in glass houses shouldn't throw stones.
(88) He who laughs last laughs longest.
(89) A stitch in time saves nine.
(90) A penny saved is a penny earned.

Such generalized advice may, in context, serve as criticism; but as criticism with the weight of tradition, it is perhaps easier on face than other kinds of rule-stating. (See Green 1975b for some examples of proverbs used in conversation.)

Strategy 14: Displace H

S may go off record as to who the target for his FTA is, or he may pretend to address the FTA to someone whom it wouldn't threaten, and hope that the *real* target will see that the FTA is aimed at him. Ervin-Tripp (1972:247) cites an example of this, where one secretary in an office asks another — but with negative politeness — to pass the stapler, in circumstances where a professor is much nearer to the stapler than the other secretary. His face is not threatened, and he *can* choose to do it himself as a bonus 'free gift'.

In Tamil villages, indirect requests are often delivered deviously in this way; S moans about his needs to a bystander in the hearing of the intended target of the request.

Strategy 15: Be incomplete, use ellipsis

This is as much a violation of the Quantity Maxim as of the Manner Maxim. Elliptical utterances are legitimated by various conversational contexts — in answers to questions, for example (where attenuation provides severe problems for linguistic theory: see Morgan 1973). But they are also warranted in FTAs. By leaving an FTA half undone, S can leave the implicature 'hanging in the air', just as with rhetorical questions:

(91) Well, if one leaves one's tea on the wobbly table . . .
(92) Well, I didn't see yóu . . .

This is in fact one of the most favoured strategies for requests and other FTAs in Tamil, especially to one's superiors. Thus:

(93) eenunka, talevali . . .
Oh sir, a headache . . .

was used by a niece to ask her father's younger brother for an aspirin. This gave him the option of telling her to go and lie down, rather than dispensing a precious pill.

5.6 Conclusion to section 5.00

In this long section, the main body of the paper, what we have done is to demonstrate in great detail the fine-grained parallelisms in the expression of politeness in three unrelated languages. We present this great bulk of material because it is far from obvious that such parallelisms should exist, and positively surprising that the similarities should penetrate so far into the minutiae of utterance construction — to include, for example, uses of negatives, subjunctives, hedging particles and tags; of manipulations of deixis and presuppositions; of plurality, tense, and person. And it is this body of striking parallels that is the motivation for the development of the theoretical account in terms of actors' strategies in section 3.00. This was our puzzle, the theory was our attempted answer, and we may now pass on to consider amplifications and applications. Our hope is that the applications, especially to sociological material, will provide ample justification for the whole investigation.

6.00 DERIVATIVE HYPOTHESES

6.1 Exploitations of strategies

Our model would predict a number of possible exploitations of the politeness strategies. We consider these briefly here.

6.1.1 Trying to re-rank R, P, or D. We mentioned in section 3.4.2, in our discussion of the nature of the sociological variables that go into assessing the seriousness of an FTA, that a speaker may exploit the fundamental ambiguity that derives from the compounding of the factors D, P, and R into a single index of risk, and attempt to redefine one of the variables.[63] That is, any FTA utterance will encode the estimated danger of the FTA, but it does not necessarily display which of the social variables is primarily responsible for the assessed weight of W_x. S and H will both have some estimate of these variables, and S may choose to try to re-rank the expectable weighting of one of the variables at the expense of the others.

In trying to re-rank R, S may take advantage of mutual-knowledge assumptions between S and H of their respective social distance D and social power P, and S may choose to act *as though* R_x is smaller than he in fact knows (and knows that H knows) it really is. He can do this by saying, for example, 'Hey, Harry, how about lending me your new car!' and hoping that the positive-politeness optimism will convince Harry that it is not a very big or unreasonable request. This is risky, as Harry may decide that it is D or P that the addressee is manipulating, rather than R, and take offence. But the fact that there are three possible variables to manipulate means that the choice of which one is manipulated is off record, and the speaker could argue (if challenged by Harry) that he didn't mean to imply that D or P was small, simply that R was small. Similarly for the other factors.

Turning to ways of re-ranking P, we may note that the relationship between going baldly on record and having power (that the speaker doesn't have to worry about threatening the addressee's face, as he is in a situation of power over him such that his (S's) face cannot easily be damaged by H) gives rise to two kinds of exploitations. On the one hand, a speaker can use a bald-on-record FTA to claim (by implicature) that he is powerful over H, and does not fear his retaliation. This is risky, but if he gets away with it (H doesn't retaliate, for whatever reason), S succeeds in actually altering the public definition of his relationship to H: that is, his successful exploitation becomes part of the history of interaction, and thereby alters the agreed values of D or P. Hence the power of making scenes, S calling on audience support to destroy H's face — a technique used, for example, by low-caste Indian wives, despite their small P, against errant husbands.

Another kind of exploitation of the power connotations of the bald-on-record strategy can be seen in offers. As mentioned above in section 5.2, direct commands (i.e. those baldly on record) may be made by non-powerful persons *only if* they are (ostensibly) in the hearer's interest and the act commanded is such that the addressee wouldn't do it unless ordered to. Thus, as we have seen, an invitation or a request for a visitor to enter one's house is a direct command (syntactically) in many different languages, and operates as an attempt to overcome H's reluctance to impose on S, by pretending that S has the power to force H to act (and perhaps, at one stage further removed, implicitly humbling the house and the speaker by pretending that the addressee has to enter under duress, as R. Lakoff (1972) has pointed out). A speaker, therefore, may exploit this fact and try to redefine something that *he* really wants (a request) as being something that *H* really would want (an offer), as in 'Come to the movies with me tonight; I insist. You'll love it.' The fact that the speaker may exploit in this manner the inverse relationship between requests and offers is evidence for the existence of the mutual knowledge of negative-face wants, for to offer something rather than request something is an advantageous strategy only if both parties know that offering is less of an imposition than requesting – and that no one wants impositions. The same holds for the redefinition of threats as advice, for example.

In trying to re-rank D, S may take advantage of the relationship between on-record strategies and intimacy, which is that in intimate relations there may be presumed to be minimal danger of face threats. This gives rise to the use of bald-on-record insults or jokes as a way of asserting such intimacy. Hence we get conventionalized (ritualized) insults as a mechanism for stressing solidarity. In addition, there is the further exploitation of insulting someone in front of an audience, so that the audience thinks the insult is merely such an assertion of intimacy, while the addressee (wounded by an accurate dart) is forced to accept it lightly even though he may know better.

Another exploitation of the relationship between intimacy and jokes may operate to redefine R as well as D. A speaker may make a very large request as a joke (implying either that it is really small or that he doesn't really mean it) – for example, 'How about lending me your new Cadillac then, eh?' The off-recordness of large requests here merges with the jokeyness of small requests; it is up to H then to decide which is meant, and his decision may determine whether the S–H relationship develops in the direction of greater intimacy (smaller D) or not.

6.1.2 Use of non-expectable strategy to insult. One final type of exploitation of the politeness strategies should be mentioned: if S is *too* polite (overestimating W_x) he may insult H (or simply wound his feelings) by implying that D or P(H) is greater than it is. He may use this form of rejection as a sanction against H's bad behaviour (for example, by switching from the usual T pronoun to the use of the formal V, to invite one's former comrade to a duel; see Friedrich 1972). On the other hand, by being too familiar (underestimating W_x), a speaker may insult H by implying that D or P(H) is smaller than it is. This may be unintentional as well; for example, when a speaker from a basically positive-politeness culture interacts with one from a negative-politeness culture, the latter may well be offended by the over-familiarity of the former. This point is further developed under 'Ethos' in section 7.2.1 below.

This use of 'marked' (unexpected) linguistic forms in the choice of titles of address has been given theoretical treatment by Geoghegan (1970). However, his rules seem to be highly specialized and do not extend to strategic choice outside simple sets of alternates; they cannot therefore provide a satisfactory general theory. In our view, rather than particular conventional rules for the conveyance of 'special affect' (anger, intimacy, insult, etc.), what is needed is a general theory of the exploitation of conventional rules and expectations, as Grice (1967) argued.

One interesting and quite widely reported phenomenon, which is perhaps evidence of the extent to which such exploitations are used, is the progressive degradation of some honorifics. Comparable to the abusive use of *my good man* in England, the abusive use of Japanese honorifics is reported by Sansom (1928). He claims that of the originally polite substitutes for the second person pronoun, *'kisama* ["noble sir"] is used in abusive as well as very familiar language, *kimi* ["king"] among intimates, *omae* ["honourable front"] to servants, children, wives, and others by whom no deference is expected' (*ibid.*:305; glosses added from earlier sentences). Similarly, use of the Swedish V pronoun *ni* is seen by members of lower classes as abusive (Paulston 1976). We suggest that such degradation may come about through the exploitative use of highly valued forms to convey insult — that is, through ironic politeness.

6.2 Mixture of strategies

The mixture of elements deriving from positive- and negative-politeness strategies in a given utterance may simply produce a kind of hybrid strategy somewhere in between the two. When token tag questions are tacked on to a presumptuous positively polite request, for example, or when hedges (e.g. *like, sort of*) are used to render more vague the expression of an extreme positive-politeness opinion, the results are basically still positive-politeness strategies, even though they make use of essentially negative-politeness techniques to soften the presumption. But there are other uses of strategy mixtures that don't hybridize, but rather move the speaker and addressee back and forth between approaching and distancing in their interaction. Such movement may be a painful jerk, if clumsily done, or it may be smoothly integrated to maintain a satisfactory balance in the quality of interaction between S and H.

6.2.1 The delicacy of the interactional balance. As we have repeatedly stressed throughout this paper, the linguistic realizations of positive- and negative-politeness strategies may operate as a social accelerator and a social brake, respectively, to modify the direction of interaction at any point in time. Interactants, in any situation where the possibility of change in their social relationship exists, are constantly assessing the current 'score' — the mutual-knowledge assessments of D and P, for example — and may make minute adjustments at any point in order to re-establish a satisfactory balance or to move the interaction in the desired direction towards greater closeness or greater distance.

For example, upon making a positively polite request S may decide that he has been *too* presumptuous and tack a long hedge onto it:

(1)   Hey Joe, let's go take in a flick tonight, OK? — I mean, if you're not too busy and would like to.

Or he may soften up an overly cautious request with a positively polite endearment:

(2)   You wouldn't happen to have a pen I could possibly borrow, by any chance, would you ol' buddy?

And as S and H may not agree in their desires (for example, in the case of a male pursuing an unwilling female, or a buyer pursuing an unwilling seller), a given interaction may juggle back and forth from moment to moment between devices for reducing and widening social distance. Thus the linguistic realizations of politeness strategies may be a very revealing index of the quality of social relationships and the course of their development.

6.2.2 Moods. Likewise, a shift from one strategy to another may reflect the speaker's momentary 'mood', not only as a function of the interaction and therefore as a part of the interactional balance, but completely extrinsically to the interaction as well. Thus one day I may look on all the world as my brother, treat all FTAs as small and regale everyone with positively polite effusions; the next day I may consider everyone my enemy and react to all contacts with the cold avoidances of negative politeness. Such mood changes reflect a changed evaluation of D, P, and

231

R, and in order for interactants to interpret utterances correctly they must have some assessment of each other's current mood. As such assessments build up over time, they enter into the interactants' assessments of one another's personality, and thus feed back into the basic interactional mutual knowledge estimations of D, P, and R.

That the idiosyncrasies of personality, the vagaries of mood, and the stabilities of social relationships might all be constructed (at least in part) out of the same highly limited basic dimensions may seem improbable. But there does seem to be a potential for genuine ambiguity in interaction between these three orders of experience: if Joe jokes, is he jokey by nature, or is he in a jokey mood, or does he stand in a joking relationship with his interlocutor? Similar questions apply to the expression of intimacy, or of respect. If this is so, it is a fundamental fact, and an understanding of the significant dimensions on which interaction varies should provide insights into the dimensions on which personality is built, as well as social relationships. It suggests that an essentially transactional or interactional theory of social life may provide a unified account of phenomena at such very different levels.

6.3 FTAs and conversational structure

In our analysis so far, we have talked as if interaction were built out of unit acts, each of which might be an FTA requiring strategic adjustment of some sort or other, and which were strung together with no more than occasional reference to prior acts (as in answers or agreements) or to succeeding acts (as in questions or requests). Such a view, promoted in no small part by the philosophy of action and by the theory of speech acts in particular, has been ably criticized by Schegloff and Sacks (1973), Turner (1975), and Schegloff (1976). They argue, essentially, that conversational location, both in terms of 'local turn-by-turn organization' (Sacks, Schegloff and Jefferson 1974) and in terms of overall conversational structure (Schegloff and Sacks 1973), is a crucial determinant of how an utterance is understood. And at various points workers in this vein have touched upon the ways in which FTA considerations impinge on conversational structure. We have already referred to Sacks's work on the preference for agreement, and we should add references to work that demonstrates that laughter in conversation is finely attuned to the occurrence of FTAs (Jefferson, Sacks and Schegloff 1976), and that compliments generate specific turn-structures (Pomerantz 1978). Finally, the conversational organizations that these workers have discovered are extremely sensitive to violation; turn-taking violations (interrupting, ignoring selection of other speakers, not responding to prior turns) are all FTAs in themselves, as are violations of opening and closing procedures.

Here we try to make some amends for our neglect of these larger structural dimensions. Implicitly we have already used such notions, especially in our definition of off-record strategies. One basic observation to be made is that FTAs do not necessarily inhere in single acts (and hence the concept might be better labelled 'face-threatening intention'). To see this, consider the following way of reproving an employee for not doing his job properly. Knowing that he has failed to deal with a whole batch of correspondence, the boss asks piece by piece whether it has been done, receiving a string of negative answers. No more need be said. The point is that a higher-level intention to issue a criticism may be conveyed by a series of acts (and responses) that are not themselves FTAs, or are not the particular FTA in question. In short, plans – including conversational plans – are hierarchical, and conversational understanding is achieved by reconstruction of levels of intent beyond and above and integrative of those that lie behind particular utterances or sentences.

Consequently, some strategies for FTA-handling are describable only in terms of sequences of acts or utterances, strung together as outputs of hierarchical plans. To take a simple case, offers in many lands are made once, refused, made again, refused, made again, and at length accepted or finally refused. Consider (3):

(3) A_1 : Would you like a drink?
     B_1 : Oh no, it's all right.
     A_2 : No, I insist.
     B_2 : OK, I'd love a double whisky.

We all recognize this sequence, the demonstration of not very reluctant reluctance. To accept an offer is an FTA, best minimized by allowing oneself to be cajoled into it. In many cultures, the polite modification of both offers and requests may be spread over a conversational sequence between two parties, instead of being confined to one utterance or turn. In Tenejapa such sequences must be played through, though at varying lengths, regardless of whether it is clear to both participants whether the offer will ultimately be accepted or refused. To offer only once would be as startling as accepting at once. The existence of such sequences illustrates an important fact – that strategic language usage cross-cuts linguistic units from the allophone to the discourse chunk.[64]

In India, to a greater extent than in England or the U.S.A., requests must follow, or be followed by, detailed reasons for requesting. But yet another strategy, much used for its off-record benefits, is simply to provide the *reasons* alone, allowing these to suggest the request. Thus, in one taped example, some women dispossessed of hearth and home by an angry land-lord recounted their woes in dramatic terms for thirty minutes to the village president, but at no point did they directly ask him to do anything. The sequential peculiarities that are introduced into discourse by such non-explicit higher-level face-threatening intentions are well illustrated by another episode. A man's wife's father's sister L comes seeking a massive loan to finance her daughter's marriage. She talks to the man's mother M, but she never asks directly or even mentions a loan; instead she recounts to M endless details of expenses that must be met. But M intersperses into L's list of expenses lists of her own expenses brought about by her son's illness (and so on). To an observer, the two participants might be com-miserating about their mutual financial troubles in an exchange of stories (another observable conversational organization). But then suddenly with startling effect the conversation takes this turn:

(4) L: cari, naan pirappaTalaam?
      OK, may I go?
    M: (Laughs): eppaTi kuTukkalaam?
      How can we give (the money)?

In fact, L's request to leave implicates in the context something like 'OK, let's come to the point: are you or aren't you going to lend me the money that I need (if not, I'm off, and don't expect to see me again . . .).' It is the abrupt implicature that draws M's laugh, and the first direct reference to the possibility that M might lend the money to L. Everything that went before was in fact L's presentation of reasons why M should lend her the money, and M's presentation of reasons why she couldn't. The two high-level strategies for requesting and refusing surface in our two utterances in (4). And the surfacing was brought about by a threat to leave, whose strategic issuance may be gauged by the fact that L only left four hours later (but without her money). The whole event was reported as: 'L came to ask us for a loan for her daughter's marriage.'

Turning to a theoretical viewpoint, a closely related observation we would like to make is this: language-usage concepts like those we have been developing (FTA, positive politeness, negative politeness, etc.) seem to be prerequisites for the description of sequencing phenomena in natural conversation. Take the following example:

(5) A_1: It could do with an onion.
    B_1: A whole one? (getting one)
    A_2: Yes, a whole one, cut fairly fine.
    B_2: Fáirly fine, or véry fine?
    A_3: Well, as fine as you can.

234

Take B_2: the informant protests he heard A_2 absolutely clearly. Why then does he question it? Clearly, he suspects A had motives for saying something a little different from what she meant; in fact he doubts her word, thinking 'I don't know whether she was just being polite.' In other words, it transpires that A_2 was an FTA and was mutually recognized to be so — B thinking that A would not impose on him to the extent of asking him to cut the onion *very* fine — and A in A_3 admits to that interpretation. The dialogue is not comprehensible without reference to the notion of an FTA.

Other FTAs can construct particular styles of verbal interchange. For instance, it appears that in English one shouldn't admit that one is feeling too bad:

(6) A: Hi, how are you?
     B: Oh, fine. Actually though . . .

nor feeling too good:

(7) A: How are you?
     B: Not too bad. Well actually pretty good . . .

These have quasi-conventional parallels in Tamil:

(8) A: eppati irukkinka?
     How are you?
     B: oNNumille. aanaa viiTTle koRantinka tolle, maaneejar tontaravu.
     It's nothing. But at home there's trouble with the kids, at the office with the boss . . .

And again in English, one shouldn't admit to wanting anything:

(9) A: What can I do for you?

   B: Oh nothing $\left\{ \begin{array}{l} \text{much.} \\ \text{, I expect.} \end{array} \right\}$ I just . . .

This is even clearer in Tzeltal, where it is enjoined that whenever one is asked what one wants or why one came, the appropriate answer is *ma'yuk* ('Nothing'); then one goes on to explain the reason.

A final point about the role of FTAs in conversational structure is that FTAs can generate well-structured sequences of turns. An initial observation here is that culturally stabilized interaction rituals with conventionalized formulae are very largely FTA-oriented, and the ritual formulae (which form no small part of members' notions of politeness) for apologies, thanks, farewells, condolences, sneezes (*God bless you*), stumbles (*whoopsy-daisy*) are evidence of the great utility and face-cost benefit of having ready-made ways of dealing with potential face-loss situations. Such formulae seem to be universally available in languages (Ferguson 1976), and frequently involve elaborate sequences of conversational turns with exploitative variations (see, for example, Irvine 1974). Such also are Goffman's (1971) 'remedial interchanges', which he treats as well-defined rituals presumably of cultural origin.

We have the hunch (and some evidence) not only that such rituals are universally available, but that their structures display remarkable parallels in organization. Moreover, these structures seem essentially similar to those observable in less ritualized FTA-generated interchanges.[65] Hence we would choose to assimilate such frozen interchanges to their interactionally generated counterparts, and provide an account of such universals in interactional organization in terms of rational attention to breaches of expected levels of face respect.

To do this we would have to posit what we may call the 'balance principle', which may be formulated as follows. If a breach of face respect occurs, this constitutes a kind of debt that must be made up by positive reparation if the original level of face respect is to be maintained. Reparation should be of an appropriate kind and paid in a degree proportionate to the breach. This principle should follow from the original assumptions of our model in just those circumstances where participants have adequate motives for caring for each others' face. Thus if A does something that damages B's face (or his assets, and thus indirectly his face), B has the right to demand reparation for A's act, and A must then provide this in adequate proportion, and B must accept it. For instance, if A treads on B's toe, B has the right to complain, A the obligation to apologize, and B (if the apologies are adequate) the obligation to accept them. Our balance principle should generate such sequences as outputs of rational strategies. Of course such sequences or parts of them may become conventionalized ready-made turn-assigned formulae of the sort 'I'm sorry' – 'That's all right'. But functionally identical sequences can be generated to fit any situation.

We may use a Tzeltal interactional episode to illustrate this and one other point. The other point is that our balance principle may (especially via interaction with other politeness strategies) trigger a chain reaction of imbalance, overcorrection, counter-overcorrection, and so on until balance is again restored.

In the following excerpt from the beginning of a Tzeltal conversation, M is an old woman and P is her middle-aged married daughter who has come to visit at M's house. After ritual greetings, P is invited into the house and seated, and the conversation begins:

> M₁: ma²yuk lom yaš tal ²a²wala ²ilotik ²ek ¢'in.
> You haven't come much to sort of see us, then.

236

P₁: maʔyuk ba šhuʔ hulbal.
　　I can't find occasion to visit.
M₂: ma šhuʔ. haʔ in –
　　You can't. It's that –
P₂: mahtek yaš tal kilatiše.
　　I have never come to see you at all.
M₃: ʔay naš baʔay ʔala ʔaʔteli.
　　It's just that there's a bit of work (you have to do).
P₃: haʔin biluk naš kala hpaspasta tey ta hnaiki.
　　It's that there are some things I just do a bit continually there
　　at my house.
M₄: haʔ yaʔwil.
　　So it is, you see.
P₄: haʔ.
　　So it is.

In M_1 the mother mildly reproaches P for not coming to visit sooner; in P_1 P proffers an excuse. Then in M_2 M confirms the excuse as if she were P, and begins to offer details as if she had all the knowledge of P's activities that only P herself has. This ends one cycle of the remedial interchange: offstage offence – reproach – excuse – acceptance. But then in P_2 (following the lead given by M's role switch in M_2), P *recycles* the remedial interchange by reproaching herself; that is, she takes the role that M assumed in M_1 and indeed, exaggerates it ('I've *never* come'). Then in M_3 M takes P's former role and offers an excuse for P (again, as if she were P and knew all about her difficulties with visiting), whereupon P replies in P_3 with an affirmation (and elaboration) of the excuse. In M_4 M emphatically affirms P's excuse (which she herself has offered her in M_3), again explaining it ('you see') as if she were P. And in P_4 P reaffirms her excuse by a repeat.

Thus the basic structure of the first few minutes of this conversation is this: M reproaches, P excuses herself, M accepts the excuse by repeating P's excuse as if she were P; then the remedial interchange is recycled, this time with a complete switch of roles, P does a self-reproach, M provides excuses, P accepts them by repetition and elaboration.

Our tentative analysis[66] is as follows. An FTA of reproach generates P_1 as reparation, and M_2 as acceptance, by the balance principle. But in M_2, partly perhaps to retrospectively minimize the FTA she did in M_1, M uses the positive-politeness strategy of taking the other's point of view, with a resultant role switch. Moreover, it seems that she is about to produce for P a better excuse than P provided for herself. Now M's role switch and the beginning she makes on elaborating P's excuse effectively undermine the force of P's reparation. (Consider how if one spills coffee on

237

someone else's clothes and they kindly point out how it could happen to anyone, one feels even more obligated to stress how sorry one is.) An apology is a debt that must be paid and cannot simply be annulled by a generous creditor. It is this, then, that makes the remedial interchange still incomplete on the first cycle, and leads P to recycle the interchange by interrupting with a self-reproach, which is itself a one-upping of M's original reproach. Although this should roundly pay off the debt, it forces M to offer excuses on P's behalf because P has now created an imbalance in the other direction; this move of M's seems to undo P's full reparation (which is perhaps further undone by the 'you see' in M_4, whereby M maintains her role switch). And this explains why, after eight more turns talk about their respective healths (beyond our chunk given above), P recycles the remedial interchange yet again by saying:

P_8: mahtek ʔa kilat, me telomat niše.
   I've never seen you, to see if you are well.

followed again by M offering her an excuse ('Well, where would we have seen each other? It's a long way between our houses') and P accepting it.

   This episode seems, then, to show that face-preserving strategies may lie not only behind well-defined conversational structures like remedial interchanges (including frozen conventional exchanges that had original rational sources) but also behind the apparently repetitive and redundant replays of such exchanges that are generated by fine and delicate adjustments of the balance of mutual face respect. And these together, we believe, should provide students of conversational organization with reason to be deeply interested in matters of face.

7.00 SOCIOLOGICAL IMPLICATIONS

We turn now to the application to sociological (including anthropological) concerns of the apparatus we have developed. In section 7.1 we consider the relevance of our theory to the traditional concerns of social anthropology; in 7.2 we turn to the analysis of significant patterns of interaction in particular social systems.

7.1 Social theory and the study of interaction

We have explored some systematic and universal properties of language use addressed to face redress. But what bearing has all this on sociological or anthropological theory or research? What is *universal* and pan-cultural cannot, at first glance, be of *cultural* significance. That which organizes such low-level orders of events can hardly, it might seem, have any bearing on the mainstream sociological concern with social structure. Indeed the study of interactional systematics has been impugned by Giddens (1973:15) on charges of being 'a resurgence of crude voluntarism, linked to what I would call a retreat from institutional analysis'. Moreover, he continues, the views 'that the most vital aspects of social existence are those relating to the triviata of "everyday life" . . . easily rationalise a withdrawal from basic issues involved in the study of macro-structural social forms and social processes' (*ibid.*).

One suspects that many social theorists, including some anthropologists, share these views. Nevertheless, in actual fact in social anthropology there has been a persistent if rather thin strand of interest in the way in which social relations of various kinds are realized in interaction. And this interest follows from the sorts of theoretical orientation that have been most influential. To take just two examples, theorists holding such widely different views of the nature of social structure as Radcliffe-Brown and Lévi-Strauss both nevertheless subscribe to the view that social relationships and their quality are the basic facts (or part of them) which a theory of social structure must account for.[67] Moreover, both theorists emphasize that the nature of the social relationship between two persons is intrinsically related to the kind and quality of the interaction that takes place between them. Thus Radcliffe-Brown stated that 'it is evident that the whole maintenance of a social order depends upon the appropriate kind and degree of respect being shown towards certain persons, things, and ideas or symbols' (1952:91); and further, 'in studying a kinship system it is possible to distinguish the different relatives by reference to the kind and degree of respect that is paid to them' (*ibid.*:95). And of course Radcliffe-Brown's tetrad (as Fortes dubs it) of joking, familiarity, respect and avoidance was adopted and adapted into Lévi-Strauss's 'kinship atom' (1968:72 and ch.2).

So for both of these influential theorists, and for the many who follow them, anthropological theory directs one to look at interactional quality with a keen eye. For the conduct of social relations, themselves units of social structure, is realized in interaction. In this context, then, it is felt to be important to specify links between abstract theories of social structure and the details of interaction. Thus Fortes can say of Radcliffe-Brown's paper on the mother's brother in South Africa (in Radcliffe-Brown 1952), which related interactional quality to jural rules, 'the seminal influence of this paper on the development of kinship theory over the past forty years has been without parallel' (Fortes 1969:47).

Yet we may ask why, in this generally favourable theoretical climate, the study of social interaction has in fact been so neglected in social anthropology. We suspect that the reasons for this are deeper than the contingencies which research is always subject to. For there seems to be a distinct ambivalence about the actual study of interaction by anthropologists. In the first place there seems to be a fear that, as indicated in the quote above from the sociologist Giddens, the study of interaction will mask a withdrawal from concern with social structure and the central mechanisms whereby societies replicate themselves across the generations. Anthropologists would then be left with nothing but the study of 'the triviata of everyday life'. But that danger seems remote.

Another line of thought that is perhaps instrumental in devaluing the study of interaction is the assumption that social structure simply does not penetrate that far down into the details of behaviour. In this view society is about the patterned or stereotyped, interaction is about the idiosyncratic, and what is idiosyncratic cannot be about the social. Of course this is a possibility, but it seems to us that it is simply false. And we believe that all students of interaction would agree that social interaction is extremely tightly and systematically structured in patterns that are daily replicated by countless individuals.

Another and more plausible line of thought that distracts the anthropologist's attention from interaction is just the opposite. Far from being idiosyncratic, in this view the systematics of interaction are universal. And what is identical in all cultures cannot distinguish between them; thus interaction is a substratum that we may simply take for granted. Rather than belonging to a field that concerns itself with the variety of human social systems, the study of interaction is the exclusive province of some other distinct discipline — ethology or social psychology, perhaps.

But this view rests on the assumption that there exists some well-defined sub-sociological level where interaction is independent of larger-scale social facts, a view apparently (and no doubt influentially) held by Goffman (1974:13). We believe this to be a cardinal error. Rather, interaction seems to be both determined by and determinant of various aspects of those social facts. That is not to say that we cannot analytically extract interactional principles from their social matrix; indeed, the overall thrust of this paper is just the reverse. The point is rather that larger-scale social facts (institutions, jural rules, rights, and duties) are embodied in, and in part exist in, interactional detail, and hence to yield this subject matter to some other discipline is to denude social anthropology of one of the slender columns by which its theoretical concepts rest on observable facts.

As we see it, the situation is this. We may identify an area of study that is essentially concerned with social structure, and another area that concentrates on the internal systematics of interaction. The first area is generally deemed to belong to social anthropology, but the second is not. Now there is a third area where these domains overlap, where social structure informs and determines interaction and where interaction creates or recreates social structure. And it is in this third area that some anthropological work has been done, and has been considered legitimate and acceptable within the discipline, indeed important and exciting (for example, E. N. Goody 1972; J. R. Goody 1959; Irvine 1974: and other work in the ethnography of speaking).

But our point is that the study of this third area cannot be properly or thoroughly undertaken until a basic understanding of *both* the other areas is achieved. Interactional systematics – the fine-grained analysis of the properties of face-to-face communicative behaviour – simply cannot be ignored if any significant progress in the third area is to be made. And anthropologists must be willing to displace some of their effort in this direction if they wish to make this progress.[68]

If such progress can be made, then there is great hope that a detailed set of principles will emerge that provide a bridge from abstract notions of social structure down to the details of interaction. That is, it should prove possible to define precise theories that will take as input socio-structural information and generate as output expectable and acceptable styles of interaction between particular participants. If this can be done, then we will have a means of testing, in the domain of social relations, whether or not hypothesized aspects of social structure are indeed in operation. This paper attempts to make some steps in this direction.

Now if our aim is to provide bridges among these three areas, we must like other anthropologists be especially interested in the third area where social structure and interaction overlap. Radcliffe-Brown's tetrad of interactional qualities remains one of the most important contributions to this area. And it is worth clarifying here the relationship that our paper has to these interactional qualities, which remain traditional concerns of social anthropology. Our paper can be seen as taking up two components of Radcliffe-Brown's tetrad – namely familiarity and respect[69] – and specifying with precision the mechanisms whereby the interactional flavour captured by such glosses is actually transmitted by participants. And, like Radcliffe-Brown, we see significant correlations with social dimensions, although from our present pan-cultural perspective we are interested in gross general social determinants rather than those particularizations of them operative in special cultural contexts.[70]

We hope to have shown in this discussion that interactional systematics do have relevance for traditional anthropological concerns. Our argument has been that in the first place anthropologists, when theorizing, recognize the importance of interactional variables in so far as they can be tied to social-structural principles (witness Radcliffe-Brown's tetrad of interactional qualities). Consequently, anthropologists occasionally attempt to do some work in the area of interaction. So, we may ask, why not do it systematically? And why not attempt to specify the link between social structure and interaction with precision? Indeed, we proffer this paper in part simply as a piece of descriptive apparatus for the recording of inter-actional quality in some more sophisticated way than the use of gross labels like 'respect' and 'familiarity', with which anthropologists have hitherto seemed content. In elaborating the apparatus, and in claiming cross-cultural validity, we do however go further: we see the endeavour as performing an explanatory role in the linking of social structure to behavioural patterns in a way that participants themselves do. And such efforts to link observables to underlying abstract social dimensions, which requires an understanding of the systematics of those observables them-selves, cannot but be part of an empirically based social theory that has a concern with social relationships. As Goodenough found for a related area (1969:327): 'Methods that allow us objectively to measure such things as anger, insult, flattery, and the gravity of offences . . . such methods, I submit, are not exercises in sterile formalism. They promise to be powerful analytical tools. They encourage me to great optimism about the possibi-lity of developing considerable precision in the science of social behavior.'

7.2 Sociological applications

Here we ask, in what ways do our claims for pan-cultural strategies of language use fit the culture-specific facts, and in what ways can they be used to describe those facts? Any comparative social theory must be at once based on universal principles and yet have culture-internal applica-tion. We wish to emphasize here that our quite specific universal principles can provide the basis for an account of diverse cultural differences in interaction. The basic resources we use to show this are two:

(i)   parameters and variables within the scheme itself;
(ii) differential distribution of the various strategies across a social population.

The first dimension of variation has to do with cultural patterns that hold for some particular population in general, whether a group or a social category. We are considering normatively stabilized expectations about how members will deal with FTAs, and especially the gravity with which they will treat them.

The second dimension is ego- rather than group-oriented. It has to do with the particular constellations of dyads that radiate out from ego, and across which ego's use of strategies varies. Looking at language usage in this way, we can map implicit categories of alters who are important to ego (a method not dissimilar to Warner's use of dyads (1937), although we are not limited to named conscious categories of alters).

We consider these two approaches in turn.

7.2.1 Ethos. Every observer in a foreign land knows that societies, or sub-cultures within societies, differ in terms of what might be called 'ethos', the affective quality of interaction characteristic of members of a society. We use the word 'ethos' in a derivative but more restrictive sense than Bateson (1958): our 'ethos' refers specifically to interactional quality.[71] In some societies interactional ethos is generally warm, easy-going, friendly; in others it is stiff, formal, deferential; in others it is characterized by displays of self-importance, bragging and showing off (the Kwakiutl as reported by Benedict (1934), the Iatmul men as reported by Bateson (1958)); in still others it is distant, hostile, suspicious (the Dobu as inter-preted by Benedict (*ibid.*)).

How does our theory provide for the observable cultural differences in ethos? Note first that the theory was couched in terms of individual acts, and presented a dyadic act-by-act account of strategic interaction. Having claimed that the acts of individuals represent the gamut of strategies from bald on record to indirectness, depending on situational factors deter-mining the assessment of W_x, how then can we generalize from particular acts to ethos, to the overall stable flavour of interaction in a society?

The link is provided by the culture-specific dimensions of social rela-tionships, as assessed by D and P. To the extent that types of social relationship are repetitive throughout a society — that there is a constancy, a stability, in such relationships — it is possible to generalize about the kinds of relationships that prevail in that society — for example, whether they generally reveal a heavy emphasis on status differentiation, so that high P values are likely to be assessed, or alternatively an egalitarian emphasis, with low P values. And similarly, since assessments of P and D crucially determine W_x, which in turn regulates the choice of politeness strategy, it is possible to generalize about the kinds of politeness that typically, in public,[72] are employed by members of that society. Thus, in our account, stability in social relations provides the explanation of regu-larities in interactional strategies,[73] just as in the accounts of Bateson and Benedict standardization of individual emotions via cultural conditioning explains the ethos or configuration that is evidenced in a culture. 'Ethos', in our sense, then, is a label for the quality of interaction characterizing groups, or social categories of persons, in a particular society.

Our politeness theory provides a descriptive and explanatory framework for such generalizations about dominant ethos in the following way. First note what our claims for 'universals' amount to:

243

(i)   The universality of face, describable as two kinds of wants.

(ii) The potential universality of rational action devoted to satisfying others' face wants.

(iii) The universality of the mutual knowledge between interactants of (i) and (ii).

From these our argument (as summarized in section 2.00) should follow *a priori*, and since it follows by the same kind of reasoning we have assumed in (ii) to be universally available, it follows that the strategies together with their abstract realizations will be potentially available to persons in any culture as rational means of dealing with the face of others.

To these *a priori* claims we add a claim based on the observation of the actual use of sentences in context: that the seriousness of an FTA is assessed as a complex function of three variables, 'distance', 'power', and 'rating of imposition'.

Now we must ask what room the model leaves for cross-cultural variation. Since we have excluded extrinsic weighting of wants (see section 4.2), we cannot account for cultural differences in terms, say, of greater desire for positive-face satisfaction than negative-face satisfaction in some society (in the U.S.A. compared with England, for example). Note that if we allowed extrinsic weighting of face wants, then cultural (emic) explanations of cross-cultural differences would supersede explanation in terms of universal (etic) social dimensions like D and P. Ours is the stronger hypothesis (it may of course be wrong) requiring a correlation between D and P levels in a society and the kind and amount of face attention.

Our model restricts the variables to a handful. The apparatus we have with which to describe cross-cultural variations is only:

(i)   The general level of W_x in a culture, as determined by the sum of P, D, and R values.

(ii) The extent to which all acts are FTAs, and the particular kinds of acts that are FTAs in a culture.

(iii) The cultural composition of W_x: the varying values (and thus importance) attached to P, D, and R_x, and the different sources for their assessment.

(iv) Different modes of assignment of members to the sets of persons whom an actor wants to pay him positive face, and the extent to which those sets are extended: are the relevant persons a highly limited and restricted class, or are they (or some of them) an extensive set?

In addition, external to our model but resulting from the application of it to particular populations, a fifth dimension of variability enters crucially into ethos:[74]

(v) The nature and distribution of strategies over the most prominent *2 people* dyadic relations in a particular society: are they distributed symmetrically? asymmetrically? in particular configurations?

Variations on these five dimensions can be shown to capture a great deal of the ethos of particular societies or groups.

Take, for instance, dimension (i), the general level of W_x in a culture. It is clear that in some cultures, due to the general high level of P, D, and R values, the assessment of the seriousness of FTAs is skewed, perhaps leaving out small FTAs entirely so that positive politeness is virtually non-existent. Thus we can distinguish (with immense crudity) between positive-politeness cultures and negative-politeness cultures. In positive-politeness cultures the general level of W_x tends to remain low; impositions are thought of as small, social distance as no insuperable boundary to easy-going interaction, and relative power as never very great. These are the friendly back-slapping cultures, as in the western U.S.A., some New Guinea cultures, and the Mbuti pygmies, for example.

In contrast, the negative-politeness cultures are those lands of stand-offish creatures like the British (in the eyes of the Americans), the Japanese (in the eyes of the British), the Malagasy (as reported by E. O. Keenan, personal comm.) and the Brahmans of India.

But of course these crass generalizations can be refined; subcultural differences can be captured to some extent also by dimension (i). In general we have a hunch that all over the world, in complex societies, dominated groups (and sometimes also majority groups) have positive-politeness cultures; dominating groups have negative-politeness cultures. That is, the world of the upper and middle groups is constructed in a stern and cold architecture of social distance, asymmetry, and resentment of impositions, while the world of the lower groups is built on social close-ness, symmetrical solidarity, and reciprocity. An index for upper-class negative-politeness ethos and lower-class positive-politeness ethos is provided by T/V pronominal usage in some Western societies, with reciprocal V usage at the top and reciprocal T usage at the bottom, as reported by Paulston (1976) for Swedish, by Friedrich (1972) for nineteenth-century Russian, and by Brown and Gilman (1960) for French and other Indo-European languages. The same holds for castes in a region of South India (Levinson 1977). We read a similar interpretation into reports of speech styles for upper and lower strata in two African societies, the Wolof (Irvine 1975) and the Burundi (Albert 1972). Geertz (1960) gives a vivid account of such class differences in language use in Java. And probably

245

much of the difference between Bernstein's (1971) 'elaborated' and 'restricted' codes can be assigned to negative-politeness versus positive-politeness preferences in linguistic expression.

If we seek to understand these patterns in stratified societies, we could try two lines of explanation. The first would be that the elaboration and aloof dignity of negative-politeness strategies is simply a natural symbol of high status and intrinsically fits aristocratic virtues. Just as the sacred is hedged around and given a protected territory in most cultures, so the bearers of high social status are given larger and more inviolable personal preserves. (And the Javanese, according to Geertz 1960, actually seem to see it this way.)

But our theory suggests another firmer line of explanation. If we find more reciprocal negative politeness in higher strata than in lower strata, then this must signify that there are higher D values in higher strata, and lower D values in lower strata. (If it were P that was responsible, then we would have asymmetrical usages of negative politeness, one way upwards.) But what does it mean to say that persons in higher social strata experience more social distance towards their fellows? Bott's (1957) analysis of networks in different social classes in England provides one plausible interpretation. She found more loosely knit networks amongst upper-class families, denser networks amongst lower-class families. A similar distinction between patterns of networks seems to be the explanation for the greater use of reciprocal V pronouns among higher castes in South India (Levinson 1977). As in England, property, mobility and ambition appear to be the divisive forces that break the solidarity of the upper strata.

This distinction between positive- and negative-politeness emphases not only marks class from class in hierarchical societies, but also marks different kinds of social roles from one another. Thus we suspect that, in most cultures, women among women have a tendency to use more elaborated positive-politeness strategies than do men among men. This is dramatically true in Madagascar (E. O. Keenan 1974b), and certainly true in Tenejapa (P. Brown 1979, 1980) and in Tamil villages (Levinson 1977), and it is reported by Bateson (1958) for Iatmul women. If this turns out to be generally true, it is perhaps partly understandable along the same lines provided by Bott's discussion in terms of networks — compared with women, men may assimilate more to upper-class dignity and competition for power, while women, excluded from this arena, maintain solidary ties with one another.[75]

Less metaphorically, we can characterize the distinction as polar types on the W_x dimension, where the 'warm' positive-politeness cultures have a subjective ideal of small values for D, R and relative P which give them their egalitarian, fraternal ethos, while the 'standoffish' negative-politeness cultures subscribe to a subjective ideal of large values for D, R and relative P which give them their hierarchical, paternal ethos.

Our cross-cultural grid can now receive a second dimension — or rather, set of dimensions — the extent to which all interactional acts in a culture are considered FTAs, and the different kinds of acts that are so considered. For instance, one subdivision is the distinction between debt-sensitive cultures and non-debt-sensitive cultures. In England and the U.S.A., for example, offers are not very threatening FTAs, but in Japan an offer as small as a glass of ice-water can occasion a tremendous debt, and may be accepted as heavily as a mortgage in a Western society (Benedict 1946). In India, Indians are often taken aback by the way in which Westerners accept offers as tokens of unrequitable metaphysical friendship instead of as coins to be punctiliously repaid. It is only in such cultures that one can express thanks by saying, in effect, 'I am humiliated, so awful is my debt.'

In this case the cultural composition of the rating of impositions seems essentially to be what is involved.[76] Other variations of R_x assessment that have fairly dramatic results on language usage are those concerning the definition of what we may call 'jousting arenas' — topics or verbal games in which risk to participants' face is greatly lessened. New York Blacks have their ritual insults (Labov 1972a), the middle-class Europeans their intellectual arguments (but note how a Frenchman's style of argument may appear vituperative to an Englishman).[77]

So also, compliments may be very big FTAs in societies where envy is very strong and where witchcraft exists as a sanction, and criticisms may be very big FTAs in 'shame' cultures.

A problematical dimension is introduced by considerations of whether S's face or H's face is more important to protect. In some societies it is a terrible FTA to allow one's own face to be threatened; hence no self-humbling strategies will be appropriate, and series of self-elevating challenges (of the form 'I'm better than *you* because . . .') characterize interaction. This seems to be what lies behind Kwakiutl interaction (as reported in Benedict 1934, and as contrasted with the deferential Zuni), as well as the behaviour of Iatmul men (Bateson 1958), and possibly partially motivates the competitive contrapuntal conversations reported by Reisman (1974) for the Antiguans.

An important consequence of this second dimension of variability is the far-reaching ramifications it may have in the usage and elaboration of particular preferences among potential linguistic outputs. For there are likely to be cultural constraints on certain outputs of the politeness strategies as a result of the treatment of some classes of acts as especially severe FTAs. Even though rationally a particular output would work as an instance, say, of negative politeness (for example, APOLOGIZE) yet in a given culture FTAs may be defined in such a way that that output will not be acceptable (for example, where pride is supreme, to apologize may be a greater FTA than to transgress on H's face without apologizing).

For the same sorts of reasons, in a given society particular techniques of face redress may become highly favoured as strategies, and therefore conventionalized. In English, for example, conventionalized indirect requests are so common that it is rare to hear a completely direct request even between equals (and in the middle classes, it is even surprisingly rare from mother to child, unless she is angry). This seems to result from the suppression of the acknowledgement of asymmetric power relations in Western dyads. (Support for this comes from Brown and Gilman's analysis (1960) of recent historical changes in the use of T/V pronouns in European languages. See also Neustupný 1968.) This suppression makes commands extreme FTAs in Western cultures. But in many cases the particular origins of cultural preferences for specific strategies are now obscure. For instance, in Tzeltal, the distancing and unsureness implications of high pitch have been highly conventionalized so that high pitch is a characteristic of most requests. The use of high pitch in English, and the use of conventionalized indirect speech acts in Tzeltal, are certainly available as viable negative-politeness techniques but are not conventionalized to the same degree.

From this it follows that there will be exploitations of high pitch in Tzeltal that would not be available in English, for example. In other words, whatever politeness techniques have been especially conventionalized in a society should give rise to conventional exploitations — implicatures derived from implicatures — which would not exist in other societies without this particular conventional association. For example, the fact that indirect speech acts are highly conventionalized in English means that in most circumstances using an indirect speech act implicates that S is trying to respect H's negative face. Therefore to say 'Would you please mind not walking on the grass' where the context makes it clear that S is not respecting H's negative face (specifically, that he will insist on H's complying with the request), can implicate sarcasm or anger. We expect that such an implicature would not be available (or would be at least far more devious) in languages without highly conventionalized indirect speech acts. This factor probably accounts for much stereotypical cross-cultural misunderstanding; it represents perhaps the major limitation to universal intelligibilities in the politeness domain.

These observations overlap with our third dimension of cross-cultural variation: the varying importances attached to P, D, and R, and the different scales for their assessment. We have said that the actual factors that go into assessing the size of these three social variables are of course culturally specific (with even some leeway for idiosyncratic variation), but we should note as well that, in different societies, different ones of these factors may overwhelm the others. In India, for example, the D variable seems to be less important (to have lower average values) than the P variable; in the U.S.A., on the other hand, P is perhaps normally insignificant relative to D.

Furthermore, cultures may differ in the degree to which wants other than face wants (such as the want for efficiency, or for the expression of power) are allowed to supersede face wants. If there is a norm of sincerity, for example, sincere disapproval is less of an FTA than it would be in societies not having such a legitimization of non-face wants. Norms in this way enter into the cultural definitions of R_x.

Turning to dimension (iv), the different ways in which positive-face wants are distributed over an ego's social network allow us to capture an important variable: in some cultures (or subcultures) there is a dramatic distinction between those whom you really want to be similar to and appreciated by as a more or less whole person, and those whom you wish to value some special trait or ability that you possess, but nothing more. In India this division would be along family and caste lines; in some African kinship systems, along lineage lines; and so on. E. O. Keenan (1974a:108) reports such a sharp dichotomy in Madagascar between *havana* ('kinsmen') and *vahiny* ('strangers', 'non-kinsmen'); 'free goods' types of requests (e.g. for a match) can occur only with *havana*. Similarly, in Tenejapa people who are *pahal sbil sok* ('have the same name') can be approached with requests which would never be asked of others. In Western culture we get a more even spread of positive-face wants across persons, and as a result have (in middle-class subcultures, at least) what we may call 'shrunken personality grooming', where an actor does exaggerated positive politeness addressed to just a few positive-face wants that he may assume the addressee would want him to desire (the roses, the good weather, the dog, the baby, for example).

Finally, we may sketch some patterns that result from the fifth dimension of variability: the distribution of strategies (from bald on record through positive and negative politeness to indirectness) across what we may crudely call 'the typical social dyad' of a particular society. Of course there are many distinct and specific kinds of dyad in any one society, but from a very general point of view, one of these types generalized in terms of P and D often receives major cultural emphasis, and predominates in public interaction. Moreover, the great majority of interactions may occur between persons whose social relationships fall within this one generalized type of dyad. And, further, it may be that this one dyadic type is the one most salient to observers by virtue of being the one that typifies 'relations in public'. We are looking here for the social basis for the predominant cultural style of interaction, while below (in section 7.2.2) we concentrate on the social basis of the *differences* between the dyads that an ego enters into.

Let us consider a set of four kinds of dyads (or generalized social relationships) specified by two polar values (high and low) attributed to S and H, on the two dimensions P and D. Now our model predicts that in such dyads strategies of language use will not be randomly distributed; rather, within each of these dyad types only the particular corresponding distribution of strategies shown in Fig. 7 will occur in any culture. In Fig. 7 we omit the pattern found in the dyad formed by high P and high D values, since this would look very similar to Dyad I (high P and low D) except that more redressive strategies would be used downwards, to inferiors. We use S and H here as our familiar participants, but the arrows show which strategy each would use when speaking to the other.

Crudely, then, in societies where the majority of public relations are dominated by high P relations (e.g. India), we would expect both extremes of our strategy array to be visibly much in operation, with bald on record (and perhaps positive politeness) going down to inferiors, and negative politeness and indirectness going up to superiors. (Such a typical dyad would be realized in India, for example, in the relation between a landowner and his low-caste labourer, and in many cultures by patron–client,

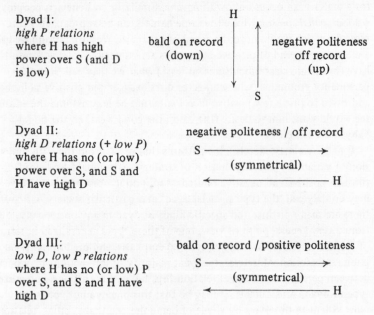

Dyad I:
high P relations
where H has high power over S (and D is low)

H

bald on record (down)   negative politeness off record (up)

S

Dyad II:
high D relations (+ low P)
where H has no (or low) power over S, and S and H have high D

negative politeness / off record
S ——————————→
(symmetrical)
←—————————— H

Dyad III:
low D, low P relations
where H has no (or low) P over S, and S and H have high D

bald on record / positive politeness
S ——————————→
(symmetrical)
←—————————— H

Fig. 7. Patterns of strategy distribution

landlord–serf, or master–servant relations.) In societies where high D relations dominate in public encounters (of which Japan by all accounts is one, Madagascar (E. O. Keenan 1974a, 1974b) another, and England to a lesser degree yet another), one would expect symmetrical use of high-numbered strategies to be most evident. In societies where low D is the emphasis and P is minimized (as perhaps in western U.S.A.), symmetrical use of bald on record and positive politeness would be expected. And where low P relations prevail without high D (as between men, or between women, in an egalitarian society), we would expect symmetrical low-numbered strategies as well.[78]

Our point here is that predominant interactional styles, which constitute a crucial part of cultural ethos, are at least in part built up of strategies for face redress that are in turn anchored to predominant types of social relationship, as measured in terms of vertical and horizontal social distance.

The factors entering into interactional ethos may be illustrated by an example from a particular culture. Research (Brown 1979, 1980) on distinctive interactional styles of men and women in Tenejapa has yielded some interesting results. Keeping topic constant so as to neutralize R_x in so far as this is possible in natural-conversation data,[79] and comparing the speech used within female dyads with that used in male dyads, it appears that the women are more positively polite: that is, their speech is highly elaborated for positive politeness, whereas the men are, relatively, more bald on record in their speech. A useful if crude index of this is provided by the use of emphatic particles: significantly higher counts of them occur in speech between women than in speech between men. In addition women use some qualitatively different positive-politeness strategies, such as the extensive use of ʔ*ala* ('a little') as a positive-politeness 'endearment' in conversation; the use of irony, rhetorical questions, and negative assertions meaning positives for emphatic expression of opinion; exaggerated empathetic intonation and prosodics. Furthermore, women use negative politeness strategies in situations where men do not, for example in hedging expressions of emphatic opinion or strong feelings. Men too have characteristic strategies not used by women (a brand of sexy joking, and a kind of preaching/lecturing style, for example). Hence a set of characteristic 'feminine styles' and a female ethos can be isolated from typical kinds of 'masculine style' and a male ethos, each generated by particular applications of strategies.

Turning to cross-sex dyads, we find that the contrast between the ethoses of each sex is maintained. For we find that women are polite to men — now mostly with the use of negative-politeness strategies — and men are brusque (relatively bald on record) to women, unless a high D demands negative politeness. Thus we have overall for women a pattern of high negative politeness and high positive politeness, attributable to the sharp dichotomizing of their social world into two categories of people, men and women, each of which requires different strategies of politeness. For men, on the other hand, the social world is less sharply divided; men treat everyone regardless of sex relatively bald on record, unless a high D or high R_x in particular circumstances forces them to choose a higher strategy. Thus women are, overall, 'more polite' than men in this society.

Tentatively (for this analysis is far from complete) we may venture that the sources for these distinct ethoses include at least the following. Women are vulnerable to men in a society where wives, sisters, and daughters may be beaten, and marriageable women may be abducted; their predominantly negatively polite speech to men derives then largely from the P variable. Turning to the contrast between women talking to women and men to men, perhaps a dominant factor is that men have a higher weighting of wants that conflict with face wants — for example, wants that support a goal of communicative efficiency which conflicts with the elaboration of face-redressive strategies. In addition, many of the women in a domestic group will be married in, since residence is patrilocal; hence there is likely to be a slightly greater D between the women of a household than between the men of a household. Moreover, women treat some FTAs more cautiously than men; the vulnerability of women means that more acts, and particular acts (such as talking to an unrelated male at all), are defined as face-threatening, motivating women to assess W_x higher than men do in general. It also motivates the particular strategies they choose, notably the ubiquitous expression denying responsibility, *maškil* ('I don't know'), as a self-protective device. One other possible factor is the process akin to Bateson's 'schismogenesis' (1958): men may stress their brusqueness as a sign of tough masculinity, and women their polite graciousness as a display of feminine values.[80]

This example has been sketched in some detail to illustrate one application of the theory developed in this paper. The comparison of the usages of two social categories of people, men and women, at the strategic level (rather than, for example, in terms of whether they follow or break certain — surface defined — rules of politeness), makes possible an analysis that links the differential usage to the social context in which the strategies are embedded. At the level of the more abstract face-redressive strategies, the determining effect of particular social-structural arrangements is much clearer than at the level of non-strategic rule descriptions of behaviour. Such an analysis focusing on the non-arbitrary order evident in linguistic styles allows the relationship between language styles and social structure to be spelled out in detail.[81]

It is along these lines, then, that we hope to be able to use our model of the universals in linguistic politeness to characterize the cross-cultural differences in ethos, the general tone of social interaction in different societies. This framework puts into perspective the ways in which societies are *not* the same interactionally, and the innumerable possibilities for cross-cultural misunderstanding that arise. For example, the French often sound rude to Englishmen because their speech is more 'aggressive', and Americans can sound boorish to Englishmen while the English may sound cold or pompous to Americans — in short, there are endless daily reminders of the social/cultural relativity of politeness and of norms of acceptable interaction. By including in our formulation the social factors P, D, and R which predict particular patterns of cultural skewing, we hope to account for such differences within our explanation of the similarities, as well as to make clear what kind of cross-cultural variability we would *not* expect to find — for instance, in no society will members use positive politeness for big FTAs and negative politeness for small ones, or positive politeness only to superiors and negative politeness only to inferiors.

The study of culture in the way Bateson and Benedict envisaged is now out of fashion. Perhaps in the sort of way outlined here, anthropologists might turn again to the analysis of cultural ethos with tools precise enough to give some concrete content to such broad but interesting generalizations.

7.2.2 Distribution of strategies. Let us now indicate an application of a less comparative and more ethnographic sort. We can use the descriptive apparatus of our politeness model to chart the significant kinds of social relationship that any ego in a structural locus enters into — significant not just to the analyst but to members of the society themselves. In other words, we can use it as a tool for *Verstehen* analysis. To begin, we can take named important categories of alters and see which strategies are used for which FTAs to each, thus testing whether the predictions in terms of independently measured dimensions of 'distance' and 'power' hold up. Then, having gained confidence in the diagnostic power of the method, we can see what can actually be learned about an ego's perception of distinct classes of alters and the behaviour appropriate to them. In this way it is possible to discover subtle distinctions that more orthodox procedures may miss or be unclear about. For instance, the controversial problem of the degree of homogeneity of alters subsumed in a category kinship term (see Fortes 1969:61; Leach 1971) might be illuminated in this way.

Research has been carried out (Levinson 1977, 1982) along these lines, on a data base of large quantities of natural conversation between known participants in a Tamil village, where ethnographic analysis had already been done (Beck 1972). The choice of pronouns of address provides a crude index of the much more subtle and variable degrees of respect and familiarity that can be communicated by the use of the strategies described in the body of this paper. Taking just two of these pronouns, we can systematically map for each ego those categories of alters that are addressed with the V or plural (respectful) second-person pronoun, and those addressed with the T or singular (non-respectful) second-person pronoun. We may take the distribution of T to indicate (very approximately) the distribution of bald-on-record and positive-politeness strategies, and the distribution of V to be very roughly coincident with the use of negative-politeness and off-record strategies, for FTAs with a low R_x. If we collect these details of T and V usage, a quite extraordinarily detailed patterning emerges. There seem to be three main types of inter-caste usage: one in which all members of one caste give T to all members of another; one in which all members of one caste give V to all members of another; and one in which members of one caste give T or V to members of another depending on the relative age of speaker and addressee. Informants provide the following social valuation of these usages: if caste A gives T to caste B, and B does not reciprocate with T, then A ranks higher than B, while if A gives V to B, and B does not reciprocate, then A ranks lower than B. If caste A uses the third pattern of usage (T or V according to relative age) to B, then A claims a measure of equality with B.[82] Given this valuation of the patterns of usage, we can infer an extremely detailed ranking of all castes in the village by counting the number of valued and disvalued usages that each caste gives or receives. And these are assessments that, given exposure to consistent patterns of use in public interactions, every member of the village can and does make – if not with the same precision and completeness that the ethnographer can achieve. In short, these overall patterns of pronominal usage chart for us what is at least potentially a members' map of the hierarchical relations that guide everyday interaction. For the most part this ranking can be shown to be consensual, but we can also identify areas of retaliative and rank-maximizing behaviour between certain castes. Moreover, pronominal usage leads us to recognize that inter-caste relations are not just structured by relations of relative rank, for there are large blocs of castes who exchange the third pattern of usage (T or V according to relative age) which effectively neutralizes caste ranking. Here we need to invoke another (hitherto unexplored) dimension of inter-caste relations, a dimension of solidarity and alliance. In this sort of way pronominal usage, as a crude index of the distribution of the more subtle gradations of politeness that are strategically available, provides us with real insights into the overall structuring of inter-caste relations within a *Verstehen* framework.

Turning to interactions between members of the same caste, the same simple pronominal alternation reveals — by means of different thresholds for transition from one usage to another — four important categories. For most castes these are household members, parallel kin, affines, and cross kin. But some castes have different internal organizations, so that (for instance) for the dominant caste, the category 'ego's clan' supersedes 'parallel kin', and the set of 'residual other clans' supersedes 'cross kin', as the categories that determine T/V usage. These differences correspond to an elusive category of castes of which village members are no longer consciously aware. Again, some interesting patterns emerge when intra-caste usage is compared between castes; essentially, the lower the caste the more use of T. Similarly, the lower the economic status of families within a caste, the greater the use of T. Low status and the use of positive polite-ness to one's fellows (which mutual T crudely indexes) seem to be clearly associated, while high-status groups insist on deference to elders and cross kin. The extremely different treatment of affines and potential affines is something that orthodox treatments of Dravidian kinship do not seem to have sufficiently emphasized. (See Levinson 1977, 1982 for further details.)

This experience suggests that the analysis of the distribution of strate-gies for language usage (even as crudely indexed by T/V pronouns) may indeed be a useful ethnographic tool. But it does more than simply pick out areas that might be missed in a standard ethnographic analysis, for it provides, in a way that standard techniques do not, an insight into the unreflective (non-exegetical) categories with which members actually operate. It reveals not just what is important for us, the observers, but also what is important for them, the observed, and it does this on a non-intuitive accountable basis.

8.00 IMPLICATIONS FOR LANGUAGE STUDIES

8.1 Face wants as functional pressures on language

This section describes some interrelations between grammar and face redress. We propose (a) that face redress is a powerful functional pressure on any linguistic system, and (b) that a particular mechanism is discernible whereby such pressures leave their imprint on language structure.

8.1.1 Functionalism in linguistic theory. Before we proceed, a few remarks on some trends in linguistic theory should be made. Recently, after a period of suppression by the methodological presuppositions of transfor-mational generative grammar, there has been a resurgence of interest in functionalist explanation — that is, in the search for a source outside the

purely linguistic system that might motivate the bulk of grammatical constraints. Most of this work attempts to locate such sources in the principles of cognitive processing, or in the interaction of language with other mental faculties.[83]

In contrast to what we may call 'internal' cognitive functionalist explanation, there are 'external' pragmatic theories that seek to link linguistic structures to the organization of communication. The theories of Grice (1971) and Searle (1969) are wholeheartedly of this latter sort, but more tentative partial pragmatic functionalisms are to be found in work stemming largely from the Lakoffs and scattered through issues of the Chicago Linguistic Society papers and in Cole and Morgan 1975. Work by sociologists on conversational structure can also be said to belong here (see, for example, Creider 1976 and Schegloff 1976 for some linguistic implications). The identification of plausible functional sources for linguistic structures remains mere correlation until the actual mechanisms whereby aspects of usage can pass into structure are substantiated; however, work that establishes mechanisms of this sort is now gradually building up (Cole 1975; Sankoff and Brown 1976; Weinreich, Labov and Herzog 1968). Similar processes in ontogenetic development are reported by E. O. Keenan (1975:293).

Despite all this interest in the functions that grammatical rules and constraints perform, remarkably little attention has been given to *social* pressures on grammar — this despite the overwhelming and pervasive evidence of such pressures preserved, for instance, in the honorific systems of the languages of South Asia, and despite the continued theoretical championship of Hymes. Sociolinguists have indeed documented cases of social impingement on language form (Friedrich 1966; Gumperz and Wilson 1971; Labov 1972c), but the social factors in these cases are either culture-specific pressures on the lexicon (as in Friedrich's work) or largely implicit sociological processes such as group-boundary maintenance, or 'social climbing' (see our remarks in section 8.2). In any case we find no arguments of a scope paralleling that of the now fashionable internal functionalisms, which attempt to provide sources for whole families of linguistic phenomena.

We can see at a glance the reason for this neglect. Linguistics is currently especially concerned to establish the general nature of a satisfactory theory of language, and the nature of linguistic universals must play a key role in such a theory. Moreover, it seems that such universals must be, given the varied tongues of man, extremely abstract. In this context, social motivations appear on the face of it to be unlikely functional sources for syntactic and derivational machinery, in that many aspects of derivational process are thought to be universal and yet cultures and social systems are diverse in the extreme, and moreover do not correlate neatly with languages or language families. It would then appear that largely unprovable historical correlations between languages and past social systems would have to be assumed.

But the unhopeful nature of the case is, we believe, due largely to the primitive state of sociological theory, for what ought to be functionally related to universal linguistic principles are of course universal sociological principles. But few of the latter have as yet been convincingly proposed — few, at least, with potential linguistic bearing.

The strategies of face redress are, we believe, precisely such a universal sociological principle.[84] It is this that puts face redress as a motive for derivational machinery on a par with other promising candidates for functional explanation in linguistics. Moreover, it meets the criterion set by the title of a paper by Bever (1975), 'Functional explanations require independently motivated functional theories', for, leaving aside completely the linguistic realizations of the politeness strategies, we believe there would be enough kinesic and behavioural data to independently support our strategies. (Indeed, Durkheim had already adduced the prototypes on the basis of ritual, Goffman on the basis of largely non-verbal interaction.) One advantage of our scheme is that it does predict some culture-specific (and therefore history-bound) variations in the applications of the universal principles (as discussed in section 7.00), and we would expect there to be correlations between overall levels and kinds of face redress in a culture and the special elaboration of grammatical devices for achieving that redress. Indeed, universal principles that did not predict constraints on the particular differences between local realizations would be little more than lowest common denominators.

We draw further encouragement for the thesis that face redress may be an important functional principle in grammatical organization from the independent references to it by linguists which have appeared, for example in the work of Costa (1975), Davison (1975), Green (1975a), Heringer (1972), R. Lakoff (1972, 1974a), Searle (1975), and Travis (1975). Indeed, it is from the linguist R. Lakoff's work that we draw the courage to promote the view that social functions are a prime candidate for the motivation of the great mass of superficial derivational machinery that characterizes a particular language.

Moreover, face preservation as a functional source has some great advantages over cognitive functions in certain areas, namely those where linguistic rules seem to increase rather than decrease the complexity of sentence-processing. In asking why these rules exist, one naturally turns to something like our proposed functional source. A very similar view has been argued by R. Lakoff (1974a).

8.1.2 Relations between structure and usage. We hope to have made a *prima facie* case for the plausibility of face preservation as a potential functional source for some linguistic structures. Now we wish to establish a mechanism whereby such a social pressure could in fact leave its imprint on grammatical structure.

Let us first characterize our terms. We distinguish linguistic structure from language usage, understanding by the former something which can be glossed as 'linguistic form and literal meaning' (or, as some would have it, 'grammar'), and by the latter the employment of linguistic forms and literal meanings in particular contexts for particular communicative purposes. We do not believe this distinction to be unproblematic; quite the contrary — in the last resort, as distinguishing mutually exclusive categories, it is almost certainly untenable. (This is in fact the thrust of a great deal of recent work in linguistics.) Nevertheless, the distinction usefully describes polar types of phenomena: morphophonemic rules in a language,, for example, may be pragmatically immune (unaffected by context),[85] while words and phrases like *hey, OK, thank you, howzat* simply cannot be adequately described without reference to their contexts of use. At the heart of the distinction, perhaps, lies the extent to which the description and explanation of some form can proceed by reference to the role that the form plays within the linguistic system (its 'structural' properties), versus the extent to which such description and explanation must make reference outside the grammar to the contexts in which it is employed (its 'usage' properties). But recent work indicates that the applications of many transformational rules can only be fully described in terms of *both* structural and contextual constraints (e.g. G. Lakoff 1974; Ross 1975; Scheintuch 1976). These developments suggest that the distinction between structure and usage, as based on the appropriate kinds of description and explanation, is a matter of degree.

For our descriptive purposes the distinction between structure and usage is not alone adequate. We shall posit three classes — 'forms', 'meanings' (which together make up 'structure')[86] and 'usages' — and two interesting relations between them. These are diagrammed in Fig. 8. Again, we do not suppose that any of these distinctions are unproblematic.[87] The first relationship (type I) is a relation between form and meaning that (hypothetically) predicts all the interesting properties of that form's usage. Let us call this 'structure-determined usage'. A case in point might be the use of *if you don't mind* in indirect requests (an output of the strategy of polite hedging), where the pragmatic effect is achieved by virtue of the meaning of the phrase. That is, *if you don't mind* means something like 'if you have no objection to doing A'; it thus straightforwardly, by virtue of its literal meaning, satisfies the strategic aim DON'T

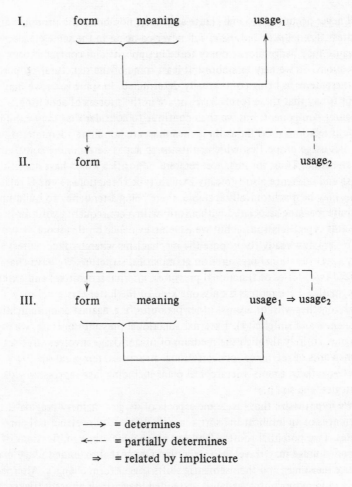

I.   form   meaning   usage₁

II.   form   usage₂

III.   form   meaning   usage₁ ⇒ usage₂

⟶ = determines
⟵--- = partially determines
⇒ = related by implicature

Fig. 8. Relations between structure and usage

ASSUME H IS WILLING TO DO ANY ACT by making the requested act conditional on H's willingness to do it.

The second interesting relationship (type II) is a direct connection between form and usage, without the mediation of meaning. Let us call this 'usage-determined structure'. Cases in point are words like *hey, oi, OK,* and some interjections, particles and honorifics in many languages. Here distributional (syntactic) facts, aspects of form, may be largely predicted by contextual constraints on usage. For example, *hey* and *oi*, being initial attention-getters, will occur only in sentence-initial position (except in self-interruptions); Tamil *-nka*, being an addressee honorific, will never occur in the same clause as *nii*, the non-honorific pronoun of address; Tzeltal *mak* and *melel* will never co-occur in the same clause because they hedge illocutionary force in opposite and contradictory directions. So we may talk about at least some of the structural properties of these items as being contextually determined. In some cases we may want to say that these forms have, or are in the process of acquiring, a meaning component, but we shall continue to consider that they exhibit type II relations in so far as these meanings are not alone adequate to predict usage properties, which continue to act as determining constraints on structure. Thus, for instance, referent honorifics which have specific sense and reference also typically exhibit type II relations. Type II relations may be diachronically instable, there being a tendency to build up a definite meaning associated with a form with a consequent evolution towards type I relations — but we have no evidence on this score.

We are now ready to propose the mechanisms whereby face redress may exert functional pressures on grammatical structure. We have characterized two classes of functional pressures, internal (cognitive) and external (pragmatic). Face redress is only one kind of the latter class, and may work together with or against other pressures (e.g. against communicative efficiency and simplicity). External functional pressures operate, we imagine, entirely through the medium of usage. Usage involves large-scale frameworks of reference: conversational structures, temporal–spatial locational facts, agents' hierarchical plans including face-redressive strategies, and so on.

We hypothesize that just some aspects of usage — namely pragmatic inferences of an implicatural sort — are likely to acquire structural correlates. Two potential routes stand out along which the ramifications of extended usage may travel into structure. One is that extended usage may change meanings, and then semantic shifts trigger form changes. Alternatively (and more controversially), extended usages may directly trigger form changes via some kind of context-sensitive syntactic or phonological rule.[88]

It is this last alternative that is of particular interest to us. Returning to patterns I and II in Fig. 8, it is our hypothesis that they are often linked together synchronically or diachronically, by implicature, into the larger configuration III which superimposes I and II. Examples of such patterns existing synchronically are almost certainly provided by indirect speech acts, where there are structural feedbacks from extended usages (Gordon and Lakoff 1971; Ross 1975). For other domains where such patterns can be found, see Heringer 1972; Horn 1972; G. Lakoff 1975. Diachronically, patterns like II may very often evolve from I via III. Many honorifics are cases in point, as we shall illustrate below. Take as an example the T/V distinction in Tamil pronouns, the development of which we have already described (see note 57). There face-redressive pressures which motivate the utilization of the strategic ambiguity of the plural soon ensure that the plural second-person pronoun becomes used as an honorific singular. We have then an extended usage beyond that predicted by the literal meaning alone. This extended usage acquires syntactic reflexes: there is no agreement of nominal predicates with polite plural pronouns (as opposed to semantically plural pronouns).[89] We have then synchronically a situation like III. Eventually a new plural is reintroduced, and the literal meaning of the original form (and the usage based on that literal meaning) atrophies, leaving a pattern like II (a once-plural 'you' used only to express deference to a singular addressee). From this a new literal meaning can in time emerge (namely, a singular honorific 'you'). Under the same pressures the other newly introduced plural comes to be used honorifically, and a situation like III re-emerges, with the extended politeness usage acquiring distinguishing agreement rules of its own. And this is how the system is today.

Our proposal, then, is this. External functional pressures are always mediated through usage. Extended patterns of usage feed back into structural properties either through changes in meaning or directly through formal reflexes of extended usages. In either case implicatures play a crucial role in the mechanism (either through causing semantic shift or through triggering form reflexes), and thus in language change. At least one of the basic mechanisms whereby functional pressures exerted by face-preserving strategies are imported into language structure is in the transition from a pattern like I, through III, to II,[90] and perhaps full circle back to I.

On this view, the relationship between structure and usage is a fluid one, and this fluidity is reflected in the state of a language at any one point in time, where various degrees of structural incorporation of extended usages and varying extents of pragmatic conditions on rule applications may be found. Implicature plays a key role in this scheme, and if (as we believe) implicature can only be given proper treatment within a broader theory of communication, then a theory of language can never be entirely separated from such a broader theory.

If this theory is correct, we would expect at least the following to be the case:

(i)   Configurations like II would preserve traces of their origin in rational exploitations of configurations like I that have passed through a configuration like III.
(ii)   Configurations like III should be discernible.

(iii) At any one point in time one would expect to find cases illustrating various degrees of transition from I to II via III.

(iv) These processes should each be correlated with one or more of our face-preserving strategies, wherever that is claimed as the functional source.

We now review some examples from our inventory of the linguistic realizations of face-redressive strategies and attempt to show that these expectations are (at least in part) fulfilled. It should be clear that such linguistic patterns will vary in the extent to which face redress may reasonably be supposed to be a major functional source. For instance, there are many possible systemic and cognitive functions for the passive, and face redress is here only (at most) a complementary source. We will make arguments for social motivations behind both kinds of linguistic machinery, but clearly the arguments must be weaker where persuasive alternative functionalist arguments exist.

8.1.3 Examples. In the following sections we organize the material by functional category (ironies, indirect speech acts, hedges, and so on). We try very roughly to order these along a dimension that runs from almost pure cases of type I (structure-determined usage), via complex configurations like III where extended usages have acquired some grammatical correlates, to pure cases of type II (usage-determined structure). But since the categories are functional, we find within some of them linguistic means of realizing that particular function which themselves range from type I to type III. If our illustrations were more thoroughly cross-linguistic this would be even more evident. And of course we try to show in each case that politeness motives are one important reason why linguistic facts are exactly the way they are. In short, we believe that the facts show that our expectations (i)–(iv) obtain.

8.1.3.1 Ironic composition and understatement. Cutler (1974:118) maintains that 'To be uttered ironically . . . a sentence must conform to the following restriction: it must, in the context in which it is produced, express on its literal reading a desirable state of affairs; the literal reading must be approbatory in tone. Thus its ironical meaning must, obviously, express the converse – disapprobation.'[91] Similarly, Grice (1967, ch.3:19) observed: 'I cannot say something ironically unless what I say is intended to reflect a hostile or derogatory judgment or a feeling such as indignation or contempt.' And Perret (1976:F2) notes that the necessary condition on a successful irony is that it should express 'a value judgement that is more positive than the circumstances deserve'.

In short, authors agree that irony has (to put it in our terms) an essential FTA content: it must express, broadly construed, a criticism. But they have failed to ask *why* this is the case. Our answer of course is that irony is an output of an off-record strategy that attends to face threat. Alternatively, in cases where the irony is disambiguated in form, it may be the output of an on-record strategy, but in all cases irony is organized around the potential face threat posed by the critical content (including evasion of unambiguous responsibility for it).

Those cases where irony is disambiguated provide examples where what is essentially a pattern of usage begins to pick up structural correlates. For instance, in some regional dialects of English ironies can apparently occur marked with heavy nasalization (G. and R. Lakoff, personal comm.). In addition the phrase *I don't think*, in an ironic statement like

(1)   John's a genius, I don't think.

can serve, partially as a bearer for prosodic clues, as a disambiguator (Cutler 1974:117). Even clearer examples of structural correlates of irony are provided by certain contradictory clusters of particles in Tzeltal:

(2)   mak yuʔ wan hp'eh naš snaik k'oel škal ¢'in č'i.
      So *perhaps* it's that *maybe* there's only one house down there, *I say, to be sure.* (c.i. Of course there are plenty of houses down there!)

Here it is the contradictory implications of 'perhaps', 'maybe', contrasting with the emphatic 'I say' and 'to be sure', that forces the ironic reading.

Understatement is another class of usages that are crucially organized around face threats. Observe the following curious facts. One can make good ironic statements in a language by going to the extreme polar opposite of what one means, as in the following:

(3)   John's a genius. (c.i. John's a fool)
      (rather than saying (e.g.) 'John's above average in intelligence.')

(4)   This hamburger is really sizzling hot. (c.i. It's stone cold)
      (rather than 'This hamburger is warm.')

Similarly, with understatement:

(5)   This hamburger is nót sizzling hot. (c.i. It's stone cold)
      (rather than 'This hamburger is not warm.')

Now note the following examples (read without heavy stress):

(6)   John's not a friend.

could easily be used as understatement to implicate that John's an enemy, but:

(7)   John's not an enemy.

cannot easily be used to implicate that John's a friend. It means, rather,
that he's neither friend nor enemy. Compare:

(8)   Bill's not a moral man. (could implicate Bill's immoral)
(9)   Bill's not an immoral man. (couldn't implicate Bill's a moral – i.e.
       virtuous – man)

and

(10) These doings are not good. (c.i. They are evil)
(11) These doings are not evil. (couldn't c.i. They are good)

   What is happening in these examples can be shown diagrammatically
(where the arrows point to the implicated meaning):

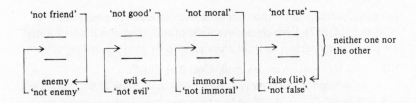

That is, with any of these value continuums, if one negates the top
members, one can implicate the bottom members of the pairs, but if one
negates the bottom members one only implicates the middle range of the
scale. There is no intrinsic reason why the scales should be this way up, so
where does the asymmetry come from?

   Our explanation is that in implicating that someone is an enemy, or is
evil or immoral, or has told a lie, one is performing an FTA, namely criticizing. In saying that someone is *not* an enemy, immoral, evil, etc., one is
not criticizing and not performing an FTA. There is a good social motive
(avoiding responsibility, etc.) for saying much less than you mean when
criticizing; this being mutual knowledge, the utterance 'John's not a
friend' can easily be used to implicate that he's an enemy, whereas if you
wanted to say that John is a friend, there would be no good motive for
not saying it directly. Therefore, if you say that he's not an enemy, he's
probably not a friend.[92]

   Apparent exceptions in fact support our argument. In just those circumstances where the fact that John is my friend could endanger my or your
face (e.g., John has just been arrested as a Commie spy), if I say 'John is
not an enemy of mine' I could implicate that he *is* a friend. So also in the

264

case of a possibly loaded FTA compliment: 'She's not bad' could implicate that she's very good.

We do not see any immediate structural correlates of these understatements. But there are some words like *exactly*, and some phrases like *that's not my idea of*, that can help to force the implicatures:

(12) John's not exactly a moral man. (can implicate immoral)
John's not exactly an immoral man. (not normally used to implicate very moral)

(13) That's not my idea of $\left\{\begin{array}{l}\text{bliss.}\\\text{heaven.}\\\text{happiness.}\end{array}\right\}$ $\left(\text{c.i. That's my idea of }\left\{\begin{array}{l}\text{hell}\\\text{misery}\end{array}\right\}\right)$

That's not my idea of hell. (is not standardly used to implicate That's my idea of heaven)

(14) John's no friend of mine. (c.i. John's an enemy)
John's no enemy of mine. (does not implicate John's my best friend)

One possible structural correlate is the absence of any single lexicalization for 'neither-friend-nor-enemy', or 'neither-good-nor-evil'. For as Horn has demonstrated (1972), what is standardly implicated is rarely lexicalized; there is simply no need for the lexical item.

In sum, we suggest that the reason ironies and understatements are associated with the critical content that they empirically have is that the expression of such content tends to be a serious FTA, calling for an off-record strategy. Such a Gricean 'flout' of conversational maxims as is involved in irony provides a realization *par excellence* of such an off-record strategy. We thus have here an area where face considerations determine the extended usages of a pattern of structure–usage relations like type I. Slowly this pattern I acquires feedback into form from these extended usages, evolving into a pattern like III (as in the Tzeltal example (2) above). But in the English examples this evolution has not fully occurred.

8.1.3.2 Lexical usage. Now let us consider a word like *quite*. Its standard dictionary entry has the meaning 'completely', 'wholly', 'entirely', with an etymological derivation from *quit*, 'to be free, clear, absolved' (*Concise Oxford Dictionary*), as in 'The tank is *quite* full, it won't hold any more.' But it seems to have a sense opposite to this one, namely 'somewhat', 'not to the fullest degree', as in:

(15) It was *quite* a good meal, but not worth a pound.
(16) The south face is *quite* easy, as long as you have vanadium pitons.

(17) New York City is *quite* a nice place to live, considering.
(18) He's *quite* nice, really, despite his millions.

Quite then seems to have both the meaning 'very' and the meaning 'not very'. Since no other etymological source is suggested for the word, we must assume that both derive from the one source. Why?

Our first observation is that, assuming that there is no intonational disambiguation, the sense that *quite* has in one particular case is not resolved purely by the linguistic context. For instance, the *but* clause in (15) presupposes a contrast between the one conjunct and the other (R. Lakoff 1971a), yet the negative evaluation in the *but* clause does not force the 'very' (absolutely positive) reading of the first conjunct. In fact, it tends to force the other reading.

We fall back then on conversational context, and we note that, as Sacks discovered (1973), there is an observable preference for agreement in conversation. Consequently one gets exchanges like those reported above (p. 119), where standardly one agrees first, then disagrees. Similarly, one minimizes criticisms by making positive evaluations first, and then negative ones afterwards:

(19) John's a good fellow, but frankly, the team will do as well without him.

Now, we speculate that markers of positive (or at least extreme) evaluation like *quite* can come, by association with the following disvaluations, to acquire standard implicatures that invert their original sense. Eventually these implicatures may become distinct senses of their own. If this or some other account in terms of implicature generated by a preference for prior agreement is invalid, it is difficult to see how else one could account for the way, for instance, the word *sure* (or the phrase *for sure*) comes to have a concessive meaning, implicating reservations:

(20) Sure, John's not a bad guy (but . . .)

And the Tamil particle -*taan* shows a similar pattern. Literally it means 'only', 'nothing else but', as in:

(21) nii enna connaalum, nii cencatu tappu*taan*.
     Whatever you say, what you did was *quite* wrong. (thoroughly)

But like English *quite*, it can be used to implicate 'somewhat':

(22) nallaa*taan* iruntatu.
     It was *quite* good (but I have reservations).
(23) avaan nallavan*taan*.
     He's *quite* a good guy (but . . .)

266

Another example is found in the word *just*, which has a literal meaning of 'exactly', but can also mean 'barely':

(24) That's just amazing. (very)
(25) This is just a little dirty. (not very)
(26) I've just come by to say hello. (simply, merely)

The Tzeltal particle *niš* has a precisely similar ambiguity between its use as 'exactly' and its use as 'simply', 'merely', 'no more than'.

The point is that when you have such shifts of sense by standardized implicature, what often lies behind them is meaning (in Grice's sense — intending) more than you say, and one crucial motive for doing that is minimization of face threats. So here are cases of structure–usage relations of pattern I acquiring standard but extended usages of a particular sort (evolving towards pattern III) under the pressure of face-attending strategies.

8.1.3.3 Phonology and prosody. Corum (1975b) describes a well-defined phonological process of palatalization in Basque, the application of which, she claims, is 'completely dependent on the context' (p. 97). 'When speaking to a good friend, a child, or anyone with whom you share a certain amount of solidarity, Basques will palatalize several consonants which are not otherwise palatalized' (*ibid.*:96). In our terms, this looks like a phonological rule which the language provides specifically for positive-politeness usage. Curiously, there seems to be a similar palatalization rule in Japanese, which applies in almost identical intimate contexts only (Sansom 1928:305; O'Neill 1966:134). The phonological processes involved in fast-spoken (allegro) English, as described by Zwicky (1972), may perhaps have close ties to casual, positive-politeness contexts in a similar way.

Similarly, as mentioned above, Tzeltal-speakers use creaky voice to express commiseration and complaint, and to invite commiseration; this too is a phonetic feature that is used only in positive-politeness situations. In a more ritualized and precisely describable way, Tzeltal-speakers use sustained falsetto as a negative-politeness honorific feature; it is enjoined in greeting formulae, and may spread over an entire formal interaction, or more often drop to be reused as an FTA is broached.

In Tamil, low-caste (Harijan) speakers addressing high-caste powerful persons, in the rural area studied, use a customary thin high-pitched voice with a trailing-off of speech volume at the end of utterances. This signifies deference, but its usage is confined not to specifiable relationships so much as to heavy-FTA circumstances. Thus a daughter may use it to her father during a request; it is not restricted to Harijans' speech to high-caste individuals. Of course a tremendous caste/power differential ensures heavy FTA assessments from a low-status speaker to a high-status addressee.

Now our point here is not simply that there are correlations of prosodic or phonological features with social contexts, but rather that there are rational reasons why these particular features are used in these particular circumstances. For instance creaky voice, having as a natural source low speech energy, can implicate calmness and assurance and thence comfort and commiseration, attitudes not suitably expressed in negative-politeness circumstances. On the other hand, high pitch has natural associations with the voice quality of children: for an adult then to use such a feature to another adult may implicate self-humbling and thus deference (Brown and Levinson 1974). We predict therefore that sustained high pitch (maintained over a number of utterances) will be a feature of negative-politeness usage, and creaky voice a feature of positive-politeness usage, and that a reversal of these associations will not occur in any culture.

8.1.3.4 Indirect speech acts.

We have already described politeness motives that lie behind the use of indirect speech acts. We should perhaps point out that some linguists trying to describe the semantics or pragmatics of indirect speech acts have noticed a fundamental politeness element (see for example Green 1975a; Heringer 1972; R. Lakoff 1974a), as has Searle (1975:74).[93]

But these writers appear to have missed the extremely systematic way in which the rational strategies of face redress, like pessimism and hedging, are able to predict the internal structure of polite indirect requests, for example, with their possibility operators, subjunctives and negative questions (see above, p. 135). No other explanatory schema that we know of predicts these usages.

There is in the literature an interesting confusion of politeness and acceptability (or even grammaticality). Thus Gordon and Lakoff (1971) write rules ('conversational postulates') to exclude 'You can (please) pass the salt.' But this of course could function as a request: it is simply an unlikely one because the normal motive for using an indirect form is to give the speaker an 'out' and/or to suspend some assumption (typically a felicity condition) that presumes cooperation with the request. But 'You can please pass the salt' does not suspend the felicity condition, it asserts it. Its apparent ungrammaticality is simply a reflection of its apparent uselessness. We would argue that indirect speech acts are just a special case of the general problem of indirect uses of language, essentially by implicature, and that as in those other cases, decoding the communicative intent relies on the mutual availability of a reasonable and particular motive for being indirect. Consequently, an indirect request that is impolite is less likely to be understood as a request at all. Questions of relative politeness as discussed above are thus likely to enter into the delimitation of any well-bounded class of indirect speech acts.

Now, since classes of indirect speech acts have syntactic correlates, all this becomes of importance to grammar. We will not review these syntactic reflexes here, but we should mention that they do not only involve processes like sentence-internal *please* insertion in English (Gordon and Lakoff 1971; Sadock 1974), or its equivalent, *koncam* insertion in Tamil (see above, pp. 139–40). In addition, it has been shown for English that sentence adverbs and reason adverbials (Davison 1973, 1975), certain *if* clauses (Heringer 1972), negative polarity items (Sadock 1974), and disjunctions with other speech acts (Sadock 1974; G. Lakoff 1974) have distributional constraints based not on 'surface' illocutionary force but on the indirect illocutionary force. Further, the syntactic rule of 'slifting' makes essential reference to the unified class of direct *and* indirect requests as a trigger for preposing embedded questions in English (Ross 1975). Sag and Liberman (1975) have demonstrated intonational correlates of indirect speech acts, which can disambiguate their conveyed meanings. On some analyses these linguistic reflexes are evidence of the incorporation of these forms into English structure as 'idioms' (Sadock 1974), but the more convincing analysis seems to be that extended *usage* can acquire direct syntactic correlates. In any case, within the class of indirect speech acts we can find evidence of degrees of structural incorporation, from usages without syntactic reflexes, to those with some (e.g. internal *koncam* insertion in Tamil), to those with many, and finally to those (like 'How about another whisky?' as an indirect suggestion) that seem to have acquired idiom status. Indirect speech acts are an area, then, where we can find the whole array of relations between form, meaning, and usage (from pattern I, through III, to II), and the linking process is once again the implicature and its acquisition of structural correlates.

A slightly different point that we may make here is that these acquired structural correlates may themselves have a systematic relation to face-redressive techniques – a systematic relation that should not be ignored by a grammar seeking significant generalizations. For instance, there are certain contractions in English, as illustrated by the following pairs:

(27) (a) Do you mind if I smoke?
     (b) Mind if I smoke?
(28) (a) Are you going to give me a ride?
     (b) Gonna give me a ride?
(29) (a) I have to go now.
     (b) Hafta go now.

(30) (a) You ought to pay your bills.
     (b) Oughta pay your bills.
(31) (a) Why don't you cut your hair?
     (b) Whyncha cut your hair?

Here the (a) sentences are contracted to (b) forms only under certain interpretations and assumptions. Not only must we refer to conveyed meanings — as in (27), where (a) will contract only if it is an indirect request for permission — we must also refer to FTA concepts if we are to give descriptions which are not simply *ad hoc* of the *classes* of conveyed meanings which trigger the transformations from (a) to (b) forms in (27)–(31). For instance, take:

(32) Oughta go get the phone.
(33) Oughta do your homework.
(34) Oughta love your parents.

and compare the following:

(35) *Oughta pay your bills on time and you do.
(36) You ought to pay your bills on time and you do.

(36) is acceptable because (30a) is contextually 'ambiguous' between a literal statement and a conveyed piece of advice. With the contraction *oughta*, (30b) can only be a speech act of advising, so since you can't advise somebody to do something which you are telling them they've already done, (35) is odd. But (32) could be a piece of advice or an excuse, (33) a warning or suggestion, and (34) could be a criticism; hence the contraction is allowed.

What we suggest is this: *you ought to* can contract to *oughta* just when the utterance is being used to perform an FTA. Moreover, it can contract appropriately only if the FTA is being done with positive politeness. This last statement holds for all the (b) sentences in examples (27)–(31).

It seems to be the case in English that the use of conventional indirectness (including indirect speech acts) extends beyond its negative-politeness limits and has positive-politeness usages too. Since its rational motivation lies in redress to negative face, this should be difficult to explain, because positive and negative politeness are, to a large extent at any rate, mutually exclusive strategies. However, it appears that as soon as conventional indirectnesses pass into positive-politeness strategic use, they become in general syntactically contracted.

Since contraction and ellipsis serve positive-politeness ends, being markers of in-group membership and casual informality, this effectively

270

stamps conventional indirectnesses (especially indirect speech acts) with a positive-politeness visa and reissues them for a different circulation.

Consider the following contrasts:

Negatively polite conventional indirectness	Positively polite contracted form
I want to	I wanna
Do you want to	Wanna
Do you need a	Needa
Do you mind if I	Mind if I
Why don't you	Wyncha
How do you feel about	How about

The boundary is also marked in other ways, especially by lexical substitutions for basic conversational phrases; for example:

Negative politeness	Positive politeness
yes	yup, uh-huh
no	nope (but this may convey obstinacy)
all right	sure

These forms in fact have slightly different distributions (see for instance James 1972, 1973).

8.1.3.5 Hedges. Hedges on Gricean Maxims and hedges on illocutionary force (the latter just a special case of the former, in our analysis) are, as we have seen, an extremely important resource for the realization of politeness strategies. This follows from the core of our thesis, that face redress is one of the basic motives for departing from the maximally efficient talk that the Maxims define.

Now, hedging can be achieved by prosodics, particles, lexical items, parentheticals, full adverbial clauses, and other means, such as embedding as complements of expressions like *I guess that, I suppose that.* Even syntactic rules like 'Neg Raising' may be involved (Scheintuch 1976). Some of these hedges involve basically predictable usages of structural phenomena; for example, a clause like 'Although I do not know this for certain' suspends a felicity condition on assertions, and achieves what it achieves by virtue of what it literally means. Hence no special pragmatic account is required, its function being predicted by its semantics which in turn is constructed out of the meanings of its parts. In short we have an instance of a configuration like type I. At the other end of the continuum are particles without any immediately specifiable literal meaning that native speakers or dictionary-makers can formulate; a syntactic–semantic description will not predict their usage, and we have to resort rather to a direct pragmatic analysis on which to base an account of syntactic distribution. We are talking here, then, rather of the structural properties of usage phenomena, i.e. a pattern like II. In between the polar types of such clauses and such particles, there are words and phrases which have literal meanings rather removed from their hedge usages but in which the gap may be, or may have been, bridged by the extended significances provided by implicature (i.e. a configuration like III). Indeed, even particles sometimes still retain possible traces of their origins in implicature. Let us take some examples of each type in the order mentioned.

Heringer (1972:55) describes a set of illocutionary-force hedges that consist of the expression of a felicity condition in an *if* clause; for example:

(36)   Give me a hand, if you can.

One would like to say that simply by virtue of the meaning of the *if* clause, it functions pragmatically as a hedge on the force of the speech act.[94] The combination of these *if* clauses with a direct or indirect request is one of the standard ways of politely requesting in Tamil, as we have seen.

Another level of phenomena is represented by *you know* and *I mean*, in sentences like:

(37)   I was coming out of the door, you know, when I mean I saw him standing there, waiting.

Although these parentheticals are clearly derived from the literal senses of *you know* and *I mean*, they behave syntactically, semantically, and pragmatically in a very different way (Corum 1975a; Goldberg 1982). They have taken on a life of their own, and their functions would be related directly to their syntactic properties. Yet one can see that the role they now play was or is related to their literal meanings, almost certainly by implicature (along the lines of pattern III). FTA sources for such implicatures are clearer in cases of hedges like *sort of*, as in:

(38)   I sort of feel I must tell you this.
(39)   I sort of hate to say this, but . . .
(40)   I really sort of think . . .

where the *sort of* serves notice of reluctance to impinge, or, in other cases, indicates a cooperative avoidance of possible disagreement. The fact that *really sort of think* is no contradiction is an indication of the degree to which this almost particle-like phrase has lost its literal meaning. These, then, are phrases which have distributions predictable essentially on pragmatic rather than semantic grounds, but which are transparently related to literal meanings that already have a hedging function.[95]

Let us now turn to hedges whose origins in implicature are more remote. We have noted no less than eighteen Tzeltal particles which operate as hedges on illocutionary force. Some have more or less well-defined meanings; *niš*, for example, can generally be glossed as 'just'. But others are more problematic: *me, kati, mak*; the meanings or significances of these are determined by usage. Even here we can make guesses at etymological sources; thus *me* is identical to the conditional morpheme, so it may be a remnant of the hedging 'if' clauses that operate in English and Tamil (discussed above). The particle *mak* might possibly be derived from *maʔyuk*, literally 'there is not any, as it were'; at least the dubitative sense of the latter is consonant with that of *mak*. But we have no evidence on this score. Similarly the Tamil particles *-ee* and *-oo* may be related to identical morphemes in the pronominal and quantifier paradigm respectively. But whatever their etymological origin, they are now fundamentally pragmatic elements, with perhaps primary FTA-redressive origins, which have direct structural implications (examples of pattern II).

We suspect that such particles are in fact to be found in the majority of the world's languages. And they are the sort of element that is used profusely in spoken utterances. Nevertheless, they are just the kind of thing that tends to escape the net of the grammarian and the lexicographer. Just recently a few studies have appeared investigating such particles in particular languages: Uyeno 1971 on Japanese particles; F. Karttunen 1975a and 1975b on Finnish clitics; Corum 1975b on Basque particles; and Van Valen 1975 on German *doch*.

8.1.3.6 Impersonalization mechanisms. Two important means of impersonalizing are the passive and impersonal models. We deal with these in turn.

The passive. R. Lakoff notes (1971b:149) that 'the principal question to be faced by anyone who wants to present a viable "passive" underlying structure and "passive" transformation is this: why passivize a sentence at all?' She suggests (*ibid.*:159) that one function of the rule might be 'an especially emphatic marking of the topicalization', but notes that this suggestion 'is apparently contradicted by the agentless passive, perhaps the most frequent form of the *be*-passive'. The question is then left unanswered in her paper.

Our suggestion is this. Impersonalization serves basic politeness ends (see above, pp. 190ff) and the passive exists (at least partially) to serve these ends. What evidence could we have? For a start, there are at least three major mechanisms involved in English and other passives: the promotion of an underlying object (to subject position); the demotion of an underlying subject; and, in addition, passive-marking and agreement rules. Our functional hypothesis claims that the basic motive is subject demotion, and possible deletion, and *not* object promotion. Thus we would hypothesize:

> Where a language has a passive or circumstantial voice, the agent may (with possible lexical exceptions) always be deleted.

In other words, the basic motive is to demote the subject to a superficial case locus where it may be deleted. Postal–Perlmutter relational grammar apparently makes exactly the contrary claim (E. L. Keenan 1975:346): the basic operation is object promotion, and this triggers subject demotion. However, recent work by E. L. Keenan (1975) and Comrie (1977) within the same theory shows that this is not the case. First, there are many languages where subject demotion without object promotion produces the 'impersonal passive' (Spanish, Latin, German, Dutch, Polish, Welsh, and Finnish are cited by Comrie; Turkish and 'Slavic' by E. L. Keenan), where the verb cannot agree with a non-existent (superficial) subject and takes the impersonal or 'unmarked' third-person morphemes (Comrie, 1977:11). Secondly, specific facts in a variety of languages strongly support the primacy of subject demotion (E. L. Keenan 1975:346-9). Further, Comrie (*ibid.*:15) notes that Latvian has obligatory deletion of the demoted subject (to this, E. L. Keenan (*ibid.*:340-1) adds Hungarian, classical Arabic, Machiguenga, Maninka). This prompts Comrie to claim that the basic motive that underlies both personal and impersonal passives can be glossed as 'subject removal'. And Costa argues convincingly (1975) that both the so-called passive and the impersonal *si* constructions in Italian are actually passives with demoted and deleted generic human agents. Noting that one primary function is the reduction of the prominence of the agent, she argues that '*si* constructions are exploited pragmatically as a means of shifting responsibility off a subject. This pragmatic use is typically a reflection of politeness and formality conventions which require that in potentially embarrassing situations speakers should avoid pinning down who is responsible for what action' (*ibid.*:120). She observes that just as English statements like 'One just doesn't do things like that' can implicate the deontic modality and the second-person pronoun of 'You must not do things like that', so similarly *si* constructions can be used as polite commands or implicated imperatives (*ibid.*:119-21). In addition, they can be used to construct passive performatives parallel to the English:

(41) It is hereby declared that . . .

A somewhat similar phenomenon occurs in Tamil, where:

(42) enna ceyratu?
What is its doing?

is understood as the impersonal passive 'what is to be done?' Thus, as mentioned above (p. 209), the use of the verbal noun with an implied deleted agent (implicating 'you') and implicated deontic modality can be used to make polite commands. For example:

(43) ate ceyratu.
(Someone's) doing it.

can be used to mean 'you do it'. As this is a form that is rapidly spreading due to its neutrality on the honorific/dishonorific dimensions (Annamalai and Ramanujan, n.d.), one may conjecture that it will develop into a fully grammaticalized impersonal passive. Here then is the special usage of a structural resource, on its way to becoming incorporated into the grammar (presumably via a structure–usage relationship pattern like III), with clear politeness pressures as a source. This suggests to us that all passives may have evolved from extended usages of other constructions acquiring structural correlates. If so, passives would be cases of a full circle of evolution through our types of structure–usage relations, back to type I, with face redress as a functional source.

Impersonal modals. Noticing that many languages express modal notions with dative agents which are usually deleted (as discussed above, pp. 191–4), we hypothesize:

> If a language has a substantial set of verbs which take oblique-case agents, this set will include verbs of obligation.

This hypothesis is based on the theory that impersonalization is a redressive device, and that statements of obligation are especially threatening FTAs. We would further guess:

> If a language has verbs of obligation taking oblique-case agents, the agent will be deletable.

Another device we would expect is this:

> Where a verb of obligation takes an agent in a subject case, that

agent may often be deletable and person and number not be marked in the verb.

If these hypotheses are substantiated (and we have no counter-evidence), a *prima facie* case for face redress as a functional source can be made. In that case, the same sort of evolutionary cycle that may lie behind passives would be a reasonable origin for impersonal verbs.

8.1.3.7 Honorifics. As stated above (in section 5.4), by 'honorifics' in an extended sense we understand direct grammatical encodings of relative social status between participants, or between participants and persons or things referred to in the communicative event. That is, these are prime examples of a direct relationship between form and usage – our pattern II. It may well be that such a relationship is mediated by some sort of social valuation or 'social semantics',[96] but we suppose this to be a different kind of thing from a standard semantic interpretation. Honorifics may also have the specific sense and reference of their non-honorific alternates – but these are by definition not their defining or interesting properties, which are relations of type II.

Our thesis here is again that honorifics typically derive from a type I pattern via a type III pattern, and thence evolve the characteristic pattern II. If this is so, then we would expect honorifics to reveal traces of their rational origin as extended usages, implicatures, or morphemes with other semantic content.

We mentioned in section 5.4 that there are a number of axes on which honorific systems are built, but the two most relevant systems here are referent honorifics and addressee honorifics. The rational sources (in face-redressive strategies) for referent honorifics are often quite transparent, but addressee honorifics are apparently more arbitrary.

Now it seems that addressee honorifics (that is, direct encodings of the speaker–addressee relationship, independent of the referential content of the utterance) are empirically much rarer than referent honorifics. The known cases (of some elaboration, at any rate) come predominantly from Southeast Asia (Geertz 1960; Martin 1964; Stevens 1965). Moreover, despite the validity of the analytical distinction between addressee and referent honorifics, on close examination it appears that there is an overlap between the two honorific systems: some honorific morphemes of languages having both systems tend to be used to encode both the speaker–addressee relation and the speaker–referent relation.[97] This prompts us to suggest that there are interesting diachronic relationships between referent and addressee honorifics; specifically, that referent honorifics are basic and – at least as encoded in address forms – universal, and that addressee honorifics are derived from these by (at least in part) the same sort of process that derives pattern II from I via III. This happens, we suggest, in the following way.

As we noted above, referent honorifics can be used to give respect to the addressee indirectly, by giving respect to the addressee's close associates or belongings. These are, if one likes, inferentially derived addressee honorifics, and they may stabilize in the way that some Japanese referent honorifics have (see p. 181 above) so that they may only be used in reference to the addressee's associates or belongings. A pattern analogous to III then emerges, where the original referent honorifics (organized in a pattern analogous to I) have acquired extended usages as addressee honorifics, and these extended usages acquire syntactic reflexes of their own.

We suggest, then, that via the recurrent use of referent honorifics in situations where the addressee–referent relation is a close one (i.e., the respected persons or things belong to H's social orbit) they may evolve into direct addressee honorifics. A simple case is provided by the single addressee honorific in Tamil, the particle *-nka* (discussed above, p. 180). The basic plural suffix in Tamil is underlying *-kaL*, colloquial *-ka*, and when preceded by a nasal consonant is realized as *-nka* (where /k/ is voiced). In the pronominal paradigm and its verbal agreements, the plurals are all marked by *-nka*, as there are preceding nasal segments. Now, as described above in detail, plural pronouns are used of singular referents to convey respect for that referent. It seems likely that the habitual use of this referent honorific *-nka* led to its acquiring an independent life of its own as a *direct* addressee honorific. It now occurs as a syntactically liberated particle that can follow virtually any and every constituent in a sentence, excepting modifiers, and gives respect to the addressee regardless of what is referred to in the sentence. Similar processes probably lie behind the overlap between addressee and referent honorifics observable in Japanese and Korean, where some morphemes participate in both systems.

The Japanese honorific morpheme *mas* provides a possible case of a further kind of transition from a signal of the speaker–addressee relation to the speaker–setting relation, for now it is a marker of formal speech independent of S and H status, as well as a relative-status marker (Uyeno 1971:14–15; Makino 1970:186). Similarly, Garvin and Riesenberg (1952:203) report a case of overlap between addressee and bystander honorifics in the use of Ponapean royal honorifics. It seems that as soon as a form acquires a stabilized usage, exploitations of that usage to convey extended significances become feasible, as Grice (1967) has predicted. In this way a referent honorific might conceivably be the source of an addressee honorific, and that in turn the source of a setting honorific.

We must now substantiate our claim that honorifics often have reconstructable rational sources as realizations of face-preserving strategies. This is particularly clear in referent honorific systems, on which we shall now concentrate. We have already argued for the rational sources underlying the use of the deferential plural in pronouns. If this were not the case it would be difficult to explain the world-wide usage of plural pronouns for respect.[98] We hypothesize that every honorific system bears traces of its strategic origin. That is, we expect that, like 'styles', honorific 'levels' will not be constructed from an arbitrary selection of contentless features but will meet or will in the past have met the conditions for successful face-redressive action that we have surveyed. General discussions of addressee honorifics point out that they are the marked forms compared to the basic language, that they are composed of longer, more elaborate alternates, and are endowed with 'a kind of stately pomp' (Geertz 1960:173; see also Martin 1964). Very similar remarks hold for the 'high' language in diglossic situations (Ferguson 1964:434).

Let us now turn to the peculiarly elaborate Japanese case[99] and see whether such traces of strategic origin are visible. Uyeno (1971:16) lists six colloquial alternates for the pronoun 'I', and five for 'you', in decreasing order of politeness. Looking into the etymology of these forms, we find that all of them are derived from circumlocutions which are exactly parallel to those now used productively in Madagascar as outputs of facepreserving strategies (E. O. Keenan 1974a, 1976). For instance, the Japanese pronoun *watakusi* ('I', most formal) meant 'slave' or 'servant', *anata* ('you', most formal) meant 'that side'; *kimi* ('you', medium formal) meant 'king', and so on (Sansom 1928:78–80,305–6), although these original meanings have long since been eclipsed by their purely pronominal function. Many other such circumlocutions have been the source of relatively stabilized pronominal systems for Japanese at various historical dates.

Turning to referent honorifics encoded in verbal inflections, we find rational sources for these as well. Take for instance the 'respectful' suffix for verbs (*-areru*), and the 'elegant' form of the copula (*de irassharu*) in Miller's array of honorifics (1967:271). The first of these, *-areru*, derives from the passive (*ibid.*:287). The polite usage of the passive (to obtain the distancing effect noted in section 5.4) may be the direct source of this usage, which had already stabilized by A D 1100, or alternatively, the extended 'possibility' sense of the passive may have been involved (Sansom 1928:160–3). The second form, *de irassharu*, is similarly derived from a passivized copula with an additional well-attested polite use of the causative (*ibid.*:172,308). The polite causative is also the source of *masu* (lit.: 'cause to be', 'honourably dwell'; *ibid.*:219,308), now a standard 'formal' suffix that encodes both the speaker–addressee and the speaker–setting relations (Uyeno 1971:14–15). Another copula (now confined to literary style), *haberu*, is self-humbling, and derives naturally enough from *han* ('to crawl') and *iru* ('to be') (Sansom 1928:214). Of course such etymological origins are quite irrelevant to the modern speaker of Japanese; they are simply honorific forms that have to be learned. Our point is that they are not arbitrary forms: they originate as productive outputs of face-preserving strategies which then become stabilized and change their meaning.

Verbs that are derived thus from polite passive or other sources come to function as auxiliaries which now merely add respect. Thus *zonji soru* (lit.: 'I am in attendance to think') is simply a formal equivalent of *zonzu* ('I think'; *ibid.*: 309–10); and *hairi kudasare* (lit.: 'hand down/bestow an entering') is just a polite version of *hairu* ('enter'). Similarly, the Japanese honorific verbs for giving and receiving may be used as auxiliaries to elevate the tone of a verb (Kuno 1973:ch.9).

It should be clear that the syntax and semantics of Japanese are profoundly affected by this impingement of social forces on the pronominal and verbal system. For instance, the free deletion of subjects and the non-existence of proper possessive pronouns can be attributed to the pragmatic encoding of person in the kind of honorific chosen (Sansom 1928:306). And in other respects the difficulties posed for a non-sociologically sensitive grammatical description of Japanese seem insuperable (see Kuno 1973:ch.9; Yamanashi 1974). The formidable challenge the system poses to the non-native speaker, who requires detailed cultural knowledge to speak with even a comprehensible level of appropriateness, may be gauged from the elaborate programmed text in O'Neill 1966.

Perhaps limiting cases to our thesis of rational strategic origin are provided by the 'mother-in-law' languages of Australia, where entire vocabularies have two distinct realizations, one for use when taboo relatives such as mothers-in-law are within hearing and the other for when they are not. But even here, as Dixon points out (1972:292–3), the much lesser degree of specification in the 'taboo' language, the higher level of generality in which things are discussed, is in keeping with its 'avoidance' function.

In any case, we hope to have made here a case for the view that honorifics, which are perhaps the most obvious and pervasive intrusion of social factors into grammar, are not in origin arbitrary markers of social status, but rather are – at least in many cases – frozen outputs of face-oriented strategies. And the freezing process involves a transition from a pattern like I, via III, to II.

In conclusion, we have argued in this section (8.1) that attention to face is an important functional pressure on language, and that in both the synchronic and diachronic patterns observable one can identify a process whereby pressures on usage acquire structural implications. But in addition to the examples raised here, in assessing the importance of this functional pressure we should point to the very remarkable parallels that one can find in language after language in very many of the linguistic realizations of our strategic outputs: in all languages that we know of we find hedges on illocutionary force and on Grice's Maxims, indirect speech acts, metaphor, irony, and so on, in many cases with precisely parallel constructions. Even where these linguistic devices perform clear conceptual operations on propositional or illocutionary content, without recourse to communicational functions we have no explanation of why *these* operations are required and independently developed. This rich and specific parallelism in the functional resources of languages suggests that there must indeed be some underlying powerful universal pressures of an interactional sort lying behind the development of those resources.

8.2 Implications for sociolinguistics

It is in action and interaction that we believe the most profound inter-relations between language and society are to be found. Despite prolonged work in this area by 'micro-sociolinguists' (notably Gumperz), ethnographers of speaking (led by Hymes) and ethnomethodologists (especially Sacks and Schegloff), its importance does not seem to have been adequately appreciated by British social anthropologists since Malinowski. Ardener (1971:xiii) catalogues three main 'levels' at which British social anthropologists have been interested in language, and the level of action is notably absent. It is with respect to this particular field of micro-sociolinguistics that we wish to draw out some implications from our study. We view the fundamental explicandum or datum here as the construction of message forms analysed at all levels, including prosodic and kinesic. This view (contrasting, for example, with that of Labov's work) — perhaps initiated by Gumperz and Hymes, formulated by Ervin-Tripp (1972), and even tacitly assumed by Bernstein (1971) — is now a fundamental doctrine of the 'ethnography of speaking', and we need not justify it here. The more controversial implications of our study follow fairly directly from our emphasis on rational strategies in language use.

The key problem in sociolinguistics is always the origin and nature of the social valence attached to linguistic form. Some sociolinguists view this as a relatively unmediated attribution of value on the basis of the social value of the group with which the linguistic forms are associated (Labov 1972c; Trudgill 1974a). Others see the choice of form determined primarily by the social characteristics of participants and setting, and thus the form's valence derives from the way in which it encapsulates those social determinants. The form may then be used outside the social context that usually determines its use, to invoke 'metaphorical' allusions to that context (Ervin-Tripp 1972; Blom and Gumperz 1972). We prefer a somewhat less mechanical and less arbitrary source for the social valence of message forms. For us communicative intentions[100] have built-in social implications, often of a threatening sort. What then becomes interesting is how such communicative intentions become constrained, for such constraints, expressed by means of the pragmatic resources of the language, show in the construction of messages. Communicative intentions, like all social goods, do not flow smoothly in all directions through a social structure; indeed part of what gives some particular social structure its form is the specific nature and distribution of such constraints, as Lévi-Strauss (1968) has argued. In language the constraints are more on form than on content (or at least form provides a more feasible area of study). The ways in which messages are hedged, hinted, made deferential, and embedded in discourse structures then become crucial areas of study. But such areas are also the concern of pragmatics, the study of the systematic relation of a language to context. The special interest of sociolinguistics in our view is in the differential use of such pragmatic resources by different categories of speakers in different situations. It is in this way that we derive our slogan 'Sociolinguistics should be applied pragmatics.'

For us, then, the social valence of linguistic form has two especially important sources: the intrinsic potential impact that a specific communicative intention may have on a social relationship, and the ways in which by modifying the expression of that intention participants seek to modify that impact — such modification measuring for participants the nature of the social relationship. On this view a very considerable intentional and strategic mediation connects linguistic form with social relationships. In short, language usages are tied to strategies rather than directly to relationships, although relationships will be characterized by the continued use of certain strategies.

A mode of analysis follows naturally from this orientation. The social value of the linguistic form of messages can only be ascertained by looking at such forms as tools for doing things, and asking what kinds of things a given form could be doing.[101] This mode of analysis has various advantages over currently prevailing methods. For instance, suppose we assume instead that patterns of message construction have purely rule-based origins. One then talks for instance in terms of 'alternation' and 'co-occurrence rules' (Ervin-Tripp 1972), or alternatively in terms of rules for speech events (e.g. Hymes 1972, and articles in Bauman and Sherzer 1974). But problems emerge: the social conditions which are supposed to determine the application of alternation rules do not always do so (cf.

Sankoff 1972). Nor do co-occurrence rules operate as systematically as the rule analogy suggests (note for example the routine mixtures of dialect or diglossic levels: Blom and Gumperz 1972; Herman 1976). If and when strict rules operate, one expects rule violations to be attended to in interaction, but such attention is notably lacking in some sociolinguistic 'rule' violations. In short, although rule-based analysis may be adequate for some cases (such as the selection of address forms from a finite set of possibilities), it does not generalize to all.

Strategic analysis has several significant advantages here. Non-occurrence of expected forms, 'exceptions' or 'breaches', can be made sense of by analysing the rational sources for those occurrences in an otherwise homogeneous style with other rational sources. For instance, a sudden warning 'Come here', interposed in a formally polite conversation, is not read as rude despite the overt imperative, if the need for efficient or urgent communication takes precedence over face redress.[102] Similarly we have talked about minute adjustments of social distance, 'brakes and accelerators', as the sort of fine-grained strategic manipulation that routinely occurs in interactions; this too will be a source of inconsistency in 'co-occurrence rules'.

But above all, rule analysis tends to accept the statement of rules as the terminal point of investigation. It thus inhibits investigation into the systematic source of patterns of message construction. A strategic analysis, on the other hand, makes claims about the non-arbitrary nature of style. On this view the features that co-occur in a 'style' are determined by strategic choices, and the coherence of a style lies not necessarily on the formal level but on the strategic level that underlies the selection of forms. (This point is argued in more detail in P. Brown 1976.) If this is so, it may explain the current failure of sociolinguistics to produce a penetrating analysis of style.[103] We do not mean to imply that there is never any normative overlay on strategically coherent patterns of speaking. There is no inconsistency; we simply argue that the analyst can push below such normative levels, where they exist, and ask why they are the way they are. Let us refer here yet again to Lewis's analysis of convention (1969), which argues for a philosophical reduction of conventions to rational origins.

These remarks hold generally for work done in the ethnography of speaking as well. But a special point here is this: rule-based analysis works very well for well-bounded ritualized speech events like greetings, as Irvine (1974) has elegantly demonstrated. But as soon as one wishes to generalize into the less well-bounded, less ritualized episodes that form the vast majority of casual interactions, tremendous difficulties arise. Informants cannot produce rules for such events in the same way that elicitation may produce rules for ritual episodes.

In developing the apparatus of this paper, then, we have the express aim of developing descriptive and analytical procedures which not only augment rule-based analyses within ritually prescribed speech events, but also extend satisfactorily to the most casual of encounters.

9.00 CONCLUSIONS

Empirical research may have ramifications in multiple directions. Here we bring together those that we foresee and make some assessment of their relative importance.

Let us first summarize what we set out to do in this paper. We wished in the first place to account for the pan-cultural interpretability of politeness phenomena, broadly defined. We argued that this interpretability derives from the universal mutual-knowledge assumptions of interacting individuals: that humans are 'rational' and that they have 'face'. On these lines we constructed an overall theory of politeness, integrating notions of polite friendliness and polite formality in a single scheme. From abstract ends, our two 'face wants', repeated application of rational means–ends reasoning will bring us down to the choice of linguistic and kinesic detail, to the minutiae of message construction. Only at the most abstract level, then, do we need to resort to concepts like 'ethological primitives', 'innate dispositions', and so on – concepts that notoriously block inquiry. Nor, interestingly, do norms play a central role in the analysis.

This is the core of the investigation, which is to be read against a set of sociological goals. The essential idea is this: interactional systematics are based largely on universal principles. But the application of the principles differs systematically across cultures, and within cultures across subcultures, categories and groups. Moreover, categories of egos distribute these universally based strategies across different categories of alters. From an interactional point of view, then, principles like those here described are some of the dimensions, the building blocks, out of which diverse and distinct social relations are constructed. Far from being a retreat from the central issues of sociology, as Giddens suggests (1973:15), the study of interactional systematics promises to be a crucial way in which abstract sociological concepts can be related in a precise way to social facts. We would like our endeavour to be seen as an attempt to build one arch in one bridge linking abstract concepts of social structure (whether these are analyst's concepts or member's concepts) to behavioural facts. The absence of such bridges is, we believe, the major omission in sociological thought and methodology.[104]

But whatever the assessment of our theoretical contribution, we would like to claim that the phenomena here described, and the methods used for that description, provide a useful ethnographic tool for the fine-grained analysis of the quality of social relations. Here we have developed the tool and have done no more than sketch the directions such analysis would take.

Notes

1   This paper was written in the summer of 1974. Since then, much has appeared which is relevant to the field of linguistic politeness, and we have incorporated references to this work. But our argument remains substantially unchanged. We are aware of many inadequacies and unevennesses of treatment, and may say — to adapt an apology of Coleridge's — that the following fragment is published at the request of a scholar of great and deserved celebrity, and as far as the authors' own opinions are concerned, rather as a psychological curiosity than on the ground of any supposed intellectual merits.

    We gratefully acknowledge our key intellectual debts in this paper to the following people: John J. Gumperz, for his emphasis on the strategic analysis of language usage; H. P. Grice, for his philosophy of communication; Jay Atlas, for his work on the logic of practical reasoning; and Robin Lakoff, for her perceptive observations on linguistic politeness. A special debt is owed to E. Annamalai for detailed help with the interpretation of the Tamil data, to Brian Stross for help with the Tzeltal, and to Elinor O. Keenan, who provided much insightful discussion as well as facts from her Malagasy data. We also wish to thank the following people who read and commented on the first draft: Gerald Gazdar, Esther Goody, Allen Grimshaw, Dell Hymes, Gillian Sankoff, and John Trim. And we owe Esther Goody a great debt for very detailed comments on the last draft of the paper.

2   We use the word 'sociological' in the sense 'of the sociological sciences'; the inclusion of social anthropology is specifically intended.

3   The distinction here referred to is this: what we call 'inclusive "we"' includes the addressee; 'exclusive "we"' excludes the addressee and refers to the speaker and some others. Many languages (e.g. Tamil, Tzeltal) distinguish these two senses with two separate pronouns. English does not; but the distinction is maintained with regard to the phrase *let us*, for only in the inclusive sense will *let us* contract to *let's*, which explains the oddness of 'Let's beat you up.'

4   We owe the inspiration for this move to Grice's intellectual programme.

5   But we can claim as intellectual ancestors some illustrious reductionists: Weber (1947), Leach (1954, 1961), Barth (1966).

6   We follow Schiffer (1972): if it is mutual knowledge between A and B that C, then A knows that B knows that A knows . . . that C.

7   Juvenile, mad, incapacitated persons partially excepted.

8   The notions and labels for positive and negative face derive ultimately from Durkheim's 'positive and negative rites' (in *The Elementary Forms of the Religious Life*, 1915), partially via Goffman.

9   A third argument in favour of a model based on 'wants' rather than 'norms' was pointed out to us by Gillian Sankoff: that it allows a dynamic to be introduced into the analysis. For particular levels of face redress characterize particular social relations (as we shall argue), and such relations have histories — are constituted, worked on,

10   negotiated. A norm-based analysis requiring a static level of face redress could not account for this.

10   We are not here suggesting a direct semantic analysis of the English surface words *want, desire, intend,* or *ought.*

11   Following Grice (1971): a communicative act is a chunk of behaviour B which is produced by S with a specific intention, which S intends H to recognize, this recognition being the communicative point of S's doing B.

12   Readers may note that many of these are responses to prior H-originated FTAs. This is because if H has made a prior FTA threatening the present S's face, whatever S now chooses to do is likely to be dealing with his own threatened face. (He could of course choose to redress his own face loss by attacking H's face, rather than by protecting his own.)

13   These acts are damaging to S's face because of his basic positive-face wants of self-control and self-respect. In evidencing failure to achieve these wants he makes it unlikely that H will approve of him, as well as threatening H's face (potentially) with embarrassment *for* S.

    The existence of these kinds of acts as face threats is exploited in the conventionalized self-face-humbling of extreme deference; cf. section 6.1 below.

14   For example:

	negative face	*positive face*
threaten S	promises	apologies
threaten H	warnings	criticisms

One might expect that redressive action to an FTA would be always directed specifically at that particular aspect of face which it threatens. Indeed, this is sometimes the case: a promise can be redressed with a hedge ('I'm sure I can do X, if you want'), an apology with support for S's positive face ('I'm not a bad guy, but I'm sorry I did that'), a warning with assurance that the *speaker* doesn't intend to impede H's actions ('It's no skin off my teeth, but Mr Jones says if he sees your son in his strawberry patch again, he'll tell the vicar!'), and a criticism with deference or assurance of a general high opinion of H ('Sorry to be so nitpicky, but you've misspelled half the words in this otherwise brilliant essay'). But in fact things are much more complicated than this simple cross-classification, and many FTAs fit into more than one category, so that redressive action may be addressed to any potential aspect of the face threat, not necessarily just to the most relevant one(s).

15   This want has a number of origins: (a) It may be considered to be part of rationality: minimize effort. (b) It may be a derivative want from wanting something that can only be achieved by efficiency or urgency (cf. section 5.2).

16   There is also a natural association (i.e., there is another means–end relation) between seeking 'common ground' (positive politeness)

and wanting to *develop* a relationship – which may be presumptuous or even threatening to H.

17   We draw encouragement for the importance of the three factors P, D, and R from Grimshaw's independent identification of very similar dimensions (Grimshaw 1980c).

18   The numerical values are here intended only as a model of relative measures of proportions of P, D, and R, and not of course as absolute values of some sort. Some writers do feel that only a small set of discriminations on such dimensions exist, within the scope of Miller's 'magical number 7 ± 2'. Thus Goodenough (1969:325) writes: 'these reasons lead me confidently to predict that the number of status dimensions in any system of social relationships will prove to be severely limited and that the number of statuses that are culturally discriminated in each dimension will prove to be in the neighborhood of seven or less.' If this is so, all our scales should run only from 1 to 7 or so.

19   The significance of these dimensions in language usage was initially explored by Brown and Gilman (1960) in their work on the T/V distinction in pronouns. That emic correlates exist can be seen in the way that informants actually talk in terms of social distance, both vertically and horizontally. Thus in Tamil one talks of *tuuram contam* (literally 'distant own-kind', i.e. distant kin) on the horizontal social dimension; and of *uyira jaati* (literally 'high kind' or 'high caste') and *kiiRe jaati* ('low kind' or 'low caste') on the vertical social dimension.

20   Gillian Sankoff points out (personal comm.) that assessments like this (whether an actor is known to enjoy being imposed upon) raise a very complex problem, that of assessing the status of 'mutual knowledge' in a given interaction. How do we know what is mutually known, and how do we know we know? While recognizing the difficulties with this notion, we consider that it is one with which a theory of interaction will have to come to grips.

21   However, there is perhaps one implicit claim, and that is that a variable like 'social distance' on at least one psychological level is not a binary choice between, say, 'in-group' and 'out-group', although it may be so conceptualized on another level. There is some psychological evidence (Rosch 1977) and some linguistic evidence (G. Lakoff 1972) that supports us in this view; it suggests that categorization is a secondary process that follows complex estimations of *degrees* of membership of an object in a set. Here we attach no great importance to the claim, but it is worth noticing that our R factor has a similar binary categorization into 'free goods' and 'non-free goods' (at least in Western society: see Goffman 1967, 1971).

22   For instance, the explanatory power of the notion 'norm' depends upon a precise specification of the way in which norms are related to normative behaviour. But this specification seems tacitly assumed to be some simple kind of class-subsumption, or 'category thinking'. That is, with norms stated as 'If X, do Y', the problem reduces to

deciding when something is in category X or category Y. Alternatively, norms might be linked to behaviour by some set of rules specific to each norm, but there is very little discussion of such points in the literature. There are extreme difficulties with either view, for the means of fulfilling a norm like 'Honour thy father and thy mother' do not seem to be limited to any finite set (nor to any simple recursively defined infinite set) of behaviours. Consequently the assumption of some pattern-matching faculty or some rule-specifications do not seem adequate to the task. In addition, as every anthropologist knows, norms are often not observed, and sometimes scarcely observed at all. Yet informants, and consequently ethnographers, continue to maintain that such norms exist.

These difficulties may be resolved by assuming that what links norms to normative behaviour is a rational assessment of whether the behaviour fulfils the normative injunction – in other words, an application of a system of practical reasoning. Such a system has two important and distinctive properties, 'ampliativeness' and 'defeasibility' (see below), which will capture just the two problematic aspects of norms we have discussed. Ampliativeness will provide the indefiniteness of means whereby norms may be fulfilled, and defeasibility – or the possibility of invalidating inferences simply by the addition of premises – will provide a systematic account of how norms can exist and yet not be applied.

To expand the last remark: in order to avoid various philosophical difficulties about the reduction of the 'moral ought' to the 'practical ought', we can allow that the former can be a reason for the latter. (One may treat 'standing orders' in a similar fashion.) Once moral oughts are on the same plane as practical oughts, non-moral practical oughts can override practical oughts of moral origin, in the way that we all know they sometimes do. Conflicting norms, and the choice between them, can be similarly handled. Such an analysis would lead us to investigate the systematicity of non-fulfilments of norms; if no such systematicity exists, nor can the norm.

23 Compare for instance the problems all 'Verstehen' sociologists face with their non-introspective informants, or social psychologists with their subjects' non-volunteered 'attitudes', or linguists with their attempts to make explicit unconscious generative processes, or structural anthropologists with their models of myth or cosmos that no informant would subscribe to.

24 That is, they don't have separate lexicalizations for the two concepts – at least not in English, Tamil, Tzeltal, or any others we have come across.

25 This informal presentation is spelled out more carefully in Atlas and Levinson 1973.

26 We owe the proof of this to Michael Gordon (personal comm.).

27 We hope that this deals with the very interesting critique of Grice's Maxims from a cross-cultural perspective by E. O. Keenan (1976).

She cites many examples of Madagascan violations of the Quantity
Maxim, for example a mother asking her son 'Is the person still
sleeping?' 'The person' in fact refers to the speaker's husband, whom
she avoids referring to more specifically because of a particular taboo
on exact identification. But if no such Quantity Maxim were operating as an underlying assumption, then the son would not assume
that he should be able to identify the referent, and all such referring
expressions would fail to denote. In fact Malagasy-speakers habitually do understand such vague expressions, and they do so only
on the assumption that the speaker is being cooperative in just the
way the Maxims demand, but not necessarily on the superficial level
(of what is actually said) at which taboo and politeness constraints
operate. In short, even if one could find a population where no
utterances at all superficially conformed to the Maxims, this would
not necessarily be evidence of their non-existence. What would be
counter-evidence would be communities where no assumption was
made that, at some level, persons were trying to convey the truth (or
be sincere), or tie their utterances to prior remarks, or provide
enough information to locate a specific proposition, or be intelligible
– in other words, communities in which the Maxims were met
neither on the level of what is literally said nor on the level of what
is implicated. The importance of Grice's Maxims for cross-cultural
study is, in our view, that they pinpoint particular motives (like
politeness) for departures from them.

28   The Tzeltal and Tamil examples are glossed underneath in English.
The Tzeltal transcription is roughly phonemic, where č represents
the sound spelled in English *ch*, š corresponds to English *sh*, ¢
represents English *ts*, ʔ indicates a glottal stop, and ' indicates
glottalization of the preceding consonant.

The Tamil transcription follows Schiffman (1971, Part II:2–4) in
adopting a transcription which is very close to an abstract phonemic
level while retaining a close relation to Tamil orthography. This
unholy alliance between linguistic and orthographic conventions is
not perhaps as dubious as it may seem, for Tamil orthography is
extremely systematic and quite close to at least one adequate
phonemic analysis. Where doubts arise we do favour a solution
consonant with the orthography. A distinct set of phonemes exists
for handling loan words. Symbols have their common values, except
for the following major departures: (a) retroflex consonants are
represented by upper-case versions of the standard symbols; (b) long
vowels are represented by reduplicated vowel symbols; (c) the contrast between intervocalic voiced lax stops and their voiceless tense
counterparts is represented by single versus reduplicated symbols.
Reduplication in the case of *cc* indicates a palatalized affricate.
Despite the adoption of these conventions based on Tamil orthography, the examples are all in colloquial Tamil (either the 'standard
colloquial' or Coimbatore dialect), not the diglossic written variant.

For both the Tzeltal and the Tamil examples, the English glosses
(i.e. the translations) are as close as can be given without providing

both a literal word-for-word gloss and a free translation. The standard linguistic conventions are followed for presenting linguistic examples: round brackets ( ) indicate optional material; curly brackets { } indicate alternative options; asterisks * indicate ungrammatical forms. In addition we have added our own conventional symbol, c.i., for indicating 'meanings' that are conversationally implicated; it is important to distinguish these from the stable meanings of words and clauses, because they are contextually dependent inferences.

29 Gerald Gazdar observes (personal comm.) that this 'as if' clause creates problems for our model, for any possible counter-example could be treated as an 'as if' case. We await a sophisticated theory of metaphor to constrain the interpretation of 'as if' so that it can be incorporated in a formal model.

30 R. Lakoff's analysis of this (1972), as equivalent to 'Have some more cake – yecch!' or a way of humbling the cake, seems to us counter-intuitive. It seems more accurate to see S's forcefulness as designed to overcome H's reluctance to devour all of S's cake.

31 To be redress it must include an implication of *cooperative* wanting of the same wants; if S communicates that he is in deadly *competition* with H over some mutual want, it can hardly be positive-politeness redress.

32 For the complexities of the semantics of Tamil reduplication, see Sangster 1968.

33 This example comes from the data of Brent Berlin.

34 Emily Post (1922) recommends topics, etc. for positive-politeness conversation.

35 The process of conventionalization can be thought of as 'short-circuiting' inferences, so that where A may be inferred from B (especially by practical reasoning), stating B with the intent to convey A can become, by routine association, an 'idiom' for A. But see our further discussion below.

36 As will become clear later, we do not think that felicity conditions are genuine isolates, but we retain the notion for heuristic purposes. For although Austin (1962) and Searle (1969) argue that these felicity conditions are conventional and presumably arbitrary, at least some of them (the most important) seem really to be nothing more than particularizations of Grice's Maxims of Quality and Relevance (which account for Searle's 'sincerity' and 'preparatory' conditions, respectively).

37 The intonation, high pitch, and kinesics of questioning serve perhaps as well as the actual syntactic marking of questions, in some cases at any rate, so that (17) may not be rude if it is thus intonationally and kinesically marked.

38 In Table 1 we have added the two preparatory conditions (ii) and (iii), even though they are not t~ be found in Searle's accounts, presumably because (ii) is a precondition on (i), and (iii) can only be stated for *certain* requested acts where doing them once, in certain conditions, is all that could be desired. This illustrates the difficulty

of working with felicity conditions (see also the next two notes).
The contents of the requests illustrated in the table differ for the
three languages, as the items reasonable to request differ.

39 For example, owing to the fact that the future in both Tamil and
Tzeltal has special aspectual and modal presuppositions, use of the
future tense in requests is highly restricted. Present tense serves for
immediate future.

40 These kinds of indirect speech acts are smuggled into Searle's
account of indirect requests (1975) under the rubric 'reasons for H
to do the action requested', even though the theory there propounded,
based on felicity conditions, does not attempt to account for them.

41 If this view is correct, yet another motivation for felicity conditions
withers away. In our view they are redundant notions in any case
for the major speech-act types, where illocutionary intentions (of
the sort envisaged by Grice (1973), corresponding approximately to
Searle's 'essential conditions'), when formulated to meet Grice's
Maxims, would automatically have the properties attributed to them
by Searle's felicity conditions.

One apparent way of extending the felicity-condition approach
to meet our objections of inadequate coverage of the types of indirect speech act would be to allow *entailments* of felicity conditions
to be used like the felicity conditions themselves. This would obtain
'Is there any salt?' from 'H can pass the salt', the ability condition on
requests. Unfortunately it would also suggest that 'Is there an
addressee?' could routinely function as a request for the salt. The
point is of course that a viable hint must contain enough information
in it to allow the inference of a particular proposition and illocutionary
force by a particular addressee in a particular context. But such
complex notions cannot be handled by the standard accounts of
indirect speech acts.

42 That this is not merely an idiosyncrasy of this Tamil word is indicated by the precisely similar usage of the word *kely* ('a little') in
Malagasy (E. O. Keenan and E. L. Keenan, personal comm.), as in:

> mba kely omeo ny moto aho.
> please a little be given the bread to me

where *kely* can co-occur with another politeness morpheme *mba*
('please'), and further softens the request.

43 Sometimes considerable play may be made on the ambiguity of
hedges between illocutionary-force modifiers and propositional-
content modifiers. In Malagasy (E. O. Keenan and E. L. Keenan,
personal comm.), a boy accused of breaking a window may respond:
'Perhaps', leaving his response ambiguous between 'Perhaps I may
have done it' and 'Perhaps I'm telling you that I did it'. Exactly the
same noncommittalness is common in Tzeltal (*yak niwan*, 'yes perhaps') even where both speaker and hearer *know* that the correct
answer is definitely 'yes'.

44 We are especially indebted to E. Annamalai for discussions of the
subtleties of these Tamil particles. See also Zvelebil 1954.

45   Use of the word 'sense' or 'meaning' is not intended to commit us to distinct lexical entries: they should be read as 'literal or implicaturally derived meaning'. An important question is how these different meanings are teased apart in the process of language understanding. Intonational patterns are an important clue, but restrict the set of possible meanings rather than selecting just one. Similarly, syntactic and semantic constraints aid disambiguation; thus for instance the emphatic-negation sense of *-ee* can only occur where the implied quantifier has some domain to range over, and is consequently blocked where there is a semantically singular count noun. But many possibilities are still left open to be narrowed by broader discourse-disambiguating processes, still unexplored. A leading question is whether for each particle there is only one central sense and a set of implicatures, or a number of actually distinct lexical entries. The tools for deciding such matters are still too primitive to provide definite answers.

46   However, just as the English sentence will not allow sentence-internal *please* insertion, the Tamil sentences will not take *koncam*; neither allows syntactic marking of illocutionary force.

47   Compare the positive-politeness versions of this — *just a sec', just a mo'* — where the abbreviation acts as a sort of onomatopoeic emphasis of the shortness of the time.

48   But see the descriptive formats suggested in Neustupný 1968 and Altmann and Riška 1966.

49   These would perhaps be realized by the distinction between Zwicky's 'calls' (Schegloff's (1972b) 'summonses') and 'addresses' in the usage of vocative forms (Zwicky 1974).

50   There are exceptions, however. Dell Hymes has pointed out to us (personal comm.) that in the area of kinship terms, Schneider and Roberts (1956) 'in a paper on Zuni kin terms, specifically argued that kin term semantics were not to be explained entirely in terms of fixed kin reference, and had to be understood as role-designating, hence variably (strategically) usable terms'. See also Weller, 1981.

51   Gillian Sankoff (personal comm.) observes that the opposite holds for Canadian French T/V usage. The modern ethos being in favour of solidarity (and hence positive politeness) rather than deference (and negative politeness), one would not find people switching from T to V to mitigate an FTA, but rather, if at all, from V to T. This would be an essentially positive-politeness strategy in line with the dominant ethos. That is, since V is the unmarked usage, to switch from T to V would be unsolidary, rude, standoffish.

52   Annamalai points out (personal comm.) that this use of the pronoun can single out one addressee from others and thus in certain circumstances can be more polite, rather like the positive-politeness use of first names in English. Of course in offers like 'You go first', the pronoun, by increasing the emphaticness, increases the politeness. But in Tamil (as in English), *nii inkirentu poo!* ('You go away from here') is more forceful and less polite than the same sentence without the 'you'.

53   Actually the affixal status of *-Num* is a current colloquial development from a literary dative verb. The underlying structure of (341)
is something close to *nii ceyya onnukku veeNTum* ('It is necessary
for you that you do it'), with both dative and nominative co-
referential agents, either but not both of which may show up in
surface structure.

54   Some languages (e.g. Kalagan) make a distinction within oblique
cases and thus have two further voices: an instrumental-time voice
and a benefactive-place voice (E. L. Keenan 1972:9–10).

55   E. O. Keenan, to whose original observations this section is much
indebted, investigated the actual usage of these forms. She found
that not only does the resource for such agent-deletive defocusing
exist, but it is used to the hilt. For instance, in one sample passage
76 per cent of verbs which could syntactically be active, passive, or
circumstantial were non-active; in another passage non-active verbs
reached 84 per cent of the total verbs in which options existed
(E. O. Keenan 1974a:89–95).

56   Dumont (1970) sees particular cultural sources for this absorption
of the individual in the group. But there are more general observations to be made of kinship-dominated social structures; as Maine
(1965:74) originally pointed out, 'the *unit* of an ancient society was
the Family, of a modern society the Individual'.

57   Annamalai (personal comm.) has pointed out to us that the facts
are really considerably more complex than this. The historical
succession was approximately this, as we now understand it:

	I. Proto- Tamil	II. Old Tamil	III. Intermediate Tamil	IV. Modern Tamil
sing.	*niin*	*nii*	*nii*	*nii*
sing. + honorific	–	*nii + yir*	*niir*	{ *niir* *niinkaL*
plural	*niim*	*nii + yir*	*niim + kaL*	*niinkaL*

In other words, the original plural *niim*, dropped out for a while as
niiyir (*-ir* = plural suffix) replaced it, and then as *niiyir* (now *niir*)
came to be used honorifically, *niim* was reintroduced with an additional plural morpheme *-kaL*, hence *niinkaL*. But once again the plural
form is having its plurality eroded as a 'you' (singular honorific) form.
The argument then remains valid, but a clearer case is provided by the
third-person pronouns:

	II. Old Tamil	III. Intermediate Tamil	III. Modern Tamil
sing.	*avaan*	*avaan*	*avaan*
sing. + honorific	–	*avaar*	{ *avaar* *avaarkaL*
plural	*avaar*	*avaar + kaL*	*avaarkaL*

The exact chronology of these transitions is complex; see Shanmugam 1971:ch.4 and references therein. Zvelebil (1962) suggests a slightly different succession which, if anything, strengthens the point. A similar pattern may be noticed in the history of English, where the second-person plural *you* replaced the old *thou*; but the distinction between *you* (plural) and *you* (honorific) was reintroduced by the use of third-person verb inflections (*you was*) with *you* (honorific) (used by Boswell and Walpole) that persisted into the nineteenth century (Traugott 1972:175).

We present these details because they illustrate a point made much of below: we see here the consistent pressure that social facts of these sorts exert on a linguistic system, the social impingement providing the motive force behind many grammatical complexities. For an African parallel, see Gregersen 1974:52.

58   A peculiar grammatical fact is that (383) is syntactically ambiguous only if the referent of *motal mantiri* is female: in that case *avaanka* could be either a genitive bracketed with *mantirikaL* (meaning 'her ministers') or a pleonastic nominative pronoun (meaning 'she'). But if the referent is male, only the latter reading is possible, because the pleonastic pronoun is obligatory; however, the ambiguity returns if the pronoun is the less honorific *avaar*. This peculiar syntactic quirk is typical of the perturbations caused in a language by honorific systems (see Comrie 1975; Corbett 1976). To understand it one has to know that a basic three-way distinction for single male referents (*avaan*, 'he'; *avaar*, 'he' + honorific; *avaanka*, 'he' + super-honorific) contrasts with a basic two-point scale for female referents (*avaa*, 'she'; *avaanka*, 'she' + honorific), so that on an honorific scale, *avaanka* to female referents corresponds to *avaar* to male referents. And the syntax is attuned to the honorific scale (i.e. treats female *avaanka* and male *avaar* as a syntactic class, omitting male *avaanka*), not to the surface form (it thus incidentally retains some syntactic marking of sex which is lost in the plural pronouns themselves).

59   The distribution of address by name, correlating approximately to the distribution of T pronouns, provides a map of the distribution of relative low status in Tamil society. To superiors there is a very strong taboo on the use of names, and an elaborate set of address terms, titles, and designators is available based on kinship, caste titles, house location, government office, names of family-owned fields, names of village of origin if elsewhere, and so on. There are also taboos of a more general sort such that an inferior in the presence of a superior is unlikely to refer by name or specific designator to any of his family or close associates. Thus in example (284) quoted on p. 184, a low-caste man used the phrase 'that girl' as an initial reference to his own daughter, such Gricean Quantity Maxim violations being interpretable on the basis of their expectability. For a vast range of precisely similar taboo-based strategies in Madagascar, see E. O. Keenan 1974a, 1976.

60   In an earlier draft we had in tandem to this section a section on the use of the presupposition of an FTA as a further means of dissociating

the speaker from the threatening act. We have removed it, however, as we do not understand all the mechanisms involved here, and indeed, presupposing an FTA seems to be only one of a family of strategies where the FTA is embedded to the right of a lot of material that serves to defocus it. Indeed, embedding as the complement of verbs that do not even promote the presuppositions of that complement seems to work even better than presupposing the FTA.

61 Since we wrote this it has come to our attention that there are a number of reports of social-psychology experiments showing that 'nouniness' increases in situations of social distance or social discomfort. See, for example, Fielding and Fraser 1978.

62 Grice (1975) gives four relations that a speaker may stand in *vis-à-vis* the Maxims: violating them, opting out of them, resolving a clash between them, and flouting (exploiting) them. Implicitly he adds a fifth: observing them. Our use of the term 'violation' is quite different; we exclude his usage of the same term, but include flouts together with any gradient inadequacy that an utterance may have *vis-à-vis* the Maxims.

63 An instance of this ambiguity between P and D as determining the use of T or V pronouns was long ago noted by Brown and Gilman (1960). Similar observations on address titles have been made, for example by Ervin-Tripp (1972), and are implicit in Geoghegan's mapping rules (1971).

64 A conversational viewpoint directs us also to the use of carefully located silence as a means of accomplishing an FTA even where our super-strategy 5 (Don't do the FTA at all) is enjoined. Thus, in Tamil, polite acceptances may be conveyed by deliberate silences, as illustrated by the glosses in this passage (where A is a man, and W is his friend's new bride):

> A: Do you sing?
> W: (silence)
> A: Hooray! Give us a song!

Similarly, in Tamil the politest refusal is simply no answer at all; hence if A writes to B for a favour and B does not reply, this signifies a polite refusal.

65 Some evidence for this can be found in parallels like the fact that the one-upping that occurs in frozen Arabic greetings (Ferguson 1976) occurs elsewhere freely as an interactional resource in English compliments (Pomerantz 1978).

66 We would need to do much more comparative work in Tzeltal conversation to be really confident of this. We would want to show from materials that members do indeed attend to such features of conversation in the way that Sacks and Schegloff and their associates have shown can be done for English. But it is interesting that work done in that way in English conversation does show a similar regard for interactional balance (see, for example, Goffman 1976; Pomerantz 1978; Jefferson, Sacks and Schegloff 1976).

67 For instance, Radcliffe-Brown held (1952:192): 'In the study of

social structure the concrete reality with which we are concerned is the set of actually existing relations . . . which link together certain human beings.' Nadel (1957:5) quotes Fortes and Eggan as having held similar views, although like Nadel himself Fortes seems to hold a somewhat more abstract view of social structure. Even those whose views of social structure are most abstract do not reject the central role of social relations as data: 'social relations consist of the raw materials out of which the models making up the social structure are built', claims Lévi-Strauss (1968:279), although he is quick to add: 'social structure can, by no means, be reduced to the ensemble of . . . social relations'. And for those who are reluctant to accord social structure the same degree of ontological substantivity, who would rather see it for instance as 'a set of ideas about the distribution of power between persons and groups of persons' (Leach 1954:4), the facts of social relationships and their interactional content have an indisputable significance.

68   Sometimes work done by others may be exploited, as we here exploit the work done by ethnomethodologists, linguists, and ethnographers of speaking. But such work is not always done in frameworks which allow direct application. Where it is, we should be grateful and not castigate such workers for not doing anthropology, as sociologists have castigated the practitioners of ethnomethodology.

69   However, respect and familiarity are in our theory subsumed in a more general explanatory scheme. Such a more general scheme was in fact adumbrated by Radcliffe-Brown himself in two respects. On the one hand he made the observation that 'The avoidance relationship is in one sense an extreme form of respect, while the joking relationship is a form of familiarity' (1952:107). The first equation we see to be correct, indeed predicted by the negative-face want and thus an automatic output of our system. The second equation is dubious; as Radcliffe-Brown himself pointed out (no doubt influenced by Freud), joking relationships are compounded out of conflicting relations of 'conjunction' and 'disjunction' (*ibid.*:98). The second respect in which our scheme is more general was also prefigured by Radcliffe-Brown when he sought to extend his analysis of joking relations beyond the kinship domain (*ibid.*:ch.5). In a similar way we relate respect and familiarity to very general considerations of social distance (D) and social hierarchy (P), which subsume as particular cases horizontal and vertical social distance measured in kinship terms (whether genealogical or categorical). As far as we can see, our scheme makes the correct predictions in the kinship domain.

70   A major point of divergence with Radcliffe-Brown is that we do not imagine a total determinism from social-structural loci (as measured on our two dimensions) to interactional behaviour. It is because we widen the social-structural correlates beyond kinship ones that the possibility of behavioural choice looms large. Indeed, the causal arrows may run in the opposite direction: it is reasonable to assume that in every society, in at least some social arenas, there is room for the creation of social relations by the choice of behavioural strate-

gies. (A similar sentiment is expressed by Leach (1962:133) and endorsed by Fortes (1969:288).) Social relations thus created are no less social relations than those ascribed. It is an empirical question to what extent and in what domains in any particular society an individual's social relations are an outcome of behavioural choice as opposed to jural prescription.

71   Our use of the term 'ethos' is based on the more general sense in which Bateson used the term, to label the 'emotional emphases of a culture' (1958). Bateson's 'ethos' (and Benedict's related term 'configuration' (1934)) were broadly used to cover all the emotional emphases that give a coherent emotional tone to a culture. Based in individual psychology, standardized in groups, their ethos was a characteristic of individuals, as members of a group (or culture) manifesting particular emotional emphases. Here we use the term to characterize interactions, the behaviour of dyads, and hence the generalizable aspects of the interaction patterns of groups. Our ethos, then, is a subset of the behavioural manifestations of Bateson's ethos, and does not involve the behaviour of individuals when alone, say, or as revealed in ritual or in myth. Note, however, that Bateson (*ibid.*:119–21) does give examples of interactional ethos: he cites the tone of interaction in a conversation (as jokey, light-hearted, non-serious, as opposed to intense and sincere), as well as the more stable tone of interaction at a college high table, with its rituals and historically based values.

72   We add 'in public' because it is the publicly viewable side of interaction that enters into generalizations about interactional ethos.

73   The rational corollary of this is E. Goody's point (1978b) that social roles provide very important clues to what in fact is communicatively intended by the production of some linguistic form.

74   We are indebted to Dell Hymes for pointing out to us the importance of this dimension.

75   Many of the linguistic features characteristic of women's speech in English (as per R. Lakoff 1975) are typical positive-politeness linguistic realizations; for example, the use of hedges like *sort of, kind of*; the use of exaggeration; the preference for agreement; the inclusive 'we'.

76   It seems that much of social ritual is devoted to indirect ways of doing big FTAs such as asking for a woman in marriage, prosecuting a breach of law, making accusations of witchcraft, negotiating a sale of land. What FTAs a particular society elevates to the status of ritual is then an interesting variable.

77   We are indebted to Maurice Bloch (personal comm.) for provocative remarks here.

78   Other possible patterns may have more complex sources than this, however. Suppose we found a society where both negative politeness and positive politeness were highly in evidence. Our theory predicts that such a pattern would result if the kinds of social relationships and/or the kinds of FTAs were sharply dichotomized, so that, for instance, a person is defined as either a bosom buddy or a total

stranger, and/or FTAs are defined so that half of them are very small and half very big, with no intermediate ground. Similarly, in a society where FTAs are defined in general as very small, we would expect a pattern of low elaboration for both positive and negative politeness.

79 The problems of getting comparable data neutralizing R are significant, since men and women have different concerns and hence talk about different things. Even more difficult is to find dyads equivalent in P and D for men and women. Thus, getting comparable data is not a matter of matching exact values for P, D, and R, but rather of matching as nearly as possible degrees of 'more' or 'less' on the scales of P, D, and R (see P. Brown, 1979, 1980). Note that if one *could* get data where the relations are all held constant, then the speech of men and women (our theory predicts) should be the same. By holding R_x constant, we expect that the different strategies used should be attributable to different P and D assessments.

80 This observation parallels that of Trudgill (1974a) for English, where he suggested that middle-class men use working-class forms (that is, they 'undercorrect' their speech) as a way of stressing their masculinity, whereas women typically 'hypercorrect', using linguistic forms characteristic of persons of higher classes than their own.

81 Another example of a study of sex ethos, along related lines, is that of E. O. Keenan (1974b) on Malagasy interaction. She phrases her conclusions in terms of 'norms': women are norm-breakers, constantly breaking the prevailing cultural norms of non-confrontation and de-emphasis of self. Her conclusion (implied rather than asserted) is that women allow some other specific interactional goals (efficiency, for example) to supersede the norms. Her analysis could be rephrased in terms of strategy selection and practical reasoning along the lines suggested above. Our analysis would claim that such abstract norms reinforce the values of various wants and thus enter into assessment of FTAs.

82 Significantly, these valuations exactly parallel the valuation of food transfers (parallel to T-giving) and the valuation of service-provision (parallel to V-giving) as already established in Indian studies, and in the village of this study (see Beck 1972). This suggests that a unified theory of social transactions incorporating both linguistic and material transfers may indeed be possible.

83 See Bever 1975 for a partisan survey, and other articles in the same volume. For a motivation of movement rules in terms of what is an implicitly psychological source, 'prominence', see Langacker 1974.

84 One can easily imagine others: for instance, the group-boundary maintenance procedures that implicitly underlie much sociolinguistic reasoning by Gumperz and Labov, or the principles of interactional management investigated, in very different ways, by Goffman and by Sacks and Schegloff.

85 Agreement rules might be a case in point. But if the language has honorific plurals, these will in fact have different agreement rules

from semantic plurals (Comrie 1975). No particular level of grammatical description, except perhaps the most abstract, is likely to be predictably pragmatically immune.

86 By 'form' we mean a morpheme or a string of morphemes and their syntactic correlates, or a phonological/prosodic pattern and its systematic correlates. By 'meaning' we intend some stable characterization of a form's sense in terms of truth conditions, atomic primitives, or whatever.

87 We are aware of the extreme crudity of the characterizations in Fig. 8. A more sophisticated mode of treatment of some of these problems may be found in Sadock's similar analysis (1974) of these relations.

88 Transderivational constraints have been proposed for this kind of operation by Gordon and Lakoff (1971), and attacked by Sadock (1974) on methodological grounds. Nevertheless, something of this sort seems necessary, and Gazdar and Klein (1976) demonstrate that they can be given a satisfactory formal interpretation. We believe that the methodology must succumb to the facts.

89 See Comrie 1975 for similar details in other languages.

90 Another mechanism is illustrated by euphemism. Here not only do forms acquire new meanings, they inherit them. Thus *lavatory* becomes replaced by *toilet* (and their original meanings wither), and then in turn by *bathroom*. But each of these was originally an extended usage whose politeness derived from its indirectness, and each was understood in the way that implicatures are — in other words, it was a configuration like III.

91 Cutler excludes from this generalization what she calls 'provoked ironies', for example 'Sure, Joe, you locked the door', which refer back to 'something which the audience has previously said or held' (*ibid.*:119).

92 The same asymmetry in implicatures on scalar predicates holds for some Tamil examples, providing support for our interpretation of the phenomenon. Thus *avaan nallavan ille* ('He's not a good man') implicates 'He's a bad man', but *avaan keTTavan ille* ('He's not a bad man') implicates only 'He's neither especially good nor especially bad.'

93 Davison (1975:153–4,174) argues that the 'semantics' of indirect speech acts involve the speaker's attitude or belief that the proposition or topic introduced is painful or intrusive, rather than involving politeness. But our analysis of politeness in terms of FTAs subsumes her 'semantic' elements.

94 However, it is not clear that one *can* say that; these *if* clauses have peculiar properties, as Heringer notes (1972:52–5). Whether these properties are automatically explained given a satisfactory semantics for the performative analysis will have to wait until that exists. For some difficulties, see for example Lewis 1972:110.

95 For syntactic rules that operate on such phrases, see Corum 1975a and the references therein.

96 But this is not the view implicit in the widely adopted treatment of

address forms by Geoghegan (1971), for instance, where address forms are determined directly by the social attributes of addressee. There are extreme problems with this view — not the least is the strategic use of such linguistic resources in FTA contexts as described above (see also Levinson 1977).

97 Comrie (1976:n.4) notes such overlaps in Javanese for *sampéjan* and *neḍa.* Arrays of verb suffixes and copulas in Japanese show the same sort of overlap. See also Martin 1964:409.

98 Brown and Gilman (1960) produced a culture-specific explanation for the European T/V systems which will not hold for Asia and Africa.

99 The sociological conditions for the emergence of elaborate honorific systems must be very particular. Why, for instance, do Indian languages have much less developed systems than Japanese, despite the much more rigid and elaborate system of social stratification in India?

100 For those disturbed by the use of such a mentalistic notion, for 'communicative intention' read 'speech act'; this particularizes our intended sense to a minimal unit.

101 This point has been made repeatedly by Hymes (e.g. 1974a), who observes that he got it from Burke (Hymes, personal comm.). Nonetheless, it has continued to be ignored in research programmes.

102 This raises severe difficulties with R. Lakoff's (1975) rule-based analysis of politeness; see P. Brown (1976) for a critique.

103 Irvine (1975) makes a similar point.

104 We do not wish to imply that it is a gap that can simply be filled without reconstruction of abstract concepts. We expect the contrary.

REFERENCES

Albert, E. 1972. Culture patterning of speech behavior in Burundi. In Gumperz and Hymes, eds. 1972, pp. 73-105.

Allen, J. 1983. Recognizing intentions from natural language utterances. In *Computational models of discourse*, ed. M. Brady and R. Berwick, pp. 107-66. Cambridge, Mass.

Alrabaa, S. 1985. The use of address pronouns by Egyptian adults. *Journal of Pragmatics* 9(5):645-57.

Altmann, G. and Riška, A. 1966. Towards a typology of courtesy in language. *Anthropological Linguistics* 8(1):1-10.

Annamalai, E. and Ramanujan, A. n.d. Reference grammar of Tamil. Unpublished mimeo, Univ. of Chicago.

Anscombe, G. E. M. 1957. *Intention*. Oxford.

Ardener, E. W., ed. 1971. *Social anthropology and language*. ASA Monograph 10. London.

Argyle, M. 1972. Non-verbal communication in human social interaction. In Hinde, ed. 1972, pp. 243-96.

Argyle, M. and Cook, M. 1976. *Gaze and mutual gaze*. Cambridge.

Aristotle. 1969. *Nicomachean ethics*, transl. J. A. K. Thomson. Harmondsworth.

Atkinson, J. M. 1979. Displaying neutrality. Paper presented at the Conference on the Possibilities and Limitations of Pragmatics, Urbino, 1979.

1982. Understanding formality: the categorization and production of 'formal' interaction. *British Journal of Sociology* 33(1):86-117.

Atkinson, J. M. and Drew, P. 1979. *Order in court*. London.

Atkinson, J. M. and Heritage, J., eds. 1984. *Structures of social action*. Cambridge.

Atlas, J. and Levinson, S. 1973. The importance of practical reasoning in language usage: an explanation of conversational implicature. Unpublished MS, Dept. of Linguistics, Univ. of Cambridge.

1981. It-clefts, informativeness and logical form. In Cole, ed. 1981, pp. 1-61.

Austin, J. L. 1962. *How to do things with words*. Harvard Univ. William James Lectures 1955. Oxford.

Bach, E. 1973. *Syntactic theory*. New York.

Baker, C. 1975. This is just a first approximation, but . . . In *Papers from the eleventh regional meeting of the Chicago Linguistic Society*, pp. 37-47. Chicago.

Barnlund, D. C. 1975. Communicative styles in two cultures: Japan and the United States. In *The organization of behaviour in face-to-face interaction*, ed. A. Kendon, R. M. Harris, and M. R. Key, pp. 427-56. The Hague.

Baroni, M. R. and D'Urso, V. 1984. Some experimental findings about the question of politeness and women's speech. *Language in Society* 13(1):67-72.

Barth, F. 1966. *Models of social organization*. RAI occasional Paper 23. London.

Basso, K. 1979. *Portraits of the Whiteman*. Cambridge.

Bateman, J. A. 1985. *Utterances in context: towards a systematic theory of the intersubjective achievement of discourse*. Unpublished Ph.D. dissertation, University of Edinburgh.

Bates, E. and Benigni, L. 1975. Rules of address in Italy: a sociological survey. *Language in Society* 4(3):271–88.

Bates, E. 1976. *Language and context: the acquisition of pragmatics*. New York.

Bateson, G. 1958 (1936). *Naven*. Stanford, Calif.

Bauman, R. and Sherzer, J., eds. 1974. *Explorations in the ethnography of speaking*. Cambridge.

Baxter, L. A. 1984. An investigation of compliance-gaining as politeness. *Human Communication Research* 10(3):427–56.

Bayraktaroglu, A. in preparation. *Troubles-telling in Turkish*. Open University Ph.D.

Beach, W. A. and Dunning, D. G. 1982. Pre-indexing — conversational organization. *Quarterly Journal of Speech* 68:170–85.

Bean, S. 1978. *Symbolic and pragmatic semantics: a Kannada system of address*. Chicago.

Beck, B. E. F. 1972. *Peasant society in Koṅku*. Vancouver.

Bell, A. 1984. Language style as audience design. *Language in Society* 13:145–204.

Benedict, R. 1934. *Patterns of culture*. Boston.
 1946. *The chrysanthemum and the sword*. London.

Benoit, P. J. 1983. The use of threats in children's discourse. *Language and Speech* 26(4):305–29.

Berk-Seligson, S. 1983. Sources of variation in Spanish verb construction usage: the active, the dative, and the reflexive passive. *Journal of Pragmatics* 7(2):145–68.

Berlin, B. and Kay, P. 1969. *Basic color terms: their universality and evolution*. Berkeley and Los Angeles.

Berne, E. L. 1968. *Games people play*. London.

Bernstein, B. 1971. *Class, codes and control*, vol. 1. London.

Berreman, G. D. 1963. *Hindus of the Himalayas*. Berkeley, Calif.

Bever, T. 1975. Functional explanations require independently motivated functional theories. In Grossman, San and Vance, eds. 1975, pp. 580–609.

Birdwhistell, R. L. 1970. *Kinesics and context*. Philadelphia.

Blau, P. M. 1964. *Exchange and power in social life*. New York.

Bleisener, T. and Siegrist, J. 1981. Greasing the wheels: conflicts on the round and how they are managed. *Journal of Pragmatics* 5:181–204.

Bloch, M. 1975. Introduction to *Political language and oratory in traditional society*. London.

Blom, J. P. and Gumperz, J. 1972. Social meaning in linguistic structures: code-switching in Norway. In Gumperz and Hymes, eds. 1972, pp. 407–34.

Blum-Kulka, S. 1982. Learning to say what you mean in a second language: a study of the speech act performance of learners of Hebrew as a second language. *Applied Linguistics* 3(1):29–59.

1983. Interpreting and performing speech acts in a second language: a cross-cultural study of Hebrew and English. In *TESOL and sociolinguistic research*. ed. N. Wolfson and J. Eliot. Rowley, Mass.

1985. Indirectness and politeness in requests: same or different? Paper presented at the International Pragmatics Conference, Viareggio, Italy, Sept. 1985. (To appear in Papi and Verschueren, eds., in press.)

Blum-Kulka, S. and Olshtain, E. 1984. Requests and apologies: a cross-cultural study of speech act realization patterns (CCSARP). *Applied Linguistics* 5(3):196-212.

Blum-Kulka, S., Danet, B. and Gherson, R. 1985. The language of requesting in Israeli society. In *Language and social situation*, ed. J. Forgas. New York.

Boggs, S. T. 1978. The development of verbal disputing in part-Hawaiian children. *Language in Society* 7:325-44.

Bolinger, D. 1967. The imperative in English. In *To honor Roman Jakobson: essays on the occasion of his 70th birthday*. Janua Linguarum ser. major 31, pp. 335-62. The Hague.

Bonikowska, M. P. 1985a. Opting out: the pragmatics of what is left unsaid. *Lancaster Papers in Linguistics* 32.

1985b. The speech act of complaining. *Lancaster Papers in Linguistics* 33.

Bott, E. 1957. *Family and social network*. New York.

Brittan, A. 1973. *Meanings and situations*. London.

Brouwer, D. 1982. The influence of the addressee's sex on politeness in language use. *Linguistics* 20(11/12):697-711.

Brouwer, D., Gerritsen, M., and de Haan, D. 1979. Speech differences between men and women: on the wrong track? *Language in Society* 8:33-50.

Brown, P. 1976. Women and politeness: a new perspective on language and society. *Reviews in Anthropology* 3(3):240-9.

1979. *Language, interaction and sex roles in a Mayan community: a study of politeness and the position of women*. Unpublished Ph.D dissertation, University of California, Berkeley.

1980. How and why are women more polite: some evidence from a Mayan community. In McConnell-Ginet, Borker and Furman, eds., 1980, pp. 111-36.

n.d. Aboriginal/Non-aboriginal interaction in Northern Queensland. Paper presented to the Anthropology Seminar, Oxford University, November 1984.

Brown, P. and Fraser, C. 1979. Speech as a marker of situation. In Scherer and Giles, eds. 1979, pp. 33-62.

Brown, P. and Levinson, S. 1974. A theory of prosodic semantics. Unpublished MS, Language Behavior Research Lab, Univ. of California, Berkeley.

1979. Social structure, groups, and interaction. In Scherer and Giles, eds. 1979, pp. 291-341.

in preparation. Communication in interethnic settings: Aboriginal/Non-Aboriginal interaction in Cape York Peninsula. Report to the Australian Institute of Aboriginal Studies, Canberra.

Brown, R. and Ford, M. 1964. Address in American English. In Hymes, ed. 1964, pp. 234-44.

Brown, R. and Gilman, A. 1960. The pronouns of power and solidarity.
    In *Style in language*, ed. T. A. Sebeok, pp. 253-76. Cambridge, Mass.
Butturff, D. and Epstein, E. L., eds. 1978. *Women's language in America.*
    (Language and style books 1). Akron, Ohio.
Candlin, C. N. 1981 (1978). Discoursal patterning and the equalizing of
    interpretive opportunity. In *English for cross-cultural communica-
    tion*, ed. L. E. Smith, pp. 166-99. London.
Carrell, P. L. and Konneker, B. H. 1981. Politeness: comparing native and
    non-native judgements. *Language Learning* 31(1):17-30.
Carter, A. T. 1984. The acquisition of social deixis: children's usages of
    'kin' terms in Maharashtra, India. *Journal of Child Language* 11(1):
    179-201.
Cazden, C. B. 1979. Language in education: variation in the teacher-talk
    register. In *Language in public life*, ed. J. E. Alatis and G. R. Tucker,
    Georgetown University Roundtable on Language and Linguistics,
    pp. 144-62. Washington, D.C.
Cheshire, J. 1982. *Variation in an English dialect.* Cambridge.
Chick, J. 1985. The interactional accomplishment of discrimination in
    South Africa. *Language in Society* 14(3):299-326.
Chomsky, N. 1965. *Aspects of the theory of syntax.* Cambridge, Mass.
    1968. *Language and mind.* New York.
    1976. *Reflections on language.* London.
Chun, A., Day, R., Chensworth, N. A. and Luppescu, S. 1982. Types of
    errors corrected in native–non-native conversations. *TESOL Quar-
    terly* 16:537-47.
Cicourel, A. V. 1968. *The social organization of juvenile justice.* New York.
Clark, H. H. and Carlson, T. 1982a. Speech acts and hearers' beliefs. In
    Mutual knowledge, ed. N. Smith. New York.
    1982b. Hearers and speech acts. *Language* 55(4):767-811.
Clark, H. H. and Gerrig, R. J. 1984. On the pretense theory of irony.
    Journal of Experimental Psychology: General, vol. 113:121-6.
Clark, H. H. and Lucy, P. 1975. Understanding what is meant from what is
    said: a study in conversationally conveyed requests. *Journal of
    Verbal Learning and Verbal Behaviour* 14:56-72.
Clark, H. H. and Schunk, D. H. 1980. Polite responses to polite requests.
    Cognition 8:111-43.
    1981. Politeness in requests: a rejoinder to Kemper and Thissen. *Cog-
    nition* 9:311-15.
Clyne, M. 1981. Culture and discourse structure. *Journal of Pragmatics*
    5:61-66.
Cody, M., McLaughlin, M. and Schneider, J. 1981. The impact of relational
    consequences and intimacy on the selection of interpersonal per-
    suasion tactics: a reanalysis. *Communication Quarterly* 29:91-106.
Cogen, C. and Herrmann, L. 1975. Interactions of the expression 'Let's
    just say' with the Gricean maxims of conversation. In *Proceedings
    of the first annual meeting of the Berkeley Linguistics Society*,
    pp. 60-8. Institute of Human Learning, Univ. of California, Berkeley.
Cohen, A. D. and Olshtain, E. 1981. Developing a measure of sociocultural
    competence: the case of apology. *Language Learning* 31(1):113-34.
Cole, P. 1975. The synchronic and diachronic status of conversational
    implicature. In Cole and Morgan, eds. 1975, pp. 257-88.

Cole, P., ed. 1978. *Syntax and semantics 9: Pragmatics.* New York.
    1981. *Radical pragmatics.* New York.
Cole, P. and Morgan, J. L., eds. 1975. *Syntax and semantics,* vol. 3:
    Speech acts. New York.
Comrie, B. 1975. Polite plurals and predicate agreement. *Language* 51(2):
    406-18.
    1976. Linguistic politeness axes: speaker–addressee, speaker–referent,
    speaker–bystander. *Pragmatics Microfiche* 1.7:A3. Dept of Linguis-
    tics, Univ. of Cambridge.
    1977. In defence of spontaneous demotion: the impersonal passive. In
    Syntax and semantics, vol. 8: Grammatical relations, eds. P. Cole
    and J. Sadock. New York.
Corbett, G. 1976. Address in Russian. *Journal of Russian Studies* 31:3-15.
Corum, C. 1974. Adverbs . . . long and tangled roots. In *Papers from the
    tenth regional meeting of the Chicago Linguistic Society,* pp. 90-102.
    Chicago.
    1975a. A pragmatic analysis of parenthetic adjuncts. In *Papers from the
    eleventh regional meeting of the Chicago Linguistic Society,* pp.
    133-41. Chicago.
    1975b. Basques, particles and babytalk: a case for pragmatics. In *Pro-
    ceedings of the first annual meeting of the Berkeley Linguistics
    Society,* pp. 90-9. Institute for Human Learning, Univ. of Califor-
    nia Berkeley.
Costa, R. 1975. A functional solution for illogical reflexives in Italian. In
    Grossman, San and Vance, eds. 1975, pp. 112-25.
Coulmas, F. 1979. On the sociolinguistic relevance of routine formulae.
    Journal of Pragmatics 3(3/4):239-66.
    1981. Poison to your soul: thanks and apologies contrastively viewed.
    In Coulmas, ed. 1981, pp. 69-92.
Coulmas, F., ed. 1981. *Conversational routine: explorations in standard-
    ized communication situations and prepatterned speech.* The
    Hague.
Coupland, N. 1980. Style-shifting in a Cardiff work-setting. *Language in
    Society* 9:1-12.
Creider, C. 1976. Thematization in Luo. *Pragmatics Microfiche* 1.7:B14.
    Dept. of Linguistics, Univ. of Cambridge.
Crosby, F. and Nyquist, L. 1977. The female register: an empirical study
    of Lakoff's hypotheses. *Language in Society* 6:313-22.
Cutler, A. 1974. On saying what you mean without meaning what you
    say. In *Papers from the tenth regional meeting of the Chicago Lin-
    guistic Society,* pp. 117-27. Chicago.
D'Amico-Reisner, L. 1983. An analysis of the surface structure of dis-
    approval exchanges. In Wolfson and Judd, eds., 1983.
Darnell, R. 1985. The language of power in Cree interethnic communica-
    tion. In *Language of inequality,* ed. N. Wolfson and J. Manes, pp.
    61-72. Berlin.
Davidson, D. and Harmon, G., eds. 1972. *Semantics of natural language.*
    Dordrecht, Holland.
Davidson, J. 1984. Subsequent versions of invitations, offers, requests
    and proposals dealing with potential or actual rejection. In Atkin-
    son and Heritage, eds. 1984, pp. 102-28.

Davison, A. 1973. *Performative verbs, adverbs and felicity conditions: an inquiry into the nature of performative verbs.* Unpublished Ph.D. dissertation, Dept of Linguistics, Univ. of Chicago.

1975. Indirect speech acts and what to do with them. In Cole and Morgan, eds. 1975, pp. 143–85.

Day, R. R., Chensworth, N. A., Chun, A. E. and Luppescu, S. 1984. Corrective feedback in native–non-native discourse. *Language Learning* 34(2):19–45.

Den Ouden, J. B. H. 1979. Social stratification as expressed through language: a case study of a South Indian village. *Contributions to Indian Sociology* NS, Vol. 13(1):33–59.

Deucher, M. 1985. A pragmatic account of women's use of standard speech. Paper presented at the International Pragmatics Conference, Viareggio, Italy, September 1985. To appear in Papi and Verschueren, eds., in press.

Dixon, R. M. W. 1972. *The Dyirbal language of North Queensland.* Cambridge Studies in Linguistics 9. Cambridge.

Drew, P. 1984. Speakers' reportings in invitation sequences. In Atkinson and Heritage, eds. 1984, pp. 129–51.

Drossou, M. 1985. *Requests in English and in Greek.* MA dissertation, University of York.

Dubois, B. L. and Crouch, I. 1975. The question of tag questions in women's speech: they don't really use more of them, do they? *Language in Society* 4(3):289–94.

Dumont, L. 1970. *Homo hierarchicus.* London.

Duranti, A. 1981. Speech-making and the organization of discourse in a Samoan fono. *The Journal of the Polynesian Society* 90(3):357–400.

1983a. Referential and social meanings of subject pronouns in Italian conversation. Unpublished MS.

1983b. Intentions, self and local theories of meaning: words and social action in a Samoan context. Unpublished MS. (revised version of paper presented at American Anthropological Association meetings, Chicago, Nov. 1983.)

1985. Sociocultural dimensions of discourse. In *Handbook of discourse analysis,* ed. T. A. van Dijk, vol. 1, pp. 193–230. London.

Durkheim, E. 1915. *The elementary forms of the religious life.* London.

Eades, D. 1982a. You gotta know how to talk. . . : information-seeking in South East Queensland aboriginal society. *Australian Journal of Linguistics* 2:61–82.

1982b. 'Where you going?' Reasons and privacy in Southeast Queensland Aboriginal Society. Unpublished MS, Department of Anthropology, University of Queensland.

Eakins, B. and Eakins, R. G. 1978. *Sex differences in human communication.* Boston.

Edelsky, C. 1977. Acquisition of an aspect of communicative competence; learning what it means to talk like a lady. In Ervin-Tripp and Mitchell-Kernan, eds. 1977, pp. 225–243.

1979. Question intonation and sex roles. *Language in Society* 8(1):15–32.

1981. Who's got the floor? *Language in Society* 10(3):383–421.

Edmondson, W. J. 1981. On saying you're sorry. In Coulmas, ed. 1981, pp. 273-88.

Eibl-Eibesfeldt, I. 1972. Similarities and differences between cultures in expressive movements. In Hinde, ed. 1972, pp. 297-314.

Erickson, F. and Schultz, J. J. 1979. *The counsellor as gatekeeper: social interaction in interviews.* New York.

Ervin-Tripp, S. 1964. An analysis of the interaction of language, topic and listener. In Gumperz and Hymes, eds. 1964, pp. 86-102.

    1972. On sociolinguistic rules: alternation and co-occurrence. In Gumperz and Hymes, eds. 1972, pp. 213-50.

    1976. Is Sybil there? The structure of some American English directives. *Language in Society* 5:25-66.

    1977. Wait for me, roller-skate! In Ervin-Tripp and Mitchell-Kernan, eds. 1977, pp. 165-88.

    1979. Children's verbal turn-taking. In Ochs and Schieffelin, eds. 1979, pp. 393-414.

    1981. How to make and understand a request. In Parret, Sbisà, and Verschueren, eds. 1981, pp. 195-210.

    1982. Structures of control. In *Communicating in the classroom*, ed. L. C. Wilkinson, pp. 27-47. New York.

Ervin-Tripp, S. and Gordon, D. P. (in press). The development of requests. In *Communicative competence: acquisition and intervention*, ed. R. L. Schiefelbusch. Baltimore.

Ervin-Tripp, S. and Mitchell-Kernan, C., eds. 1977. *Child discourse.* New York.

Ervin-Tripp, S., O'Connor, M. C. and Rosenberg, J. 1984. Language and power in the family. In Kramarae, Shultz and O'Barr, eds. 1984, pp. 116-35.

Faerch, C. and Kasper, G. 1984. Two ways of defining communicative strategies. *Language Learning* 34(1):45-63.

Fairhurst, G. T., Green, S. T. and Snavely, B. K. 1984. Face support in controlling poor performance. *Human Communication Research* 11(2):272-95.

Falbo, T. and Peplau, L. A. 1980. Power strategies in intimate relationships. *Journal of Personality and Social Psychology* 38:618-28.

Fang, H. Q. and Hen, J. H. 1983. Social changes and changing address norms in China. *Language in Society* 12(4):495-509.

Feld, S. 1982. *Sound and sentiment.* Philadephia.

Ferguson, C. A. 1964. Diglossia. In Hymes, ed. 1964, pp. 429-39.

    1976. The structure and use of politeness formulas. *Language in Society* 5:137-51. (Also in Coulmas, ed. 1981, pp. 21-36.)

    1978. Talking to children: a search for universals. In J. H. Greenberg, et al., eds. 1978, vol. 1, pp. 203-224.

Fielding, G. and Fraser, C. 1978. Language and interpersonal relations. In *The social context of language*, ed. I. Markova. London.

Fillmore, C. J. 1971a. Verbs of judging: an exercise in semantic description. In Fillmore and Langendoen, eds. 1971, pp. 273-89.

    1971b. Toward a theory of deixis. In *Working Papers in Linguistics*, vol. 3(4). Honolulu.

    1972. How to know whether you're coming or going. In *Linguistik* 1971, ed. K. Hyldgaard-Jensen, pp. 369-79.

1974. Pragmatics and the description of discourse. In *Berkeley studies in syntax and semantics*, vol. 1:V.1-21. Institute of Human Learning, Univ. of California, Berkeley.

1975. Santa Cruz lectures on deixis. *Indiana Univ. Linguistics Club Papers*. Bloomington.

Fillmore, C. J. and Langendoen, D. T., eds. 1971. *Studies in linguistic semantics*. New York.

Firth, J. R. 1972. Verbal and bodily rituals of greeting and parting. In *The interpretation of ritual*, ed. J. S. LaFontaine, pp. 1-38.

Foley, W. and Van Valin, R. 1983. *Functional syntax and universal grammar*. Cambridge, England.

Fortes, M. 1945. *The dynamics of clanship among the Tallensi*. London.

1949. *The web of kinship among the Tallensi*. London.

1969. *Kinship and the social order*. London.

Fraser, B. 1975. Hedged performatives. In Cole and Morgan, eds. 1975, pp. 187-210.

1980. Conversational mitigation. *Journal of Pragmatics* 4:341-50.

1981. On apologizing. In Coulmas, ed. 1981, pp. 259-71.

Fraser, B. and Nolan, W. 1981. The association of deference with linguistic form. In Walters, ed. 1981, pp. 93-111.

Friedrich, P. 1966. The linguistic reflex of social change: from Tsarist to Soviet Russian kinship. In *Explorations in sociolinguistics*, ed. S. Lieberson, pp. 31-57. Bloomington, Indiana.

1972. Social context and semantic feature: the Russian pronominal usage. In Gumperz and Hymes, eds. 1972, pp. 270-300.

Gal, S. 1979. *Linguistic shift: social determinants of linguistic change in bilingual Austria*. New York.

1983. 'Comment' on L. B. Breitborde, Levels of analysis in sociolinguistic explanation: bilingual code switching, social relations and domain theory. *International Journal of the Sociology of Language* 39:63-72.

Garfinkel, H. 1972. Remarks on ethnomethodology. In Gumperz and Hymes, eds. 1972, pp. 301-24.

Garvey, C. 1975. Requests and responses in children's speech. *Journal of Child Language* 2:41-63.

Garvin, R. L. and Riesenberg, S. H. 1952. Respect behavior on Ponape: an ethnolinguistic study. *American Anthropologist* 54:201-20.

Gazdar, G. and Klein, E. 1976. How to formalize transderivational constraints. Paper presented at the 3rd Groningen Roundtable on Mathematical Linguistics: Semantics for Natural Language.

Geertz, C. 1960. *The religion of Java*. Glencoe, Ill.

Geoghegan, W. 1970. A theory of marking rules. Working Paper no. 37, Language Behaviour Research Lab, Univ. of California, Berkeley.

1971. Information processing systems in culture. In *Explorations in mathematical anthropology*, ed. P. Kay, pp. 3-35. Cambridge, Mass.

Gibbons, J. 1980. A tentative framework for speech act description of the utterance particle in Cantonese. *Linguistics* 18:763-76.

Gibbs, R. W. 1979. Contextual effects in understanding indirect requests. *Discourse Processes* 2:1-10.

Giddens, A. 1973. *The class structure of the advanced societies*. London.

1984. *The constitution of society: outline of the theory of structuration.* Cambridge.

Giles, H. 1980. Accommodation theory: some new directions. *York Papers in Linguistics* 9:105–36.

Giles, H., ed. 1984. The dynamics of speech accommodation. *International Journal of the Sociology of Language,* special issue, 46.

Givon, T., ed. 1979. *Syntax and semantics 12: Discourse and syntax.* New York.

Gleason, J. B. 1980. The acquisition of social speech: routines and politeness formulas. In *Language: Social psychological perspectives,* ed. H. Giles, P. Robinson, and P. Smith. Oxford.

Goffman, E. 1967. *Interaction ritual: essays on face to face behavior.* Garden City, New York.

1971. *Relations in public: microstudies of the public order.* New York.

1974. *Frame analysis.* Cambridge, Mass.

1976. Replies and responses. *Language in Society* 5:257–313.

1981. *Forms of talk.* Philadelphia.

Goldberg, J. 1982. *Discourse particles: an analysis of the role of 'Y'know', 'I mean', 'Well', and 'Actually' in conversation.* Unpublished Ph.D. dissertation, University of Cambridge.

Good, D. 1985. On why being more cognitive requires you to be more social. In *Social action and artificial intelligence,* ed. G. N. Gilbert and C. Heath. Aldershot.

in press. Conversation and social skill. In *Handbook of social skills training,* vol. 2: *Clinical application and new directions,* ch. 9, ed. C. R. Hollin and P. Trouwer. Oxford.

Goodenough, W. 1969. Rethinking 'status' and 'role': toward a general model of the cultural organization of social relationships. In *Cognitive anthropology,* ed. S. A. Tyler, pp. 311–30. New York.

Goodwin, C. 1979. The interactive construction of a sentence in natural conversation. In *Everyday language: studies in ethnomethdology,* ed. G. Psathas, pp. 97–121.

Goodwin, M. H. 1980a. Directive response sequences in girls' and boys' task activities. In McConnell-Ginet et al. 1980, pp. 157–73.

1980b. He-said, she-said: formal cultural procedures for the construction of a gossip dispute activity. *American Ethnologist* 7:674–95.

1982. Processes of dispute management among Urban Black children. *American Ethnologist* 9:76–96.

1983. Aggravated other-correction and disagreement in children's conversations. *Journal of Pragmatics* 7(6):657–77.

Goodwin, M. and Goodwin, C., in press. Children's arguing. In Philips, Steele and Tanz, eds., in press.

Goody, E. N. 1972. 'Greeting', 'begging' and the presentation of respect. In *The interpretation of ritual: essays in honour of A. I. Richards,* ed. J. S. La Fontaine, pp. 39–72. London.

1978a. Introduction to *Questions and politeness,* ed. E. Goody, pp. 1–16.

1978b. Towards a theory of questions. In Goody, ed. 1978, pp. 17–43.

Goody, E., ed. 1978. *Questions and politeness: strategies in social interaction.* Cambridge.

Goody, J. R. 1959. The mother's brother and the sister's son in West Africa. *Journal of the Royal Anthropological Institute* 89:61–88.

Gordon, D. 1983. Hospital slang for patients. *Language in Society* 12:173–85.

Gordon, D. and Lakoff, G. 1971. Conversational postulates. In *Papers from the seventh regional meeting of the Chicago Linguistic Society*, pp. 63–84. Chicago.

Green, G. 1975a. How to get people to do things with words: the Whim-perative question. In Cole and Morgan, eds. 1975, pp. 107–41.

1975b. Nonsense and reference; or, the conversational use of proverbs. In *Papers from the eleventh regional meeting of the Chicago Linguistic Society*, pp. 226–39. Chicago.

Greenberg, J. H., Ferguson, C. A. and Moravcsik, E. A., eds. 1978. *Universals of human language*, vols. 1–4. Stanford.

Gregersen, E. A. 1974. The signalling of social distance in African languages. In *Language in its social setting*, ed. W. W. Gage, pp. 47–55. Washington, D.C.

Grice, H. P. 1967. Logic and conversation. Unpublished MS, from the William James Lectures 1967. (Chapter 3 is published separately: see Grice 1975.)

1971 (1957). Meaning. In *Semantics: an interdisciplinary reader*, eds. D. D. Steinberg and L. A. Jakobovits, pp. 53–9. Cambridge.

1973. Probability, desirability, and mood operators. Paper presented at the Texas Conference on Pragmatics. Univ. of Texas, Austin.

1975. Logic and conversation. In Cole and Morgan, eds. 1975, pp. 41–58. (Cf. Grice 1967).

Griffiths, P. 1974. *That, there,* deixis I: *That.* MS, Univ. of Newcastle upon Tyne.

Grimshaw, A. D. 1980a. Mishearings, misunderstandings, and other non-successes in talk: a plea for redress of speaker-oriented bias. *Sociological Inquiry* 50:31–74.

1980b. Selection and labelling of INSTRUMENTALITIES of verbal manipulation. *Discourse Processes* 3:203–29.

1980c. Social interactional and sociolinguistic rules. *Social Forces* 58(3):789–810.

1983. 'Comment' on L. B. Breitborde, Levels of analysis in sociolinguistic explanation. *International Journal of the Sociology of Language* 39:73–87.

Grossman, R. E., San, L. J. and Vance, T. J., eds. 1975. *Papers from the parasession on functionalism.* Chicago Linguistic Society. Chicago.

Guilbaud, G. T. 1959. *What is cybernetics?* New York.

Gumperz, J. J. 1970. Verbal strategies in multilingual communication. In *Monograph series on languages and linguistics*, 21st annual round-table, Georgetown University, no. 23. Washington, D.C.

1971. *Language in social groups.* Stanford, Calif.

1975. Code-switching in conversation. *Pragmatics Microfiche* 1.4:A2. Dept of Linguistics, Univ. of Cambridge.

1978a. The conversational analysis of interethnic communication. In *Interethnic communication*, ed. E. Lamar Ross. Athens, Ga.

1978b. Dialect and conversational inference in an urban community. *Language in Society* 7(3):393–409.

1982a. *Discourse strategies.* Cambridge.

1982b. *Language, interaction and social identity.* Cambridge.

Gumperz, J. J. and Hymes, D., eds. 1964. *The ethnography of communication. American Anthropologist,* 66.vi, pt 2, Special publ. Washington, D.C.

1972. *Directions in sociolinguistics.* New York.

Gumperz, J. J. and Wilson, R. 1971. Convergence and creolization: a case from the Indo-Aryan/Dravidian border in India. In Gumperz 1971, pp. 251–73.

Haas, M. 1964. Men's and women's speech in Koasati. In Hymes, ed. 1964, pp. 228–33.

Haiman, J. 1985. *Iconicity in syntax.* Amsterdam.

Harada, S. I. 1976. Honorifics. In *Syntax and semantics 5: Japanese generative grammar,* ed. M. Shibatani, pp. 499–561. New York.

Harris, R. 1984. *Truth and politeness: a study in the pragmatics of Egyptian Arabic conversation.* Unpublished Ph.D. dissertation, University of Cambridge.

Haverkate, H. 1979. *Impositive sentences in Spanish: theory and description in pragmatics.* Amsterdam.

Haviland, J. B. 1977. *Gossip, reputation and knowledge in Zinacantan.* Chicago.

1979a. How to talk to your brother-in-law in Guugu Yimidhirr. In *Languages and their speakers,* ed. T. Shopen, Ch. IV. Cambridge, Mass.

1979b. Guugu–Yimidhirr brother-in-law language. *Language in Society* 8:365–93.

1982. Kin and country at Wakooka outstation: an exercise in rich interpretation. *International Journal of the Sociology of Language* 36:53–72.

in preparation. Work on Tzotzil and Guugu Yimidhirr conversation.

Head, B. F. 1978. Respect degrees in pronominal reference. In J. H. Greenberg et al., eds. vol. 3, pp. 151–211.

Heringer, J. T. 1972. *Some grammatical correlates of felicity conditions and presuppositions.* Ph.D. dissertation; Ohio State Univ. Working Papers in Linguistics 11:1–110.

Heritage, J. 1981. Strategies in interaction: a response to Riley. Paper presented at the 1981 BAAL conference.

1984a. Recent developments in conversation analysis. *Warwick Working Papers in Sociology.* University of Warwick, Coventry.

1984b. *Garfinkel and ethnomethodology.* Cambridge.

Herman, V. 1976. Code switching in Tamil. Diploma dissertation, Dept of Linguistics, Univ. of Cambridge.

Hill, J. H. and Hill, K. C. 1978. Honorific usage in modern Nahuatl: the expression of social distance and respect in the Nahuatl of the Malinche. *Language* 54(1):123–55.

Hinde, R. A., ed. 1972. *Non-verbal communication.* Cambridge.

Hogg, M. A. 1985. Masculine and feminine speech in dyads and groups: a study of speech style and gender salience. *Journal of Language and Social Psychology* 4(2):99–112.

Hollos, M. 1977. Comprehension and use of social rules in pronoun selection by Hungarian children. In Ervin-Tripp and Mitchell-Kernan, eds. 1977, pp. 211–23.

Hollos, M. and Beeman, W. 1974. The development of directives among Norwegian and Hungarian children: an example of communicative style in culture. *Language in Society* 7:345–55.

Holmes, J. 1984. Modifying illocutionary force. *Journal of Pragmatics* 8(3):345–65.

Holtgraves, T. M., 1984. *The role of direct and indirect speech acts in social interaction.* Unpublished Ph.D. thesis, University of Nevada – Reno.

Horn, L. 1972. *On the semantic properties of logical operators in English.* Unpublished Ph.D. dissertation. Univ. of California, Los Angeles.

  1978. Some aspects of negation. In J. H. Greenberg et al., eds. 1978, vol. 4:127–210.

  1984. Toward a new taxonomy for pragmatic inference: Q-based and R-based implicature. In Schiffren, ed. 1984, pp. 11–42.

Horne, E. C. 1974. *Javanese dictionary.* New Haven, Conn.

House, J. and Kasper, G. 1981. Politeness markers in English and German. In Coulmas, ed. 1981, pp. 157–85.

Hymes, D. 1972. Models of the interaction of language and social life. In Gumperz and Hymes, eds. 1972, pp. 35–71.

  1974a. *Foundations in sociolinguistics: an ethnographic approach.* Philadelphia.

  1974b. Ways of speaking. In Bauman and Sherzer, eds. 1974, pp. 433–51.

Hymes, D., ed. 1964. *Language in culture and society.* New York.

Ide, S. 1982. Japanese sociolinguistics: politeness and women's language. *Lingua* 57:357–85.

  1983. Two functional aspects of politeness in women's language. *Proceedings of the 13th International Congress of Linguists*, Tokyo, 1982. The Hague.

Ide, S., Hori, M., Kawasaki, A., Ikuta, S. and Haga, H. 1986. Sex differences: politeness in Japanese. *International Journal of the Sociology of Language* 58 (special issue on Japanese sociolinguistics), pp. 25–36.

Irvine, J. T. 1974. Strategies of status manipulation in the Wolof greeting. In Bauman and Sherzer, eds. 1974, pp. 167–91.

  1975. Wolof speech styles and social status. *Working papers in sociolinguistics*, no. 23. Southwest Educational Development Lab, Austin, Texas.

  1979. Formality and informality in communicative events. *American Anthropologist* 81(4):773–90. (Reprinted in J. Baugh and J. Sherzer, eds. *Language in use*, pp. 211–28.)

  1981. Semantics and context in Wolof insults. Paper delivered at the meetings of the Australian Linguistics Society and the Australian Anthropological Association, Canberra, August, 1981.

  1982. Language and affect: some cross-cultural issues. In *Contemporary perceptions of Language: interdisciplinary dimensions*, ed. H. Byrnes, pp. 31–47. Washington, D.C.

  1985. How not to ask for a favor in Wolof. *Papers in Linguistics* 13:3–50.

Jackson, S. and Jacobs, S. 1980. Structure of conversational argument: pragmatic bases for the enthymeme. *Quarterly Journal of Speech* 66:251–65.

1981. The collaborative production of proposals in conversational argument and persuasion: a study of disagreement regulation. *The Journal of the American Forensic Association* 18:77–90.

Jacobs, S. and Jackson, S. 1982. Conversational argument: a discourse analytic approach. In *Advances in argumentation theory and research*, ed. R. Cox and C. A. Willard. Carbondale, Ill.

1983. Strategy and structure in conversational influence attempts. *Communication Monographs* 50(4):285–304.

Jahangiri, N. 1980. *A sociolinguistic study of Persian in Tehran.* Univ. of London Ph.D. thesis.

Jain, D. K. 1969. Verbalization of respect in Hindi. *Anthropological Linguistics* 11(3):79–97.

James, A. R. 1983. Compromisers in English: a cross-disciplinary approach to their interpersonal significance. *Journal of Pragmatics* 7:191–203.

James, D. 1972. Some aspects of the syntax and semantics of interjections. In *Papers form the eighth regional meeting of the Chicago Linguistic Society*, pp. 162–72. Chicago.

1973. Another look at, say, some grammatical constraints on, oh, interjections and hesitations. In *Papers from the ninth regional meeting of the Chicago Linguistic Society*, pp. 242–51. Chicago.

James, S. L. 1978. Effect of listener age and situation on the politeness of children's directives. *Journal of Psycholinguistic Research* 7:307–17.

Jefferson, G. 1979. A technique for inviting laughter — its subsequent acceptance/declination. In *Everyday language: studies in ethnomethodology*, ed. G. Psathas, pp. 79–96. New York.

1980. On 'trouble-premonitory' response to inquiry. *Social Inquiry* 50(3/4):153–85.

1984a. On stepwise transition from talk about a trouble to inappropriately next-positioned matters. In Atkinson and Heritage, eds. 1984, pp. 191–222.

1984b. On the organization of laughter in talk-troubles. In Atkinson and Heritage, eds. 1984, pp. 346–69.

n.d. On exposed and embedded correction in conversation. Unpublished MS, University of Manchester, Dept. of Sociology.

Jefferson, G. and Lee, J. R. E. 1981. The rejection of advice: managing the problematic convergence of a 'troubles-telling' and a 'service encounter'. *Journal of Pragmatics* 5(5):399–422.

Jefferson, G., Sacks, H. and Schegloff, E. 1976. Some notes on laughing together. *Pragmatics Microfiche* 1.8:A2. Dept of Linguistics, Univ. of Cambridge.

Jefferson, G. and Schenkein, J. N. 1977. Some sequential negotations in conversation: unexpanded and expanded versions of projected action sequences. *Sociology* 11:87–103.

Johnstone, B. n.d. 'He says . . . so I said': past/present tense alternation in narrative depictions of authority. Unpublished MS, Georgetown University.

Kachru, B. B. *et al.*, eds. 1973. *Issues in linguistics: papers in honor of Henry and Renée Kahane.* Urbana, Ill.

Kapferer, B., ed. 1976. *Transaction and meaning.* Institute for the Study of Human Issues, Philadelphia.

Karttunen, F. 1975a. More Finnish clitics: syntax and pragmatics. *Indiana Univ. Linguistics Club Papers.* Bloomington.

1975b. Functional constraints in Finnish syntax. In Grossman, San and Vance, eds. 1975, pp. 232–43.

Kasher, A. in press. Politeness and rationality. In Papi and Verschueren, in press.

Katriel, T. 1985. *Brogez*: ritual and strategy in Israeli children's conflicts. *Language in Society* 14(4):467–90.

(forthcoming). 'Dugri' speech: talking straight in Israeli 'Sabra' culture. Oxford.

Kaufer, D. S. 1981. Understanding ironic communication. *Journal of Pragmatics* 5(6):495–510.

Keenan, E. L. 1972. Relative clause formation in Malagasy. In *The Chicago Which Hunt*, pp. 169–89. Chicago Linguistic Society, Chicago.

1975. Some universals of passive in relational grammars. In *Papers from the eleventh regional meeting of the Chicago Linguistic Society*, pp. 340–52. Chicago.

Keenan, E. Ochs, 1974a. *Conversation and oratory in Vakinankaratra, Madagascar.* Unpublished Ph.D. dissertation, Dept of Anthropology, Univ. of Pennsylvania.

1974b. Norm-makers, norm-breakers: uses of speech by men and women in a Malagasy community. In Bauman and Sherzer, eds. 1974, pp. 125–43.

1975. Making it last: repetition in children's discourse. In *Proceedings of the first annual meeting of the Berkeley Linguistic Society*, pp. 279–94. Institute for Human Learning, Univ. of California, Berkeley.

1976. The universality of conversational implicature. *Language in Society* 5:67–80.

Kemper, S. and Thissen, D. 1981. How polite? a reply to Clark and Schunk. *Cognition* 9:305–9.

Kenny, A. J. 1966. Practical inference. *Analysis* 26:65–75.

Kline, S. L. 1981. Construct system development and face support in persuasive messages: two empirical investigations. Paper presented at the annual meeting of the International Communications Association, Minneapolis, Minn.

Kochman, T. 1981. *Black and white styles in conflict.* Chicago.

1983. The boundary between play and non-play in black verbal dueling. *Language in Society* 12(3):329–37.

1984. The politics of politeness: social warrants in mainstream American public etiquette. In Schiffrin, ed. 1984, pp. 200–209.

Körner, S. 1974. *Practical reason.* Oxford.

Kramarae, C. 1981. *Women and men speaking: frameworks for analysis.* Rowland, Mass.

Kramarae, C., Shultz, M. and O'Barr, W., eds. 1984. *Language and power.* Beverly Hills, Calif.

Kramer, C., Thorne, B and Henley, N. 1978. Review essay: Perspectives on language and communication. *Signs: Journal of Women in Culture and Society* 3(3):638–51. Chicago.

Kuno, S. 1973. *The structure of the Japanese language.* Current Studies in Linguistics ser. 3. Cambridge, Mass.

La Barre, W. 1972 (1947). The cultural basis of emotions and gestures. In *Communication in face-to-face interaction*, eds. J. Laver and S. Hutcheson, pp. 207-24. Harmondsworth.

Laberge, S. 1977. Etude de la variation des pronouns sujets définis et indéfinis dans le français parlé de Montréal. Ph.D. dissertation, Univ. of Montreal.

Labov, W. 1966. *The social stratification of English in New York City.* Washington, D.C.

　　1972a. Rules for ritual insults. In Sudnow, ed. 1972, pp. 120-69.

　　1972b. The logic of nonstandard English. In *Language in the inner city: studies in the Black English vernacular*, pp. 201-40. Philadelphia.

　　1972c. *Sociolinguistic patterns.* Philadelphia.

　　1978. Modes of mitigation and politeness. In *A pluralistic nation: the language issue*, ed. M. A. Lowrie and N. F. Conklin. Rowley, Mass.

　　1984. Intensity. In Schiffren, ed. 1984, pp. 43-70.

Labov, W. and Fanshel, D. 1977. *Therapeutic discourse: psychotherapy as conversation.* New York.

Lakoff, G. 1972. Hedges: a study in meaning criteria and the logic of fuzzy concepts. In *Papers from the eighth regional meeting of the Chicago Linguistic Society*, pp. 183-228. Chicago.

　　1973. Fuzzy grammar and the performance/competence terminology game. In *Papers from the ninth regional meeting of the Chicago Linguistic Society*, pp. 271-91. Chicago.

　　1974. Syntactic amalgams. In *Papers from the tenth regional meeting of the Chicago Linguistic Society*, pp. 321-44. Chicago.

　　1975. Pragmatics in natural logic. In *Formal semantics of natural language*, ed. E. L. Keenan, pp. 253-86. Cambridge

Lakoff, R. T. 1970. Tense and its relation to participants. *Language* 46(4):838-49.

　　1971a. If's, and's, and but's about conjunction. In Fillmore and Langendoen, eds. 1971, pp. 115-50.

　　1971b. Passive resistance. In *Papers from the seventh regional meeting of the Chicago Linguistic Society*, pp. 149-62. Chicago.

　　1972. Language in context. *Language* 48(4):907-27.

　　1973a. The logic of politeness; or minding your p's and q's. In *Papers from the ninth regional meeting of the Chicago Linguistic Society*, pp. 292-305. Chicago.

　　1973b. Questionable answers and answerable questions. In Kachru et. al., eds. 1973, pp. 453-67.

　　1974a. What you can do with words: politeness, pragmatics and performatives. In *Berkeley studies in syntax and semantics*, vol. 1: XVI:1-55. Institute of Human Learning, Univ. of California, Berkeley.

　　1974b. Remarks on this and that. In *Papers from the tenth regional meeting of the Chicago Linguistic Society*, pp. 345-56. Chicago.

　　1975. *Language and women's place.* New York.

　　1977a. Women's language. *Language and Style* 10(4):222-48.

　　1977b. Politeness, pragmatics and performatives. In *Proceedings of the Texas Conference on Performatives, Presupposition and Implicatures,* ed. A. Rogers, B. Wall and J. P. Murphy, pp. 79–106. Washington, D.C.: Center for Applied Linguistics.

1979. Stylistic strategies within a grammar of style. In Orasanu, Slater, and Adler, eds. 1979, pp. 53–80.

Lakoff, R. T. and Tannen, D. 1979. Communicative strategies in conversation: the case of 'Scenes from a marriage'. *Proceedings of the 5th Annual Meeting of the Berkeley Linguistics Society* 5:581–92.

Lambert, W. E and Tucker, G. R. 1976. *Tu, vous, usted: a social psychological study of address patterns.* Rowley, Mass.

Langacker, R. W. 1974. Movement rules in functional perspective. *Language* 50(4):630–64.

Lavandera, B. in press. The social pragmatics of politeness forms. In *Sociolinguistics: an international handbook of the science of language and society*, ed. V. Ammon, N. Dittmar and K. J. Mattheier. Berlin.

Laver, J. 1968. Voice quality and indexical information. *British Journal of Disorders of Communication*, 3:43–54.

1981. Linguistic routines and politeness in greeting and parting. In Coulmas, ed. 1981, pp. 289–304.

Leach, E. R. 1954. *Political systems of highland Burma.* London.

1961. *Pul Eliya: a village in Ceylon.* Cambridge.

1962. On certain unconsidered aspects of double descent systems. *Man* 62(214):130–4.

1964. Anthropological aspects of language: animal categories and verbal abuse. In *New directions in the study of language*, ed. E. Lenneberg, pp. 23–64. Cambridge, Mass.

1966. Ritualization in man. *Philosophical Transactions of the Royal Society*, Series B, vol. 251, No. 722, pp. 403–8.

1971. Concerning Trobriand clans and the kinship category *tabu*. In *The developmental cycle in domestic groups*, ed. J. Goody, pp. 120–45. Cambridge.

1972. The influence of cultural context on non-verbal communication in man. In Hinde, ed. 1972, pp. 315–47.

1976. *Culture and communication: the logic by which symbols are connected.* Cambridge.

Leech, G. N. 1977. Language and tact. L.A.U.T. paper 46. (Reprinted as Leech 1980.)

1980. *Language and tact.* Amsterdam.

1983. *Principles of pragmatics.* London.

Lefebvre, C. 1975. Report on a case of T/V alternation in Cuzco, Quechua. Paper delivered at the 74th annual meeting of the American Anthropological Association, San Francisco, December.

1979. 'Quechua's loss, Spanish's gain'. *Language in Society* 8:395–407.

Lein, L. and Brenneis, D. 1978. Children's disputes in three speech communities. *Language in Society* 7:299–323.

Levinson, S. C. 1973. Felicity conditions as particularizations of Grice's maxims. Unpublished MS, Language Behavior Research Lab, Univ. of California, Berkeley.

1977. *Social deixis in a Tamil village.* Unpublished Ph.D. dissertation, Dept of Anthropology, Univ. of California, Berkeley.

1978. Sociolinguistic universals. Unpublished paper, Department of Linguistics, University of Cambridge.

1979a. Activity types and language. *Linguistics* 17(5/6):356-99.

1979b. Pragmatics and social deixis. *Proceedings of the 5th Annual Meeting of the Berkeley Linguistics Society*, 206-23.

1980. Speech act theory: the state of the art. *Language and Linguistics Technical Teaching: Abstracts*, 13(1):5-24.

1981a. Explicating concepts of participant role: on the infelicity of S and H. Paper presented at the meetings of the Australian Linguistics Society and the Australian Anthropological Association, Canberra, August 1981.

1981b. Some pre-observations on the modelling of dialogue. *Discourse Processes* 4:93-116.

1982. Caste rank and verbal interaction in western Tamilnadu. In *Caste ideology and interaction*, ed. D. B. McGilvray, pp. 98-203. Cambridge.

1983. *Pragmatics.* Cambridge.

1985. What's special about conversational inference? Paper presented to the British Psychological Society annual meetings, Swansea, April 1985.

1986. Conceptual problems in the study of regional and cultural style. In *Methods of sociolinguistic description: the case of Berlin urban vernacular*, ed. N. Dittmar and P. Schlobinski. Berlin.

in press. Minimization and conversational inference. In Papi and Verschueren, eds., in press.

Lévi-Strauss, C. 1968 (1963). *Structural anthropology.* London.

1969 (1949). *The elementary structures of kinship.* London.

Lewis, D. 1969. *Convention: a philosophical study.* Cambridge, Mass.

1972. General semantics. In Davidson and Harmon, eds. 1972, pp. 169-218.

Loveday, L. 1981. Pitch, politeness, and sexual role: an exploratory investigation into the pitch correlates of English and Japanese politeness formulae. *Language and Speech* 24(1):71-89.

1982. *The sociolinguistics of learning and using a non-native language.* Oxford.

1983. Rhetorical patterns in conflict: the sociocultural relativity of discourse-organizing processes. *Journal of Pragmatics* 7:169-90.

Lustig, M. W. and King, S. 1980. The effect of communication apprehension and situation on communication strategy choices. *Human Communication Research* 7:74-82.

Lyons, J. 1972. Human language. In Hinde, ed. 1972, pp. 49-85.

Lycan, W. C. 1977. Conversational politeness and interruption. *Papers in Linguistics* 10(1/2):23-53.

MacKay, D. M. 1972. Formal analysis of communication processes. In Hinde, ed. 1972, pp. 3-25.

Mackie, V. C. 1983. Japanese children and politeness. *Papers of the Japanese Studies Center* 6, Melbourne.

Maine, L. H. 1965 (1861). *Ancient law.* London.

Makino, S. 1970. Two proposals about Japanese polite expressions. In *Studies presented to R. B. Lees by his students*, eds. J. Sadock and A. Vanek, pp. 163-87. Edmonton, Alberta.

317

Malinowski, B. 1923. The problem of meaning in primitive languages. In *The meaning of meaning*, eds. C. K. Ogden and I. A. Richards. London.

Maltz, D. N. and Borker, R. A. 1982. A cultural approach to male-female miscommunication. In Gumperz, ed. 1982b, pp. 196-216.

Manes, J. 1983. Compliments: a mirror of cultural values. In Wolfson and Judd, eds. 1983.

Manes, J. and Wolfson, N. 1981. The compliment formula. In Coulmas, ed. 1981, pp. 115-32.

Mannheim, B. 1982. A note on 'Inclusive/Exclusive' in 16th century Peru. *International Journal of American Linguistics* 48(4):450-89.

Mark, R. A. 1971. Coding communication at the relationship level. *Journal of Communication* 21:221-32.

Marriott, M. 1976. *Hindu transactions: diversity without dualism.* In Kapferer, ed. 1976, pp. 109-42.

Martin, S. 1964. Speech levels in Japan and Korea. In Hymes, ed. 1964, pp. 407-15.

Mathiot, M. 1982. Review of E. N. Goody, ed. *Questions and politeness. Journal of Pragmatics* 6:70-3.

Mauss, M. 1966 (1925). *The gift*, transl. I. Cunningham. London.

Maynard, D. W. 1985. How children start arguments. *Language in Society* 14(1):1-30.

Maynard-Smith, J. Origins of social behaviour. Lecture delivered at Darwin College, Cambridge. In Fabian, A., ed. *Origins*, in press.

McClean, A. C. 1973. Modes of address in Nepali. *Archivum Linguisticum* NS 4:89-102.

McConnell-Ginet, S. 1983. Review article: on *Language, sex and gender*, ed. by J. Orasanu et al. 1979, and *Sexist language*, ed. by M. Vetterling-Braggin, 1981. *Language* 59(2):373-91.

McConnell-Ginet, S., Borker, R. and Furman, N., eds. 1980. *Women and language in literature and society.* New York.

McLaughlin, M. L., Cody, M. J. and Rosenstein, N. E. 1983. Account sequences in conversations between strangers. *Communication Monographs* 50(2):102-25.

McLaughlin, M. L., Cody, M. J. and O'Hair, H. D. 1983. The management of failure events: some contextual determinants of accounting behaviour. *Human Communication Research* 9:208-24.

Mead, G. H. 1934. *Mind, self and society*, ed. C. W. Morris. Chicago.

Mehotra, 1981. Non-kin forms of address in Hindi. *International Journal of the Sociology of Language* 32:121-37.

Miller, G. A., Galanter, E. and Pribram, K. H. 1960. *Plans and the structure of behavior.* New York.

Miller, R. A. 1967. *The Japanese language.* Chicago.

Miller, W. R. 1980. Speaking for two: respect speech in the Guarijio of Northwest Mexico. *Proceedings of the 6th Annual Meeting of the Berkeley Linguistics Society* 6:196-206.

Milroy, L. 1980. *Language and social networks.* Oxford.

Moerman, M. 1977. The preference for self-correction in a Tai conversational corpus. *Language* 53(4):872-82.

in press. *Talking culture: ethnography and conversational analysis.* Cambridge.

Mohan, B. A. 1974. Principles, postulates, politeness. In *Papers from the tenth regional meeting of the Chicago Linguistic Society*, pp. 446–59. Chicago.

Morgan, J. L. 1973. Sentence fragments and the notion 'sentence'. In Kachru et al., eds. 1973, pp. 719–51.

Nadel, S. F. 1957. *The theory of social structure.* London.

Nakhimovsky, A. D. 1976. Social distribution of forms of address in contemporary Russian. In *International Review of Slavic Linguistics* 1:79–118.

Neustupný, J. V. 1968. Politeness patterns in the system of communication. In *Proceedings of the eighth international congress of anthropological and ethnological sciences*, pp. 412–19. Tokyo and Kyoto.

1978. *Poststructural approaches to language.* Tokyo.

New York Times. 1973. *The Watergate hearings.* New York.

1974. *The White House transcripts.* New York.

Newcombe, N. and Zaslow, M. 1981. Do 2½-year-olds hint? a study of directive forms in the speech of 2½-year-old children to adults. *Discourse Processes* 4:239–52.

O'Barr, W. M. 1982. *Linguistic evidence: language, power and strategy in the courtroom.* New York.

O'Neill, P. G. 1966. *A programmed guide to respect language in modern Japanese.* London.

Ochs (Keenan), E. 1982. Talking to children in Western Samoa. *Language in Society* 11:77–104.

1984. Clarification and culture. In Schiffren, ed. 1984, pp. 325–41.

in press a. The impact of stratification and socialization on men's and women's speech in Western Samoa. In Philips, Steele and Tanz, eds., in press.

in press b. *Culture and language acquisition: acquisition of communicative competence in a Western Samoan village.* New York.

Ochs, E. and Schieffelin, B. B., eds. 1979. *Developmental pragmatics.* New York.

Ogino, T. 1986. Quantification of politeness based on the usage patterns of honorific expressions. *International Journal of the Sociology of Language* 58:37–58.

Olshtain, E. 1983. Sociocultural competence and language transfer: the case of apology. In *Language transfer in language learning*, ed. S. Gass and L. Selinker, pp. 232–49. Rowley, Mass.

Olshtain, E. and Blum-Kulka, S. 1983. Cross-linguistic speech act studies: theoretical and empirical issues. In *Language across cultures*, ed. L. M. Mathuna and D. Singleton, pp. 235–48.

Orasanu, J., Slater, M. and Adler, L., eds. 1979. *Language, sex and gender.* Annals of the New York Academy of Science, 327.

Ortner, S. B. 1984. Theory in anthropology since the 60s. *Comparative Studies in Society and History* 26(1):126–66.

Owen, M. 1983. *Apologies and remedial interchanges.* Berlin.

Papi, M. and Verschueren, J. in press. *Proceedings of the International Conference at Viareggio, Sept. 1985.* Amsterdam.

Parkin, D. 1976. Exchanging words. In Kapferer, ed. 1976, pp. 163–90.

1980. The creativity of abuse. *Man* (N.S.) 15:45–64.

Parsons, T. 1951. *The social system.* Glencoe, Ill.

Parret, H., Sbisà, M. and Verschueren, J., eds. 1981. *Possibilities and limitations of pragmatics: Proceedings of the Conference on Pragmatics, Urbino, 1979.* Amsterdam.

Pateman, T. 1982a. David Lewis's theory of convention and the social life of language. *Journal of Pragmatics* 6:135-57.

1982b. Communicating with computer programs. *Journal of Pragmatics* 6:225-39.

Paulston, C. B. 1976. Pronouns of address in Swedish: social class semantics and a changing system. In *Language in Society* 5:359-86.

Peristiany, J., ed. 1965. *Honor and shame: the values of Mediterranean society.* Chicago.

Perret, D. 1976. On irony. *Pragmatics Microfiche* 1.7:D3. Dept of Linguistics, Univ. of Cambridge.

Philips, S. 1974. Warm Springs 'Indian time': how the regulation of participation affects the progress of events. In *Explorations in the ethnography of speaking*, ed. R. Bauman and J. Sherzer, pp. 92-109. New York.

1980. Sex differences and language. *Annual Review of Anthropology* 9:523-44.

Philips, S. V., Steele, S. and Tanz, C., eds., in press. *Language, gender, and sex in comparative perspective.* Cambridge.

Pitt-Rivers, J. 1977. *The fate of Shechem, or the politics of sex.* Cambridge.

Polanyi, L. 1982. Linguistic and social constraints on story-telling. *Journal of Pragmatics* 6:509-24.

Pomerantz, A. 1975. *Second assessments: a study of some features of agreements/disagreements.* Unpublished Ph.D. dissertation, University of California, Irvine.

1978. Compliment responses: notes on the cooperation of multiple constraints. In *Studies in the organization of conversational interaction*, ed. J. Schenkein, pp. 79-112. New York.

1980. Telling my side: limited access as a 'fishing' device. *Sociological Inquiry* 50:186-98.

1984a. Agreeing and disagreeing with assessments: some features of preferred/dispreferred turn shapes. In Atkinson and Heritage, eds., pp. 57-101.

1984b. Pursuing a response. In Atkinson and Heritage, eds. 1984, pp. 152-63.

Post, E. 1922. *Etiquette in society, in business, in politics and at home.* New York.

Radcliffe-Brown, A. R. 1952. *Structure and function in primitive society.* London.

Read, B. K. and Cherry, L. J. 1978. Preschool children's production of directive forms. *Discourse Processes* 1:233-45.

Rehbein, J., 1981. Announcing – on formulating plans. In Coulmas, ed. 1981, pp. 215-58.

Reisman, K. 1974. Contrapuntal conversations in an Antiguan village. In Bauman and Sherzer, eds. 1974, pp. 110-24.

Richards, J. C. and Sukwiwat, M. 1983. Language transfer and conversational competence. *Applied Linguistics* 4(2):113-25.

320

Riley, P. 1981. Strategy: collaboration or conflict? Paper presented at the 1981 BAAL conference.

Rintell, E. 1979. Getting your speech act together: the pragmatic ability of second language learners. In *Working Papers on Bilingualism*, No. 17, ed. M. Swain, pp. 97-106. Ontario Institute for Studies in Education.

1981. Sociolinguistic variation and pragmatic ability. In Walters, ed., 1981, pp. 11-34.

Romney, A. K. and D'Andrade, R. G. 1964. *Transcultural studies in cognition. American Anthropologist* 66.iii, pt 2, Special publ. Washington, D.C.

Rosaldo, M. Z. 1982. The things we do with words: Ilongot speech acts and speech act theory in philosophy. *Language in Society* 11:203-37.

Rosch, E. 1977. Human categorization. In *Cross-cultural studies in psychology*, vol. 1, ed. N. Warren. London.

Ross, J. R. 1972. The category squish: endstation Hauptwort. In *Papers from the eighth regional meeting of the Chicago Linguistic Society*, pp. 316-28. Chicago.

1973. Nouniness. In *Three dimensions of linguistic theory*, ed. Osamu Fujimura, pp. 137-257. The TEC Company, Tokyo.

1975. Where to do things with words. In Cole and Morgan, eds. 1975, pp. 233-56.

Roy, A. M. 1976. On the function of irony in conversation. *University of Michigan Papers in Linguistics* 2(2):64-71.

1977. Towards a definition of irony. In *Studies in language variation*, ed. R. W. Fasold and R. Shuy. Washington, D.C.

1978. *Irony in conversation.* University of Michigan Ph.D. dissertation.

Sacks, H. 1967. Lecture notes. Dittoed MSS, Univ. of California, Irvine.

1973. Lecture notes. Summer Institute of Linguistics, Ann Arbor, Michigan.

1975. Everyone has to lie. In *Sociocultural dimensions of language use*, ed. M. Sanches and B. Blount, pp. 57-80. New York.

Sacks, H., Schegloff, E. A. and Jefferson, G. 1974. A simplest systematics for the organization of turn-taking for conversation. *Language* 50(4):696-735.

Sadock, J. 1972. Speech act idioms. In *Papers from the eighth regional meeting of the Chicago Linguistic Society*, pp. 329-39. Chicago.

1974. *Towards a linguistic theory of speech acts.* New York.

Sag, I. A. and Liberman, M. 1975. The intonational disambiguation of indirect speech acts. In *Papers from the eleventh regional meeting of the Chicago Linguistic Society*, pp. 487-97. Chicago.

Sangster, B. C. 1968. Homonymy in Tamil reduplication. Unpublished M.A. thesis, Univ. of Chicago.

Sankoff, G. 1972 (1971). Language use in multilingual societies: some alternative approaches. In *Sociolinguistics*, eds. J. B. Pride and J. Holmes, pp. 33-51. Harmondsworth.

Sankoff, G. and Brown, P. 1976. The origins of syntax in discourse: a case study of *Tok Pisin* relatives. *Language* 53(3):631-66.

Sansom, G. B. 1928. *An historical grammar of Japanese.* Oxford.

Scarcella, R., 1980. On speaking politely in a second language. In *The learner in focus: the issue of the decade*, (on TESOL, ser. '79) ed. C. Yorio, K. Perkins and J. Schachter, pp. 275–87. Washington DC:TESOL.

Scarcella, R. and Brunak, J. 1981. On speaking politely in a second language. In Walters, ed. 1981, pp. 59–75.

Schank, R. C. and Colby, K. M. 1973. *Computer models of thought and language.* San Francisco.

Schegloff, E. A. 1972a. Notes on a conversational practice: formulating ؛ place. In Sudnow, ed. 1972, pp. 75–119.

1972b. Sequencing in conversational openings. In Gumperz and Hymes, eds. 1972, pp. 346–80.

1976. On some questions and ambiguities in conversation. *Pragmatics Microfiche* 2.2:D8. Dept of Linguistics, Univ. of Cambridge.

1979. Presequence and indirection: applying speech act theory to ordinary conversation. Paper presented at the Conference on Pragmatics, Urbino, 1979.

in press. Between macro and micro: contexts and other connections. In *The macro-micro link*, ed. J. Alexander, B. Giesen, R. Munch and N. Smelser. Berkeley and Los Angeles.

n.d. Some sources of misunderstanding in talk-in-interaction. Unpublished MS, UCLA.

Schegloff, E., Jefferson, G. and Sacks, H. 1977. The preference for self-correction in the organization of repair in conversation. *Language* 53:361–82.

Schegloff, E. A. and Sacks, H. 1973. Opening up closings. *Semiotica* 8:289–327.

Scheintuch, G. 1976. Some pragmatic conditions on applications of NEG-Movement. *Pragmatics Microfiche* 1.7:B2. Dept of Linguistics, Univ. of Cambridge.

Schelling, T. C. 1960. *The strategy of conflict.* Cambridge, Mass.

Scherer, K. and Giles, H., eds. 1979. *Social markers in speech.* Cambridge.

Schieffelin, B. B. 1979. Getting it together: an ethnographic approach to the study of the development of communicative competence. In Ochs and Schieffelin, eds. 1979, pp. 73–108.

1984. Ade: a sociolinguistic analysis of a relationship. In *Language in use*, ed. J. Baugh and J. Sherzer, pp. 229–43. Englewood Cliffs, N.J.

in press. *How Kaluli children learn what to say, what to do, and how to feel.* New York.

Schieffelin, B. and Feld, S. in press. Do different worlds mean different words? In Philips, Steele and Tanz, eds., in press.

Schieffelin, E. L. 1980. Anger and shame in the tropical rainforest. Paper presented at the AAA meetings, 1980, Washington, D.C.

Schiffer, S. R. 1972. *Meaning.* Oxford.

Schiffman, H. F. 1971. *Reader for advanced spoken Tamil, Parts I and II.* U.S. Dept of Health, Education and Welfare, Office of Education, Institute of International Studies, Washington, D.C.

Schiffrin, D. 1980. Meta-talk: organizational and evaluative brackets in discourse. *Sociological Inquiry* 50:199–236.

1981. Tense variation in narrative. *Language* 57:45–62.

1984. Jewish argument as sociability. *Language in Society* 13:311–334.

ed., 1984. *Meaning, form and use in context: Linguistic applications.* Washington, D.C.

Schneider, D. M. and Roberts, J. M. 1956. Zuni kin terms. Monograph 1, Notebook no. 3, Laboratory of Anthropology, Univ. of Nebraska. Lincoln.

Schubiger, M. 1972 (1965). English intonation and German model particles: a comparative study. In *Intonation*, ed. D. Bolinger, pp. 1975-93. Harmondsworth.

Scollon, R. and Scollon, S. B. K. 1980. *Athabaskan-English interethnic communication.* Center for Cross-cultural Studies, University of Alaska, Fairbanks.

  1981. *Narrative, literacy and face in interethnic communication.* Norwood, N.J.

  1983. Face in interethnic communication. In *Language and communication*, ed. I. C. Richards and R. W. Schmidt. London.

Scotton, C. M. and Wanjin, Z. 1983. *Tongzhi* in China: language change and its conversational consequences. *Language and Society* 12(4): 477-94.

Searle, J. R. 1969. *Speech acts.* Cambridge.

  1975. Indirect speech acts. In Cole and Morgan, eds. 1975, pp. 59-82.

  1976. A classification of illocutionary acts. *Language in Society* 5:1-23.

Sen, A. K. 1979 (1976-7). Rational fools. In *Philosophy and economic theory*, eds. F. H. Hahn and M. Hollis, pp. 87-109. Oxford Readings in Philosophy. Oxford. (Also in *Philosophy and Public Affairs* 6(1976-7):317-44.)

Shanmugam, S. V. 1971. *Dravidian nouns: a comparative study.* Annamalai Univ., Annamalainagar, Madras.

Shibamoto, J. S. 1985. *Japanese women's language.* New York.

  in press. The womanly woman: manipulation of stereotypical and non-stereotypical features of Japanese female speech. In Philips, Steele and Tanz, eds., in press.

Shimanoff, S. 1977. Investigating politeness. In *Discourse across time and space*, ed. E. O. Keenan and T. L. Bennett. Southern California occasional Papers in Linguistics No. 5, pp. 213-41.

Silverstein, M. 1979. Language structure and linguistic ideology. *CLS: The elements: parasession on linguistic units and levels*, pp. 193-247.

Sinclair, A. 1976. An empirical study of indirect speech acts in usage. Diploma dissertation in linguistics. Dept of Linguistics, Univ. of Cambridge.

Slobin, D. I. 1963. Some aspects of the use of pronouns of address in Yiddish. *Word* 19:193-202.

Slugoski, B. R. 1985. *Grice's theory of conversation as a social psychological model.* D.Phil, Oxford.

Slugoski, B. R. and Turnbull, W. 1985. Grice and social context. Paper presented at the International Pragmatics Conference, Viarregio, Italy, Sept. 1985. To appear in Papi and Verschueren, eds., in press.

Smith, P. M. 1985. *Language, the sexes, and society.* Oxford.

Smith-Hefner, N. 1981. To level or not to level: codes of politeness and prestige in rural Java. *CLS:Papers from the parasession on Language and Behavior.* pp. 211-17.

Sperber, D. 1984. Verbal irony: pretense or echoic mention? *Journal of Experimental Psychology: General*, vol. 113:130-6.

Sperber, D. and Wilson, D. 1981. Irony and the use/mention distinction. In Cole, ed. pp. 295-318.

1982. Mutual knowledge and relevance in theories of comprehension. In *Mutual knowledge*, ed. N. Smith, pp. 61-87. London.

1986. *Relevance: Communication and cognition*. Oxford.

Stalnaker, R. 1972. Pragmatics. In Davidson and Harmon, eds. 1972, pp. 380-97.

Stevens, A. M. 1965. Language levels in Madurese. *Language* 41(2):294-302.

Stiles, W. B. 1981. Classification of intersubjective illocutionary acts. *Language in Society* 10:227-249.

Strecker, I. in preparation. *Symbolization: an anthropological analysis*. To be published by Athlone Press, London.

Street, R. L. Jr. and Giles, H. 1982. Speech accommodation theory: a social cognitive approach to language and speech behaviour. In *Social cognition and communication*, ed. M. E. Roloff and C. R. Berber, pp. 193-226. Beverly Hills, Calif.

Stubbs, M. 1983. Can I have that in writing please? Some neglected topics in speech act theory. *Journal of Pragmatics* 7(5):479-94.

Suchman, L. A. in press. *Plans and situated actions: the problems of human-machine communication*. Cambridge.

Sudnow, D., ed. 1972. *Studies in social interaction*. New York.

Tannen, D. 1981a. The machine-gun question: an example of a conversational style. *Journal of Pragmatics* 5:383-97.

1981b. NY Jewish conversational style. *International Journal of the Sociology of Language* 30:133-49.

1981c. Indirectness as discourse: ethnicity as conversational style. *Discourse Processes* 4:221-38.

1982. Ethnic style in male-female conversation. In Gumperz, ed. 1982a, pp. 217-31.

1984a. *Conversational style: analysing talk among friends*. Norwood, N.J.

1984b. The pragmatics of cross-cultural communication. *Applied Linguistics* 5(3):189-95.

Tannen, D. and Öztek, P. C. 1981. In Coulmas, ed. 1981, pp. 37-54.

Thomas, J. 1983a. Cross-cultural pragmatic failure. *Applied Linguistics* 4(2):91-112.

1983b. The language of unequal encounters: a pragmatic analysis of a police interview. Paper read at the Hatfield Conference on Discourse Analysis, Hatfield Polytechnic, May 1983.

1984. Cross-cultural discourse as 'unequal encounter': towards a pragmatic analysis. *Applied Linguistics* 5(3):226-35.

1985. The language of power: towards a dynamic pragmatics. *Journal of Pragmatics* 9(6):199-216.

Thorne, B. et al., eds. 1983. *Language, gender and society*. Rowley, Mass.

Thorne, D. 1975-6. Arwyddocâd y rhagenwau personal ail berson unigol ym Maenor Berwig, Cwmwd Carnwyllion (The significance of the second-person singular pronoun on the Manor of Berwig in the Commute of Carnwyllion). *Studia Celtica* 10-11:383-7.

Torode, B. 1974. Teacher's talk in classroom discourse. In *Explanation in classroom conversation*, eds. M. Stubbs and S. Delamont. New York.

Traugott, E. C. 1972. *A history of English syntax: a transformational approach to the history of English sentence structure.* New York.

Travis, A. 1975. Pushing forms and meaning around: on the non-standard interpretation of surface structures. In Grossman, San and Vance, eds. 1975, pp. 512-26.

Treichler, P. A., Frankel, R. M., Kramerae, C., Zoppi, K. and Beckman, H. B. 1985. Problems and *problems*: power relationships in a medical encounter. In Kramerae, Shultz, and O'Barr, eds. 1984, pp. 62-88.

Trudgill, P. 1974a. *Sociolinguistics: an introduction.* London.

  1974b. *The social differentiation of English in Norwich.* Cambridge.

  1981. Linguistic accommodation: sociolinguistic observations on a sociopsychological theory. In *CLS:Papers from the parasession on language and behavior*, ed. C. S. Masek, R. A. Hendrick and M. F. Miller, pp. 218-37. Chicago.

Turner, R. 1975. Speech act theory and natural language use. *Pragmatics Microfiche* 1.1:A3. Dept. of Linguistics, Univ. of Cambridge.

Turner, V. W. 1967. *The forest of symbols: aspects of Ndembu ritual.* Ithaca, N.Y.

Uyeno, T. 1971. *A study of Japanese modality: a performative analysis of sentence particles.* Unpublished Ph.D. dissertation, Dept of Linguistics, Univ. of Michigan, Ann Arbor.

Valdés, G. and Pino, C. 1981. Muy a tus órdenes: compliment reponses among Mexican-American bilinguals. *Language in Society* 10:53-72.

Van Dijk, T. A., ed. 1985. *Handbook of Discourse Analysis*, 4 vols. London.

Van Valen, R. D., Jr. 1975. German *doch*: the basic phenomena. In *Papers from the eleventh regional meeting of the Chicago Linguistic Society*, pp. 625-37. Chicago.

  1980. Review of Greenberg, J. et al., eds. in *Journal of Pragmatics* 4:185-93.

Varonis, E. M. and Gass, S. M. 1985. Miscommunication in native/non-native conversation. *Language in Society* 14(3):327-43.

Verschueren, J. 1978. *Pragmatics: an annotated bibliography.* Amsterdam: Benjamins. (and yearly supplements in Journal of Pragmatics).

  1984. Linguistics and crosscultural communication (Review article). *Language in Society* 13(4):489-509.

  in press. *A comprehensive bibliography of pragmatics.* Amsterdam.

Vetterling-Braggin, M., ed. 1981. *Sexist language: a modern philosophical analysis.* Totowa, N.J.

Walters, J. 1979. Strategies for requesting in Spanish and English: structural similarities and pragmatic differences. *Language Learning* 29(2):277-94.

  1980. The perception of politeness in English and Spanish. In Yorio et al., eds., pp. 288-96.

  1981. Variation in the requesting behaviour of bilingual children, In Walters, ed. 1981, pp. 77-92.

Walters, J., ed. 1981. *The sociolinguistics of deference and politeness.* Special issue of *The International Journal of the Sociology of Language*, 27. The Hague.

Warner, W. L. 1937. *A black civilization*. New York.

Weber, M. 1947. *The theory of social and economic organization*, ed. T. Parsons. London.

Weigel, M. M. and Weigel, R. M. 1985. Directive use in a migrant agricultural community. *Language in Society* 14(1):63-79.

Weinreich, U., Labov, W. and Herzog, M. 1968. Empirical foundations for a theory of language change. In *Directions for historical linguistics: a symposium*, eds. W. Lehman and Y. Malkiel, pp. 97-195. Austin, Texas.

Weiser, A. 1974. Deliberate ambiguity. In *Papers from the tenth regional meeting of the Chicago Linguistic Society* pp. 723-31. Chicago.

1975. How not to answer a question: purposive devices in conversational strategy. In *Papers from the eleventh regional meeting of the Chicago Linguistic Society*, pp. 649-60. Chicago.

Weller, R. P. 1981. Affines, ambiguity and meaning in Hokkein kin terms. *Ethnology* 20:15-29.

Wenger, J. R. 1982. *Some universals of honorific language with special reference to Japanese*. Unpublished Ph.D. dissertation, University of Arizona.

West, C. 1979. Against our will: male interruptions of females in cross-sex conversation. In Orasanu, Slater and Adler, eds. 1979, pp. 81-97.

Wierzbicka, A. 1985a. A semantic metalanguage for a crosscultural comparison of speech acts and speech genres. *Language in Society* 14(4):491-514.

1985b. Different cultures, different language, different speech acts: Polish vs. English. *Journal of Pragmatics* 9(2/3):145-78.

Wierzbicka, A., ed. in preparation. Special issue of the *International Journal of the Sociology of Language* on particles.

Wilson, D. and Sperber, D. 1981 (1978). On Grice's theory of conversation. In *Conversation and discourse – structure and interpretation*, ed. P. Werth, pp. 155-78. London.

Wolfson, N. 1982. *CHP: The conversational historical present in American English*. Dordrecht.

Wolfson, N., D'Amico-Reisner, L. and Huber, L. 1983. How to arrange for social commitments in American English: the invitation. In Wolfson and Judd, eds. 1983.

Wolfson, N. and Judd, E., eds. 1983. *Sociolinguistics and language acquisition*. Rowley, Mass.

Wood, B. S. and Gardner, R. 1980. How children 'get their way': directives in communication. *Communication Education* 29:264-72.

Wootton, A. 1981. The management of grantings and rejections by parents in request sequences. *Semiotica* 37:59-89.

Yamanashi, Masa-aki. 1974. On minding your p's and q's in Japanese: a case study from honorifics. In *Papers from the tenth regional meeting of the Chicago Linguistic Society*, pp. 760-71. Chicago.

Yang, M. C. 1945. *A Chinese village*. New York.

Yorio, C., Perkins, K. and Schachter, J. eds. 1980. *The learner in focus: the issue of the decade*. (On TESOL 1979). Washington, D.C.

Youssouf, I., Grimshaw, A. and Bird, C. 1976. Greetings in the desert. *American Ethnologist* 3:797-824.

Zimin, S. 1981. Sex and politeness: factors in first- and second-language use. In Walters, ed. 1981, pp. 35–58.

Zimmerman, D. H. and West, C. 1975. Sex roles, interruptions and silences in conversations. In B. Thorne and N. Henley, eds. *Language and sex: difference or dominance?* Rowley, Mass.

Zvelebil, K. 1954. The enclitic vowels (*-ā, -ē, -ō*) in modern Tamil. *Archiv Orientální* 22:375–405.

1962. Personal pronouns in Tamil and Dravidian. *Indo-Iranian Journal* 6:65–9.

Zwicky, A. M. 1972. On casual speech. In *Papers from the eighth regional meeting of the Chicago Linguistic Society*, pp. 607–15. Chicago.

1974. Hey, Whatsyourname! In *Papers from the tenth regional meeting of the Chicago Linguistic Society*, pp. 787–801. Chicago.

AUTHOR INDEX

331

339

orders, 66, 76, 96, 108, 132, 147, 152, 153-4, 164, 209, 229, 248, 274-5; *see also* bald on-record, requests
overhearers, *see* bystanders
overstatement, 107, **219-20**

P, *see* power
Pacific Island societies, 9; *see also* Ponape, Samoa, etc.
palatalization, 267
paralanguage, 92; and speaker identity, 29
parentheticals, 120, 271, 272
participant(s), 280; roles, 113, 118
particles, **146-62**, 259, 263, 266-7, 292n.45; discourse, 28; as hedges, 105-6, 109-10, 113, 117, 119, 142, **146-62**, 177, 211, 219, 222, 223, 225, 271-3; honorific, 180, 184, 277; as an index of politeness strategies, 251
partings, *see* closings, conversational
passive, 27, 70, 94, 192, 194-7, 208, 262, 273-5, 278
payoffs, *see* strategy, choice of
pauses, 38-9; *see also* hesitation, silence
perception, of politeness, *see under* politeness *and also* hierarchy (of polite expressions)
performative(s), 190; acts, 57; adverbs, 146-72, 269; hypothesis, 146, 299n.94
permissions, 98, 152
person: grammatical, *see under* pronoun; social, 1, 9-10, 13, 14, 34, 35, 44, 50, 182, 246
personality, 61, 62, 101, 232
pessimism, interactional, 11, 136, 143, 144, **172-6**, 268
philosophy, 84, 232, 282, 288n.22
phonology, 267-8
pitch, high, 86, 94, 106, 140, 172, 175, 248, 267-8, 290n.37
please, 37, 101, 133, 134, 135-6, 139-40, 158, 177, 190, 210, 269, 291n.42, 292n.46
pluralization, 23, **198-204**, 227, 261, 277-8, 293n.57
point of view, 9-10, 28, **118-22**, 202, **204-6**; switching of, 28, 118-22, 126, 198, 202, 210, 237-8; and tense, 28, 118, 120-1, 204-5
Polish, 274
polite pronouns, *see* pronouns (polite); *see also* address
politeness: absence of, *see* bald on-record, rudeness; acquisition of, *see*

under acquisition; applications of the theory of, 3, 33-6, 227, 238-55; asymmetrical use of, 12, 24-5, 34, 45-6, 178; concepts of, 13-15, 101-3, 129-30, 211-13; *see also under* negative politeness, positive politeness, off-record; definitions of, 6, 68-71, 101-3, 129-30, 211-12; degrees of, 6-7, 15, 17, 29-31, 35, 41-2, 57, 71-4, 93, 134-6, 139, 142-4, 200-1, 203; discourse and, *see* discourse; distribution of, in society, 4-5, 12, 107, 242, 245, 249-50, 253-5; *see also* gender, social class, stratification; folk concepts of, 13-15, 43, 48, 52n.12, 57, 61, 235; formal, *see* negative politeness; formula, *see* formula; implicated nature of, 5-7; indirect, *see* indirection, off-record; and language structure, *see* grammar, language change, morphology, phonology, syntax, *and under* language; motivations for, 60, 61, 68; negative, *see* negative politeness; perception of, 17, 22, 33, 35; positive, *see* positive politeness; redundant expression of, 25; semantic field of, 53n.14; strategy, 4-7, 15, 25, 37, 42, 53n.15, 85-7, 281-2; successive upgrading of, 37, 42-3, 233, 295n.65; *vs.* tact, *see* tact; theories of, 4-7; universal *vs.* language-specific, *see under* universals
politics, 47, 67
Polynesian languages, 195, *see also* Samoan, etc.
Ponapean, 179, 200, 201, 277
possibly, *see* modals
positive politeness, 2, 14, **17-21**, 23, 31, 60, 62-4, 70, 71-2, 73-4, 79, 81, **101-29**, 237, 267, 270; asymmetrical *vs.* symmetrical use of, 34, 46, 250-1; contrasted with negative politeness, 101, 104, 110, 112, 119, 126, 129, 142, 230, 270; cultures with emphasis on, 14, 34, 230, 243, 245-6, 292n.51, *see also* ethos; escalation of, in interaction, 18; and Gricean maxims, 4, 218; 'grooming', 249; linguistic realizations of, 28, **101-129**; and performance, 32; as social accellerator, 93, 103, 231; and stratification, 245-6, 255; and women, 31-2, 246, 251, 297n.75; *see also* face (positive)

power (P), **15-17**, 30-3, 35, 69, **74-84**, 91, 108, 109, 138, 172, 176, 178, 202, 228-31, 243-4; and bald on-record usage, 97, 250-1; and control, 29-33, 47; cultural composition of, 35, 76-7; cultures with emphasis on, 249-50; and gender, 29-33; in institutions, 32; symbolism of, 45-6

powerless groups and persons, 29-33

practical reasoning, 8, 11, 58, **64-5**, 68, 84, **87-91**, 91-2, 130, 138, 212, 215, 216, 288n.22; *see also* Kenny logic, rationality

pragmatics, 2-7, 33, 48-9, 256, 281; applied, 56; contrastive, 35-6; and politeness, 48-9, 272; *see also under* grammar

praise, self-, 39

preconditions, for speech acts, 40, 41-2; *see also* felicity conditions

preference organization, **38-41**; for agreement, 27, 37, 113-14

preferred turns, *see* preference organization

preparatory condition, *see under* felicity conditions

pre-requests, 40

pre-sequences, 8, 40-2

presupposition, 101, 134, 138, 144, 146, 176, 182, **217**, 227; manipulation of, **122-4**, 291n.39; as strategy, 117, 122-4, 125, 294-5n.60

principles: of politeness, 4-7, 55, 57; of language use, 3-7, *see also* maxims

promises, 66, 68, 69, 125, 146, 171, 286n.14

pronouns: first, 179, 204, 278; plural inclusive, 53n.18, 57, 72, 119-20, **127-8**, 199, 202-3, 285n.3, 297n.75; plural exclusive, 119-20, 180, 199, 203, 285n.3; second, 179, 204, 278, 292n.52; polite (T/V), 23-5, 36-7, 45-6, 107, 110, 144, 179, 180-1, 184, **198-204**, 230, 245, 253-5, 260-1, 278, 287n.19, 292n.51, 293-4n.57, 294n.58, 295n.63, 298n.82, 300n.98; possessive, 119-20, 279; *see also* address, honorifics

prosody, 33, 37, 94, 104-6, 119, 172, 186-7, 188, 212, 222, 251, 263, 267-8, 271, 280; *see also* intonation, paralanguage, stress, voice quality

proverbs, 226

psychology, 9, 55, 94, 287n.21, 298n.83; cognitive, 56, 84, 256-7; experi-

ments in, **15-22**, 295n.61; and plausibility of model, 7-8; social, 2, 240, 288n.23

Quality, maxim of, 3-4, 95, 148, 162, 164-6, 214, 221-5, 290n.36

quantitative methods, *see under* methodology

Quantity, maxim of, 3, 95, 162, 164, 166-8, 214, 217-21, 289n.27

quarrels, *see* arguments, conflict, rudeness

questions, 132, 136, 143-4, 147, 151, 153, 154, 156, 160, 170, 205, 290n.37; answers preferred, 5, 38, 114; cultural use of, 26; negative, **122-3**, 268; polite use of, 6, 135-6, 143, **145-72**; rhetorical, 69, 132, 155, 212, **223-5**, 251

Quechua, 53n.18, 198, 202

quoted speech, 107, 122, 152-3; *vs.* indirect reported speech, 206

R, *see* rating of imposition

rank: of imposition, *see* rating; of politeness, *see under* indirect speech acts, politeness (strategy): social, 9, 78, 253; *see also* social status, power

rating of imposition (R), 12, **15-17**, 18, 32, 34, 74-84, 172, 176, 228-9, 232, 244, 247, 249

rationality, 9, 55, 56, 58-9, 61, 64-5, 83, 85, 87-91, 280; and convention, 59; definition of, 58, 64-5; deviation from, 5, 55; and intention, 7; *vs.* irrationality, 9, 55; and politeness, 3, 4-5, 55, 59-60, 86; *see also* practical reasoning

reasoning: inductive, 212; reflexive, *see under* mutual knowledge

reasons, giving of, 116, **128-9**, 170, 189, 215, 233-5, 291n.40; *see also* excuses

reciprocity, 70, 72, 77, 101, 129

recognition, in greetings, 38-9

redress, for imposition, *see under* face

redundancy, of politeness, 25

reduplication, 105, 167, 290n.32

referent honorifics, *see under* honorifics

reflexivity, of S's and H's wants, 101, 128

refusals, 38, 72, 216, 220, 233-4

rejections, 39

relationship, *see* social relationship

Relevance, maxim of, 3-4, 95, 164, 168-71, 213-17, 290n.36

342

religion, 13, 43-4; *see also* person (social), sacred

reluctance, expressing, 91, 93-4, 188, 272

remedial interchanges, 26, 42, 236-8; *see also* apologies

remindings, 66

repair, conversational, 9, 21, 34, 35-6, 38

repetition, 43, **112-13**, 237-8

reprimands, 66, 233; *see also* criticisms

requests, 10, 12, 19, 20, 24, 25-6, 27, 35, 36-7, 38-9, 40, 41, 57, 66, 67, 69, 72, 76, 81, 108, 111, 112, 115, 117-18, 124, 125, 126-7, 132, 135, 146, 163, 164, 171, 174, 184, 185, 190, 204, 210, 227, 228-9, 248, 249, 267, 272, 291n.39 and 42; conditions on, 40, 41-2; and conversational sequencing, 233-5; displacement of, 168; for 'free goods', 80, 249; indirect, 12, 19, 35, 36-7, 40, 41-2, 69, 70, 81, 111-12, **132-44**, 153, 173, 175-6, 189, 212, 213, 215, 216, 227, 248, 258, 268-9; for information, 132; for permission, 123, 270

respect, *see* honorifics, politeness, *and under* social relationship

rhetoric, 4, 35, 221

ridicule, 66

risk, assessment of in strategy-choice, 17, 60, 71-5, 76, 78, 83

rites, *see* ritual

ritual, 3, 18, **43-7**, 204, 257, 297n.76; of approach *vs.* avoidance, 18, 43, 129; formula *see* formula; *vs.* instrumental acts, 44; nature of, 44; politeness as prototype for, 43-7; positive *vs.* negative, 43-4, 285n.8; *see also* remedial interchanges

role, social, 15, 17, 78-9, 181, 246, 297n.73

routine, polite, 43, 85; *see also* formula

rudeness, 5, 11, 12, 14, 19, 22, 26-7, 36-7, 62, 66, 97, 121, 122, 134, 135, 144, 174, 176, 178, 191, 203, 211, 223, 229-30, 268, 282, 290n.37, 292n.51; ritual, 28, 72, 229, 247

rural, *vs.* urban usage: of conventional indirect speech acts, 138; of T/V, 24

Russian, 184, 198, 245

S, *see* speaker

S. E. Asian languages, 275; *see also* Japanese, Javanese, etc.

sacred, concepts of, 43-4: nature of the person, *see under* person

Samoa, 9-10, 24, 28, 31, 36, 53n.18

sarcasm, 212, 220, 248

satisfactoriness, 64-5, 87-90

Saussurean perspective, 23

scalar predicates, 123, 264, 299n.92

scenes, making, 228-9

second-language learning, 3, 21, **35-6**, *see also* acquisition

self-esteem, preservation of, 41, *see also* face (cooperative preservation of)

self-identifications, 38-9

semantics, and politeness, 6-7, 22, 176; *see also* logical form

semiotics, of politeness, 1-2, 47; *see also* symbolism

Senegal, *see* Wolof

sentence-type, *see* speech acts

sequence, conversational, 26, 38-42, 47, 168, 212, 224, 232-8; *see also* conversation (structure)

setting, *see* context, formality, situation

sex: and language, *see* gender, men's speech, women's speech; talk about, 52n.11

sexism, and language, 29

shame, 13-14, 52n.12, 247

silence, 39, 295n.64; *see also* hesitation, pauses

sincerity, of expression of feelings, 101, 107, 149-51, 177, 183, 222, 249

situation: effects on politeness level, 12, 15-17, 28, 77, 78-81, 142, 176, 180-1, 280; *see also* context

slang, 28, 111

Slavic languages, 198, 274; *see also* Russian, etc.

small talk, 109-10, 112, **117-18**

social class, 24, 31, 245-6, 298n.80; middle, 32, 247, 248, 249; and pronoun use, 24, 245; working, 31, 122, 230; *see also* caste, stratification

social constraints on language use; *see* social determinants

social control, 1-2, 47, 239

social determinants, of politeness level, 2, 15-17, 38-41, 74-8

social deixis, *see under* deixis

social group, 103, 179, 191, 202-3, 242, 243, 253, 256, 280, 293n.56, 298n.84; and stratification, 245

social network, 24, 31, 249; and dialect, 31; and gender, 31-2; and rank, 31, 246

social relationship, 12, 72, 232, 239,